# THE LAW AND PRACTICE OF GLOBAL ICT STANDARDIZATION

This book presents a first comprehensive effort to explore the mechanics and fundamentals of global ICT standardization. It offers a comprehensive study of legal rules governing ICT standardization, systematically analyses governance and institutional features of some most prominent Standards Development Organizations, and presents qualitative empirical evidence on implementation of these rules in practice. By evaluating legal and procedural rules in light of current practices and tendencies in the industry, the book explores various options available for disciplining ICT standardization from the viewpoint of the applicable legislation, judiciary, and internal governance rules of Standards Development Organizations and offers practical solutions on how to increase the legitimacy of ICT standards. Adding to the previous theoretical approach to the field of standardization from historical, legal, and political science perspective, this book applies theoretical considerations to unexplored scenarios, offering a holistic picture of ICT standardization and providing a novel contribution to the field.

DR. OLIA KANEVSKAIA is an Assistant Professor at Utrecht University. She is an author of multiple academic articles on standardization governance. Her work on trade and economic law is recognized by multiple international awards and fellowships. She previously held academic positions at Tilburg Law and Economics Center, KU Leuven Center for IT and IP Law, and NYU School of Law.

CAMBRIDGE INTERNATIONAL TRADE AND ECONOMIC LAW



Processes of economic regionalisation and globalisation have intensified over the last decades, accompanied by increases in the regulation of international trade and economics at the levels of international, regional and national laws. At the same time, significant challenges have arisen with respect to economic liberalization, rule-based systems of trade and investment, and their political and social impacts. The subject matter of this series is international economic law, in this contemporary context. Its core is the regulation of international trade, investment, finance and cognate areas such as intellectual property and competition policy. The series publishes books on related regulatory areas, in particular human rights, labour, environment and culture, as well as sustainable development. These areas are horizontally interconnected and vertically linked at the international, regional and national levels. The series also includes works on governance, dealing with the structure and operation of international organisations related to the field of international economic law, and the way they interact with other subjects of international and national law. The series aims to include excellent legal doctrinal treatises, as well as cutting-edge interdisciplinary works that engage law and the social sciences and humanities.

*Books in the series*

*The Law and Practice of Global ICT Standardization*
Olia Kanevskaia

*Between Market Economy and State Capitalism:*
*China's State-Owned Enterprises and the World Trading System*
Henry S. Gao and Weihuan Zhou

*New Asian Regionalism in International Economic Law*
Pasha L. Hsieh

*Essential Interoperability Standards: Interfacing Intellectual Property and Competition in International Economic Law*
Simon Brinsmead

*Digital Services in International Trade Law*
Ines Willemyns

*Law and Politics on Export Restrictions: WTO and Beyond*
Chien-Huei Wu

*Energy in International Trade Law: Concepts, Regulation and Changing Markets*
Anna-Alexandra Marhold

*Shareholders' Claims for Reflective Loss in International Investment Law*
Lukas Vanhonnaeker

*Transparency in the WTO SPS and TBT Agreements: The Real Jewel in the Crown*
Marianna B. Karttunen

*Preferential Services Liberalization: The Case of the European Union and Federal States*
Johanna Jacobsson

*Emerging Powers in International Economic Law: Cooperation, Competition and Transformation*
Sonia E. Rolland and David M. Trubek

*Commitments and Flexibilities in the WTO Agreement on Subsidies and Countervailing Measures*
José Guilherme Moreno Caiado

*The Return of the Home State to Investor-State Disputes: Bringing Back Diplomatic Protection?*
Rodrigo Polanco

*Industrial Policy and the World Trade Organization: Between Legal Constraints and Flexibilities*
Sherzod Shadikhodjaev

*The Public International Law of Trade in Legal Services*
David Collins

*The Prudential Carve-Out for Financial Services: Rationale and Practice in the GATS and Preferential Trade Agreements*
Carlo Maria Cantore

*Preferential Services Liberalization: The Case of the European Union and Federal States*
Johanna Jacobsson

*Judicial Acts and Investment Treaty Arbitration*
Berk Demirkol

*Distributive Justice and World Trade Law: A Political Theory of International Trade Regulation*
Oisin Suttle

*Freedom of Transit and Access to Gas Pipeline Networks under WTO Law*
Vitaliy Pogoretskyy

*Reclaiming Development in the World Trading System, 2^nd edition*
Yong-Shik Lee

*Developing Countries and Preferential Services Trade*
Charlotte Sieber-Gasser

*Establishing Judicial Authority in International Economic Law* Edited by Joanna Jemielniak, Laura Nielsen and Henrik Palmer Olsen

*WTO Dispute Settlement and the TRIPS Agreement: Applying Intellectual Property Standards in a Trade Law Framework*
Matthew Kennedy

*Trade, Investment, Innovation and their Impact on Access to Medicines: An Asian Perspective*
Locknie Hsu

*The WTO and International Investment Law: Converging Systems*
Jürgen Kurtz

*The Law, Economics and Politics of International Standardisation* Edited by Panagiotis Delimatsis

*Export Restrictions on Critical Minerals and Metals: Testing the Adequacy of WTO Disciplines*
Ilaria Espa

*Optimal Regulation and the Law of International Trade: The Interface between the Right to Regulate and WTO Law*
Boris Rigod

*The Social Foundations of World Trade: Norms, Community, and Constitution*
Sungjoon Cho

*Public Participation and Legitimacy in the WTO*
Yves Bonzon

*The Challenge of Safeguards in the WTO*
Fernando Piérola

*General Interests of Host States in International Investment Law* Edited by Giorgio Sacerdoti, with Pia Acconci, Mara Valenti and Anna De Luca

*WTO Disciplines on Subsidies and Countervailing Measures: Balancing Policy Space and Legal Constraints*
Dominic Coppens

*The Law of Development Cooperation: A Comparative Analysis of the World Bank, the EU and Germany*
Philipp Dann

*Liberalizing International Trade after Doha: Multilateral, Plurilateral, Regional, and Unilateral Initiatives*
David A. Gantz

*Domestic Judicial Review of Trade Remedies: Experiences of the Most Active WTO Members* Edited by Müslüm Yilmaz

*The Relevant Market in International Economic Law: A Comparative Antitrust and GATT Analysis*
Christian A. Melischek

*International Organizations in WTO Dispute Settlement: How Much Institutional Sensitivity?*
Marina Foltea

*Public Services and International Trade Liberalization: Human Rights and Gender Implications*
Barnali Choudhury

*The Law and Politics of WTO Waivers: Stability and Flexibility in Public International Law*
Isabel Feichtner

*African Regional Trade Agreements as Legal Regimes*
James Thuo Gathii

*Processes and Production Methods (PPMs) in WTO Law: Interfacing Trade and Social Goals*
Christiane R. Conrad

*Non-Discrimination in International Trade in Services: 'Likeness' in WTO/GATS*
Nicolas F. Diebold

*The Law, Economics and Politics of Retaliation in WTO Dispute Settlement* Edited by Chad P. Bown and Joost Pauwelyn

*The Multilateralization of International Investment Law*
Stephan W. Schill

*Trade Policy Flexibility and Enforcement in the WTO: A Law and Economics Analysis*
Simon A. B. Schropp

# THE LAW AND PRACTICE OF GLOBAL ICT STANDARDIZATION

OLIA KANEVSKAIA
*Utrecht University*

CAMBRIDGE
UNIVERSITY PRESS

CAMBRIDGE
UNIVERSITY PRESS

Shaftesbury Road, Cambridge CB2 8EA, United Kingdom

One Liberty Plaza, 20th Floor, New York, NY 10006, USA

477 Williamstown Road, Port Melbourne, VIC 3207, Australia

314–321, 3rd Floor, Plot 3, Splendor Forum, Jasola District Centre, New Delhi – 110025, India

103 Penang Road, #05–06/07, Visioncrest Commercial, Singapore 238467

Cambridge University Press is part of Cambridge University Press & Assessment, a department of the University of Cambridge.

We share the University's mission to contribute to society through the pursuit of education, learning and research at the highest international levels of excellence.

www.cambridge.org
Information on this title: www.cambridge.org/9781009300575

DOI: 10.1017/9781009300551



First published 2023

*A catalogue record for this publication is available from the British Library.*

ISBN 978-1-009-30057-5 Hardback

*To Greg and Leia, who taught me that not everything can be standardized – and that's fine.*

CONTENTS

# TABLES

# TABLE OF CASES

## WTO Appellate Body Reports

Appellate Body Report, European Communities – Regime for the Importation, Sale and Distribution of Bananas, WTO Doc. WT/DS27/AB/R (September 9, 1997)

Appellate Body Report, EC-Measures Affecting Asbestos and Asbestos-Containing Products, WT/DS135/AB/R (March 12, 2001)

Appellate Body Report, Anti-Dumping Measures on Certain Hot-Rolled Steel Products from Japan, WT/DS184/AB/R (July 24, 2001)

Appellate Body Report, European Communities – Trade Description of Sardines, WT/DS231/AB/R (September 26, 2002)

Appellate Body Report, United States – Measures Affecting the Production and Sale of Clove Cigarettes, WTO Doc. WT/DS406/AB/R (April 4, 2012)

Appellate Body Report, United States – Measures Concerning the Importation, Marketing and Sale of Tuna and Tuna Products, WTO Doc. WT/DS381/AB/R (June 13, 2012)

Appellate Body Report, United States – Certain Country of Origin Labelling (COOL) Requirements, WTO Doc. WT/DS384/ARB, WT/DS386/ARB (June 29, 2012)

## European Courts

Cases 9/56 and 10/56, Meroni & Co, Industrie Metallurgiche *v.* High Authority [1957–1958] ECR 133

Case 48/69, Imperial Chemical Industries Ltd. *v.* Commission [1972] ECLI:EU:C:1972:70

Case C-120/78, Rewe-Zentral AG *v.* Bundesmonopolverwaltung für Branntwein [1979] ECR 1979–00649.

Joined Cases 96 to 102, 104, 105, 108, and 110/82, N V IAZ International Belgium e.a. *v.* Commission [1983] ECLI: ECLI:EU:C:1983:310

Joined Cases 89/85, 104/85, 114/85, 116/85, 117/85, and 125/85 to 129/85 Ahlstrom and Others *v.* Commission [1988] ECLI:EU:C:1993:120

Case C-41/90, Klaus Höfner and Fritz Elser *v.* Macrotron GmbH [1991] ECLI:EU:C:1991:161

Case T-66/89, Publishers Association *v.* Commission [1992] ECLI:EU:T:1992:84

Case T-4/92, Evangelos Vardakas *v.* Commission [1993] ECLI:EU:T:1993:29

Joined Cases T-213/95 and T-18/96, Stichting Certificatie Kraanverhuurbedrijf (SCK), Federatie van Nederlandse Kraanverhuurbedrijven (FNK) *v.* Commission [1997] ECLI:EU:T:1997:157

Case T-102/96, Gencor *v.* Commission [1999] ECR II-753

Case C-67/96, Albany International BV and Stichting Bedrijfspensioenfonds Textielindustrie [1999] ECLI:EU:C:1999:430

Case C-309/99, J.C.J. Wouters, J.W. Savelbergh, Price Waterhouse Belastingadviseurs BV and Algemene Raad van de Nederlandse Orde van Advocaten [2002] ECLI:EU:C:2002:98

Joined Cases T-217/03 and T-245/03, Fédération nationale de la coopération bétail and viande (FNCBV) e.a. *v.* Commission [2006] ECLI:EU:T:2006:391

Case T-155/04, SELEX Sistemi Integrati SpA *v.* Commission of the European Communities [2006] ECLI:EU:T:2006:387

Case C-227/06, Commission *v.* Belgium [2008] ECR 2008 I-00046.

Case C-113/07, SELEX Sistemi Integrati SpA *v.* Commission of the European Communities [2009] ECLI:EU:C:2009:191

Case T-432/05, EMC Development AB *v.* European Commission [2010] ECLI:EU:T:2010:189

Case C-185/08, Latchways plc and Eurosafe Solutions BV *v.* Kedge Safety Systems BV and Consolidated Nederland BV [2010] ECLI:EU:C:2010:619

Case T-286/09, Intel Corp. *v.* Commission [2014] ECLI:EU:T:2014:547

Case C-171/11, Fra.bo SpA *v.* Deutsche Vereinigung des Gas- und Wasserfaches [2012] ECLI:EU:C:2012:453

Case C-1/12, Ordem dos Técnicos Oficiais de Contas *v.* Autoridade da Concorrência [2013] ECLI:EU:C:2013:127

Case C-270/12, United Kingdom of Great Britain and Northern Ireland *v.* European Parliament and Council (ESMA) [2014] ECLI:EU:C:2014:18

Case C-170/13, Huawei Technologies Co. Ltd *v.* ZTE Corp [2015] ECLI: EU:C:2015:477.
Case C-613/14, James Elliott Construction Ltd *v.* Irish Asphalt Ltd [2016] ECLI:EU:C:2016:821
Case C-413/14, Intel Corp. *v.* European Commission [2017] CLI:EU: C:2017:632
Case C-219/15, Elisabeth Schmitt *v.* TÜV Rheinland LGA Products GmbH [2017] ECLI:EU:C:2017:128
Case C-310/17, Levola Hengelo BV. *v.* Smilde Foods BV [2018] ECLI:EU: C:2018:899
Case T-185/19, Public.Resource.Org and Right to Know *v.* Commission [2021] ECLI:EU:T:2021:445

## EU National Courts

### *Germany*

Bundesgerichtshof [BGH] (June 30, 1983), GRUR 1984
Bundesverfassungsgericht [BVerfGE] (July 29, 1998), ZUM 1998
Bundesgerichtshof [BGH] (2009) 180 BGHZ 312
OLG Düsseldorf (2017) I-2 U 23/17

### *Netherlands*

Hoge Raad (June 22, 2012), LJN: BW0393
Raad van State, Uitspraak 201903780/1/A1, ECLI:NL:RVS:2020:924

### *UK*

Unwired Planet Int Ltd and Unwired Planet LLC *v.* Huawei Technologies Co ltd and Huawei Technologies UK Co Ltd (2017) EWHC 711 (Pat).
Unwired Planet Int Ltd and Unwired Planet LLC *v.* Huawei Technologies Co Ltd and Huawei Technologies UK Co Ltd (2017) [2018] EWCA Civ 2344.

## US Courts

Wheaton *v.* Peters, 33 U.S. (8 Pet.) 591 [1834]
Addyston Pipe and Steel Co. *v.* United States, 175 U.S. 211 [1899]
Standard Oil Co. *v.* United States, 337 U.S. 293 [1949]

C-O-Two Fire Equip. *v.* United States 197 F2d [1952]
Radiant Burners, Inc. *v.* Peoples Gas Co. 364 U.S. 656 [1961]
Eastern Railroad Presidents Conference *v.* Noerr Motor Freight, Inc., 365 U.S. 127, 135 [1961]
National Macaroni Manufacturers Association, et al. *v.* Federal Trade Commission, No. 14713 [1965]
United States *v.* Am Radiator and Standard Sanitary Corp 433 F2d 174 [1971]
Bldg. Officials and Code Admin. v. Code Tech., Inc., 628 F.2d 730 I st Cir. [1980]
American Society of Mechanical Engineers *v.* Hydrolevel Corporation, 456 U.S. 556 [1982]
Allied Tube *v.* Indian Head, Inc., 486 U.S. 492 [1988]
Hartford Fire Insurance Co. *v.* California. 113 S. Ct. 2891 [1993]
CCC Info. Servs. Inc. *v.* MacLean Hunter Mkt. Rep., Inc., 44 F.3d 6 1 2d Cir. (1994)
Dell Computer Corp., 121 F.T.C. 616, 618 [1996]
Practice Mgmt. Info. Corp. *v.* Am. Med. Ass'n, 1 2 1 F.3d 5 1 6 9th Cir. (1997), amended by 133 F.3d 1 1 40 9th Cir. [1998]
Adamaxx *v.* Open Software Foundation, No. 97-1807 [1998]
Yahoo!, Inc. *v.* La Ligue Contre Le Racisme, 169 F. Supp. 2d 1181, N.D. Cal. [2001]
En banc, Veeck *v.* S. Bldg. Code Cong. Int'I, Inc., 293 F.3d 791 (5th Cir. 2002) *cert. denied*, 539 U.S. 969 [2003]
MGM Studios, Inc. *v.* Grokster, Ltd., 545 U.S. 913 [2005]
eBay Inc. *v.* MercExchange, L.L.C., 547 U.S. 388 [2006]
United States Courts of Appeals for the Federal Circuit, Qualcomm Inc. *v.* Broadcom Corp. [2007]
Broadcom Corporation *v.* Qualcomm Incorporated, 543 F3d 683 Fed. Cir [2008]
Golden Bridge Technology Inc. *v.* Motorola, Inc., 547 F.3d 266, Fed. Cir [2008]
US Court of Appeals of DC Circuit, No. 07-1086, Rambus Incorporated *v.* Federal Trade Commission [2008]
Microsoft Corp. *v.* Motorola Inc., 2:10-cv-01823-JLR, 871 F. Supp. 2d 1089, W.D. Wash [2012]
Shell's Disposal & Recycling, Inc. *v.* City of Lancaster, 504 F. App'x 194, 202, 3d Cir [2012]
TruePosition, Inc. *v.* LM Ericsson Tel. Co. (Jan. 6, 2012), No. 11-4574, 2012 WL 33075 [2012]

TruePosition, Inc. *v.* LM Ericsson Tel. Co. (Aug. 21, 2012), No. 11-4574, 2012 WL 3584626 [2012]

Innovatio IP Ventures, LLC Patent Litig., 921 F. Supp. 2d 903 N.D. Ill. [2013]

TruePosition, Inc. *v.* LM Ericsson Tel. Co. (Oct. 9, 2012) 977 F. Supp. 2d 462 [2013]

TCL Comm'n *v.* Ericsson, C.A. No. 14-CV-341, C.D. Cal. [2017]

American Society for Testing & Materials *v.* Public.Resource.org, Inc. No. 1:13-cv-01215 (TSC), 2017 WL 473822, (D.D.C. Feb. 2, 2017), *amended by* No. 17-7035, D.C. Cir. [2018]

NSS Labs, Inc. *v.* Crowdstrike, Inc., Case No. 3:18-cv-05711, Statement of Interest of the United States (N.D. Cal., filed June 26, 2019)

# ABBREVIATIONS

| | |
|---|---|
| 3G | third generation of wireless mobile telecommunications technology |
| 3GPP | 3rd Generation Partnership Project |
| 4G | fourth generation of wireless mobile telecommunications technology |
| 5G | fifth generation of wireless mobile telecommunications technology |
| AD | Area Director |
| AG | Advocate General |
| AFNOR | Association Française de Normalisation |
| AMA | American Medical Association |
| AMD | Associate Member Director |
| ANS | American National Standard |
| ANSI | American National Standards Institute |
| ARIB | Association of Radio Industries and Businesses |
| ASA | American Standards Association |
| ASD | Accredited Standards Developer |
| ASME | American Society of Mechanical Engineers |
| ASTM | American Society for Testing and Materials |
| ATIS | Alliance for Telecommunications Industry Solutions |
| ATM | air traffic management |
| AudCom | Audit Committee |
| BARB | Bluetooth Architectural Review Board |
| BCP | Best Current Practices |
| BoG | Board of Governors |
| BQRB | Bluetooth Qualification Review Board |
| BRI | Belt and Road Initiative |
| BRL | Business Review Letter |
| BSI | British Standards Institution |
| BTI | Bluetooth Test and Interoperability Group |
| CARB | California Air Resources Board |
| CASE | Cyber-investigation Analysis Standard Expression |
| CCSA | China Communications Standards Association |
| CDMA | Code Division Multiple Access |
| CECED | Conseil Européen de la Construction d'Appareils Domestiques |

| | |
|---|---|
| CEG | Communauté de l'Électricité |
| CEN | European Committee for Standardization |
| CENELEC | European Committee for Electrotechnical Standardization |
| CEPT | European Conference of Postal and Telecommunications |
| CJEU | Court of Justice of the European Union |
| CPSA | Consumer Product Safety Act |
| DCMA | Digital Millennium Copyright Act |
| DICOM | Digital Imaging Communication |
| DIN | Deutsche Institut für Normstellung |
| DIPD | Draft Improvement Proposal Document |
| DoJ | Department of Justice |
| DRM | Digital Rights Management |
| DVGW | Deutsche Vereinigung des Gas- und Wasserfaches |
| E-OTD | Enhanced Observed Time Difference |
| EAB | Educational Activities Board |
| EAR | Export Administration Regulation |
| EC | European Commission |
| ECMA | European Computer Manufacturers Association |
| EDGE | Enhanced Data Rates for GSM Evolution |
| EFF | Electronic Frontier Foundation |
| EFTA | European Free Trade Association |
| EME | Encrypted Media Extensions |
| EN | Harmonized European Standard |
| ENISA | European Agency for Cybersecurity |
| ERCIM | European Research Consortium for Informatics and Mathematics |
| ESO | European Standards Organization |
| ETSI | European Telecommunications Standards Institute |
| EU | European Union |
| EV-DO | Evolution-Data Optimized |
| ExSC | ANSI Executive Council |
| FCC | Federal Communications Commission |
| FDA | Food and Drug Administration |
| FIPD | Final Improvement Proposal Document |
| FRAND | fair, reasonable, and nondiscriminatory |
| FRD | Functional Requirements Document |
| FSC | Forest Stewardship Council |
| FTC | Federal Trade Commission |
| GATT | General Agreement on Tariffs and Trade |
| GDPR | General Data Protection Regulation |
| GPRS | General Packet Radio Service |
| GSM | Global System for Mobile Telecommunication |
| HCFA | Health Care Financing Administration |

| | |
|---|---|
| HES | Harmonized European Standard |
| HEVC | High Efficiency Video Coding |
| HTML | HyperText Markup Language |
| HTTP | HyperText Transfer Protocol |
| HUD | Department of Housing and Urban Development |
| IAB | Internet Architecture Board |
| IAOC | IETF Administrative Oversight Committee |
| IASA | IETF Administrative Support Activity |
| IASB | International Accounting Standards Board |
| IATM | International Association for Testing Materials |
| ICANN | Internet Corporation for Assigned Names and Numbers |
| ICT | Information and Communications Technology |
| IEC | International Electrotechnical Commission |
| IEEE | Institute of Electrical and Electronics Engineers |
| IEEE-SA | Institute of Electrical and Electronics Engineers Standards Association |
| IESG | Internet Engineering Steering Group |
| IETF | Internet Engineering Task Force |
| IMS | IP Multimedia Sub System |
| IOP | Interoperability Testing |
| IoT | Internet of Things |
| IP | internet protocol |
| IPR | Intellectual Property Rights |
| IrDA | Infrared Data Association |
| IRTF | Internet Research Task Force |
| ISB | International Standards Body |
| ISO | International Organization for Standardization |
| ISOC | Internet Society |
| ITC | International Trade Commission |
| ITU | International Telecommunications Union |
| JEDEC | Joint Electron Device Engineering Council |
| JISC | Japanese Industrial Standards Committee |
| JRC | Joint Research Centre |
| JTC | Joint Technical Committee |
| JVT | Joint Video Team |
| LAN | local area network |
| LMU | Location Measurement Unit |
| LoA | Letter of Assurance |
| LTE | Long-Term Evolution |
| MCPTT | Mission-Critical Push to Talk |
| MGAB | Member and Geographic Activities Board |
| MFN | Most Favoured Nation |
| MoU | Memorandum of Understanding |

| | |
|---|---|
| MPEG | Moving Picture Experts Group |
| MS | mobile station |
| NCRPA | National Cooperative Research and Production Act |
| NEN | Nederlandse Normalisatie Instituut |
| NesCom | New Standards Committee |
| NFPA | National Fire Protection Association |
| NGO | nongovernmental organization |
| NIST | National Institute of Standards and Technology |
| NomCom | Nominating Committee |
| NSO | National Standardization Organizations |
| NTTAA | National Technology Transfer and Advancement Act |
| NWP | New Work Proposal |
| OASIS | Organization for the Advancement of Structured Information Standards |
| OECD | Organization for Economic Cooperation and Development |
| OFDM | Orthogonal Frequency-Division Multiplexing |
| OFR | Office of the Federal Register |
| OJ | Official Journal |
| OMB | Office of Management and Budget |
| OSI | Open Systems Interconnection |
| OSF | Open Software Foundation |
| OTDOA | Observed Time Difference of Arrival |
| OTOC | Ordem dos Técnicos Oficiais de Contas |
| OXML | Open EXtended Markup Language |
| P&P | Policies and Procedures |
| PAG | Patent Advisory Group |
| PAN | personal area network |
| PAR | Project Authorization Request |
| PatCom | Patent Committee |
| PCG | Project Coordination Group |
| PDF | Portable Document Format |
| ProCom | Procedures Committee |
| PSPB | Publication Services and Products Board |
| R&D | research and development |
| RAN | radio access network |
| RAND | reasonable and nondiscriminatory |
| RevCom | Review Committee |
| RFC | Request for Comments |
| SAC | Standardization Administration of China |
| SASB | IEEE-SA Standards Board |
| SBC | Southern Building Code |
| SBCCI | Southern Building Code Congress International |
| SCK | Stichting Certificatie Kraanverhuurbedrijf |

| | |
|---|---|
| SDO | Standard Development Organization |
| SDOAA | Standards Development Organization Advancement Act |
| SEP | Standard Essential Patent |
| SIG | Special Interest Group |
| SME | small and medium-sized enterprises |
| SMPD | Specification Management Process Document |
| SMS | Short Message Services |
| SPS | Sanitary and Phytosanitary Measures |
| SSO | Standard-Setting Organization |
| SSPPU | Smallest Saleable Patent Practicing Unit |
| STC | Specific Trade concern |
| TAB | Technical Activities Board |
| TAG | Technical Architecture Group |
| TBT | Technical Barriers to Trade |
| TBT NSS | TBT Notification Submission System |
| TCP | Transmission Control Protocol |
| TFEU | Treaty of Functioning of the European Union |
| TRIPS | Trade-Related Aspects of Intellectual Property |
| TSDSI | Telecommunications Standards Development Society of India |
| TSG | Technical Study Group |
| TÜV | Technischer Überwachungsverein |
| UK | United Kingdom |
| UL-TOA | Uplink Time of Arrival |
| UN | United Nations |
| US | United States |
| USB | Universal Serial Bus |
| USTR | US Trade Representative |
| UTDOA | Uplink-Time Difference of Arrival |
| VCR | videocassette recorder |
| VESA | Video Electronics Standards Association |
| VITA | VMEbus International Trade Association |
| W3C | World Wide Web Consortium |
| WAPI | WLAN Authentication and Privacy Infrastructure |
| WCDMA | Wideband Code Division Multiple Access |
| WHATWG | Web Hypertext Application Technology Working Group |
| WiMAX | Worldwide Interoperability for Microwave Access |
| WIPI | Wireless Internet Platform for Interoperability |
| WLAN | wireless local area network |
| WSN | wireless sensor network |
| WTO | World Trade Organization |
| XHTML | EXtensible HyperText Markup Language |
| XML | EXtensible Markup Language |

# Introduction

When we think about connectivity, we usually imagine complex IT infrastructure and high-tech devices powered by cutting-edge scientific research. Rarely do we consider these technologies as a form of regulation, or the power behind them as regulators. And yet, what would our daily life be without the ability to transfer data from one device to another? How will we be able to interact with different people, operate complex electronic equipment, and take part in almost all modern activities without interconnection between different electronic systems?

Connectivity as an enabler of global economic activity is not merely an attribute of the modern digitalized society. Decades and centuries ago, inventions such as telegraphs, telephones, and the first internet network protocols have shaped interactions between various stakeholders of the global economy. This trend continues today with the 5th generation cellular networks (5G) and the Internet of Things (IoT), a new ecosystem of connected environment.[1] These and many other technological and societal innovations cut across different fields and influence the behavior of States and companies alike.

Connectivity technologies are codified in technical documents and specifications: Information and Communication Technologies (ICT) standards.[2] By prescribing methods applied in electronic devices, coordinating transmission frequencies and defining protocols and procedures for internet connection, ICT standards provide written "rules" that hardware and software developers should follow for their products to operate properly and be compatible with other products on the market. The functioning of many electronic machines is based on hundreds of

[1] Organization for Economic Cooperation and Development (OECD), 'The internet of things: seizing the benefits and addressing the challenges' (May 24, 2016) (DSTI/ICCP/CISP(2015)3/FINAL), 9–11.

[2] This research takes a broad definition of the term "standard" that encompasses technical specifications, protocols, and languages.

such ICT standards developed by different actors in technical committees of various industry-driven organizations.[3] Being the product of science and market demands, ICT standards impose de facto norms on community, setting uniform expectations for manufacturers, consumers, and governments.

Not surprisingly, due to their far-reaching implications, ICT standards are characterized by the presence of many, often conflicting, interests. Companies compete for market power,[4] governments express security concerns related to the increased network's connectivity,[5] and civil society demands more say in technical decisions that are of societal importance. Moreover, ICT standards are paradoxical: they are neutral, yet extremely politicized; they are for everyone's benefit, yet they exclude; they have profound business impact, yet they are developed by noncommercial organizations. Developed by engineers as a part of digital infrastructure, ICT standards are not an isolated technological phenomenon; rather, they have far-reaching regulatory, political, economic, and societal consequences. As ICT standards are increasingly becoming endowed with policy-making and public interest functions, they should be analyzed in the broader institutional and regulatory context in which they are developed and enforced.[6]

Academic scholarship in the field of ICT standardization is typically devoted to analyzing interactions and competitive forces among industry players in standards development committees, for instance, when

[3] A study estimated that a modern laptop relies on 250–500 interoperability standards, see B. Biddle, A. White and S. Woods, 'How many standards in a laptop? (and other empirical questions)' (2010) in *Proceedings from K-2010: ITU Kaleidoscope Academic Conference – Beyond the Internet? Innovations and for Future Networks and Services*, Pune, India, December 13–15, 2010.

[4] IPlytics GmbH, 'Who is leading in the 5G patent race? Analysis on declared standard essential patents, 3GPP contributions and attendance data' (February 2019).

[5] NIS Cooperation Group, 'EU coordinated risk assessment of the cybersecurity of 5G networks' (October 9, 2019), available at https://europa.eu/rapid/press-release_IP-19-6049_en.htm; Europol, 'Position paper of 5G' (April 10, 2019) EDOC #1038503; US National Institute of Standards and Technology, 'Interagency report on strategic U.S. government engagement in international standardization to achieve U.S. objectives for cybersecurity' (2015) NIST Interagency Report 8074, vol. 1, available at http://dx.doi.org/10.6028/NIST.IR.8074v1.

[6] See W. Mattli and N. Woods, 'In whose benefit? Explaining regulatory change in global politics', in W. Mattli and N. Woods (eds.), *The Politics of Global Regulation* (Princeton: Princeton University Press, 2009), pp. 1–43.

selecting technologies that are essential for standards' functioning.[7] There has been hitherto little research on how these technical committees are governed and which procedural guarantees do they offer to those affected by their standards.[8] Likewise, a qualitative analysis of Standards Development Organizations' (SDOs) rules and processes remains strikingly missing from the relevant literature, creating a growing gap between the theory and practice of ICT standardization. A holistic inquiry into the ecosystem of ICT standardization, its law, and practice is necessary for the broader understanding of the resilience of standardization as a mechanism of global governance and the evolvement of SDOs as regulatory institutions.

This book explores to what extent does current ICT standardization comply with the applicable procedural and substantive requirements, and whether increased scrutiny of SDOs operating in the ICT sector is desirable to guarantee due process. In this endeavor, it goes beyond theoretical consideration by evaluating SDOs' rules and procedures in the light of current practices and tendencies in the industry. On the normative side, this book defines the rules for SDOs to follow under the current regulatory frameworks, focusing on procedural and substantive guarantees that should be respected in standards development. A further descriptive analysis explores the extent to which SDOs comply with these rules by analyzing their mechanics and institutional architecture in the context of the applicable regulatory frameworks. To understand whether and how SDOs' processes affect the legitimacy, effectiveness, and quality of their standards, the book continues with a qualitative empirical study that reveals experiences of industry experts with the processes of different SDOs.

The study is premised on two hypotheses: first, that, given the increased regulatory importance of ICT standards, it has become challenging for SDOs to offer sufficient procedural and substantive

[7] See, among many others, L. Cabral and D. Salant, 'Evolving technologies and standards regulation' (2014) 36 *International Journal of Industrial Organization* 48–56; J. Farrell, J. Hayes, C. Shapiro and T. Sullivan, 'Standard setting, patents, and hold-up' (2007) 74 *Antitrust Law Review* 603–70.

[8] Previous studies include the report on the governance and IPR policies of SDOs: J. Baron, J. L. Contreras, M. Husovec, P. Larouche and N. Thumm, 'Making the rules: the governance of standard development organizations and their policies on intellectual property rights' (2019) JRC Science for Policy Report, EUR 29655 EN, available at https://publications.jrc.ec.europa.eu/repository/bitstream/JRC115004/sdo_governance_final_electronic_version.pdf (hereinafter: JRC Report).

guarantees to satisfy all stakeholders that have varying – and sometimes even conflicting – interests in standards development; and, second, that increased scrutiny of SDOs' process by governmental authorities, when performed with caution and respect to the industry demands, can improve the quality of SDOs' decision-making and, ultimately, the effectiveness of their standards.

## Methodology

Largely conducted from a legal perspective, this study relies on an interdisciplinary methodological approach.[9] It combines desk research that involves reviewing the relevant primary and secondary sources of law and an evaluation of theoretical findings in an empirical study performed by two types of qualitative research methods, namely, case studies on procedural disputes in SDOs and semistructured interviews with experts from SDOs and private companies.

This study starts from the premise that SDOs are subject to external constrains placed on them by public law, and internal constraints that stem from the operational rules established by the SDOs' governing authorities. While the latter are developed through the mechanisms of self-regulation and can be influenced by SDOs' members and participants, the former are in principle not controlled by the SDOs. Yet, as the rules of public law affect the design of SDOs' governance, so do the operational rules of SDOs affect the instruments of public law. For this reason, it is crucial to analyze all layers of standardization regulation, their interactions and linkages, and the ways in which they influence each other and challenge each other's relevance and appropriateness. And while this study is rather limited due to a small number of SDOs it examines, its findings facilitate broader understanding of the institutional context in which ICT standards are developed and invite to view SDOs' governance from a broader perspective of ICT standards as suppliers of private regulation.

Despite certain methodological and technical limitations, the empirical study adds practical relevance to the theory. When juxtaposed with the findings of the normative and descriptive parts of this research, the findings of the empirical study, albeit anecdotal, allow to draw further conclusions regarding the current state of due process in ICT

[9] The methodological choices are further explained in Parts III and IV.

standardization, noting some possible and feasible improvements of SDOs' governance and processes and introducing further challenges associated with procedural guarantees in global SDOs.

## Outline of the Book

This book is divided into four parts. Part I presents the ecosystem of ICT standardization. Chapter 1 discusses ICT standardization as a normative regime and explains how voluntary standards created in committee processes of different types of SDOs may acquire binding force. Chapter 2 offers a normative account of legitimacy of ICT standardization as a form of private transnational (i.e., increasingly international, but not States-centered) regulation and introduces an inexhaustive list of procedural meta-principles through which private regulatory regimes can be legitimized.

Part II proceeds with examining the regulatory frameworks that apply to global ICT SDOs and provides detailed research into the applicable legislation, policy, and case law, focusing on the procedural instruments that these regulatory frameworks offer to SDOs to legitimize their standards and to limit or escape liability. Chapter 3 discusses the relevant agreements of the World Trade Organization (WTO) (Technical Barriers to Trade, TBT); Chapters 4 and 5, respectively, discuss the relevant domains of the EU and US regional regulatory frameworks. While noting that there are certain differences and similarities in how the law treats voluntary standards and SDOs producing them, Chapter 6 offers a holistic analysis of the procedural principles introduced in the examined frameworks, to which it collectively refers to as "due process" principles and further explores the relevance and suitability of these principles to ICT SDOs, identifying the shortcomings of each of the legal mechanism with regard to the current challenges in ICT standardization.

Part III explores the procedural and substantive guarantees offered in leading SDOs. Chapters 7 and 8 provide a detailed systematic overview of the operational frameworks of seven SDOs, each having different institutional background and producing different types of ICT standards. In particular, this analysis differentiates between SDOs' administrative rules ("policies" and "policy-making") and technical ("standards development)" processes. Chapter 9 then analyzes the extent to which the legal instruments discussed in Part II apply to the SDOs at issue and evaluates SDOs' rules and procedures against the due process requirements of these legal instruments.

Building on the descriptive findings of the previous chapters, Part IV contributes with practical considerations from qualitative empirical research. The findings of this part increase our understanding of current practices in ICT standardization and offer food for thought for both public and private regulators with respect to the design and scrutiny of SDOs' processes. Upon discussing the methodology for the empirical study in the introduction to Part IV, Chapter 10 offers three case studies on recent disagreements in SDOs bodies and committees where procedural guarantees were at stake and that were resolved either by the SDOs' internal dispute resolution bodies or by the courts. Chapter 11 then reveals experiences of individuals that are actively involved in ICT standardization, mostly experts from leading private companies, with the processes of different SDOs, discussing such aspects as procedural guarantees in technical committees, dispute resolution by SDOs' governance bodies and the differences between drafting SDOs' internal rules and drafting standards. This chapter seeks to understand, from a practical viewpoint, how SDOs' compliance with due process requirements relates to the effectiveness of their standards. Chapter 12 brings together theoretical and practical considerations and offers a new perspective on legitimacy of ICT standardization as a private regulatory regime. It further suggests what should be the role of different stakeholders (e.g., SDOs, governments, and courts) in strengthening the different types of legitimacy in ICT standardization, underscoring the importance of feedback mechanisms for SDOs' decision-making that is currently insufficient or absent from the SDOs' operational frameworks.

## Contributions

Without any pretense of exhaustiveness, this book explores the ecosystem and regulatory landscape of ICT standardization. Its title, *The Law and Practice of Global ICT Standardization*, was chosen to demonstrate the comprehensiveness of the study as well as its connection to practice, rather than as an attempt to make a definite contribution to the extensive field of law and standardization. This book also does not aim to make any explicit statements regarding SDOs' compliance with the applicable laws and regulatory requirements. Rather, it aspires to become a reference point by providing a comprehensive analysis of legal rules, governance, and technical processes in global ICT standardization in a manner that is explanatory as well as explorative, especially focusing on procedural guarantees in SDOs and their practical application.

The contribution of this study is threefold. Firstly, it offers a holistic analysis of legal rules and procedural principles that different regulatory frameworks have in place for industry-driven SDOs, building on the existing literature in the field as well as examining updated legal documents. Secondly, it provides a systematic overview of SDOs' governance and standards development procedures, introducing different implementation mechanisms for procedural safeguards. Lastly, it gives due account to practical considerations from qualitative empirical evidence, attempting to bring theoretical legal research a step closer to reality, and, by this means, contributing to the understanding of the ecology of ICT standardization.

The evolution of ICT standardization as a form of governance, together with the great diversity of SDOs' institutional landscape, poses the question whether due process principles, as currently formulated by the regulatory frameworks, are still fit for purpose and offer meaningful tools for their implementation and enforcement. Arguably, these principles can be bent to suit a particular industry and tailored to a particular organizational structure. Arguably, the excessive involvement of governmental actors in the design of SDOs' rules, while certainly facilitating due process, is undesirable and may distort SDOs' technical decision-making. In this regard, SDOs' are faced with a considerable challenge to follow due process requirements while being sufficiently flexible to adapt to market developments and to ever-evolving industry needs.

# PART I

## The Ecosystem of ICT Standardization

Amid many types of standards, ICT standards clearly stand out, not least for their capacity to generate network effects and stimulate innovation.[1] Their increasing regulatory importance did not go unnoticed in the age of the forth industrial revolution,[2] where the distinction between physical and digital worlds is blurred and where technological advancement is ever-growing.[3] Conceptualization of ICT standards as merely technical requirements developed "by engineers and for engineers" thus can no longer hold, and legal analysis of ICT standards should not only be devoted to the question how they are regulated, but also, *how they regulate.*

Unlike many national and regional initiatives of technology regulation,[4] ICT standardization typically takes place at the global level, with national and regional industry actors and institutions as its facilitators or implementors. In this context, by far most standardization initiatives are *private* rather than governmental: indeed, while States may have a role to play when designing the overarching rules and processes to be followed by standards developers, the driving force behind ICT standards are companies with human capital and capabilities of R&D spending. Hence, ICT standardization is one of the many examples of rule-making beyond the State, where the industry develops the rules by which it abides but even more, where such rules affect a wide range of stakeholders by regulating the most important economic and social sectors.

[1] P. Curran, 'Standard-setting organizations: patents, price fixing, and per se legality' (2003) 70 *The University of Chicago Law Review* 983–1009 at 987.

[2] K. Schwab, 'The fourth industrial revolution: what it means, how to respond' (World Economic Forum, 2016), available at www.weforum.org/agenda/2016/01/the-fourth-industrial-revolution-what-it-means-and-how-to-respond/.

[3] See L. DeNardis, *The Internet in Everything. Freedom and Security in a World with No Off Switch* (New Haven and London: Yale University Press, 2020).

[4] E.g., Regulation 2016/679 on the protection of natural persons with regard to the processing of personal data and on the free movement of such data (General Data Protection Regulation, or GDPR).

Much ink has been spilled on such nongovernmental regulatory arrangements, their benefits as opposed to governmental regulation, and the perils of misbalancing traditional governance structure and changing the patterns of authority.[5] Private regulation is especially prone to the capture by particular interests, which is further aggravated in ICT standardization due to the homogeneity of the group developing these standards and the presence of competitive forces and vested interests in standards development groups. Moreover, despite the infinitely large group of stakeholders affected by ICT standards, most noncommercial interests are not represented in standardization committees, or represented only marginally;[6] after all, standardization is not strictly a democratic process, but rather a type of epistemic regulation bound to create tensions with democratic control of public and regulatory policy, since the ultimate decision-making is entrusted to the experts, and not representatives of the whole community affected by the regulation.

Against this backdrop, the question arises regarding the legitimacy of standardization as a regulatory technique and a mechanism of private rule-making. How do standards developers gain their authority to regulate, and how can they be held accountable for their decisions? The concept of legitimacy in private regulation is not straightforward and revolves around the rule-making authority where the rules originate as well as their ability to achieve the pursued regulatory goals.[7] In ICT standardization, where rule-making takes place at the global level and is driven by expertise rather than democracy, the question of legitimacy becomes particularly salient. The changing use of connectivity standards in the era of IoT and the subsequent changes in competitive dynamics on the markets[8] affect legitimacy demands of ICT standardization and requires unpacking the characteristics and functions of ICT standards as well as revisiting their legitimization techniques.

[5] For example, H. Schepel, *The Constitution of Private Governance: Product Standards in the Regulation of Integrating Markets* (Oxford and Portland: Hart Publishing, 2005), and many others discussed in this chapters.

[6] See the literature review in A. Harcourt, G. Christou and S. Simpson, *Global Standard Setting in Internet Governance* (Oxford: Oxford University Press, 2020), pp. 19–20.

[7] See J. Black, 'Constructing and contesting legitimacy and accountability in polycentric regulatory regimes' (2008) LSE Law, Society and Economy Working Papers, n. 02-2008.

[8] See B. Conde Gallego and J. Drexl, 'IoT connectivity standards: how adaptive is the current SEP regulatory framework?' (2019) 50 *IIC – International Review of Intellectual Property and Competition Law* 135–56 at 137.

# 1

# ICT Standardization as a Normative Regime

## Characteristics of Technical Standards

### *Standards' Types and Functions*

Standards are technical documents that refer to a common set of characteristics of a particular good or service,[1] and that are voluntary. Standards exist in a bewildering variety of forms[2] and run across many domains, from quality of service in public passenger transport to technical protocols supporting data transmission across the internet. To name a few examples: the ISO 9001 standard series provide guidance for companies' quality management,[3] the Codex Alimentarius standard

[1] OECD, 'Standard setting' (March 8, 2011) (DAF/COMP(2010)), available at www.oecd.org/daf/competition/47381304.pdf, p. 9. The common definition of standards is provided by ISO/IEC Guide 2: "... a document, established by consensus and approved by a recognized body, that provides, for common and repeated use, rules, guidelines or characteristics for activities or their results, aimed at the achievement of the optimum degree of order in a given context ..." and that "should be based on the consolidated results of science, technology and experience, and aimed at the promotion of optimum community benefits," Article 3.2 of the ISO/IEC Guide 2, Standardization and Related Activities: General Vocabulary (2004), available at https://isotc.iso.org/livelink/livelink?func=ll&objId=8389141&objAction=browse&sort=name; Brunsson et al. acknowledge that the term "standard" may have several definitions and may highlight different aspects of practice and theory. See N. Brunsson, A. Rasche and D. Seidl, 'The dynamics of standardization: three perspectives on standards in organization studies' (2012) 33 *Organizational Studies* 613–32 at 615.

[2] Classification of standards would typically depend upon the scientific field, or the approach taken by organizations or scholars. For instance, OECD classifies standards as quality, informational, uniformity, professional conduct, and interoperability standards (see OECD, 'Standard setting', p. 21), whereas Werle refers to standards for products or processes that are either design-based or performance-based and have coordinative or regulative function; see R. Werle, 'Standards in the international telecommunications regime' (2001) Hamburg Institute of International Economics (HWWA) Discussion Paper 157, pp. 8–10.

[3] Series on Quality Management, ISO 9001, available at www.iso.org/iso-9001-quality-management.html.

107-1981[8] lays down requirements for labeling of food additives,[4] and international financial reporting standards of the International Accounting Standards Board (IASB) govern companies' financial accountability.[5] Standards can be "nontechnical," setting requirements for quality control, management, and financial reporting, or "technical," enabling coordination between multiple products or processes.[6] In each field, standards represent the appropriate expertise,[7] which makes them essential for almost all scientific, economic, and social activities.

Scholarship is rich on studies that unpack the variety of standards' types, roles, and purposes, where standards are praised for integrating diverse interests and providing uniform solutions for interconnecting things, methods, and people.[8] Standards control and modify behavior of different stakeholders (so-called regulative function), coordinate industry practices, and encourage cooperation (so-called normative function).[9] Technical standards in particular are considered imperative in ensuring quality of goods and services, protecting consumer from hazardous risks (by excluding nonqualifying products or providing information on products' quality),[10] and enabling the functioning of user networks.[11] By systemizing production, operation, and transfer methods, technical standards expedite supply chain and lead to economies of

[4] Codex General Standard for the Labelling of Food Additives When Sold as Such, CODEX STAN 107-1981[8], available at www.fao.org/docrep/005/Y2770E/y2770e03.htm.

[5] See the list of IFRS Standards, available at www.ifrs.org/issued-standards/list-of-standards/.

[6] I.e. Brunsson et al., 'Dynamics of standardization', p. 616; OECD, 'Standard setting', p. 23.

[7] S. Botzem and L. Dobusch, 'Standardization cycles: a process perspective on the formation and diffusion of transnational standards' (2012) 33 *Organizational Studies* 735–60.

[8] In this regard, see also H. De Vries, 'Standardization: what's in a name?' (1997) 4 *Terminology: International Journal of Theoretical and Applied Issues in Specialized Communication* 55–83, who notes that standards are solving 'matching' problems.

[9] P. Delimatsis, 'Global standard-setting 2.0: how the WTO spotlights ISO and impacts the transnational standard-setting process' (2018) 28 *Duke Journal of Comparative and International Law* 273–326 at 275, citing C. Lane, 'The social regulation of inter-firm relations in Britain and Germany: market rules, legal norms and technical standards' (1997) 21 *Cambridge Journal of Economics* 197–215.

[10] For example, the Chinese Taipei delegation to the OECD Standard Setting Roundtable noted that the use of standards for mineral water production provided better information for consumers, OECD, 'Standard setting', p. 10.

[11] See the functional typology of standards introduced in P. A. David, 'Some new standards for the economics of standardization in the information age', in P. Dasgupta and P. Stoneman (eds.), *Economic Policy and Technological Performance* (Cambridge: Cambridge University Press, 1987), pp. 154–68.

scale;[12] likewise, they generate network effects, allowing more users to join the networks and augmenting the demand for complementary production due to the increase in networks' value.[13] At the global level, technical standards harmonize States' technical regulations and enable market access,[14] encouraging liberalization of global trade.[15]

Save for few examples,[16] standards are usually created by private actors on the relevant markets.[17] They can be developed either through an extensive cooperation in groups and committees ("de jure" standardization)[18] or by means of market-based processes, where the industry chooses from among competing technologies brought on the market by different firms ("de facto" standardization).[19] The former aims to strike a

[12] The costs for developing and commercializing of a product are reduced when producers comply with a standard that is already integrated on the market. Curran, 'Standard-setting organizations', p. 988; OECD, 'Standard setting', p. 28.

[13] Curran, 'Standard-setting organizations', p. 987.

[14] Without this harmonization, exporters need to comply with trade regulation of each of their trade partners; see A. Muir, 'The race to safety: how private lawmaking and voluntary-standard adoption can inspire a global regime that strengthens and harmonizes product safety standards' (2016) 23 *Indiana Journal of Global Legal Studies* 323–47; see also J. L. Funk and D. T. Methe, 'Market- and committee-based mechanisms in the creation and diffusion of global industry standards: the case of mobile communication' (2001) 30 *Research Policy* 589–610.

[15] WTO, 'Trade and public policies: a closer look at non-tariff measures in the 21st century', World Trade Report (2012), available at www.wto.org/english/res_e/booksp_e/anrep_e/world_trade_report12_e.pdf, at 21; W. Mattli and T. Büthe, 'Setting international standards: technological rationality or primacy of power' (2003) 56 *World Politics* 1–42 at 2.

[16] For instance, the food safety industry in Latin American states has been governed by standards established by governmental authorities. P. Wiegmann, K. Blind and H. De Vries, 'Multi-mode standardization: a critical review and a research agenda' (2017) 46 *Research Policy* 1370–86, citing E. M. M. Q. Farina, G. E. Gutman, P. J. Lavarello, R. Nunes and T. Reardon, 'Private and public milk standards in Argentina and Brazil' (2005) 30 *Food Policy* 302–15.

[17] Cabral and Salant observed that market-based standards result in a faster innovation than standards regulation, and that the regulatory policy mandating compatible standards reduces investment incentives, retards innovation, and may reduce consumer and social welfare; Cabral and Salant, 'Evolving technologies'.

[18] The term "de jure" is used in this context as the opposite to "de facto" standardization, to highlight the differences between standards that are first developed and then brought on the market and standards that are developed in market-based processes.

[19] See Brunsson et al., 'Dynamics of standardization', p. 619; I. Oshri and C. Weeber, 'Cooperation and competition standard-setting activities in the digitalized era: the case of wireless information devices' (2006) 18 *Technology Analysis and Strategic Management* 265–83 at 267; T. Keil, 'De facto standardization through alliances: lessons from Bluetooth' (2002) 26 *Telecommunications Policy* 205–13 at 206; J. Farrell and G. Saloner, 'Coordination through committees and markets' (1998) 19 *The RAND Journal of Economics* 235–52. Some prominent examples of market-driven selection of

balance between various conflicting interests;[20] the latter mostly prevails in efficiency and positive externalities.[21] Preference for standards development schemes depends on multiple factors, such as regulatory choices and market characteristics, but also historical, regional, or even cultural aspects.[22] However, many standards emerge in interwoven processes containing the elements of committee- and market-based solutions and constitute a mixture of different standardization cultures and modes.[23]

## *ICT Standards*

In the domain of ICT), standards codify specifications for interoperability among various technological components.[24] More specifically, they prescribe methods applied in electronic devices and enable connections between networks, interfaces, and products of different vendors;[25]

a standard are the rivalry between AC and DC electric currents in the nineteenth century, and between VHS and Betamax, and, more recently, Blu-ray and HD-DVD video formats. To the contrary, new generations of wireless cellular standards were first developed in technical committees.

[20] As noted by Layne-Ferrar et al., collaboration among various industries is needed due to the global shift towards increasing products complexity; see A. Layne-Farrar, G. Llobet and J. Padilla, 'Payment and participation: the incentive to join cooperating standard setting efforts' (2014) 23 *Journal of Economics and Management Strategy* 24–49.

[21] Brunsson et al., 'Dynamics of standardization', p. 617.

[22] See N. Gandal, D. Salant and L. Waverman, 'Standards in wireless telephone networks' (2003) 27 *Telecommunications Policy* 325–32; J. Tate, 'National varieties of standardization', in P. A. Hall and D. Soskic (eds.), *Varieties of Capitalism* (Oxford: Oxford University Press, 2001), pp. 442–73.

[23] Wiegmann et al., 'Multi-mode standardization'. Moreover, standards developed in committees may need to compete with the rival standards to win the market; see J. van den Ende, G. Van den Kaa, S. Den Uijl and H. J. De Vries, 'The paradox of standard flexibility: the effects of co-evolution between standard and interorganizational network' (2012) 33 *Organization Studies* 705–36.

[24] See M. A. Lemley, 'Intellectual property rights and standard-setting organizations' (2002) 90 *California Law Review* 1889–980; Werle, 'Standards'. Interoperability is best defined as a "capability of two or more networks, systems, devices, application or components to exchange and readily use meaningful actionable information in a secure and effective way"; National Institute of Standards and Technology, 'NIST framework and roadmap for smart grid interoperability standards, release 1.0' (January 2010) NIST Special Publication 1108, p. 19; See W. A. Sheremata, 'Competing through innovation in network markets: strategies for challengers' (2004) 29 *The Academy of Management Review* 359–77.

[25] Lemley, 'Intellectual property rights', p. 1898; Werle, 'Standards', p. 8; R. Garud and A. Kumaraswamy, 'Changing competitive dynamics in network industries: an exploration of Sun Microsystems' open systems strategy' (1993) 14 *Strategic Management* 351–69 at 353.

coordinate radio frequencies and encryption software; and support data transmission across the internet.[26] More than other types of standards, ICT standards are subjected to continuous updates, modifications, and adjustment to market needs: after all, ICT standardization is an ongoing process where technologies are developed in parallel with, or "on top of," other technologies, often through the work of multiple committees and institutions.[27] In the past decades, ICT standards have particularly risen in prominence due to the increased digitalization, technological advancement, and commercialization of the internet.

ICT standards may range from general guidelines to definitions of complex technical features.[28] Some examples are the set of technical specifications for wireless local area networks (WLANs), commonly known as the Wi-Fi standards family; Bluetooth wireless specifications for personal area networks (PANs); third and fourth generation of wireless mobile telecommunications standards (3G and 4G); MP3 audio encoding format; TCP/IP internet protocols; and telecommunications standards for voice and data communications, such as Evolution-Data Optimized (EV-DO) standards or 1x network.[29] Among less familiar standards, IEEE 802.15.4 provides a wireless sensor network (WSN) for emergency notifications – a short-range communications system that

[26] See, among others, H. R. Delcamp and A. Leiponen, 'Innovating standards through informal consortia: the case of wireless telecommunications' (2014) 36 *International Journal of Industrial Organization* 36–47; T. Weitzel, D. Beimborn and W. König, 'A unified economic model of standard diffusion: the impact of standardization cost, network effects, and network topology' (2006) 30 *MIS Quarterly* 489–514; Gandal et al., 'Standards in wireless telephone networks'; Werle, 'Standards'; M. Tushman and L. Rosenkopf, 'Organizational determinants of technological change: towards a sociology of technological evolution' (1992) 14 *Research in Organizational Behaviour* 311–47; P. A. David and S. Greenstein, 'The economics of compatibility standards: an introduction to recent research' (1990) 1 *Economics of Innovation and New Technology* 3–41.

[27] Compare, for instance, standards for maximum or minimum requirements – measurements, length, weight, amount of food additives, which are modified less often.

[28] By way of illustration, see the difference between Design Guidelines for Balanced Technology Extended (BTX) Chassis, Revision 1.1 (February 2007) and Digital Cellular Telecommunications System (Phase 2+); Mobile Station (MS) Conformance Specification; Part 1: Conformance Specification (3GPP TS 51.010-1 version 10.3.0 Release 10), ETSI Technical Specification (February 2013).

[29] The two standards have different bandwidth characteristics and allow users to place a call either through the public switched telephone network (1x network) or through an application routed through the internet (EV-DO). For further explanation, see *Broadcom Corporation* v. *Qualcomm Incorporated*, 543 F 3d 683 (Fed. Cir. 2008).

gathers information from the monitored field and communicates it through wireless links, often used in health care and environment monitoring[30] – and IEEE 802.21 allows for seamless handovers among Wi-Fi or 3G-based networks, whereby cellphone users do not experience any interruption of information stream when changing within network hotspots.[31]

ICT standards are traditionally considered to perform a coordinative function: developed by high-tech companies and business associations, they reflect key industry requirements, reduce transaction costs, and prevent negative externalities while creating positive ones.[32] For instance, to enable compatibility and synchronization between various electronic devices, companies on the downstream market have to design their products in a way suitable for implementation of common technological solutions.[33] To that end, ICT standards provide a common platform for the production of multiple, and even competing, products; push back technological frontiers; and promote dissemination of innovation and development of new technologies. At the same time, due to the inherent power of interoperability standards to constrain the behavior of various market players,[34] they also perform a regulative function by preventing negative externalities through internalization, even without reliance on market functioning. In other words, ICT standards create normative expectations with a purpose to achieve a particular aim or economic effect.[35] This effect may even go beyond the intended regulation of

[30] See C. Buratti, A. Conti, D. Dardari and R. Verdone, 'An overview on wireless sensor networks technology and evolution' (2009) 9 *Sensors* 6869–96.

[31] See N. Dimitriou, L. Sarakis, D. Loukatos, G. Kormentzas and C. Skianis, 'Vertical Handover (VHO) framework for future collaborative wireless networks' (2011) 21 *International Journal of Network Management* 548–64.

[32] Werle, 'Standards', pp. 8–9. See also Abbott and Snidal discussing technological and regulatory externalities in standardization: K. W. Abbott and D. Snidal, 'International "standards" and international governance' (2011) 8 *Journal of European Public Policy* 345–70.

[33] An ordinary example is the possibility to access e-mails and messages through connecting to the internet network from different devices.

[34] After all, devices can only allow accessing e-mail through (wireless) networks if they support the relevant standards.

[35] Werle, 'Standards', p. 8; P. Delimatsis, 'Into the abyss of standard-setting: an analysis of procedural and substantive guarantees within ISO' (November 2014) TILEC Discussion Paper 0042-2014, p. 2.

certain markets: internet standards, for instance, have played an increasing role in shaping modern communication rights.[36]

Some ICT standards, such as Wi-Fi specifications and standards for broadband cellular networks, are developed and published by voluntary associations driven by the industry actors with the necessary expertise and resources. Others, such as Betamax and VHS videotape recording formats, have emerged in the market as a consequence of "standard battles" – competition between technologies, either by means of spontaneous adoption by users and producers or by the extensive promotion by dominant firms.[37] While this study considers ICT standardization as a holistic process, its main focus lies on standardization in technical committees of industry organizations: "standards development organizations" (hereinafter: SDOs).

## Characteristics of Standards Development Organizations

SDOs are voluntary platforms that enable cooperation and coordination among those wishing to establish a standard.[38] Standardization through SDOs is commended by many scholars and industry players due to voluntary participation in their standard-setting processes as well as the relative flexibility of SDOs' institutional rules.[39] Like standards, SDOs come in different types, which affects their institutional characteristics and governance rules and which deserve further elaboration.

[36] DeNardis provides examples of standards designing policies on privacy, access for disabled persons, and the use of internet space; see L. DeNardis, *The Global War for Internet Governance* (New Haven: Yale University Press, 2014), p. 65.

[37] S. Park, 'Quantitative analysis of network externalities in competing technologies: the VCR Case' (2004) 86 *The Review of Economics and Statistics* 937–45; M. A. Cusumano, Y. Mylonadis and R. S. Rosenbloom, 'Strategic maneuvering and mass-market dynamics: the triumph of VHS over beta' (1992) 66 *Business History Review* 51–94. David and Greenstein distinguish between "sponsored" and "unsponsored" standards: whereas the latter exist in public domain without identified author(s) holding proprietary interest, sponsored standards are established by entities, suppliers, or users; see David and Greenstein, 'The economics of compatibility standards', p. 4.

[38] J. A. Baron and T. Pohlmann, 'Who cooperates in standards consortia: rivals or complementors?' (2013) 9 *Journal of Competition Law and Economics* 905–29 at 906; see also A. Leiponen, 'Competing through cooperation: the organization of standard setting in wireless telecommunications' (2008) 54 *Management Science* 1904–19.

[39] See Mattli and Büthe, 'Setting international standards'; Curran, 'Standard-setting organizations'; Farrell and Saloner, 'Coordination through committees'.

### *Formal and Informal SDOs*

Generally, SDOs may take the form of private or semipublic bodies (implicitly) recognized by governmental authorities, or of loosely organized, informal interest groups and industry consortia. The International Organization for Standardization (ISO) and the International Electrotechnical Commission (IEC) are the prominent examples of the former: the fact that these two sister organizations are referred to in the Annexes of the Agreement on Technical Barriers to Trade (hereinafter: TBT Agreement) grants them authority to issue standards that are presumed compatible with international trade law.[40] The third recognized global SDO, the International Telecommunications Union (ITU), is a specialized agency of the United Nations that holds a monopoly over spectrum allocation and has been hosting a number of key ICT standardization activities, including the recent initiatives on 5G standardization. Within the European system, the ISO, IEC, and ITU are recognized as the only international standardization bodies;[41] their standards are quoted in national policy statements and enjoy a high profile within multinational corporations. Other examples of SDOs that enjoy a certain type of governmental recognition are regional and national bodies, discussed later.

Regardless of their status in national or international legal order, most of the formal SDOs share numerous institutional features. These include member-driven character, openness towards a large number of industry players, and consensus-based decision-making.[42] Standards adopted using transparent and consensus-driven methods are believed to be more accurate than arbitrary decisions taken through an opaque process.[43] At the same time, formal international SDOs are frequently put at a disadvantage due to their inflexibility and dominance by industrialized countries.[44]

[40] For explanation of the TBT Agreement, see Chapter 3.

[41] Article 2 of Regulation 1025/2012, OJ 2012 No. L316/12.

[42] For further elaboration on consensus, see Chapter 6.

[43] T. Simcoe, 'Standard setting committees: consensus governance for shared technology platforms' (2012) 102 *American Economic Review* 305–36; Farrell and Saloner, 'Coordination through committees'.

[44] ISO and IEC only open their membership to the National Bodies/Committees of UN Members States; Article 3.3 of ISO Statutes (20th ed., 2022), available at www.iso.org/obp/ui#iso:pub:PUB100322; and Article 4 of IEC Statutes and Rules of Procedure (2021 ed., 2021), available at www.iec.ch/members_experts/refdocs/. In ITU, only UN Member States have voting power, Article 2 of ITU Constitution, Constitution and Convention of the International Telecommunication Union adopted by the 2018 Plenipotentiary Conference (2018 ed., 2019), available at www.itu.int/en/history/Pages/ConstitutionAndConvention.aspx. For the commentary, see Delimatsis, 'Global

In turn, informal SDOs are industry consortia focused on narrow technological fields. These relatively closed committees are typically comprised of companies sharing a particular interest to develop technology or markets, and started to bloom in mid-2000s as a response to bureaucratic and stagnant standard-setting processes in larger and more "formalized" SDOs.[45] The main institutional characteristic of these platforms is the difference between actors developing ("promotors") and implementing ("adopters") technical specifications.[46] Consortia may adopt various forms: scholarship identifies single- and multiple-promoter consortia, the latter governed by promoters' agreement; incorporated consortia, where the rules of stakeholders' participation are provided by multilateral contracts; and hybrid consortia, independent incorporated nonprofit entities whose work is overseen by another organization.[47]

In the realm of ICT and wireless technologies, industry consortia appear to prevail over their formal counterparts due to their rapid standards development processes.[48] Empirical research has demonstrated an overall correlation between the narrow spectrum of a consortium's

standard-setting 2.0'; J. Braun and C. Koenig, 'The international regulatory framework of EC telecommunications law: the law of the WTO and the ITU as a yardstick for the EC law', in A. Bartosch, J. Braun, C. Koenig and M. Romes (eds.), *EC Competition and Telecommunications Law* (Netherlands: Kluwer Law International, 2009), p. 21; C. Murphy and J. Yates, *The International Organization for Standardization (ISO): Global Governance through Voluntary Consensus* (London: Routledge, 2009); J. Hinricher, 'The law-making of the International Telecommunication Union (ITU): providing a new source of international law?' (2004) 64 *ZaöR* 489–501.

45 T. Pohlmann, 'The evolution of ICT standards consortia' (2014) 93 *Digiworld Economic Journal* 17–40.

46 B. Biddle, F. X. Curci, T. F. Haslach, G. E. Marchant, A. Askland and L. Gaudet, 'The expanding role and importance of standards in the information and communications technology industry' (2012) 52 *Jurimetrics* 177–208.

47 In the US, incorporated consortia enjoy tax-exemption and nonprofit corporation status; they also allow for owning and licensing trademarks, associated with their technical specifications; see Biddle et al., 'The expanding role', pp. 188–9. Teubner et al. propose a different taxonomy of telecommunications consortia, namely: large industry and technology influencers, high-level concept developers, established standards developers, young technology specialists, small industry and technology influencers, and SSO-hosted industry drivers, L. K. Teubner, J. Henkel and R. Bekkers, 'Industry consortia in mobile telecommunications standards setting: purpose, organization and diversity' (2021) 45 *Telecommunications Policy* 1–20.

48 The increasing central role of technical consortia in the ICT sector was suggested, inter alia, in Delcamp and Leiponen, 'Innovating standards'; Pohlmann, 'Evolution'; and Biddle et al., 'The expanding role'. Blind and Gauch demonstrated that while narrow consortia can usually be found more often in the telecom and e-commerce industry, manufacturing usually has a broader focus; K. Blind and S. Gauch, 'Trends in ICT

standardization activity and the low amount of its members;[49] in such small homogeneous groups, decision-making occurs faster.[50] Especially when it concerns Intellectual Property Rights (IPR) issues, consortia have demonstrated their ability to provide quick and satisfactory solutions.

In spite of these advantages, informal SDOs are presumed to fall short on procedural and substantive guarantees compared to the formal alternatives.[51] For instance, standards development in informal groups often lack consensus, and decisions taken by these groups cannot be challenged due to the absence of dispute resolution mechanisms.[52] Moreover, the clear separation between promoters and other members suggests limited participation opportunities for stakeholders who may be interested in a standardization activity or become affected by it.[53]

The choice of a standards development platform largely depends on stakeholders' ambition for their particular standardization project. Companies wishing to rapidly promote their technology typically opt for informal committees,[54] while those pursuing bigger network externalities or seeking formal endorsement would carry out their projects in larger organizations.[55] By the same token, companies that attach more weight to quality of a standard than to the pace of its development are likely to join SDOs that follow consensus-based procedures.[56] Loosely organized groups with lower institutional costs may attract less internationally competitive firms aspiring to develop regional standards, whereas formal organizations are considered

standards in European standardization bodies and standards consortia' (2008) 32 *Telecommunications Policy* 503–13.

49 Pohlmann, 'Evolution'.

50 See, in general, A. Dixit, 'Trade expansion and contract enforcement' (2003) 111 *Journal of Political Economy* 1293–317; M. Boström and K. Tamm Hallström, 'Global multi-stakeholder standard setters: how fragile are they?' (2013) 9 *Journal of Global Ethics* 93–110.

51 Delcamp and Leiponen, 'Innovating standards', pp. 38–9.

52 Ibid.; B. Chiao, J. Lerner and J. Tirole, 'The rules of standard-setting organizations: an empirical analysis' (2007) 38 *The RAND Journal of Economics* 905–30.

53 Biddle et al., 'The expanding role', p. 184.

54 Delcamp and Leiponen, 'Innovating standards'; Pohlmann, 'Evolution'; Biddle et al., 'The expanding role'.

55 See, for instance, Pohlmann, 'Evolution'; J. Lerner and J. Tirole, 'A model of forum shopping' (2006) 96 *American Economic Review* 1091–113; N. Brunsson and B. Jacobsson, 'The contemporary expansion of standardization', in N. Brunsson and B. Jacobsson (eds.), *A World of Standards* (New York: Oxford University Press, 2000), p. 1; M. Weiss and M. Sirbu, 'Technological choice in voluntary standards committees: an empirical analysis' (1990) 1 *Economics of Innovation and New Technologies* 111–33.

56 Simcoe, 'Standard setting committees'.

to provide fertile ground for the establishment of global standards.[57] It may also occur that recognized SDOs, despite their alleged weaknesses, yield better results than informal groups: for instance, the ITU managed to complete standardization of 56K modems, initially carried out in two competing consortia, due to the support from all major market players and successful resolution of patent issues.[58]

## *Hierarchy of SDOs*

An SDO rarely operates independently from other SDOs: as such, institutions of standardizations are entwined in a system of networks.[59] The most typical approach to systematize SDOs is to follow a vertical, "top-down" hierarchical structure of international, regional, and national organizations developing, accordingly, international, regional, and national standards.[60] In this system, general rules and principles are defined at the highest hierarchical level in accordance with hard and soft law instruments of public law,[61] and standards developed at the "lower" hierarchical level gain increased legitimacy when endorsed by an SDO at the higher hierarchical order.

At the top of this hierarchy are the three International Standards Bodies (ISBs), the ISO, IEC, and ITU, whose infrastructure is founded on the national level and, when necessary, extends to regional activities.[62]

57 M. T. Austin and H. V. Milner, 'Strategies of European standardization' (2001) 8 *Journal of European Public Policy* 411–31.

58 S. M. Greenstein and M. Rysman, 'Coordination costs and standard setting: lessons from 56K modems' (2004) Center for the Study of Industrial Organization Working Paper #0056, p. 23.

59 Note that there can be different, not necessarily conflicting, and not necessarily hierarchical, approaches to systematize SDOs. For instance, Lazanski distinguishes between multilateral and multistakeholder SDOs, D. Lazanski, 'Governance in international technical standards making: a tripartite model' (2019) 4 *Journal of Cyber Policy* 362–79; while Baron and Kanevskaia contrast entity and individual-based models of SDOs governance, J. Baron and O. Kanevskaia, 'Global rivalry over the leadership in ICT standardization: SDO governance amid changing patterns of participation', in P. Delimatsis, S. Bijlmakers and M. K. Borowicz (eds.), *The Evolution of Transnational Rule-Makers through Crises* (Cambridge: Cambridge University Press, forthcoming).

60 See Articles 3.2 and 3.3 of ISO/IEC Guide 2 (2004).

61 See JRC Report, p. 60.

62 Article 1.2 of ISO/IEC Guide 59 – Code of Good Practice for Standardization (1st ed., 1994). Such terminology is also maintained in the other ISO/IEC Guides, for instance ISO/IEC Guide 21-1, Regional or National Adoption of International Standards and Other International Deliverables - Part 1: Adoption of International Standards (1st ed., 2005)

Lower down the hierarchical ladder are regional bodies, common examples being the three European Standards Organizations (hereinafter: ESOs): the European Committee for Standardization (CEN), the European Committee for Electrotechnical Standardization (CENELEC), and the European Telecommunications Standards Institute (ETSI). The ESOs typically follow a hierarchical structure set by EU law and the European Commission (EC). At the third level are National Standards Organizations (hereinafter: NSOs),[63] designated to represent national interests in the regional or international standardization fora:[64] in ISO, for example, the UK is represented by the British Standards Institute (BSI), Japan by the Japanese Industrial Standards Committee (JISC), and China by the Standardization Administration of China (SAC).[65] Depending on a country's standardization regime, NSOs can be either privately driven associations or a part of a governmental agency,[66] and may be entrusted with defining national standardization strategies.[67] In the EU, NSOs typically follow the rules and procedures of ESOs.[68]

Naturally, standardization work of the SDOs at the different hierarchical levels can overlap. In this regard, there are various mechanisms to preserve coherence and consistency of global standardization. NSOs hold membership of regional and international bodies, which, in turn, have

[63] The ISO taxonomy used to distinguish between a standardizing body, which can be many in one country, and a national standards body, which can be the member of regional and international organizations; Article 1.3 of ISO/IEC Guide 59 (1994).

[64] Note that while the European NSOs represent the interests of their respective countries by participating in ISO's committees and working groups, ANSI represents the interests of the US by appointing the Technical Advisory Groups (TAGs); see ANSI, 'ANSI procedures for U.S. participation in the international standards activities of ISO' (January 2019), available at https://share.ansi.org/Shared%20Documents/Standards%20Activities/International%20Standardization/2019-ANSI-International-Procedures.pdf. International SDOs also maintain different terminology for their memberships: for instance, ISO speaks of "Member Bodies," IEC refers to its members as "National Committees" and ITU distinguishes between "Member States" and "Sector Members."

[65] Note that SAC as such does not create standards.

[66] For example, German DIN is a nonprofit association, which signed the *Normenvertrag* with the government where it is recognized as a competent standards body; BSI is a nonprofit organization recognized in the MoU in 1982; AFNOR is an association under private law but subject to governmental control and fulfils a public function under the French Administrative Law. See Schepel, *The Constitution of Private Governance*, pp. 111–44.

[67] See JRC Report, p. 78.

[68] Ibid.

cooperation agreements and memoranda of understanding at different hierarchical levels (i.e., regional and international, or international and international).[69] Moreover, the applicable legislation often requires national SDOs to adopt standards produced at the higher hierarchical levels.[70] In ICT standardization at the highest hierarchical level, ISO and IEC join forces in the Joint Technical Committee (JTC), the ISO/IEC JTC1, which endorses prominent global ICT standards in the voting procedure by national bodies.[71]

However, such a "top-down" hierarchical approach does not take into account the institutional variety of the ICT standardization ecosystem. In this regard, SDOs' networks can also be systematized as a "bottom-up" vertical hierarchy, where groups of professionals or academics establish themselves as informal associations or consortia operating separately from their "formalized" counterparts and according to their own governance models.[72] Internet and web SDOs are typical examples of such "bottom-up" hierarchy. While most of these consortia do not seek any formal accreditation in the hierarchical ledger, they nevertheless may have liaisons or partnership with other formal organizations or consortia or seek legitimization of their standards by formal bodies.[73]

Due to their sheer abundance and the overlap of their technical activities, SDO networks are also interlinked through horizontal relationships: as will be demonstrated further in this book, SDOs cooperate and compete with each other, endorse and absorb each other's standards, and adopt each other's governance rules, such as intellectual property policies. In future, these networks may become even more complex due to standardization of IoT systems that relies on increased cooperation among various types of SDOs and governmental actors.

[69] That is, Agreement on Technical Cooperation between ISO and CEN (Vienna Agreement) (1991); IEC-CENELEC Agreement on Common Planning of New Work and Parallel Voting (Frankfurt Cooperation Agreement) (2016); MoU between IEC, ISO, ITU, and UN/ECE concerning standardization in the field of electronic business (2000).

[70] See Part II discussing obligations to adopt international standards as a basis for a country's technical regulations to preclude unnecessary trade barriers, as well to withdraw national standards conflicting with European harmonized standards.

[71] See 'About', available at https://jtc1info.org/page-3/.

[72] JRC Report, pp. 59–60.

[73] For instance, some IETF standards have been endorsed by ISO, and standards of the DVB Forum by ETSI.

### *Competitive Forces in SDOs*

The fact that standardization is driven by commercial interests of global industry players should come as no surprise. Firms become involved in standardization processes by joining SDOs as members or participants and take part in standardization activities by sending their employees to SDOs' meetings, where they contribute to decision-making. Needless to say, many of the companies participating in SDOs' processes are often rivals and have vested interests to strengthen their competitive advantage through standardization efforts, which gives rise to a number of concerns associated with strategic behavior in SDOs.

First and foremost, in committee-based standards development, information sharing between competitors is nearly unavoidable. While in the realm of network industries, coordination of technologies is critical for innovative efficiency,[74] standardization decisions can in principle conceal collusive practices and harm economic competition on the market as well as consumers.[75] For this reason, SDOs that allow collusive behavior risk breaching national competition rules.[76] Furthermore, companies may employ business practices that are not necessarily illegal, but affect the long-term dynamics in SDOs, such as sending multiple experts to the meetings or "hiring away" employees of other companies to wield more influence in standardization committees.[77] In this context, the threat to global standardization emerges when standard development processes become unbalanced or dominated by a particular group of interests, and when other groups are excluded: arguably, a standard established in such processes does not represent the view of the industry and runs afoul with the idea of open, consensus-based standardization.

Yet, the largest concerns in ICT standardization are centered around the strategic use of functional utility patents in standards development. A single electronic device may run on more than hundred standards, and

[74] See C. Shapiro and H. W. Varian, *Information Rules: A Strategic Guide to the Network Economy* (Cambridge, MA: Harvard Business Review Press, 1998).

[75] US Department of Justice, Antitrust Division, 'Can there be a "one-world approach" to competition law?' Remarks of principal Deputy Assistant Attorney General Renata B. Hesse at the Chatham House Conference on Globalization of Competition Policy (2016), available at www.justice.gov/opa/speech/principal-deputy-assistant-attorney-general-renata-b-hesse-delivers-remarks-chatham-house, which highlights the near unanimity around the world about the importance of discovering and prosecuting cartels.

[76] More on this in Chapters 4 and 5.

[77] See J. L. Contreras, 'Divergent patterns of engagement in internet standardization: Japan, Korea and China' (2014) 38 *Telecommunications Policy* 916–34.

each of these standards may embody numerous proprietary technologies essential for its proper implementation. This is particularly the case for the mobile communications sector, which accounts for the largest number of standards essential patents (SEP) declarations,[78] as well as for standards developed in consortia.[79] Since the functioning of a standard often relies on essential technologies implemented in it, access to such standards depends on access to these technologies, which patent-holders provide by granting licenses to implementers. At the same time, patent-holders may seek injunctions against companies breaching their patents by using their technologies without obtaining a valid license. A situation where a standard runs on a large number of SEPs is known as "patent thicket:" arguably, the increased transaction costs resulting from the patent thickets may discourage the standard's use and create an entry barrier for new firms.[80]

A widespread concern associated with SEPs relates to the threat of opportunism from patent-holders, who may employ various strategies to abuse their position on the market. In this regard, most of the discussions are centered around the risk of patent hold-up, described as a situation when a patent-holder increases royalty rates after its technology was adopted into a standard, while the industry is "locked into" the technology since sunk costs of implementing a standard have already been made,[81] and the risk of royalty stacking – "accumulation of hold-up positions" when individual SEP holders collectively demand royalties

[78] J. Baron and T. Pohlmann, 'Mapping standards to patents using databases of declared standard-essential patents and systems of technological classification' (2015), available at www.law.northwestern.edu/research-faculty/searlecenter/innovationeconomics/documents/Baron_Pohlmann_Mapping_Standards.pdf, at 18; D. Geradin, 'The European Commission policy towards the licensing of standard-essential patents: where do we stand?' (2013) 9 *Journal of Competition Law and Economics* 1125–45.

[79] J. Baron, Y. Ménière and T. Pohlmann, 'Standards, consortia and innovation' (2014) 36 *International Journal of Industrial Organization* 22–35.

[80] C. Shapiro, 'Navigating the patent thicket: cross licenses, patent pools, and standard setting' (2001) 1 *Innovation Policy and the Economy* 119–50. But the effect is difficult to predict due to limited empirical evidence; K. Gupta, 'The patent policy debate in a high-tech world' (2013) 9 *Journal of Competition Law and Economics* 827–58 at 841; N. Gandal and R. Régibeau, 'Standard-setting organizations', in P. Delimatsis (ed.), *The Law, Economics and Politics of International Standardization* (Cambridge: Cambridge University Press, 2015), pp. 394–433.

[81] Cabral and Salant, 'Evolving technologies'; M. A. Lemley and C. Shapiro, 'Patent holdup and royalty stacking' (2007) 85 *Texas Law Review* 1991–2049; Farrell et al., 'Standard setting'.

that cumulatively are excessive.[82] These strategies, however, have been put into question by several scholars, predominantly due to the lack of conclusive empirical evidence on the matter.[83] Furthermore, SEP-holders, having extreme bargaining power due to the relationship-specific investments, may engage in patent ambush by deciding not to declare the relevant patents prior to the adoption of a standard.[84]

Similar to patent implementers, patent-holders deal with a number of uncertainties: once a patent application is filed, it remains unclear whether the patent will actually be granted, and to which release of technical specification it will be relevant, if at all.[85] Moreover, patent-holders rely on the return of their R&D investments to continue innovating. At the same time, it should be mentioned that the effect of patents on the industry may differ per sector as well as per licensing practices: in the software industry, large patent portfolios are deemed to affect a firm's market value in a positive way, whereas fragmentation of patents rights is believed to reduce a firm's market value but, at the same time, increase

[82] See for further discussion, J. Lerner and J. Tirole, 'Standard-essential patents' (2015) 123 *Journal of Political Economy* 547–86; Gupta, 'The patent policy'; D. Geradin, A. Layne-Farrar and J. Padilla, 'Royalty stacking in high tech industries: separating myth from reality' (2007) CEPR Discussion Paper No. DP6091. Gandal and Régibeau note that royalty stacking is not a competition policy issue, since it arises from the suboptimality of independent price setting decisions in the presence of strong complementarity links; Gandal and Régibeau, 'Standard-setting organizations'.

[83] See, for instance, Gupta, 'The patent policy'; CEN-CENELEC's position paper 'Standard essential patents and fair, reasonable and non-discriminatory commitments' (September 2016), available at www.cencenelec.eu/News/Policy_Opinions/PolicyOpinions/EssentialPatents.pdf, p. 3. Gupta and Snyder found the litigation in smart phone industry to be driven by disputes arising from the implementation of design patents rather than functional utility patents, and that litigation outcomes are driven by patent quality rather than patent essentiality; K. Gupta and M. Snyder, 'Smart phone litigation and standard essential patents' (2014) Working Paper Series No. 14006, Hoover Institution Working Group on Intellectual Property, Innovation, and Prosperity, Stanford University. It has also been suggested that patent-holders' risk being subject to "patent holdout" once implementers are allowed to escape licensing negotiations; A. Layne-Farrar, 'Why patent holdout is not just a fancy name for plain old patent infringement' (February 2016) *Competition Policy International*, available at www.competitionpolicyinternational.com/why-patent-holdout-is-not-just-a-fancy-name-for-plain-old-patent-infringement. But see, more recently, C. Shapiro and M. Lemley, 'The role of antitrust in preventing patent holdup' (2020) 168 *University of Pennsylvania Law Review* 2019–63.

[84] E.g., M. Rysman and T. Simcoe, 'Patents and the performance of voluntary standard-setting organizations' (2008) 54 *Management Science* 1920–34.

[85] Interview with an industry expert, February 1, 2018.

their R&D.[86] Moreover, patent-holders may also choose to license their patents collaboratively through patents pools, independently from SDOs.[87] All this adds to the overall complexity of SEP issues and arising concerns under competition law.

To strike a balance between the rights of patent-holders and patent implementers, SDOs adopt Intellectual Property Rights (hereinafter: IPR) policies that prescribe the rules and the procedures applicable to SEPs' identification and disclosure. Disclosure obligation requires SDO members or participants to reveal existing patents and patent applications that might become essential to the standard in the development process.[88] Patent disclosure is a continuous process,[89] and while generally aiming to provide SDOs' members with more clarity, it does not tell much about the actual quality of patents, or may create even more uncertainty by risking over- and under-disclosure.[90] In turn, a licensing obligation requires patent-holders to license their SEPs either on fair, reasonable, and nondiscriminatory terms (FRAND),[91] or on royalty-free basis, the latter often being a common practice in internet and software SDOs.[92]

[86] M. Noel and M. Schankerman, 'Strategic patenting and software innovation' (2013) 61 *The Journal of Industrial Economics* 481–520.

[87] JRC Report, p. 153, which also notes that an objective evaluator must find the patents that have been contributed to be pool, be essential to the standard, which is not the case with SEPs subject to licensing commitment by patent-holders.

[88] See J. Contreras, 'An empirical study of the effects of ex ante licensing disclosure policies on the development of voluntary technical standards' (2011) Conducted for the National Institute of Standards and Technology (NIST), US Department of Commerce, available at www.nist.gov/sites/default/files/nistgcr_11_934_empircalstudyofeffectsexantelicensing2011_0.pdf.

[89] Gandal and Régibeau, 'Standard-setting organizations'.

[90] Ibid.; Rysman and Simcoe, 'Patents and the performance of voluntary standard-setting organizations', p. 1920. This was also confirmed by experts interviewed for this study.

[91] While some studies refer to "RAND," both FRAND and RAND are typically used interchangeably. Under the US doctrine, FRAND is regarded as a form of "contractual" commitment. For further clarification, see J. L. Contreras, 'Patent pledge enforcement theories', in J. L. Contreras and M. Jacob (eds.), *Patent Pledges: Global Perspectives on Patent Law's Private Ordering Frontier* (Cheltenham: Edward Elgar, 2017), pp. 101–116. Along similar lines, some scholars have described SDOs' licensing policies as "incomplete contracts"; T. S. Simcoe and A. L. Shampine, 'Economics of patents and standardization: network effects, hold-up, hold-out, stacking', in J. L. Contreras (ed.), *The Cambridge Handbook of Technical Standardization Law: Competition, Antitrust and Patents* (Cambridge: Cambridge University Press, 2018), p. 111.

[92] T. Stoll, 'Are you still in? The impact of licensing requirements on the composition of standards setting organizations' (2014) Max Planck Institute for Innovation and Competition Research Paper No. 14.

The FRAND commitment is well-accepted in the industry and by national courts that, in the course of the years, have interpreted FRAND differently.[93] At the same time, the ambiguity of FRAND's concept, and attempts to clarify it, including the levels of production chain at which licensing should take place[94] and the possibility to establish aggregate licensing rates outside the SDOs,[95] have often been in the limelight of recent legal and policy discussions. Arguably, IPR concerns are becoming even more relevant in the debate of open standards and open-source licensing practices,[96] which also question the fitness of current regional and national IPR regulation and practices in ICT standardization.

## Voluntary Standards as Normative Requirements

In the seminal scholarship, standards are referred to as "microcosms of social practices, political preferences, economic calculations, scientific necessity and professional judgment,"[97] situated in a "grey zone of law, morals, economics and politics."[98] Since standards development occurs through lengthy discussions, bargaining, deliberation, and compromise processes, to some extent it resembles drafting of a legislation:[99] this does not mean, however, that standards development should be seen as equal

93 K. F. Tsang and J. A. Lee, 'Unfriendly choice of law in FRAND' (2019) 59 *Virginia Journal of International Law* 220–305.

94 See, among many others, A. Layne-Farrar and R. Stark, 'License to all or access to all? A law and economics assessment of standard development organizations' licensing rules' (2020) 88 *George Washington Law Review* 1307–49; J. S. Borghetti, I. Nikolic and N. Petit, 'FRAND licensing levels under EU law' (2021) 17 *European Competition Journal* 205–68.

95 J. Contreras, 'Intellectual property pools and aggregation' (2021) University of Utah College of Law Research Paper No. 408, available at https://papers.ssrn.com/sol3/papers.cfm?abstract_id=3716569.

96 See M. Husovec, 'Standardization, open source and innovation: sketching the effect of IPR policies', in J. L. Contreras (ed.), *The Cambridge Handbook of Technical Standardization Law: Further Intersection of Public and Private Law* (Cambridge: Cambridge University Press, 2019), pp. 177–197.

97 Schepel, *The Constitution of Private Governance*, p. 6.

98 A. Peters, L. Koechlin, and G. Fenner Zinkernagel, 'Non-state actors as standard setters: framing the issue in an interdisciplinary fashion', in A. Peters, L. Koechlin, T. Foester and G. Fenner Zinkernagel (eds.), *Non-State Actors as Standard Setters* (Cambridge: Cambridge University Press, 2009), pp. 1–32.

99 B. Kingsbury, N. Krisch and R. B. Stewart, 'The emergence of global administrative law' (2005) 68 *Law and Contemporary Problems* 15–61; yet standard-setting is generally carried out by more diverse actors than lawmaking.

to lawmaking.[100] At the same time, "standards retain certain legal features" and "in practical terms, may be seen as hard legal obligations,"[101] despite their voluntary character. For example, developers of internet specifications for different levels of network architecture are sometimes compared to lawmakers, as they affect the behavior of actors in a way similar to the legislators: the idea that "code is law" is not unfamiliar among the scholars of internet governance.[102] As such, the normative power of standards may emerge from a range of factors, and follows the three main routes: standards' use as a regulatory technique through the reference in a governmental regulation, adoption of an industry standard by a competent organization, and compliance pull towards an industry norm from the relevant market.

### *Regulatory Incorporation*

Voluntary standards may be implemented into national legislation, or referenced by governments in any other way, with a purpose of facilitating industry regulation, providing consumer protection or safeguarding certain health and safety requirements.[103] The recourse of lawmakers to industry expertise is understandable: by and large, regulatory agencies prefer using existing industry standards due to their own inefficacy in defining detailed technical norms.[104] Likewise, strictly governmental standards can be inefficient: unlike private standards, they typically are crafted in endogenous processes, bypassing market competition.[105]

But even when developed by bodies specifically designated by States, standards may only exert legal obligations by virtue of a regulatory

[100] See ibid.; Schepel, *The Constitution of Private Governance.*

[101] Schepel, *The Constitution of Private Governance*, pp. 12–13.

[102] See L. Lessig, *Codes and Other Laws of Cyberspace* (New York: Basic Books, 1999).

[103] T. Büthe, 'Engineering uncontestedness? The origins and institutional development of the International Electrotechnical Commission (IEC)' (2010) 12 *Business and Politics* 1–62 at 3; M. De Bellis, 'The public enforcement of global private standard setting: the role of credit rating agencies in Basel II', in S. Cassese, B. Carotti, L. Casini, M. Macchi, E. MacDonald and M. Savino (eds.), *Global Administrative Law: Cases, Materials and Issues*, 2nd ed., (Rome: IRPA/IILJ, 2008), at pp. 23–8; C. Murphy and J. Yates, 'Coordinating international standards: the formation of the ISO' (2006), available at http://web.mit.edu/iandeseminar/Papers/Fall2006/Yates.pdf, at 26.

[104] S. Cassese, 'Administrative law without the state? The challenge of global regulation' (2005) 37 *N.Y.U. International Law and Politics* 663–94 at 671.

[105] D. F. Spulber, 'Innovation economics: the interplay among technology standards, competitive conduct, and economic performance' (2013) 9 *Journal of Competition Law and Economics* 777–825 at 787–8.

citation. In the EU, it is the publication of a reference to a Harmonized European Standard (HES) in the Official Journal (OJ) of the European Union that increases the normative value of these standards;[106] regardless, the use of such standards remains voluntary.[107] The US standardization system, in turn, furnishes the adoption of private model codes by semipublic organizations as well as a direct reference to private standards by federal authorities. To provide an example, the American Bar Association's Model Code of Professional Responsibility has been adopted by many States' Supreme Courts, and standards established by the Gas Industry Standards Board are embedded in regulations of the Federal Energy Regulatory Commission.[108] Unlike the case in the EU system, the application of referenced standards in the US is not voluntary: the requirement of "voluntary consensus" rather applies to the standards development process.[109]

It should also be noted that the use of a particular standard may also be mandated by a legal contract between private or governmental parties.[110] Such practices are common in many industry sectors, including construction and energy, where firms incorporate "minimum requirements" of global standards into their codes.

### *Virtue of a Force of Another Organization*

Even in the absence of a regulatory reference or an explicit delegation of powers, private norms can harden into mandatory requirements when appropriated by a recognized organization. This type of transformation is demonstrated by the WTO obligation to use relevant international

[106] See Case C-613/14, *James Elliott Construction Ltd* v. *Irish Asphalt Ltd* [2016] ECR – 821; for further analysis and explanation of HES, see Chapter 4.

[107] Case C-613/14, *James Elliott Construction Ltd* v. *Irish Asphalt Ltd*, para. 42. This did not preclude the CJEU from issuing a preliminary ruling on a HES.

[108] See Schepel, *The Constitution of Private Governance*, pp. 158–9; E. S. Bremer, 'American and European perspectives on private standards in public law' (2016) 91 *Tulane Law Review* 325–70 at 364–5.

[109] P. C. Mavroidis and R. Wolfe, 'Private standards and the WTO: reclusive no more' (2017) 16 *World Trade Review* 1–24. See also ANSI, 'Overview of the US Standardization System: voluntary consensus standards and conformity assessment activities' (2007), available at https://share.ansi.org/Shared%20Documents/News%20and%20Publications/Brochures/U.S.%20Standardization%20System-07.pdf, p. 3.

[110] P. Verbruggen, 'Introduction: regulating private regulators: understanding the role of private law' (2019) 2 *European Review of Private Law* 175–96 at 181; B. Van Leeuwen, *European Standardization of Services and Its Impact on Private Law: Paradoxes of Convergence* (Oxford: Bloomsbury Publishing, 2017), pp. 17–18.

standards as a basis for countries' mandatory technical regulations.[111] Measures adopted in accordance with such standards, meaning that there is a "very strong and substantial relationship between a regulation and the substance of the international standard,"[112] enjoy a rebuttable presumption of conformity with applicable provisions of WTO law.[113]

Private sector standards may also be endorsed ex post in a "fast-track" process of SDOs in high vertical hierarchical position, such as the ISO or IEC: in this case, a technical document is directly submitted for the (final) approval of a working group or even the whole SDO membership, sidestepping the initial stages of standards development.[114] Examples are the Linux standard for operating systems, which was formally adopted by the ISO/IEC;[115] the Portable Document Format (PDF) developed by Adobe and incorporated into an ISO standard;[116] and specifications drafted by the International Color Consortium that were used as a basis for the IEC 61966-series of "color management" standards.[117]

Endorsement by a recognized organization or SDO grants private sector standards a certain degree of legitimacy, enlarges their scope of application,[118] and, arguably, strengthens their enforcement.[119]

111 Article 2.4 of the Agreement on Technical Barriers to Trade, 1868 UNTS 120 (hereinafter: TBT Agreement); R. Howse and R. Teitel, 'Beyond compliance: rethinking why international law really matters' (2010) 1 *Global Policy* 127–36 at 132.

112 Appellate Body Report, European Communities – Trade Description of Sardines, WT/DS231/AB/R (September 26, 2002) para. 245.

113 See Chapter 3 for further elaboration.

114 Article F2 of the ISO/IEC Directives Part 1 (12th ed., 2021), available at www.iso.org/directives-and-policies.html.

115 ISO/IEC 23360, Linux Standard Base (LSB) core specification 3.1 – Parts 1 to 8.

116 ISO 19005 series, Document management – Electronic document file format for long-term preservation (PDF/A-1, PDF/A-2, PDF/A-3).

117 Büthe, 'Engineering uncontestedness?', p. 14, n. 65.

118 Brunsson and Jacobsson, 'The contemporary expansion'.

119 Some authors have argued that due to this transformation, there is a shift in implementation, monitoring, and enforcement of standards: while in voluntary standardization, these functions are typically performed by private sector or market actors, once standards are "hardened" through the WTO endorsement, these tasks become the matter of States, relevant WTO Committees and Dispute Settlement Bodies. See F. Fontanelli, 'ISO and Codex standards and international trade law: what gets said is not what's heard' (2011) 60 *International and Comparative Law Quarterly* 895–932, who analyzes the regulatory processes of ISO and Codex Alimentarius using the ANIME approach (Agenda-setting, Negotiation and adoption, Implementation, Monitoring and Enforcement), referring to K. W. Abbott and D. Snidal, 'The governance triangle: regulatory standards institution and the shadow of the state', in W. Mattli and N. Woods (eds.), *The Politics of Global Regulation* (Princeton: Princeton University Press, 2009), pp. 44–88.

Moreover, when going through a fast-track process of a formal SDO, such industry norms arguably become subjected to a greater level of scrutiny, which improves their quality and consistency.[120] Yet, it should be noted that while increasing legitimacy and quality, this practice as such does not render a standard mandatory, without it being referenced in, or used as a basis for national legislation.[121] At the same time, due to its increased legitimacy, a standard that is endorsed by a recognized organization is more likely to be incorporated into law or to provide a groundwork for regulators to build on.

### *Compliance Pull and Market Pressure*

To acquire binding force, standards require an act of *recognition*, such as a reference to a standard in a contract or national legislation, decision of a (national) court, or endorsement as an international standard within the WTO system. Yet, the use of certain voluntary standards may also be compulsory when they ensure the functioning of the market or are preferred by consumers in the absence of other regulatory alternatives.[122] The obligatory nature of standards then stems from industry-mediated processes and reflects the requirements of specific markets.[123] The extent to which these standards mirror a legal obligation depends on product or process characteristics: for instance, technical specifications are more likely to exert normative pull in a culture where they are connected with wider normative and cognitive frames, which in turn put a strong emphasis on technical skills.[124]

[120] For industry's view on the legitimacy of standards approved via "fast-track" procedures, see Part IV.

[121] However, some authors have argued that absorbance of standards into the WTO regulatory framework may be viewed as an interaction between the WTO and SDOs at the instance of a regulatory delegation; see T. Büthe, 'The globalization of health and safety standards: delegation of regulatory authority in the SPS Agreement of 1994 Agreement Establishing the World Trade Organization' (2008) 71 *Law and Contemporary Problems* 219–55.

[122] See Schepel, *The Constitution of Private Governance*, pp. 3–6.

[123] Büthe, 'Engineering uncontestedness?', p. 2.

[124] See Lane, 'Social regulation'. In this regard, see also Pauwelyn, Wessel and Wouters, who argue that there is "informal law" that may still have legal effects and/or be subject to legal constraints, and therefore needs justification by law; J. Pauwelyn, R. A. Wessel and J. Wouters, 'When structures become shackles: stagnation and dynamics in international law-making' (2014) 25 *The European Journal of International Law* 733–63 at 755–9.

While the market pressure is not sufficient to realize convergence in law,[125] these types of standards may still considerably influence firms' capacity to innovate and conduct business overseas.[126] Companies that comply with de facto standards have good reputation among their business partners.[127] On a global scale, such standards may serve as indirect trade instruments and are likely to bear similar practical consequences as mandated standards, being prerequisites for market access and shaping international commerce.[128]

### *Binding Force of ICT Standards*

Although voluntary ICT standards may become binding following the first two paths,[129] they are mostly capable of creating normative orders by the third method. The decisive factors behind the market power of an ICT standard are its network effects and switching costs,[130] as well as the willingness of consumers to adopt certain technology.[131] Interoperability of technological platforms is crucial for achieving a critical mass of actors to expand the size of the market.[132] Take the example of Bluetooth and

125 Van Leeuwen, *European Standardization*, p. 20.

126 According to the European Commission, this also applies to SMEs, which may not have been involved in standard-setting processes nor have any operational interest in using the standard; see 'Independent review of the European standardization system', Final Report of the European Commission, Directorate-General for Internal Market, Industry, Entrepreneurship and SMEs (March 2015), available at ec.europa.eu/DocsRoom/documents/10444/attachments/2/translations/en/. . ./pdf. For further research on SMEs in technology standardization, see also K. Gupta, 'The role of SMEs and startups in standards development' (2017), available at https://papers.ssrn.com/sol3/papers.cfm?abstract_id=3001513.

127 Büthe, 'Engineering uncontestedness?', p. 3.

128 WTO, 'Trade and public policies', p. 21; S. Bernstein and E. Hannah, 'Non-state global standard-setting and the WTO: legitimacy and the need for regulatory space' (2008) 11 *Journal of International Economic Law* 575–608 at 586.

129 For instance, WLAN specifications developed in IEEE are submitted to ISO/IEC/JTC1 and become international standards through ISO endorsement.

130 Curran, 'Standard-setting organizations', p. 987.

131 See L. Fuentelsaz, J. P. Maicas and Y. Polo, 'Switching costs, network effects, and competition in the European mobile telecommunications industry' (2012) 23 *Information Systems Research* 93–108. Yet, Cabral and Salant suggested that consumers are more concerned with prices rather than with network effects; Cabral and Salant, 'Evolving technologies', p. 52.

132 This is illustrated by an example of cellular phone users; E. M. Rogers, *Diffusion of Innovations: Modifications of a Model for Telecommunications* (New York: The Free Press New York, 1995), p. 245.

USB technical specifications: there exists no law that obliges a device manufacturer to implement these standards; and yet, selling smartphones or laptops that do not support these technologies is doomed to failure. In this regard, even a single-actor scheme may gain popularity amongst the industry,[133] as long as a group of actors sharing interest or preference for a certain standard is established. For instance, prior to its acknowledgment by the ISO, the aforementioned PDF standard developed by Adobe has already become a de facto market requirement.[134]

## Governance Characteristics of Voluntary Standards

Standardization is not unique in transforming voluntary specifications into normative requirements. Many governance regimes are established and maintained by nongovernmental players acting either autonomously, or together with (or under supervision of) the State.[135] Examples of such normative arrangements range from the diamond industry and private prisons to professional societies and internet routine.[136] Regulation "in the shadow" of legislation commonly emerges as a response to the inefficiencies of States in protecting property rights[137] or

133 K. A. Jakobsen, 'Revisiting standard-setting organizations' patent policies' (2004) 3 *Northwestern Journal of Technology and Intellectual Property* 43–60 at 59.

134 E. Wijkstrom and D. McDaniels, 'International standards and the WTO TBT Agreement: improving governance for regulatory alignment' (2013) World Trade Organization Staff Working Paper ERSD-2013-06, available at www.wto.org/english/res_e/reser_e/ersd201306_e.pdf, p. 17.

135 M. Mataija, *Private Regulation and the Internal Market: Sports, Legal Services and Standard Setting in EU Economic Law* (Oxford: Oxford University Press, 2016), p. 2; T. G. Weiss and R. Thakur, *The UN and Global Governance: An Unfinished Journey* (Bloomington: Indiana University Press, 2010), p. 10. See also Mattli and Woods, 'In whose benefit?'.

136 For example, P. Delimatsis, 'The future of transnational self-regulation enforcement and compliance in professional services' (2017) 40 *Hasting International and Comparative Law Review* 1–67; O. Hart, A. Shleifer and R. W. Vishny, 'The proper scope of government: theory and an application to prisons' (1997) 112 *Quarterly Journal of Economics* 1127–61; L. Bernstein, 'Opting out of the legal system: extralegal contractual relations in the diamond industry' (1992) 21 *Journal of Legal Studies* 115–57.

137 For example, the inability of medieval national laws to regulate geographically dynamic activities gave rise to the system of *lex mercatoria*, formed by merchants' communities executing rule-making, adjudicative, and enforcement tasks. See S. E. Masten and J. Prüfer, 'On the evolution of collective enforcement institutions: communities and courts' (2014) 43 *Journal of Legal Studies* 359–400 at 379, who refer to H. J. Berman, *Law and Revolution: The Formation of the Western Legal Tradition* (Cambridge, MA: Harvard University Press, 1983), p. 347; and C. Cutler, *Private Power and Global*

addressing market failures,[138] or simply due to their lack of expertise in a particular regulatory field.[139] Legal and economic orders are then shaped by various institutions:[140] while driven by expert-community or industry actors, such institutions[141] do not only provide benefits for their members, but also generate positive externalities[142] and offer (nonexcludable and nonrivalrous) public goods.[143]

As such, nonlegal forms of regulatory arrangements pertain to the realm of international and global governance – the provision of formal and informal rules, relationships and institutions by networks of legislative bodies, business and civil society actors.[144] They complement State-

*Authority: Transnational Merchant Law in the Global Political Economy* (Cambridge: Cambridge University Press, 2003), pp. 111, 138.

138 Those market failures typically stem from uncertainty and information asymmetry; see R. O. Keohane, *After Hegemony* (Princeton: Princeton University Press, 1984), p. 93.

139 See Peters et al., 'Non-state actors as standard setters', pp. 1–32.

140 At least, from a neoliberal perspective, see K. O'Neill, J. Balsiger and S. D. VanDeveer, 'Actors, norms, and impact: recent international cooperation theory and the influence of the agent-structure debate' (2004) 7 *Annual Review of Political Science* 149–75 at 164.

141 Note that "institutions" are defined broadly, covering not only organizations but also markets or companies coordinating economic activity, akin to "cognitive and moral structures, rules, norms, conventions or operating procedures which are regarded as socially or legally binding but are not self-enforcing"; J. Black, 'Legitimacy, accountability and polycentric regulation: dilemmas, trilemmas and organisational response', in A. Peters, L. Koechlin, T. Foester and G. Fenner Zinkernagel (eds.), *Non-State Actors as Standard Setters* (Cambridge: Cambridge University Press, 2009), pp. 250–1.

142 M. Larrain Aylwin and J. Prüfer, 'Trade associations, lobbying and endogenous institutions' (2015) 7 *Journal of Legal Analysis* 467–516. Historical examples are discussed in the scholarship on private ordering: see, for instance, A. Greif, P. Milgrom and B. Weingast, 'Coordination, commitment and enforcement: the case of the merchant guild' (1994) 102 *The Journal of Political Economy* 745–76; P. Milgrom, D. C. North and B. R. Weingast, 'The role of institutions in the revival of trade: the law merchant, private judges, and the champagne fairs' (199) 2 *Economics and Politics* 1–23.

143 See M. Olson, *The Logic of Collective Action: Public Goods and the Theory of Groups* (Cambridge, MA: Harvard University Press, 1965), who suggests that the actors provide public goods only if underlying costs are lower than expected benefits. In the scholarship of governance of collective action, the stance is taken that institutions should specify certain behavior as "wrong" and generate mechanisms whereby their members collectively punish "wrongdoers"; see G. K. Hadfield and B. R. Weingast, 'What is law? A coordination model of the characteristics of legal order' (2012) 4 *Journal of Legal Analysis* 471–514.

144 This terminology is suggested for "international governance" in Abbott and Snidal, 'International "standards"', p. 346. For global governance, see G. F. Callies and M. Renner, 'Between law and social norms: the evolution of global governance' (2009) 22 *Ratio Juris* 260–80, referring to O. E. Williamson, 'The economics of governance' (2005) 95 *American Economic Review* 1–18; J. A. Scholte, 'Global governance, accountability and civil society', in J. A. Scholte (ed.), *Building Global Democracy: Civil Society*

driven regulation by allocating resources and coordinating activities in a society or economy.[145] SDOs and their standards are viewed as subcategories of this type of governance:[146] situated between contract and property,[147] SDOs create standards that reach far beyond their membership.[148] By facilitating legal and economic integration, such standards often manage to create normative orders. The following examples illustrate how private and semipublic standardization schemes may exert normative requirements and result in an uptake by "regulated" communities.

### *Private Actors as Governance Suppliers*

Rules, practices, and processes laid down by sector-specific communities other than national governments or interstate organizations, and those that produce strong distributional effects between private actors, have been extensively addressed in scholarship on international and transnational governance[149] and transnational private regulation.[150] As such, transnational private regulation is marked by redistribution of the regulatory power from domestic governments to private actors operating at the global level.[151] It is generally believed to resolve collective action failures and to facilitate compromises between conflicting interests[152]

*and Accountable Global Governance* (Cambridge: Cambridge University Press, 2011), pp. 8–41.

145 See M. Bexell, 'Global governance, legitimacy and (de-)legitimation' (2014) 11 *Globalization* 289–99, who highlights that such private arrangements do not aim to *replace* State-driven regulation.

146 Abbott and Snidal, 'International "standards"', p. 346.

147 H. E. Smith, 'Property as platform: coordinating standards as technological innovation' (2013) 9 *Journal of Competition Law and Economics* 1057–89 at 1071.

148 However, it becomes problematic when a firm lets its individual interests influence standards development process to the detriment of the group and society, Smith, 'Property as platform', p. 1072.

149 See, among many others, K. W. Abbott and D. Snidal, 'Hard and soft law in international governance' (2000) 54 *International Organizations* 421–56.

150 I.e., F. Cafaggi, 'New foundations of transnational private regulation' (2011) 38 *Journal of Law and Society* 20–49; C. Scott, F. Cafaggi and L. Senden, 'The conceptual and constitutional challenge of transnational private regulation' (2011) 38 *Journal of Law and Society* 1–19. For an elaborative literature review, see P. W. J. Verbruggen and P. M. Paiement, 'Transnational private regulation', in *Oxford Bibliographies in Political Science* (July 2017), available at www.oxfordbibliographies.com/view/document/obo-9780199756223/obo-9780199756223-0226.xml.

151 Cafaggi, 'New foundations', p. 21.

152 Ibid., pp. 48–54.

and, as a consequence, offers more advantages than an uncoordinated action by all relevant actors.[153] For the very same reason, transnational regulation may be prone to escape governmental influence and to be guided by technocratic decision-making: the legitimacy of transnational private regulatory regimes then relies on general consent, participatory commitment, and mutual monitoring.[154]

Over the past decades, transnational private regimes grew in importance due to the emergence of new regulatory spaces and advancement of industry domains that have typically been under hegemony of private actors. Where balkanized domestic laws are often inadequate at addressing regulatory challenges of globalization and increased market liberalization, transnational private regulation proves more dynamic and adjustable to industry requirements.[155] Implementation of such normative schemes yet depends on a large number of factors, including the balance of power in a particular sector and the willingness of stakeholders to reach compromises.[156]

Sector-specific communities, in particular professional associations and business networks, may as well prefer to abide by the rules developed by themselves and for themselves. Regulatory regimes where industry actors are both norm-setters and norm-addressees are commonly referred to as self-regulation;[157] they are considered more business friendly than other types of private regulatory arrangements since they

[153] In this regard, transnational regulatory regimes can be compared to cartels, where members join and stay because the existence of a joint initiative is more beneficial, despite a constant temptation to seek self-interest. M. Shapiro, '"Deliberative," "independent" technocracy v. democratic politics: will the globe echo the EU?' (2005) 68 *Law and Contemporary Problems* 341–56 at 349.

[154] Cafaggi, 'New foundations', p. 47.

[155] In this regard, Trubek predicts that in the future of law there will be less attention to courts, and more to the regulatory agencies; D. M. Trubek, 'The political economy of the rule of law: the challenge of the new developmental state' (2009) 1 *Hague Journal on the Rule of Law* 28–32 at 30–1.

[156] See, for example, T. Bartley, 'Institutional emergence in an era of globalization: the rise of transnational private regulation of labor and environmental conditions' (2009) 113 *American Journal of Sociology* 297–351 at 300 (on forest certification and labor standards).

[157] See J. A. Cannataci and J. P. M. Bonnici, 'Can self-regulation satisfy the transnational requisite of successful internet regulation?' (2010) 17 *International Review of Law Computers & Technology* 51–61 at 54 (who, however, also note that a single definition of self-regulation does not exist); and F. Cafaggi and A. Janczuk, 'Private regulation and legal integration: the European example' (2010) 12 *Business and Politics*, (3), 1–40.

can be fine-tuned to individual situations, while minimizing compliance costs and avoiding damaging intrusions from outsiders.[158] Similar to transnational private regulation, self-regulation is characterized by increased flexibility and nonbinding outcomes, which may nevertheless "harden" into compulsory sector-specific rules. Having been witnessed already in Medieval times,[159] self-regulation currently spans from market governance mechanisms to product safety regulation and designing of software and internet protocols.[160]

Arguably, the absence of non-State regulation in emerging regulatory field, together with limited entry possibility for industry actors, is likely to incentivize less effective governmental action: this "legislative threat" may have as well served as a background factor for the widespread recognition of many private or self-regulatory regimes.[161] However, regulation in the shadow of States does not per se exclude governmental actors, who may encourage the adoption of self-regulatory arrangements by private sector – a so-called "meta-regulation."[162] Governments may even act as initiators of private or self-regulation: in fact, "co-regulation," where private normative regimes are underpinned by legislation, are witnessed even more often than pure self-regulatory regimes.[163]

158 See Mattli and Woods, 'In whose benefit?'; Abbott and Snidal, 'Hard and soft law'.

159 See n. 137 on *lex mercatoria*.

160 Gunningham and Rees call it economic and social self-regulation; N. Gunningham and J. Rees, 'Industry self-regulation: an institutional perspective' (1997) 19 *Law and Policy* 363–414 at 364.

161 A. Héritier and S. Eckert, 'New modes of governance in the shadow of hierarchy: self-regulation by industry in Europe' (2007) 28 *Journal of Public Policy* 113–38; E. Meidinger, 'Administrative law of global private–public regulation: the case of forestry' (2006) 17 *European Journal of International Law* 47–87 at 59.

162 See C. Coglianese and E. Mendelson, 'Meta-regulation and self-regulation' (2012) U of Penn Law School, Public Law Research Paper No. 12-11.

163 M. E. Price and S. G. Verhulst, 'In search of the self: charting the course of self-regulation on the internet in a global environment' (2000) Cardozo Law School, Public Law Working Paper No. 015, available at https://papers.ssrn.com/sol3/papers.cfm?abstract_id=216111. Ernst in this regard mentions the role of government in US standardization as enabler, coordinator, or enforcer, while noting that a clear definition of government role in standardization is absent: rather, it is direct and indirect influences to consider; see D. Ernst, 'America's voluntary standards system: a "best practice" model for innovation policy?' (February 2012) East-West Center Working Paper No. 128, available at www.eastwestcenter.org/ewcworkingpapers, p. 3. For examples of co-regulation in standard-setting, see P. J. Weiser, 'Internet governance, standard setting and self-regulation' (2001) 28 *Northern Kentucky Law Review* 822–46.

### *Governance by ICT Standardization*

While technical, and especially ICT standardization has traditionally been considered a matter of industry expertise,[164] it has also been accompanied by the presence of public sector.[165] With increased digital convergence,[166] ICT standards became linked to governmental policies: in the EU, for instance, they convey technological requirements for privacy, security, and accessibility, but also support the objectives of the Digital Single Market.[167] Similar to all technical standards, ICT standards can obscure commercial and political preferences and moral evaluations.[168]

ICT standards are developed by a great variety of stakeholders, including manufacturers of components for network systems, software and hardware developers, network operators, national regulatory agencies, consumers and even societal actors. Many of these stakeholders often have vested interests in standardization processes: for instance, some companies may offer their proprietary technologies for inclusion into a standard and as a consequence, will expect to monetize their patents once the standard is adopted; others, to the contrary, would be interested in a less restrictive access to those technologies. But eventually, for almost

[164] See P. Larouche and G. Van Overwalle, 'Interoperability standards, patents and competition policy', in P. Delimatsis (ed.), *The Law, Economics and Politics of International Standardization* (Cambridge: Cambridge University Press, 2015), pp. 367–93; L. Casini and R. Carotti, 'A hybrid public–private regime: the Internet Corporation for Assigned Names and Numbers (ICANN) and the governance of the internet', in S. Cassese, B. Carotti, L. Casini, M. Macchi, E. MacDonald and M. Savino (eds.), *Global Administrative Law: Cases, Materials and Issues*, 2nd ed., (Rome: IRPA/IILJ, 2008), pp. 29–37; K. Nadvi, 'Global standards, global governance and the organization of global value chains' (2008) 8 *Journal of Economic Geography* 323–43 at 330; Mattli and Büthe, 'Setting international standards', pp. 1, 4.

[165] In fact, with increased economic integration, trade expansion and industry transformation in the second half of the twentieth century, national administrations were allowed to have their share in formulation of technical standards. R. van Gestel and H. Micklitz, 'European integration through standardization: how judicial review is breaking down the club house of private standardization bodies' (2013) 50 *Common Market Law Review* 145–81 at 154–5.

[166] Digitalization, or digital convergence, refers to conversion of information into digital form, and subsequent possibility to access this information from everywhere; see Oshri and Weeber, 'Cooperation and competition', p. 269.

[167] See the yearly updates of the European Commission's 'Rolling plan for ICT standardization', March 2019, available at https://joinup.ec.europa.eu/collection/rolling-plan-ict-standardisation.

[168] R. Werle and E. J. Iversen, 'Promoting legitimacy in technical standardization' (2006) 2 *Science, Technology and Innovation Studies* 19–39, at 23.

each and every stakeholder, ICT devices form an essential part of their quotidian life: traffic lights should manage the traffic at roads and crosswalks; phone calls should be placed; internet connection should be present to perform many daily activities (i.e., paying utility bills, sending work- or leisure-related e-mails, booking flight tickets). With many devices interconnected through different technological layers, ICT standards constitute building blocks of information society and are ubiquitous in modern society.[169]

Perhaps the best example to appreciate the range of actors affected by ICT standards is the development of 5th generation (5G) specifications for cellular networks. Being the backbone of IoT innovation, 5G reaches a great variety of nontraditional ICT players, including such sectors as automotive and agriculture, with the objectives of enabling connected society and socioeconomic transformations.[170] Due to this long reach, 5G is likely to influence and reshape network society, international commerce, and technology innovation to the extent much greater than its predecessors.

Against this backdrop, the question arises whether (ICT) standards supplied by SDOs may be considered public goods. Such designation is supposedly precluded by the fact that standards by definition provide some sort of exclusion – either due to limitations for participation in standards development processes,[171] or due to access limitation resulting from intellectual property rights, which may grant some actors stronger bargaining power (i.e., SEPs or copyrights over standard documents). Scholarship typically characterizes standards as collective goods or club goods – excludable but nonrivalrous.[172]

A different picture emerges if one does not consider standards but rather the general outcome they aim to achieve; for ICT standards, this outcome is interoperability. As illustrated by the example of 5G and IoT, but also by the past generations of wireless standards and protocols,

169 Ibid.

170 See European Commission, '2019 Rolling plan for ICT standardization'.

171 Especially in consortia, where standards may be used to block competitors and deter market entrants and are thus "impure public goods"; see P. A. Samuelson, 'The pure theory of public expenditures' (1954) 36 *The Review of Economics and Statistics* 387–9.

172 See ibid., on collective goods; and R. Cornes and T. Sandler, *The Theory of Externalities, Public Goods, and Club Goods* (Cambridge: Cambridge University Press, 1996) on club goods. Some authors find that standards can be either private or collective goods; C. P. Kindleberger, 'Standards as public, collective and private goods' (1983) 36 *Kyklos* 377–96.

interoperability is multidimensional; interoperability ensures network externalities, shapes competition on the market, and enables communication between people and devices.[173] Although supplied by ICT standards, interoperability still possesses characteristics of a public good – nonexcludable and nonrivalry.

Less unambiguous is the likely classification of SDOs as institutions of collective action. Despite their different interests and characteristics, stakeholders join SDO activities with a common goal to develop and diffuse a standard. It has even been argued in earlier standardization literature that the heterogeneity of interests involved in standardization processes, together with competition among SDOs, ensures that the standard satisfies industry-wide connectivity needs.[174] In this regard, governance by SDOs is enabled by the normative power of their standards, but also through law and jurisdiction, as discussed in Part II of this book.

[173] See Sheremata, 'Competing through innovation in network markets'.

[174] M. L. Markus, C. W. Steinfield and R. T. Wigard, 'Industry-wide information systems standardization as collective action: the case of the U.S. residential mortgage industry' (2006) 30 *MIS Quarterly* 439–65.

# 2

# Legitimacy of ICT Standardization

## Defining and Measuring Legitimacy of Private Normative Orders

In the context of non State regulation, legitimacy as a property attributed to an organization has been subjected to a wider academic debate.[1] Typically understood as one of the elements of the rule's validity[2] and as a justification for the authority's capacity to govern,[3] legitimacy has different faces. In a democracy, legitimacy is an aspect of governance that is exercised through the right process, which initiates a pull towards compliance with the rules.[4] By the same token, legitimacy informs States' obedience to the rules of international law.[5] In multilateral organizations, legitimacy claims are typically substantiated by the inclusion of all affected interests,[6] which in turn also strengthens the effectiveness of

1 While the legitimacy of private regulatory frameworks was discussed by numerous scholars, the very concept of legitimacy is multidimensional and preserves certain obscurity. See A. Hurrelmann, S. Schneider and J. Steffek, 'Conclusion: legitimacy: making sense of an essentially contested concept', in A. Hurrelmann, S. Schneider and J. Steffek (eds.), *Legitimacy in an Age of Global Politics* (London: Palgrave Macmillan, 2007), pp. 229–37; see also Bexell, 'Global governance', p. 292, discussing legitimacy as organizational property.

2 See N. Hachez and J. Wouters, 'Promoting the rule of law: a benchmarks approach' (2013) KU Leuven Centre for Global Governance Studies Working Paper No. 105.

3 See A. Buchannan and R. O. Keohane, 'The legitimacy of global governance institutions' (2006) 20 *Ethics and International Affairs* 405–37. See also Lessig, *Codes and Other Laws*, on that the processes of behavior shaping should be justified by those they constrain.

4 See the definition in T. M. Franck, 'Democracy, legitimacy and the rule of law: linkages' (1999) Working Paper 2, New York University School of Law Public Law and Legal Theory Working Papers Series. Franck uses an example or an open debate of statutes in congress after public hearing, and the passing of statutes by majority.

5 See, in general, T. M. Franck, *The Power of Legitimacy among Nations* (Oxford: Oxford University Press, 1990).

6 This is a "necessary but not sufficient" condition for legitimacy; R. O. Keohane, 'The contingent legitimacy of multilateralism' (2006) GARNET Working Paper No. 09/06, p. 14.

the organization's decisions.[7] Since the perception of the relevance and the validity of institutional activities may vary per actor, legitimacy claims may be competing, posing a challenge on an institution of satisfying them all.[8]

In rule-making beyond States, legitimacy claims are informed differently from governance schemes that are democratic or underpinned by cross-governmental arrangements,[9] and typically concern the relationship between the rule-maker and the stakeholder group that it intends to govern.[10] In transnational private regulation, legitimacy depends on the number of market-based mechanisms it deploys (market legitimacy)[11] as well as on its voluntary nature and consent of those affected by the regulation (legitimacy of arrangement).[12]

Legitimacy may also be based on the nature of distributional consequences of the regulation: in this regard, account should be taken of whether a regulation meets the shared broader norms and values of a particular community (substantive legitimacy).[13] In epistemic rule-making, legitimacy is often derived from the reference to the relevant expertise (expert-based legitimacy).[14] Moreover, when non-State rule-making takes place in nongovernmental organizations or professional associations, its legitimacy can be derived from organizations' constitutional documents, such as bylaws and rules of procedure.

Most recent studies offer a holistic approach to legitimacy and introduce three types of mechanisms on which private rule-making can justify

[7] In this context, legitimacy, quality effectiveness, and enforcement are interrelated. F. Cafaggi, 'A comparative analysis of transnational private regulation: legitimacy, quality, effectiveness and enforcement' (2014) EUI Department of Law Research Paper No. 2014/145. However, inclusiveness may also have negative consequences for effectiveness due to cost externalization; ibid., p. 52.

[8] Black, 'Legitimacy, accountability and polycentric regulation', p. 253.

[9] See D. Curtin and L. Senden, 'Public accountability of transnational private regulation: chimera or reality?' (2011) Amsterdam Centre for European Law and Governance Working Paper Series 2011-06.

[10] P. Nanz and J. Steffek, 'Global governance, participation and the public sphere' (2004) 39 *Government and Opposition* 314–35 at 314.

[11] Cafaggi, 'A comparative analysis', p. 55.

[12] Note that this applies to consent as much as to descent. Value and forms of consent may differ according to institutional environment of the organization and regulatory space; Cafaggi, 'A comparative analysis', p. 1.

[13] Bexell, 'Global governance', p. 2.

[14] See A. C. Cutler, 'The legitimacy of private transnational governance: experts and the transnational market for force' (2010) 8 *Socio-Economic Review* 157–85.

its authority, namely: input, output, and throughput legitimacy,[15] whereby stakeholders of the regulatory regimes are, respectively, participants, users, and compliance agents.[16] Input legitimacy[17] concerns representation of interests in the regulatory bodies, and output legitimacy concerns the quality of rules and outcomes of the regulatory regimes: in other words, input legitimacy is a political criterium whereas output legitimacy is a criterium for performance.[18] In turn, throughput legitimacy concerns the quality of *processes* that steer the exercise of the regulatory authority, and is based on efficacy, accountability, and transparency.[19] While it enhances input and output legitimacy, throughput legitimacy is arguably insufficient on its own to legitimize private governance when viewed independently from political and performance elements.[20] However, a lack of input legitimacy as a consequence of a democratic deficit may arguably be compensated for by increased output legitimacy.[21]

The normative framework of input, output, and throughput legitimacy has been applied to many regulatory regimes invoked by technical standardization;[22] yet, ICT standards deserve some elaboration. ICT

[15] M. Eliantonio and C. Cauffman, 'The legitimacy of standardization as a regulatory technique in the EU – a cross-disciplinary and multi-level analysis: an introduction', in M. Eliantonio and C. Cauffman (eds.), *The Legitimacy of Standardization as a Regulatory Technique in the EU: A Cross-disciplinary and Multi-level Analysis* (Cheltenham and Northampton: Edward Elgar Publishing, 2020), pp. 1–19, using the definitions of V. Schmidt, 'Democracy and legitimacy in the European Union revisited: input, output and "throughput"' (2013) 61 *Political Studies* 2–22.

[16] Senden, with regard to standardization in the EU, stretches this analogy to citizens; L. Senden, 'Towards a more holistic legitimacy approach to technical standardization in the EU', in M. Eliantonio and C. Cauffman (eds.), *The Legitimacy of Standardization as a Regulatory Technique in the EU: A Cross-disciplinary and Multi-level Analysis* (Cheltenham and Northampton: Edward Elgar Publishing, 2020), pp. 20–47, at p. 26.

[17] See Cafaggi, 'A comparative analysis'; Bexell, 'Global governance'.

[18] Output legitimacy debate was initially sparked in political science by Fritz Scharpf; see A. Hurrell, 'Legitimacy and the use of force: can the circle be squared?' (2005) 31 *Review of International Studies* 15–32. Steffek, however, sees output legitimacy as an important democratic dimension, rather than merely the synonym for effectiveness; J. Steffek, 'The output legitimacy of international organizations and the global public interest' (2015) 7 *International Theory* 263–93.

[19] See Senden, 'Towards a more holistic legitimacy approach', p. 35, referencing Schmidt.

[20] The most common critique as outed by Steffek is that such approach leads to proceduralism and not necessarily the quality of regulatory input and output.

[21] See F. Scharpf, *Governing in Europe: Effective and Democratic?* (Oxford: Oxford University Press, 1999).

[22] Eliantonio and Cauffman, *The Legitimacy of Standardization*.

standardization develops extremely rapidly and as a consequence, legitimacy demands and supplies may not always link. Increased network effects, competitive dynamics, and reliance on other standards makes legitimacy of ICT standardization even more complex. In addition, despite the shift of ICT standardization from a purely technical to regulative and policy-making function, its political legitimacy is rarely achievable, since the continuous need to keep specifications, networks, and infrastructure up-to-date requires a rapid and flexible process that often occurs at the cost of inclusiveness and due process in SDOs' decision-making.

## Effectiveness of ICT Standardization

Governance regimes can only exist if they are successful in addressing market failures and achieving the goals they were set up to achieve: in that respect, regulation is *effective* when it succeeds in the objectives it pursues.[23] In scholarship on private ordering, effectiveness is strongly correlated with the performance of institutions: the fundamental elements of successful governance of collective action are the stability of the group[24] and good information flow among its members.[25] From the viewpoint of transnational private regulation, effectiveness of a regulatory regime is affected by such governance elements as functional separation, membership diversity, inclusiveness, transparency, and balanced funding that, altogether, ensure balanced and effective decision-making.[26]

By incentivizing cooperation among different actors, controlling free riding and balancing diverse interests, institutions facilitate compliance

[23] See Cafaggi, 'A comparative analysis', p. 5.

[24] Next to stability, a group's size and homogeneity are important: the larger the group, the more challenging is it for information flows; the more diversified the group, the more difficult it is to coordinate. A. Dixit, 'Governance institutions and economic activity' (2009) 99 *American Economic Review* 5–24 at 16.

[25] Ibid.; Information should be available regarding their identify, behavior, but also which decision is considered wrong. Importantly, classification of unacceptable behavior must match with the information available for the actors, see Dixit, 'Trade expansion'. This is also supported by the fact that heterogenous institutions may often lack lobbying strength and struggle to coordinate members behavior; see, in general, E. Ostrom, *Governing the Commons: The Evolution of Institutions for Collective Action* (Cambridge: Cambridge University Press, 1990).

[26] See Cafaggi, 'A comparative analysis'.

with their regulatory regimes.[27] Compliance, in turn, is considered one of the key indicators for the effectiveness of transnational private regulation:[28] the more a regulatory regime is trusted and accepted, the more effective it is. The opposite also holds: trust and acceptance are more likely to be gained by regimes that are effective.[29]

It has been suggested that regulation's effectiveness can be measured by assessing whether a particular rule resolves the intended regulatory challenge through its impact, cost-effectiveness, net benefits, and distributional fairness (not necessarily placed into monetary terms),[30] and whether it manages to change actors' behavior in a way that solves, reduces, or ameliorates the identified regulatory problem.[31] Therefore, effectiveness of a regulatory regime is linked to its (output) legitimacy in shaping success of rule-making and providing a regulatory solution to address collective action problems.

In the ICT industry, where success or failure are defined by return on investment and speed-to-market,[32] assessing the effectiveness of a particular standardization regime is an immensely complex multidisciplinary exercise. Hence, rather than delving on an in-depth analysis whether a regulatory regime invoked by each particular ICT standard scores high

[27] Ibid.; Abbott and Snidal, 'Hard and soft law'.

[28] Other indicators mentioned in the established body of literature are the degree of regulatory competition, power concentration, number of participants in a regulatory scheme, enforcement, quality of rules and self-assessment; see Cafaggi, 'A comparative analysis'. Note, however, that a regime may be ineffective when individuals do not engage in joint problem-solving, even though their individual compliance with the norm is high; ibid., p. 5.

[29] Senden, 'Towards a more holistic legitimacy approach', p. 27, and accompanying footnotes.

[30] Namely, the OECD Expert Paper of 2012 introduces a framework that systematically evaluated the performance of regulation and regulatory policies. It describes regulation either as a form adopted by governments or other institutional sources, acknowledging that regulation can take different forms, and can be a "collection of rules." OECD, 'Measuring regulatory performance: evaluating the impact of regulation and regulatory policy' (August 2012) Expert Paper No. 1 by C. Coglianese, available at www.oecd.org/gov/regulatory-policy/1_coglianese%20web.pdf.

[31] Ibid., pp. 9–10. While this study does not aim to evaluate the effectiveness of different standardization regimes as regulation, further studies on process and effectiveness of standards using this framework may be helpful to assess specific cases. Note, however, that this framework may not be fitting to measure the effectiveness of ICT standards due to the time lapse between bringing the standard on the market and standards' uptake by the industry, as it was explained by the experts.

[32] Ernst, 'America's voluntary standards system', p. 5.

or low for each of the possible indicators, this study follows a less systematic, but *holistic* approach to effectiveness. It assumes that from the regulator's perspective, a rule's effectiveness is observed through its uptake and actual implementation: accordingly, in a voluntary regulatory setting, the relevant question to ask would be "why do the regulated actors chose to comply with the 'rules'?" (meaning, in this context, standards). From the perspective of the regulated, a rule is effective and will induce compliance when it achieves its objectives: adapted for ICT standardization, a standard is effective when it provides the intended technological compatibility, connections or functions; in other words, when it "works."[33]

## Legitimation by Good Governance Principles and SDOs' Procedures

Effectiveness of global governance regimes is often inseparable from their legitimacy: the uptake of regulation depends on the process of its legitimation, and whether it meets the expectations, beliefs, and interests of its addressees.[34] In this regard, a large body of scholarship on transnational regulation and on global administrative law[35] has devoted scrupulous attention to procedural attributes of global institutions and the process of legitimation of their regimes, justifying or challenging their rule-making authority.

[33] This is in line with Senden's approach to output effectiveness of EU standardization, Senden, 'Towards a more holistic legitimacy approach', p. 27.

[34] See Curtin and Senden, 'Public accountability', p. 10.

[35] Accountability of non-State regimes has been discussed in the scholarship on global administrative law. which is best defined as a normative framework for developing and using specific institutional arrangements to address accountability, inequity, and imbalance of decision-making of the global regulatory bodies, which introduces normative elements that may function as mechanisms of constrain and control global rule-making. Cassese, 'Administrative law without the state', p. 688. Procedural principles discussed in the scholarship on global administrative law are rooted in national administrative law and can be accommodated in the procedures of many institutions, ranging from private bodies to hybrid, heterogeneous groupings with regulatory function, C. Harlow, 'Global administrative law: the quest for principles and values' (2006) 17 *The European Journal of International Law* 187–214 at 201. E. Benvenisti, 'The interplay between actors as determinant of the evolution of administrative law in international institutions' (2005) 68 *Law and Contemporary Problems* 319–40.

### *The Limits of Accountability*

One of the crucial components of legitimacy in globalized institutions is accountability.[36] Accountability in essence represents the provision of information by the rule-making authority and the prospect of its deliberations.[37] From the perspective of the regulated, accountability is a process of "holding an authority to account" and seeking justification for its actions and decisions,[38] whereas from the regulators' viewpoint, accountability implies "giving account," whereby regulators are judged based on prior established rules and may face consequences in a form of formal or informal sanctions.[39] A rather prevalent premise is that all power wielders, irrespective of the nature of their regulative capacity and the regulatory regime in which they operate, should be held accountable to those affected by their decisions,[40] although such accountability mechanisms may vary depending on the impact, forum, and authority:[41] for instance, at the supranational level, accountability can be provided by multiple fora, including specialized experts groups that assess the quality of processes and outputs.[42]

In traditional governance models, accountability helps prevent abuse of power.[43] This "constitutional" function cannot be easily transformed to international law where, due to the limited democratic setting, accountability has been provided through State responsibility and

36 Curtin and Senden mention accountability alongside with such principles as authorization and representation; Curtin and Senden, 'Public accountability', p. 6.

37 M. Bovens, T. Schillemans and P. 't Hart, 'Does public accountability work? An assessment tool' (2008) 86 *Public Administration* 225–42.

38 R. W. Grant and R. O. Keohane, 'Accountability and abuses of power in world politics' (2005) 99 *American Political Science Review* 29–43; R. Mulgan, 'Accountability: an ever-expanding concept?' (2000) 78 *Public Administration* 555–73.

39 M. Bovens, 'Analysing and accessing accountability: a conceptual framework' (2007) 13 *European Law Review* 447–68.

40 R. O. Keohane, 'Global governance and democratic accountability', in D. Held and M. Koenig-Archibugi (eds.), *Taming Globalization: Frontiers of Governance* (Oxford: Polity Press, 2003), pp. 130–59.

41 See A. Peters, T. Föster and L. Koechlin, 'Towards non-state actors as effective, legitimate and accountable standard setters', in A. Peters, L. Koechlin, T. Foester and G. Fenner Zinkernagel (eds.), *Non-State Actors as Standard Setters* (Cambridge: Cambridge University Press, 2009), pp. 492–557.

42 V. Schmidt and M. Wood, 'Conceptualizing throughput legitimacy: procedural mechanisms of accountability, transparency, inclusiveness and openness in EU governance' (2019) 97 *Public Administration* 727–40, at 731, on the example of the EU.

43 Grant and Keohane, 'Accountability and abuses of power'.

liability.[44] In global regulatory space, accountability serves as a control mechanism for stakeholders affected by regulatory decisions,[45] providing (semi-) regulatory institutions with the external scrutiny grip and offering opportunities for further learning through improvement or public exposure of failure.[46] In this regard, accountability represents a form of social mechanism that focuses on institutional arrangements where an actor or an organization can justify their conduct ex post,[47] and is often tied in with such procedural principles as transparency, participation, and review.[48]

While accountability is argued to be a participative and ongoing process that provides ample information for the regulated to require justifications from the regulators,[49] it is sometimes insufficient to address the challenges of global regulation. Concerns of global governance bodies giving greater regard to interests of stronger economic actors, while ignoring those of less powerful actors, may outweigh the alleged "accountability crisis" of global governance.[50] In certain instances, as when the global regulator is pursuing specialized tasks, such "disregard" of some interests may be justifiable once the specialized interests' group is narrowed down to those effectively affected by the regulatory decision; yet, the so-called "unjustified disregard" that emerges as a consequence of institutional circumstances of global regulatory governance may become particularly harmful and disadvantageous to those weaker parties that are

[44] See P. A. Nollkaemper and D. Curtin, 'Conceptualizing accountability in international and European law' (2007) 36 *Netherlands Yearbook of International Law* 3–20.

[45] Pauwelyn et al. refer to it as "external accountability" and note that the weakness of this kind of accountability in informal international law making is that the general public is quite broad, which might render the whole concept of accountability illusive; J. Pauwelyn, R. A. Wessel and J. Wouters, 'Global governance as public authority: structures, contestation and normative change' (2011) Jean Monnet Working Paper No. 06/11, p. 30.

[46] Ibid., p. 26; see also J. Black, 'Learning from regulatory disasters' (2014) LSE Law, Society and Economy Working Papers 24/2014.

[47] Curtin and Senden call it "accountability in a narrow sense" as opposed to a "broader sense," and explain it as a normative concept for evaluation of actors' behavior and setting certain benchmarks for quality of decision-making; Curtin and Senden, 'Public accountability', p. 6.

[48] Meidinger, 'Administrative law', p. 81; Kingsbury et al., 'The emergence of global administrative law', p. 17.

[49] Peters et al., 'Towards non-state actors', p. 524.

[50] See R. B. Stewart, 'Remedying disregard in global regulatory governance: accountability, participation and responsiveness' (2014) 108 *The American Journal of International Law* 211–70.

directly affected by the regulatory decision,[51] and lack any effective safeguards to challenge them.

Global regulatory bodies may be governed by different institutional mechanisms and use different tools to hold them or their officials accountable, including regard-promoting practices such as reason-giving, market competition, or reputational influences.[52] The existence and relevance of these mechanisms may vary per sector;[53] nevertheless, some normative elements are often regarded by scholars as fundamental procedural principles of globalized rule-making.

### *Legitimacy and Accountability through Good Governance Processes*

One of the most essential mechanisms for accountability in global governance is participation. Participation facilitates effective policy shaping by providing possibilities to consult those affected by a regulatory outcome at the early stage of rule-making and to exchange past regulatory experiences.[54] Participation can be decisional, relating to the right to vote or have an active role in decision-making, and nondecisional, implying the possibilities to provide input or submit views to decision-makers.[55] At the same time, it is believed that participation should be meaningful and effective in the sense that it should allow actors to *change* the outcome by approval or acceptance processes.[56]

Depending on the setting and decision to be made, active and effective participation has certain flaws. Making international bargaining more accessible might have detrimental effects, possibly leading to breakdowns in negotiations.[57] To support organizational effectiveness, global institutions with specialized tasks may restrict decision-making authority to those actors having specific knowledge and expertise in the matter.[58]

[51] Ibid.

[52] Ibid., p. 214.

[53] For instance, transparency, reason-giving, and nondecisional participation are less feasible in harmonization of technical standards and security regulations, see ibid.

[54] Harlow, 'Global administrative law', p. 202.

[55] Stewart, 'Remedying disregard', p. 235.

[56] O'Neill, Balsiger and VanDeveer, 'Actors, norms, and impact', p. 155; for participation in democratic societies, see also A. Moravczik, 'Is there a "democratic deficit" in world politics? A framework for analysis' (2004) 39 *Government and Opposition* 336–63.

[57] D. Stasavage, 'Open-door or closed-door? Transparency in domestic and international bargaining' (2004) 58 *International Organization* 667–703 at 668.

[58] See Stewart, 'Remedying disregard'. Gulbrandsen suggests this as the main critique on the Forest Stewardship Council (FSC); see L. H. Gulbrandsen, 'Accountability arrangements

However, while such institutional setting may seem beneficial for some sectors, cherry-picking of participation rules may jeopardize the functioning of accountability mechanisms, rendering them "a meaningless ritual of justifying conduct by answering only those questions that the answer-able party has decided upon."[59]

When discussing participation in regulatory decision-making, political science and theory often make a recourse to the so-called "all affected principle" – a rationale that those affected by a decision should be able to take part in the processes that reached that decision.[60] While initially understood as providing for democratic legitimation,[61] the all affected principle remains of relevance in a nondemocratic setting.[62] Naturally, the critique on the principle is its impracticality to involve virtually everyone in decision-making processes,[63] possible constraints of legal systems due to extraterritorial application of many national laws,[64] as well as its incoherence and uncertainty with regard to the benchmark of "being affected."[65] And while some scholars argued for a broad, "possibilist" interpretation of this principle,[66] others suggest that exclusion of certain actors does not per se generate a democratic deficit; rather, those effectively affected by a particular regulatory choice should be identified

in non-state standards organizations: instrumental design and imitation' (2008) 15 *Organization* 563–83.

59 Gulbrandsen, 'Accountability arrangements', p. 578. In her study on accountability of regulatory institutions in the UK, Black notices that "not only are the lines between independence, accountability and control often blurred, the roles of organizations which are acting as accounters can also be fluid"; J. Black, 'Calling regulators to account: challenges, capacities and prospects' (2012) LSE Law, Society and Economy Working Papers 15/2012.

60 See R. E. Goodin, 'Enfranchising all affected interests and its alternatives' (2007) 35 *Philosophy and Public Affairs* 40–68 at 41.

61 See M. Koenig-Archibugi, 'How to diagnose democratic deficits in global politics: the use of the "all-affected" principle' (2017) 9 *International Theory* 171–202 at 172.

62 E. Erman, 'Global political legitimacy beyond justice and democracy?' (2016) 8 *International Theory* 29–62.

63 Goodin, 'Enfranchising all affected interests', p. 56. Note however that this critique is limited to participation, and not accountability claims.

64 Ibid., p. 49.

65 Which, in fact, can often only be clarified after the decision is implemented.

66 "[. . .] a say [should be given] to anyone who might possibly be affected by any possible decision arising out of any possible agenda" (Goodin, 'Enfranchising all affected interests', p. 55).

empirically, and their involvement in decision-making should then be assessed on the basis of this empirical analysis.[67]

Another institutional tool of global governance is transparency. To be transparent, an organization should provide its stakeholders with information that is accessible and timely:[68] to facilitate the operation of accountability mechanisms, such information should include, for example, financial statements, evaluations, and reports.[69] In terms of public scrutiny, transparency would imply, inter alia, the availability of an organization's regulatory outcomes, the visibility of its decisions, and access to the resources that motivate the regulatory outcomes.[70] The provision of this information may be "active" as well as "passive," the latter meaning that the information is supplied upon request.[71] Transparency is essential for the functioning of a multi-stakeholder organization,[72] for its absence generally results in information asymmetry within the group of interested actors, and affects the uptake of the regulation.[73]

Accountability of global governance regimes is further facilitated by the requirement to give reasons for regulatory decisions.[74] Justifying regulatory choices increases the quality of the rule and its chance to be endorsed by the regulated actors.[75] It also restrains the power of stronger parties and, ideally, ensures the balance between regulatory actors.[76] Since reason-giving requires financial, human, and regulatory resources,

67 Koenig-Archibugi explains it by an "upstream" decision-making that narrows down "downstream" decision-making by imposing a variety of constraints; since the size of the affected group is shrinking, the decision becomes constrained by prior decisions and effectively restricted agendas. See Koenig-Archibugi, 'How to diagnose democratic deficits'.

68 M. Blagescu and R. Lloyd, 'Accountability of transnational actors: is there scope for cross-sector principles?', in A. Peters, L. Koechlin, T. Foester and G. Fenner Zinkernagel (eds.), *Non-State Actors as Standard Setters* (Cambridge: Cambridge University Press, 2009), pp. 270–303.

69 Ibid.

70 See E. Fisher, 'Transparency and administrative law: a critical evolution' (2010) 63 *Current Legal Problems* 272–314.

71 Stewart, 'Remedying disregard', p. 258.

72 See Boström and Tamm Hallström, 'Global multi-stakeholder standard setters'.

73 A. Dixit, *Lawlessness and Economics: Alternative Modes of Governance* (Princeton: Princeton University Press, 2004), p. 65.

74 A. van Aaken and R. Chambers, 'The accountability and independence of international election observers' (2009) 6 *International Organizations Law Review* 541–80.

75 See Stewart, 'Remedying disregard'.

76 Benvenisti, 'The interplay between actors', pp. 325–6.

possibilities to comment on proposed decisions and obtain review of these comments is mostly used in better financed and better organized institutions; in many global regimes, the lack of obligation of reason-giving is restricted not only by resource constraints, but also by consideration of confidentiality or administrative efficiency.[77] To avoid organizational inefficiency and unnecessary administrative or legal burdens, reason-giving should fit the specialized mission and goals of the regulator.[78]

Availability of appeal and/or review mechanism, while being an important part of contemporary Western administrative systems, is also relevant in the context of global governance.[79] Yet, whereas in domestic administrative law, the right of an individual affected by a decision to have it reviewed by an *independent* tribunal is essential,[80] this is not always the case for global and transnational setting, where organizations might maintain their own adjudication or review mechanisms. In this regard, review can be either direct – to determine the validity of a particular regulatory decision – or indirect, when the decision is invoked in the proceedings before a court.[81] It should be noted, however, that adjudicatory review of an institution's decision may sometimes disrupt interactions within this institution and impede its proper societal functioning, since such independent reviewer often lacks knowledge of the special needs of the specific transaction.[82]

The suggested list of normative elements for global governance is rather illustrative and should be viewed as meta-regulation: the discussed procedural principles provide guidance to global regulatory bodies when designing their governance frameworks and prove extremely useful when setting the benchmark for good governance practices in global regulatory space. Implementation of these principles will largely depend on the institutions' mission, specialized tasks, and operational sector.

[77] Stewart, 'Remedying disregard', p. 264.
[78] Ibid., p. 265.
[79] Meidinger, 'Administrative law', p. 79.
[80] Kingsbury et al., 'The emergence of global administrative law', p. 39.
[81] Stewart, 'Remedying disregard', p. 249.
[82] As suggested by Williamson, who refers to Justice Rehnquist, this concerns mostly collective bargaining agreements; O. Williamson, 'Transaction-cost economics: the governance of contractual relations' (1979) 22 *The Journal of Law and Economics* 233–61 at 256.

## SYNOPSIS

The complexity of ICT standards lies not only in their multifaceted technological features, but also the mixed institutional, legal, and organizational questions that pretrain their rule-making authority. Similar to all technical standards, ICT standards can obscure commercial and political preferences and moral evaluations.[83] Yet, by shaping and coordinating interactions between people and devices, ICT standards do not only influence competition and innovation, but affect normative conditions under which firms, governments, and societal actors operate. Even if an ICT community indeed functions by consent rather than coercion,[84] a certain degree of coercion is still present in voluntary ICT standards, since those wishing to be a part of network society should choose to comply with particular standards.[85] SDOs in the ICT sector thus set normative obligations that govern global network society through an amalgam of formal and informal rules and regulative arrangements that go beyond governmental legislation.

In this setting, the question of legitimacy of ICT standardization as a form of private governance regime naturally arises, together with the inquiries into how standards developers safeguard the interests of those affected by their decisions, and whether accountability mechanisms for ICT standardization governance are sufficient to address the arising regulatory concerns. ICT standards may be legitimized by their voluntary adoption, inclusiveness, and technical quality,[86] but crucially, by their acceptance by the industry. Yet, there are more dimensions to the legitimacy of ICT standards than merely their technical excellence. As a non-State regulatory regime, ICT standards are legitimized through the institutional and procedural settings of the organizations that create them,[87] including such features as participation of affected stakeholders, transparency, and review of decisions. In this context, procedural

[83] Werle and Iversen, 'Promoting legitimacy', p. 23.

[84] Ibid.

[85] This compliance and market pressure is what makes firms to engage in "peer-monitoring" and ostracism (i.e., when the market rejects a product) when a device is not compliant with a standard.

[86] Botzem and Dobusch, 'Standardization cycles'; M. Boström and K. Tamm Hallström, 'NGO power in global social and environmental standard-setting' (2010) 10 *Global Environmental Politics* 36–59; N. Brunsson, 'Organizations, markets and standardization', in N. Brunsson and B. Jacobsson (eds.), *A World of Standards* (New York: Oxford University Press, 2000), p. 23.

[87] See also Callies and Renner, 'Between law and social norms'.

mechanisms in SDOs serve as plausible tools to address and balance this disregard, as long as the "weaker" parties make an effective use of such mechanisms; it takes both the regulators and the regulated to ensure that the good governance principles are implemented and functioning in various global governance regimes.

That said, good rule-making processes may not always lead to good regulatory outcomes, and a strong pull towards compliance with a rule does not necessarily imply that the rule was created following the "correct processes":[88] procedural legitimacy hence may not suffice, and a deeper dive into legal, institutional, and empirical settings is required to properly appreciate the different patterns of legitimacy of the global ecosystem of ICT standardization.

[88] In this regard, Bodansky notes that even when governance norms enjoy popular acceptance, they may still be hardly justified from the normative viewpoint, and vice versa. D. Bodansky, 'The legitimacy of international governance: a coming challenge for international environmental law?' (1999) 93 *American Journal of International Law* 596–624. From the perspective of legal pluralism, Berman calls procedural mechanisms, institutions and practices important sites for managing pluralism, and not just a "necessary but regrettable" compromise; P. S. Berman, *Global Legal Pluralism: A Jurisprudence of Law beyond Borders* (Cambridge: Cambridge University Press, 2012), p. 189.

# PART II

## The Law of ICT Standardization

Although voluntary, standards may penetrate public law by being transformed into binding requirements and used to pursue public interest objectives that are typically promoted by States, such as product safety or consumer protection.[1] Since technical standardization by industry-driven bodies possesses attributes of public function,[2] it comes as no surprise that SDOs, while enjoying a high degree of self-regulation, operate under certain legal constraints imposed by public law frameworks.

The public dimension of ICT and interoperability standards also arises from their effects on trade and competition. Standards may be manipulated to create trade barriers by imposing regulatory requirements that are unnecessarily stringent or discriminative, or by pushing up compliance costs for companies,[3] which is especially burdensome for producers and exporters from developing countries due to lack of resources, knowledge, or infrastructure, and contributes to their isolation from Western markets.[4] Recent years have also witnessed mounting concerns of trade

[1] See, for instance, J. L. Contreras, 'From private ordering to public law: the legal frameworks governing Standards-Essential Patents' (2017) 30 *Harvard Journal of Law and Technology* 211–31 at 224.

[2] Ibid., 231.

[3] See, for instance, R. W. Staiger and A. Sykes, 'International trade, national treatment and domestic regulation' (2011) 40 *Journal of Legal Studies* 149–203; R. Howse, 'A new device for creating international legal normativity: the technical barriers to trade agreement and international standards', in C. Joerges and E.-U. Petersmann (eds.), *Constitutionalism, Multilevel Trade Governance and Social Regulation* (Oxford: Hart Publishing, 2006), pp. 383–95. In the past decade, the amount of regulatory measures based on standards and those that were notified to TBT Committee, as well as the number of Specific Trade Concerns (STCs) raised by Members in the TBT Committee meetings, have increased; see G/TBT/46; Ninth Triennial Review of the Operation and Implementation of the Agreement on Technical Barriers to Trade under Article 15.4 (November 2021) WTO Doc. G/TBT/37, Chart 1 – Total TBT Notifications per Triennial Review period.

[4] Think of mandatory testing in the laboratories of importing countries as well as the requirements for laboratories of exporting countries; see Committee on Technical

obstacles arising from the use of technologies: measures related to the prevention of cyber-attacks or espionage – such as mandatory security certification of network elements,[5] prohibition for governmental agencies to use hardware supplied by foreign manufacturers,[6] and refusal to cooperate with certain infrastructure suppliers in the rollout of the new generation of cellular networks due to the threat to national security[7] – are gradually emerging into the wider arena of international trade.

In turn, competitive forces and strategies to influence decision-making in standardization committees, as well as (allegations of) abuse of dominance by SEP holders through setting excessive licensing fees and seeking injunctions against implementers that are not willing to accept the proposed royalty rates,[8] have brought ICT standards into the realm of competition and antitrust law. In particular, while royalty payments protect innovators against free riding on their creations and, ideally, ensure their appropriate reward[9] and encourage future innovative contributions, access to technologies incorporated into standards for the reason of their technical or commercial essentiality remains imperative for making devices standard-compliant.[10] This may result in a two-dimensional problem: from the one side, technology-owners may employ strategies that effectively preclude access to a standard; from the other,

Barriers to Trade, Minutes of the Meeting of March 9–10, 2016, G/TBT/M/68, paras. 2.2.3.39, 2.2.3.49, and more specifically para. 2.322.

5 Committee on Technical Barriers to Trade, Minutes of the Meeting of March 9–10, 2016, G/TBT/M/68, para. 2.2.3.3, where India deviates from Common Criteria Recognition Arrangements (CCRA) for testing procedures: www.commoncriteriaportal.org/ccra/.

6 H.R. 4747, 115th Cong. (2018); Federal Acquisition Regulation; FAR Case 2018-017, Prohibition on Contracting for Certain Telecommunications and Video Surveillance Services or Equipment (August 7, 2019) (to be codified at 48 C.F.R. pts. 1, 3, 12, 13, 39, & 52).

7 For further explanation of 5G and national security issues, see J. P. Kleinhans, '5G vs. national security: a European perspective' (February 2019), available at www.stiftung-nv.de/sites/default/files/5g_vs._national_security.pdf.

8 License disputes generally take place more often than injunctions; see R. Sikorski, 'Enforcing patent pledges under EU law', in J. L. Contreras and M. Jacob (eds.), *Patent Pledges: Global Perspectives on Patent Law's Private Ordering Frontier* (Cheltenham: Edward Elgar, 2017), pp. 168–88. Note that competition law concerns discussed here arise not as much as regarding patents but their application.

9 Cabral and Salant, 'Evolving technologies', p. 51.

10 Note that technical essentiality implies that technologies become essential due to the lack of any alternative methods, while commercial essentiality implies that the alternative methods are commercial or substantially inferior. Baron and Pohlmann, 'Mapping standards to patents' at p. 2, n. 3.

technology-implementers may agree on practices that will devaluate technology and result in licensing rates that are extremely low in the current market context.[11]

Furthermore, every SDO that has offices and is administered by staff members operates under constraints of national laws: for instance, a standard-setting institution may be incorporated as a nongovernmental organization (NGO) (i.e., Institute of Electrical and Electronics Engineers (IEEE), USB Implementers Forum), an association of professionals (i.e., International Bar Association, Association of Climate Change Officers), or a semi public body (i.e., ISO/IEC, ETSI). In a similar vein, mandatory use of standards may lead to administrative or contractual law issues to be dealt with by national legislators and courts.[12] Hence, even when producing global standards, SDOs cannot escape legal requirements stemming from national legislation. In this context, most global ICT SDOs are incorporated, or hold their secretariat offices, in the US and the EU,[13] whose competition rules moreover apply extraterritorially,[14]

[11] See N. Zingales and O. Kanevskaia, 'The IEEE-SA patent policy update under the lens of EU competition law' (2016) 12 *European Competition Journal* 195–235 at 205.

[12] In most countries, disputes on licensing rates of intellectual property embedded into standards typically take place in the realm of contractual law; while the obligatory nature of private ICT standards, such as ISO 14001 for cybersecurity, arises in the realm of national administrative law.

[13] Some important organizations that are partners in the leading global SDOs developing 5G and IoT standards, such as 3GPP and OneM2M, are located in other regions, e.g., China Communications Standards Association (CCSA) and Telecommunications Standards Development Society of India (TSDSI).

[14] Extraterritorial application of EU competition law has been previously accepted on many occasions by the CJEU, e.g., Case 48/69, *Imperial Chemical Industries Ltd.* v. *Commission* [1972] ECR 619 (Dyestuffs), establishing an "economic entity" doctrine (a "ratione personae," when subsidiary and parent company are regarded as one economic entity); Joined Cases 89/85, 104/85, 114/85, 116/85, 117/85 and 125/85 to 129/85 *Ahlstrom and Others* v. *Commission* [1988] ECR 5193 (Woodpulp), establishing "implementation doctrine" (when, regardless of their origin, agreements between companies are implemented in the EU territory and trade between Member States is affected). The General Court has also endorsed a theory of "qualified effects," extending Commission's jurisdiction to conducts that have immediate, substantial, and foreseeable effects in the EU; see Case T-102/96, *Gencor* v. *Commission* [1999] ECR II-753 and Case T-286/09, *Intel Corp.* v. *Commission* [2014] In its recent decision, the General Court held that "implementation doctrine" and "effects doctrine" are alternative principles, while the latter was accepted by the Court on appeal, Case C-413/14, *Intel Corp* v. *European Commission* [2017] 5 CMLR 18; and has been confirmed by the Commission in Guidelines on the Effect on Trade Concept Contained in Articles 81 and 82 of the Treaty (April 27, 2004) OJ 2004 No. C101/81. Likewise, the US Sherman Act of 1890 applies to a conduct involving trade or commerce with foreign nations, when that conduct has a direct, substantial, and

making these two jurisdictions particularly important for legal analysis.[15]

There is little likelihood for the *content* of standards to be regulated by legal frameworks or interpreted by courts: such an active governmental involvement in the substance of industry requirements may undermine expertise-driven processes and risks regulatory capture. Instead, legal constraints and mechanisms for judicial review are directed at the *processes* of developing, adopting, and implementing technical standards, and aim to ensure that those do not emerge from an unlawful conduct. SDOs are thus constrained by multiple legal frameworks, each of them offering a mechanism for legitimization of standards in a particular legal domain.

foreseeable effect on trade or commerce in the US, or when a foreign conduct was meant to produce and indeed produced substantial effects in the US territory, *Hartford Fire Insurance Co.* v. *California*, 113 S. Ct 2891 (1993). US antitrust laws may also be applied in case a foreign regulation impedes market access for US companies, see M. Matsushita, 'The structural impediments initiative: an example of bilateral trade negotiation' (1991) 12 *Michigan Journal of International Law* 436–49.

[15] Moreover, the US and EU systems served as examples for the emerging standardization regimes, see Ernst, 'America's voluntary standards system'.

# 3

# The WTO Regulatory Framework

Addressing standards under WTO law appears rather controversial: the WTO is a government-driven international organization that addresses States' measures and policies, while standardization in itself is a private sector activity. Nevertheless, standards' potential to both encourage international commerce through harmonization of technical requirements as well as to impede market access through trade barriers[1] has laid them at the heart of many issues arising from the WTO Agreements.

At the outset, it should be noted that WTO provides for its Members mechanisms to establish a common framework for trade-related measures, as well as to seek solutions to arising concerns, either by means of discussions in one of the WTO Committees[2] or through the unique dispute settlement mechanism.[3] In this regard, the WTO system attaches cardinal importance to regulatory consistency in Members' trade policies. The requirements of eliminating discriminatory, unnecessary trade-restrictive regulations were introduced already with the establishment of the General Agreement on Tariffs and Trade (GATT)[4] and are widely employed in WTO Agreements and case laws.[5]

[1] See J. Swinnen and T. Vandermoortele, 'Trade and the political economy of standards' (2012) 11 *World Trade Review* 390–400.

[2] The WTO Committees cover different topics and provide a forum to discuss measures adopted by Members and to seek resolutions to arising disputes.

[3] For further discussion of the WTO dispute settlement, see, among many others, D. McRae, 'Measuring the effectiveness of WTO dispute settlement system' (2008) 3 *Asian Journal of WTO & International Health Law and Policy* 1–20 and J. Weiler, 'The rule of lawyers and the ethos of diplomats: reflections on the internal and external legitimacy of WTO dispute settlement' (2000) Harvard Jean Monnet Working Paper 9/00.

[4] General Agreement on Tariffs and Trade (1947) 61 Stat. pt. 5 TIAS 1700 55 UNTS 194 (hereinafter: GATT).

[5] A. O. Sykes, 'Regulatory consistency requirements in international trade' (2017) 49 *Arizona State Law Journal* 821–66. The principles of Most-Favored Nations and National Treatment of GATT, Articles I and III:4, respectively, are fundamental in the WTO system, and require no discrimination for foreign imports either against their own products or products from other Members.

Legal provisions governing the application and *preparation* of standards are introduced in the TBT Agreement, its Annexes and decisions, and are often referred to in global SDOs. In this context, it has been argued that the TBT Agreement provides mechanisms to extend substantive obligations of WTO Members as regards standards development processes to various types of SDOs.[6] This chapter aims to cast light on these obligations with regard to SDOs developing ICT standards.[7]

## Standards under the TBT Agreement

The TBT Agreement entered into force in 1995, replacing the – comparatively limited – plurilateral "Standards Code" of 1979. Requirements imposed by the TBT Agreement are supplementary to those arising from the GATT.[8] Yet, unlike the GATT, the TBT Agreement explicitly addresses private sector activity: what the TBT drafters had in mind were voluntary standards,[9] which, as demonstrated in the previous chapters, are prepared beyond public regulatory processes. Moreover, unlike the GATT, the TBT Agreement not only assesses whether a certain measure constitutes an unjustifiable trade obstacle, but also deals with its preparation.

The Agreement covers three types of measures: technical regulations, (international) standards, and conformity assessment procedures (the latter used to determine whether requirements in the technical regulations or standards are fulfilled).[10] The main distinction between technical regulations and standards appears from Annex 1 of the TBT Agreement

[6] See, among others, M. Mataija, 'Leveraging trade law for governance reform: the impact of the WTO agreement on technical barriers to trade on private standard-setting' (2019) 2 *European Review of Private Law* 293–318; E. van der Zee, 'Disciplining private standards under the SPS and TBT Agreement: a plea for market-state procedural guidelines' (2018) 52 *Journal of World Trade* 393–414; E. Partiti, 'What use of an unloaded gun? The substantive discipline of the WTO TBT code of good practice and its application to private standards pursuing public objectives' (2017) 20 *Journal of International Economic Law* 829–54.

[7] The other WTO Agreement covering standards, and which falls outside the scope of this study, is the Agreement on the Application of Sanitary and Phytosanitary Measures, 1867 UNTS 493 (hereinafter: SPS Agreement), which only applies to binding measures and, while containing provisions that are parallel to TBT Agreement, has a narrower scope.

[8] Appellate Body Report, EC-Measures Affecting Asbestos and Asbestos-Containing Products, WT/DS135/AB/R (March 12, 2001) (hereinafter: *EC-Asbestos*), para. 80.

[9] M. Du, *The Regulation of Product Standards in World Trade Law* (Oxford: Hart Publishing, 2020), p. 20.

[10] See the definitions in Annex 1.3 of the TBT Agreement.

that mirrors the definitions of the ISO/IEC Guide 2 (2004)[11] and characterizes technical regulations as "mandatory," and standards as "not mandatory."[12] The difference between these two types of measures is crucial for the proper application of the TBT provisions and was further clarified by WTO case law.

### *Technical Regulation*

Annex 1 of the TBT Agreement defines technical regulation as a document that lays down characteristics for products and processes, such as terminology, packaging, or labelling, with which compliance is mandatory.[13] In *EC-Asbestos*, the Appellate Body, the main WTO adjudicator, noted that technical regulations should cover identifiable products and provide for mandatory compliance.[14] This case law was further developed in *EC-Sardines*, which took a rather broad approach and put forward three conditions for a measure to be considered technical regulation under the TBT Agreement: (1) application to an identifiable product or group of products, (2) specification of one or more product characteristics, (3) mandatory compliance.[15] With regard to the second prong, the Appellate Body appears to accept a broad range of requirements as product characteristics;[16] with regard to the third prong, the Appellate Body emphasized legal implications of a measure for product's marketing as a significant factor of its classification as a technical regulation.[17] Remarkably, the Appellate Body has also accepted classification of measures that were seemingly voluntary as "technical regulation," when

[11] ISO/IEC Guide 2, Standardization and Related Activities – General Vocabulary (2004).

[12] Annex 1.1 and 2 of the TBT Agreement.

[13] Ibid., Annex 1.1.

[14] *EC-Asbestos*, paras. 68, 70–2.

[15] Appellate Body Report, European Communities – Trade Description of Sardines, WT/DS231/AB/R (September 26, 2002) (hereinafter: *EC-Sardines*), paras. 176–86.

[16] The examples are the measures discussed in Appellate Body Report, US – Certain Country of Origin Labelling (COOL) Requirements, WTO Doc. WT/DS384/ARB, WT/DS386/ARB (June 29, 2012) (hereinafter: *US-COOL*) and Appellate Body Report, United States – Measures Concerning the Importation, Marketing and Sale of Tuna and Tuna Products, WTO Doc. WT/DS381/AB/R (June 13, 2012) (hereinafter: *US-Tuna II*), which went beyond physical characteristics of products or the method of their production.

[17] *EC-Sardines*, paras. 251–7.

the use of alternative measures to prove compliance with certain legal requirements was prohibited.[18]

The TBT Agreement essentially aims to balance Members' right to adopt technical regulations pursuing legitimate objectives of its Article 2.2, such as protection of human health or safety, with the WTO's aim to promote liberalization of international trade.[19] Consequently, it provides Members with a certain flexibility to develop restrictive policies while acting in accordance with the Agreement,[20] and ensures that such policy space is not abused by Members seeking to protect their own markets. Next to the Most Favoured Nation (MFN) treatment and National Treatment obligations,[21] the TBT Agreement includes elements of negative integration, requiring that Members' technical regulations are not designed to frustrate trade,[22] are not more trade restrictive than necessary for fulfilling legitimate policy objectives,[23] and are not maintained in case the objective of circumstances have changed.[24] In debates on standardization and trade, technical regulations become especially relevant when voluntary standards are converted into mandatory requirements.[25]

### *Standards and International Standards*

The TBT Agreement defines "a standard" as document that is approved by a recognized body and with which compliance is *not* mandatory,[26] but

18 *US-Tuna II*; Mataija, 'Leveraging trade law', p. 301. Furthermore, a measure qualifying as a technical regulation, discussed under the TBT Agreement, should also be dealt with under Article XX(b) of GATT when it relates to health concerns; see M. Matsushita, T. J. Schoenenbaum and P. C. Mavroidis, *The World Trade Organization: Law, Practice, and Policy* (Oxford: Oxford International Law Library, 2015), p. 488, with reference to Appellate Body Report European Communities – Regime for the Importation, Sale and Distribution of Bananas, issued September 9, 1997. However, when a technical regulation constitutes an SPS measure, it is considered under the SPS Agreement; see Article 1.5 of TBT Agreement.

19 Appellate Body Report United States – Measures Affecting the Production and Sale of Clove Cigarettes, WTO Doc. WT/DS406/AB/R (April 4, 2012), para. 96. Note that this list is not limited – the *EC-Sardines* specified market transparency, consumer protection, and fair competition as legitimate objectives.

20 Wijkstrom and McDaniels, 'International standards', p. 4.

21 Article 2.1 of TBT Agreement.

22 Ibid., Article 2.2.

23 Ibid. For the definition of necessity under Article 2.2, see *US-COOL*, paras. 374–9.

24 Article 2.3 of TBT Agreement.

25 See Chapter 1.

26 Annex 1.2 of TBT Agreement. Note that although relying on ISO/IEC Guide 2 (2004), the WTO definition of standards deviates from it: for instance, it does not deal with standards for services (which is expectable since the TBT Agreement deals with goods); also, ISO/

provides no definition of "international standard," except for that this is prepared by an international standardization community and approved by an international body or system offering its membership to the *relevant bodies* all WTO members,[27] which also recognize these bodies' standardization activities.[28] The concepts of a "recognized" and "relevant" body are likewise not defined under the TBT Agreement.[29] Pursuant to the Appellate Body in *US-Tuna II*, international bodies with "recognized standardization activities" retain certain procedural and substantive features encompassed in the TBT Committee Decision.[30]

While Annex 1 of the TBT Agreement further stipulates that standards prepared by the international standardization community are based on consensus, the Agreement also appears to cover standards that are not consensus-based.[31] In its ruling in *US -Tuna II*, the Appellate Body clarified that for the purpose of the TBT Agreement, international standards do not need to be based on consensus, as long as the usual procedure of the body that has adopted the standard follows the consensus requirement.[32] While discussions on whether an international

IEC Guide 2 (2004) covers standards that are both mandatory and voluntary; see explanatory note to Annex 1 of the TBT Agreement. Mataija argues that the TBT Agreement applies only to standards adopted by recognized bodies; see Mataija, 'Leveraging trade law'.

27 Annex 1.4 of TBT Agreement and the note.

28 Appellate Body Report *US-Tuna II*, paras. 361 and 376. This is the so-called "factual" dimension, which means that WTO Members are aware of the existence of the body's standardization activities; Mataija, 'Leveraging trade law', p. 309. Note that while Annex 1 provides definitions of "central" or "governmental" bodies, it does not as such provide what "recognized" means. For further discussion on "recognized bodies" see P. Delimatsis, 'Relevant international standards and "recognized standardization bodies" under the TBT Agreement', in P. Delimatsis (ed.), *The Law, Economics and Politics of International Standardization* (Cambridge: Cambridge University Press, 2015), pp. 104–36; and O. Kanevskaia, 'ICT standards bodies and international trade: what role for the WTO' 56 *Journal of World Trade* 429–52.

29 Unlike the SPS Agreement, which introduces the (inexhaustive) list of covered standards bodies.

30 Mataija terms it as a "normative" dimension; Mataija, 'Leveraging trade law', p. 309. *US-Tuna II*, para. 376, referring to the Committee on Technical Barriers to Trade, Second Triennial Review of the Operation and Implementation of the Agreement on Technical Barriers to Trade, Annex 4: Decision on Principles for the Development of International Standards, Guides and Recommendations with Relation to Articles 2, 5, and Annex 3 of TBT Agreement, WTO Doc. G/TBT/9 (November 13, 2000) (hereinafter: TBT Committee Decision).

31 See the Explanatory Note to Annex 1.2 of TBT Agreement.

32 *US-Tuna II*, para. 353. Earlier on, *EC-Sardines* extended the scope of the TBT Agreement beyond standards crafted in ISO and IEC, but nevertheless referred to the ISO/IEC Guide 2 (2004) for the definition of a standard; *EC-Sardines*, paras. 219–33 and 255.

standard should be based on consensus arose even before the *US-Tuna II* report was adopted,[33] the reasoning of the Appellate Body was claimed to be unsettling not only due to its departure from entrenched consensus-based nature of standards, but also because it opened avenues for those organizations whose standards are not widely used to be considered as relevant standards bodies, possibly aggravating concerns of legitimacy of international standards regimes.[34]

The regulatory transformation of *international* standards into technical regulations is enabled by Article 2.4 of the TBT Agreement that obliges Members to use *international* (emphasis added) standards as a basis for their technical regulations,[35] meaning that there should be "a very strong and substantive relationship between the regulation and the substance of a standard."[36] Technical regulations adopted in accordance with this provision enjoy a rebuttable presumption of not impeding international trade. Members may depart from international standards when those are "ineffective or inappropriate" for the fulfilment of the legitimate objectives pursued by Members' technical regulation:[37] a lion's share of trade concerns raised in the TBT Committee deals exactly with Members' technical regulations deviating from international standards, for instance, for the reason of security.

## Procedural Mechanisms of the TBT Agreement

The distinction between "standards" and "international standards" becomes particularly important in the light of the procedural mechanisms that apply to the processes of their preparation. The TBT

[33] Wijkstrom and McDaniels, 'International standards', p. 7, describing that the US argued that a standard for transportation packaging of lithium batteries established by the International Civil Aviation Organization was not an international standard for the reason that it was adopted by voting, and not consensus, and hence this document should not have been used as a basis for national technical regulation.

[34] Howse, 'A new device', pointing out that a broad range of normative material may be converted into international obligations. For the overall critique of the AB reading of the TBT Agreement, see P. Mavroidis, 'Last mile for tuna (to a safe harbour): what is the TBT Agreement all about?' (2019) 30 *The European Journal of International Law* 279–301.

[35] According to Howse, this requirement should be understood in terms of reasonableness, meaning that there must be a reasonable relationship between the international standard and the domestic regulation; see Howse, 'A new device'. Note, however, that the notion of reasonable relationship was rejected by the Appellate Body in *EC-Sardines*, paras. 247–8.

[36] *EC-Sardines*, para. 245.

[37] Article 2.4 of TBT Agreement.

Committee Decision (2000) introduces principles to be adhered to by *international* standards bodies for the purpose of Article 2.4 of the TBT Agreement. In turn, organizations producing standards that are not "international" *can* be covered by Article 4 of the TBT Agreement. In the TBT realm, the mechanics of these instruments plays an important role of assessment of ICT standards as private standards under the TBT Agreement, and ICT SDOs as "recognized bodies."[38]

### *TBT Code of Good Practice*

The adoption of the TBT Code of Good Practice is believed to have been instigated by the European Commission's wish to expand the Agreement to nongovernmental bodies.[39] Essentially, Article 4 of the TBTAgreement addresses the WTO Members, and not standards organizations, with an obligation to ensure that their central government standardizing bodies accept and comply with the Code of Good Practice, and take "reasonable measures as may be available to them"[40] to ensure that the local and nongovernmental bodies within their territories do so as well.[41] The "benefits" of compliance with this Article, however, are received by standards bodies: organizations that have accepted the Code of Good Practice and comply with its provisions are presumed to act in conformity with the TBT Agreement.[42]

Members' obligations to ensure compliance of (non)governmental standardizing bodies with the Code of Good Practice apply regardless of whether or not these bodies have accepted the Code.[43] Yet, it remains unclear which "reasonable measures" should be taken by Members to

[38] For instance, some WTO Members, like Canada, linked the concept of recognition to the principles of the TBT Committee Decisions, Delimatsis, 'Relevant international standards'.

[39] Du, *The Regulation*, p. 26, referencing Proposal by the European Economic Community, 'A Code of Good Practice for Non-Governmental Bodies in the Agreement on Technical Barriers to Trade', TBT/W/110 (July 7, 1988) and Revised Proposal by the European Economic Community, 'A Code of Good Practice for Non-Governmental Bodies in the Agreement on Technical Barriers to Trade', MTN/GNC/NG8/W/71 (February 20, 1990).

[40] Code of Good Practice for the Preparation, Adoption and Application of Standards, Annex of TBT Agreement (hereinafter: Code of Good Practice).

[41] Article 4.1 of TBT Agreement and Annex 3 (B) of Code of Good Practice. For the definition of standardization bodies, see Annex 1.4–8 of TBT Agreement.

[42] Article 4.2 of TBT Agreement.

[43] Ibid., Article 4.1. For requirements related to the notification of acceptance of or withdrawal from the Code of Good Practice, see Annex 3(C) TBT Agreement.

ensure that their local and nongovernmental bodies fulfil the requirements of Article 4.1 and Annex 3 of the TBT Agreement,[44] and which consequences will be faced by Members who do not comply with this obligation.[45] Until December 2018, no Member has notified the acceptance of the Code of Good Practice by a nongovernmental body within its territory: the first ever private body accepting the Code is the US-based Calendaring and Scheduling Consortium "CalConnect."[46]

The substantive requirements of the Code of Good Practice that apply to standards bodies generally mirror the TBT obligations for technical regulations, such as MFN and national treatment.[47] By the same token, the Code requires standards bodies to ensure that their standards do no result in unnecessary trade barriers,[48] are based on international standards, unless those are ineffective or inappropriate,[49] and that national

[44] V. Thorstensen, R. Weissinger and X. Sun, 'Private standards: implications for trade, development and governance' (2015) Think Piece of E15 Initiative on Regulatory Systems Coherence, International Centre for Trade and Sustainable Development, p. 2. Partiti notes that "reasonable" implies "a degree of flexibility that involves consideration of all of the circumstances of a particular case" and "involves consideration of economic and technical feasibilities," referring to the Appellate Body Report, Anti-Dumping Measures on Certain Hot-Rolled Steel Products from Japan, WT/ DS184/AB/R (July 24, 2001), para. 84, and suggests that identifications whether the measure is reasonably available may be costs of enforcement or capacity of members in question. Partiti, 'What use of an unloaded gun?', p. 837. Some scholars have argued that taking "reasonable measures to ensure compliance" is an "empty obligation," or at least just an obligation of process or as a result; van der Zee, 'Disciplining private standards', p. 409.

[45] See Partiti, 'What use of an unloaded gun?'.

[46] See Committee on Technical Barriers to Trade, Notification under paragraph C of the WTO TBT Code of Good Practice, G/TBT/CS/N/199 (February 20, 2019). While no specific reasons have been provided for the decision to accept the Code of Good Practice, close cooperation between CallConnect and ISO may perhaps have been one of the factors that have triggered the acceptance of the Code. See further 'Alignment to international principles – WTO TBT principles for the development of international standards, guides and recommendations', CallConnect Report CC/R/WD 10100:2018, available at https://standards.calconnect.org/csd/csd-wto-tbt-principles.html#toc16. For the full list of SDOs that have accepted the Code of Good Practice, see https://tbtcode.iso.org/sites/wto-tbt/list-of-standardizing-bodies.html.

[47] Annex 3(D) of TBT Agreement also implemented by Article 5.3 of ISO/IEC Guide 59 – ISO and IEC Recommended Practices for Standardization by National Bodies (2nd ed., 2019).

[48] Annex 3(E) of TBT Agreement, also implemented by Article 5.4 of ISO/IEC Guide 59 (2019), which suggests broader participation of representatives from other countries in national bodies, to understand global trade implications of national standards.

[49] Annex 3(F) of TBT Agreement. Article 5.5 of ISO/IEC Guide 59 (2019) specifies that such standards are developed by ISO or IEC.

standards bodies are engaged, to the extent possible, in the development of such international standards by ISBs.[50] Other procedural and substantive obligations imposed by the Code include harmonization of international standards; coherence at the national, regional, and international level; transparency, submission, and review of comments; and consultations with other standards bodies.[51]

### *TBT Committee Decision*

The TBT Committee Decision (2000) introduces procedural principles that bodies adopting *international* standards should adhere to. In order to act in accordance with the TBT Agreement, Members should base their technical regulations on international standards developed by these bodies.[52] The introduction of the Decision and its principles was incited by the lacunae of the TBT Agreement as well as by concerns regarding standards' effectiveness and relevance for the global trade development, which were frequently raised at the TBT Committee meetings.[53] Contrary to the TBT Code, the Decision is believed to be largely driven by the US as counterweight to the alleged domination of the EU in international standardization.[54]

Despite its nonbinding character, the Decision serves as a tool for interpretation and application of the TBT Agreement, since the Appellate Body considered it as a subsequent agreement within the meaning of

[50] Annex 3(G) of TBT Agreement implemented by Article 5.6 of ISO/IEC Guide 59 (2019). Partiti argues that these "good governance" requirements of the TBT are carried over to the Code and to the bodies accepting it, and that by this means the code extends Members' obligations to private standardization activity unconnected to public authority. Partiti, 'What use of an unloaded gun?'.

[51] Note that similar requirements were taken over in ISO/IEC Guide 59 (1994).

[52] Article 2.4 of TBT Agreement.

[53] See First Triennial Review of the Operation and Implementation of the Agreement on Technical Barriers to Trade (November 19, 1997) WTO Doc. G/TBT/5.

[54] Delimatsis, 'Global standard-setting 2.0', p. 12. It should be noted that the Decision did not eliminate frictions between the US, the WTO Secretariat and other Members; see, for instance, the letter of 23 June 2006 from the US Permanent Mission to the WTO to Director-General Singh expressing concerns of the broad interpretation of the term "standard" and the lack of identification of standard-setting bodies in the TBT Agreement.

Article 31(3)(a) of the Vienna Convention.[55] The six procedural principles for international standards development set forth by the Committee Decision (transparency, openness, impartiality and consensus, effectiveness and relevance, coherence, and development dimension) are widely implemented in national legal requirements and operational frameworks of many SDOs.[56]

### *ISO/IEC Guide 59*

The third instrument to be discussed in the context of the WTO framework is the ISO/IEC Guide 59 on recommended practices for standardization. The first version of the Guide was adopted by ISO/IEC members in 1993[57] and predated the TBT Agreement and the Code of Good Practice.[58] In 2019, ISO/IEC Guide 59 was updated with provisions implementing the TBT instruments: as carefully noted in Guide 59 (2019), the new edition does not intend to replace nor interpret the TBT documents, but rather provides recommendations on their implementation.[59] Compliance with Guide 59 (2019) is thus insufficient to guarantee compliance with the TBT instruments.

One of the most remarkable changes of the updated Guide 59 is the clarification of its scope. While the previous version of Guide 59 was to be used by "any standardization body, whether governmental or non-governmental, at international, regional, national or sub-national level,"[60] the updated Guide 59 is intended to be used by the *national*

[55] *US-Tuna II*, para. 371. Recall that adherence to the principles introduced in the Decision is one of the conditions for a body to be considered as having "recognized standardization activities"; *US-Tuna II*, para. 376.

[56] For example, Rec. 2 of EU Regulation 1025/2012.

[57] See Introduction, ISO/IEC Guide 59 (2019).

[58] Note that The Tokyo Round "Standards Code" of 1979 did not have a comparable "Code of Good Practice" and that the Code was introduced with the TBT Agreement only in 1995. European Commission, Press Release, 'Balance sheet of seven years of negotiations', available at https://europa.eu/rapid/press-release_MEMO-94-24_en.htm; Tokyo Round Standards Code (1979) Document coce LT/TR/A/5, available at www.wto.org/english/docs_e/legal_e/prewto_legal_e.htm. Curiously, similar to the TBT Committee Decision, the Standards Code is also believed to have been driven by the US; see 'Standards Code of the Trade Agreement Act of 1979, Hearing before the Subcommittee on Transportation and Commerce and the Committee on Interstate and Foreign Commerce House of Representatives. Ninety-sixth Congress, First Session,' US Government Printing Office (June 28, 1979), at 38.

[59] Introduction, ISO/IEC Guide 59 (2019).

[60] Article 3.1 of ISO/IEC Guide 59 (1994).

*bodies* (emphasis added),[61] which it defines as any current or future national members of ISO and IEC.[62] Furthermore, where the previous version merely stated that the adoption of the Guide 59 is voluntary and intends to "ensure openness and transparency, together with an optimum degree of order, and coherence and effectiveness in worldwide standardization processes,"[63] the new version adds that it is further up to national bodies to set guidelines on their organizational culture and to follow the ISO/IEC Codes of Conduct that include responsibilities to consider inclusiveness, consensus-building attitude and skills, compliance with the procedures, efficiency, impartiality, commitment to quality, and dedication of personnel and experts.[64]

While the updated Guide 59 implements a number of definitions from ISO/IEC Guide 2 (2004) (i.e., those of a "standard" and "consensus"), it also introduces some new concepts. For instance, the term "stakeholder" is defined as an "organization, company public entity or individual that can affect, be affected by or perceive itself to be affected by a decision or activity coming from a standardization process or its deliverables," and is deemed equivalent to the term "interested party";[65] in turn, a "participant" is a stakeholder that becomes involved in the standards development process.[66]

## WTO and ICT Standardization

ICT standards are private standards and are principally developed by nongovernmental bodies comprised of enterprises and individuals.[67] At first glance, these characteristics alone render their coverage by the TBT Agreement problematic. Hence, despite their evident role in multilateral trade, ICT standards, like many other types of private standards, have for a long time managed to escape the direct purview of the WTO.[68] While

61 Article 1 of ISO/IEC Guide 59 (2019).
62 Ibid., Article 3.8.
63 Article 1.4 of ISO/IEC Guide 59 (1994).
64 Introduction, ISO/IEC Guide 59 (2019).
65 Ibid., Article 3.
66 Ibid., Article 3.7.
67 That said, these voluntary specifications can become international standards within the meaning of TBT by approval of ISO, as it is the case for the WLAN/Wi-Fi standards. See Chapter 1.
68 Scholarship has even suggested that implicit governmental endorsement of a private standards body could allow that government to escape its WTO obligations (unless the measure at issue could indeed be attributed to the government, that is). J. Wouters and

the debate on private standards and the WTO deserves specific attention, whether a standard falls within the scope of WTO law, and whether WTO obligations apply to the SDO developing this standard, will depend on this SDOs' acceptance of the Code of Good Practice or, in case of *international* standards to be used by States as a basis of their technical regulations, on the SDO's classification as "an international body or system with recognized standardization activities." Arguably, scrutinizing ICT standards against TBT norms will mitigate their risk of becoming trade obstacles by ensuring that these standards are developed in a transparent and open manner with due respect to procedural guarantees.[69]

### *ICT Standards as Trade Barriers: The Case of WAPI*

Concerns related to ICT standards are being increasingly discussed in the WTO Committees, especially when these standards become mandatory under Members' national law and thus take the form of "technical regulations."[70] One of the most remarkable examples was the case of China's WLAN Authentication and Privacy Infrastructure (WAPI) standard. Asserting that the global WLAN (or simply, Wi-Fi) specifications did not meet the objectives of ensuring safety of wireless networks,[71] China drafted its own homegrown proprietary encryption standard for WLAN.[72] The standard was developed in a secret procedure,

D. Geraets, 'Private food standards and the World Trade Organization: some legal considerations' (2012) 11 *World Trade Review* 479–89 at 485.

[69] See by analogy, Mavroidis and Wolfe, 'Private standards and the WTO', p. 21 (on the perils of poor standards development processes).

[70] Note, however, that Members seemed reluctant to discuss issues related to interoperability standards in the TBT Committee. For instance, when US expressed concerns regarding Korea's draft regulation to mandate the standard on Wireless Internet Platform for Interoperability (WIPI), Korea believed that this issue should be raised under the GATS and not the TBT Agreement, since WIPI was "a technical interface standard that governed interconnection among networks of wireless Internet service providers," adding that the notification of the measure under the TBT Agreement was submitted merely for transparency purposes. Minutes of the Meeting held on March 20, 2003, G/TBT/M/29 (May 19, 2003), paras. 54–5.

[71] T. Berger, 'Balancing barriers to trade and technical standards: potential impact on ICT industries' (2015) 17 *International Trade and Business Law Review* 315 at 338. Apparently, the reported flaws were corrected by a new IEEE standard.

[72] USTR, '2005 Report to Congress on China's WTO Compliance' (2005), available at https://china.usc.edu/2005-report-congress-china%E2%80%99s-wto-compliance, p. 43; For the overview of WAPI case study, see C. S. Gibson, 'Globalization and technology

which however followed Chinese standardization law of that time, ran on a different security protocol that its "Western" counterpart, and embedded a number of proprietary encryption algorithms owned by Chinese companies.[73]

Upon WAPI's approval, which was initially scheduled for May 2003,[74] all WLAN devices marketed in China were obliged to comply with WAPI standard. Since WAPI was not interoperable with WLAN specifications developed by IEEE, this resulted in a practical nightmare for all foreign equipment vendors: in order to maintain their presence at both global and Chinese markets, wireless devices had to be equipped with technologies reading two sets of specifications.[75] The lack of licensing obligations for Chinese companies, some of which were rivals to foreign producers, and their freedom to set royalty rates without adhering to any FRAND-type commitment added fuel to the fire.[76] From the trade law perspective, the issue was complicated by the fact that IEEE's WLAN specifications were formally approved as ISO/IEC 8802-11, while WAPI's adoption as an ISO standard was rejected.[77] This led some WTO members to claim that WAPI is not compliant with Article 2.4 of TBT Agreement since it is not based on the existing international standard.[78] It is perhaps this failure to promote WAPI as an international standard, as well as a strong

standards game: balancing concerns of protectionism and intellectual property in international standards' (2007) 22 *Berkley Technology Law Review* 1403–84.

73 The Standardization Administration of China (SAC) Directive 237 issued by China's State Council, the country's highest administrative body; see S. Lawson, 'Clouds hang low over Chinese WLAN standard' (December 19, 2003) *Computerworld*, available at www.computerworld.com/article/2804354/clouds-hang-low-over-chinese-wlan-standard.

74 Eventually, the transition period was extended and the deadline for mandatory compliance became June 2004.

75 See Berger, 'Balancing barriers'.

76 H. W. Liu, 'International standards in flux: a Balkanized ICT standard-setting paradigm and its implications for the WTO' (2014) 13 *Journal of International Economic Law* 551–600. It is therefore also not surprising that trade concerns were raised by the US and the EU.

77 See Gibson, 'Globalization and technology standards game'. Arguably, the reason for the rejection was that WAPI development lacked openness, although China submitted that the reason behind the rejection was Western bias against China.

78 Committee on Technical Barriers to Trade, Note by the Secretariat: Minutes of the Meeting of November 10–11, 2011, 39–42, WTO Doc. G/TBT/M/55 (February 9, 2012); Committee on Technical Barriers to Trade, Note by the Secretariat: Minutes of the Meeting of March 20–21, 2012, 237–41, WTO Doc. G/TBT/M/56 (May 16, 2012); Committee on Technical Barriers to Trade, Note by the Secretariat: Minutes of the Meeting of June 13–15, 2012, 204–9, WTO Doc. G/TBTIM/57 (September 18, 2012).

counterbalance from the US and EU delegations in the WTO, that led China to abandon the mandatory nature of WAPI.[79]

It is true that in a multilateral trading system, import restrictions may be justified by legitimate concerns of, for instance, national security or protection of human health or safety; same national or regional trade policies may, however, incarnate protectionism by promoting domestic manufacturers and suppliers and discouraging imports.[80] Given the size of Chinese market for wireless devices, the distributional effects of wireless networks, and revenues generated from licensing of intellectual property, it may be speculated that mandated WAPI specifications intended to target foreign importers, rather than increase national security. That said, it should be noted that the effects of standards on international trade generally depend on many factors and may vary per sector.[81] In any event, to understand whether and how trade barriers created by ICT standards can be addressed by the TBT Agreement, it is necessary to understand the application of the TBT rules to private standards.

### *Private Standards Conundrum*

Coverage of private standards by the TBT Agreement has been a matter of a long-standing discussion in the TBT Committee as well as in the

[79] See D. Ernst and S. Martin, 'Adjusting to the global knowledge economy? Recent developments in China's WAPI Standard' (2010) Unpublished manuscript, East-West Center, Honolulu. EU–China IPR2 2009, 'Third revision of China's patent law: legal texts and documents on the drafting process, 2006–2009', available at www.ipr2.org/im-ages/eu_patent_law-final.pdf. N. Sun, 'Piercing the veil of national security: does China's banking IT security regulation violate the TBT Agreement' (2016) 11 *Asian Journal of WTO and International Health Law and Policy* 2995–236.

[80] For example, a standard adopted by the Japanese Consumer Product Safety Association provided that in order to get a consumer safety seal (and thus gain access to the Japanese market), skis had to comply with particular product design specifications, which in turn were impossible to reach by foreign ski producers; P. Mavroidis, *Trade in Goods* (Oxford: Oxford University Press, 2012), p. 673; T. Büthe and W. Mattli, *The New Global Rulers: The Privatization of Regulation in the World Economy* (Princeton: Princeton University Press, 2011), p. 135.

[81] In this regard, see Trachtman discussing standards and welfare: for instance, standards may both support the provision of public goods and diminish welfare through suppression of efficient variation and regulatory competition, depending on the particular type of product, and the preferences of individuals and states; J. P. Trachtman, 'Toward open recognition? Standardization and regional integration under Article XXIV of GATT' (2003) 6 *Journal of International Economic Law* 459–92.

relevant scholarship. Compliance with private standards is becoming increasingly important for international commerce since it is often a prerequisite for accessing a large number of developed country markets, which creates confusion for exporters who already have to comply with requirements set by other "recognized" standard setters.[82] Concerns regarding the absence of a coherent WTO framework for private standards are regularly expressed by WTO Members,[83] but even meagre attempts have not been met with a great enthusiasm by the wider WTO community.[84]

Currently, the discussion on private standards seems to have reached an impasse. On the one hand, extending the scope of the TBT Agreement and its principles to private standards would inevitably require increased governmental involvement in industry-driven processes, since the obligations imposed by the TBT Agreement and its instruments are designed for WTO Members.[85] This may shake the intergovernmental structure of the WTO system and provoke widespread discontent among industry actors. On the other hand, allowing private standards to avoid WTO scrutiny opens a Pandora box of unresolved issues: is it legitimate that exporters and producers from developing countries, which are typically unable to participate in private standards bodies, should bear additional compliance costs to access developed markets? Do private standards bodies weaken the roles of ISBs? Does the low degree of openness and

[82] 'Effects of SPS-related private standards: compilation of replies', Note by the WTO Secretariat. G/SPS/GEN/932/Rev.1 (December 10, 2009); Thorstensen et al., 'Private standards', p. 4.

[83] That is, Fifth Triennial Review of the Operation and Implementation of the Agreement on Technical Barriers to Trade under Article 15.4 (November 13, 2009) WTO Doc. G/TBT/26, para. 26. A discussion on private standards in TBT Committee was recently suggested by China; however, China's proposal to draft a TBT guide on the use of private voluntary standards was actively opposed by the US and the EU; see Committee on Technical Barriers to Trade, Minutes of the Meetings, G/TBT/M/69 (June 15–16, 2016), para. 3.2.4.3.2. Members also expressed concerns under the SPS Agreement: in particular, Saint Vincent and the Grenadines were concerned that the operation of a EurepGAP scheme in relation to trade in bananas with supermarkets in the UK was not covered by WTO provisions; see 'Private Standards and the SPS Agreement', Note by the Secretariat, G/SPS/GEN/746 (January 24, 2007).

[84] Curiously, for the purpose of the SPS Agreement, Members failed to agree even on the definition of a "private standard"; Mavroidis and Wolfe, 'Private standards and the WTO', p. 12.

[85] Article 1 of TBT Agreement.

inclusiveness in private standards bodies undermine the legitimacy of international trading system?[86]

Some scholars stressed the importance of creating informal guidelines or recommendations of good practices for the preparation and application of private standards.[87] Such arrangements, however, should be sufficiently flexible to preserve the advantages of industry standardization.[88] As a solution to address capacity constraints in developing countries and to maximize positive effects of private standards, while still allowing the WTO to act as an ultimate arbiter of standards affecting international trade, it was proposed to launch an international body or forum on private standards, potentially outside the WTO, which will negotiate rules for standards, represent interests of stakeholders, and ensure better cooperation between SDOs, governments, and stakeholders. This will arguably promote regulatory cooperation as resource sharing and transparency.[89] The question remains whether such an initiative will be welcomed by private standards bodies and WTO Members.

### *SDOs in the ICT Sector as Recognized Bodies*

According to the Appellate Body, both governmental and nongovernmental SDOs can be categorized as "recognized bodies" under the TBT Agreement.[90] The concept of a "body" is rather broad: pursuant to ISO, it entails a legal or administrative entity with a specific task or composition.[91] International recognition of this body follows through the factual dimension, when WTO Members are aware of its standardization activities, and through the normative dimension, when they participate in the

[86] Mavroidis and Wolfe, 'Private standards and the WTO'; Thorstensen et al., 'Private standards', p. 6.

[87] Ibid. (both references).

[88] Mavroidis and Wolfe, 'Private standards and the WTO'; Trachtman, 'Toward open recognition?'

[89] United Nations Forum on Sustainability Standards (UNFSS), 'Voluntary Sustainability Standards' (2013), available at https://unfss.files.wordpress.com/2012/05/unfss-report-initiatives-2_draft_lores.pdf.

[90] *US-Tuna II*, para. 36.

[91] Ibid., para. 356. Delimatsis suggested that the Appellate Body has misread the narrow definition of Art 4.2 ISO Guide, Delimatsis, 'Relevant international standards', p. 20.

body's standards development activities.[92] While there is no obligation to seek WTO Members to join, a membership invitation should be automatically extended once the Member expressed its interest to join the standards body, without obstacles for accession.[93] Alternatively, recognition of a standards body can also be signaled by referencing its standards in laws and governmental documents,[94] or by their approval by an organization that has already gained the acknowledgment of all WTO Members, such as the ISO.[95]

Whether a body's standardization activities are recognized by the WTO Members appears crucial for its categorization as an ISB. However, standardization in general, and ICT standardization in particular, remains inherently a private sector activity, and the global use of ICT standards largely depends on their recognition by the *industry* rather than States. By the same token, while it has been argued that it is essential for a recognized body to have its standards adopted by a large number of governments and national standards bodies,[96] the global uptake of ICT standards carries more weight to their recognition:[97] for instance, it is hard to argue that Bluetooth and USB specifications are not internationally recognized, while they have never been endorsed as governmental standards.

Furthermore, rendering recognition depended on the number of WTO Members joining SDO membership elides the reality of standardization processes, where the large share of the work is carried out by a few Members and is offered to the membership-wide approval only at the later stages. In this regard, the ITU, which can be claimed a "recognized body" due to the wide recognition of its standards and its intergovernmental membership open to all WTO Members, has been recently criticized for China's dominance in developing standards for facial recognition.[98] In another instance, ITU's adoption of China's domestic

[92] *US-Tuna II*, paras. 358 and 390. Note that the Appellate Body in US-Tuna did not establish a "de minimis" test for recognition; rather, the more members participate, the more likely it is for the body to be "recognized."

[93] *US-Tuna II*, para. 398.

[94] Du, *The Regulation*, p. 134. Such reading is also supported by the wording of Art. 2.4 TBT Agreement, that focuses on standards rather than standards bodies.

[95] This recognition is evident, among others, from the explicit reference of the TBT Annexes to ISO and IEC.

[96] Du, *The Regulation*, p. 134.

[97] See Part IV.

[98] J. Wouters, 'Corporations and the making of public standards in international law: the case of China in the ITU', in P. Delimatsis, S. Bijlmakers and M. K. Borowicz (eds.), *The*

standards for 3G networks, TD-SCDMA,[99] did not lead to the global use of these standards, since the European WCDMA and US-driven Code Driven Multiple Access (CDMA) prevailed in the respective regions. The Appellate Body's arguments on recognition in *US-Tuna II* thus fall short on broader considerations when it comes to ICT standards bodies.

Given the abovementioned, the extent to which the six principles of the TBT Committee Decision (2000) can safeguard procedural and substantive guarantees in global ICT SDOs remains questionable.[100] The Decision indeed applies to the ISO and IEC, which the TBT Agreement implicitly recognizes by referring to the ISO/IEC Guide in its Annex 1,[101] and to the intergovernmental ICT standards bodies as ITU and JTC1. Arguably, private standards could be scrutinized with regard to their openness, transparency, and inclusiveness when endorsed by these bodies; the question remains whether such endorsement, which often occurs through "fast track" procedures, will address procedural irregularities at the lower level of standards development. Moreover, such endorsement is completely voluntary, meaning that a great number of prominent ICT standards developed outside these initiatives may not seek it. Accordingly, a further case-by-case analysis of institutional features of SDOs is necessary to determine whether they qualify as "recognized" according to the current Appellate Body's test.

*Evolution of Transnational Rule-makers through Crises* (Cambridge: Cambridge University Press, forthcoming).

[99] D. Ernst, 'Indigenous Innovation and Globalization. The Challenge for China's Standardization Strategy' (2011), available at www.eastwestcenter.org/sites/default/files/private/ernstindigenousinnovation.pdf. According to Sun, this meant that domestic regulation based on this standard could not be challenged by virtue of Article 2.5 of TBT Agreement , Sun, 'Piercing the veil'. The author however would like to point out the possibility of the existence of multiple competing international standards, which then would render this obligation meaningless for trade harmonization purposes.

[100] The rationale is that if a standard is an international standard, the body developing it should adhere to the six principles. At the same time, it is compliance with the six procedural principles of the Decision that enables the SDOs to develop "international standards."

[101] Likewise, the Committee Decision applies to ISBs listed in Annex A of the SPS Agreement, namely Codex Alimentarius Commission, International Office of Epizootics and International Plant Protection Convention. Annex A (3) of SPS Agreement. Following the reasoning of the Appellate Body in *US-Tuna II, the fact* that those bodies were listed by the SPS Committee which consists of whole WTO membership serves as proof as they have "recognized activities" in standardization; *US-Tuna II*, paras. 360–3.

There is, however, another path to subject ICT SDOs that are not "recognized bodies" within the meaning of the TBT Agreement, and hence do not produce "international" standards, to the TBT disciplines of due process, namely through these bodies' acceptance of the Code of Good Practice.[102] Yet, since the obligation to ensure the acceptance of the Code is addressed to the WTO Members rather than the SDOs themselves, and due to its ambiguities and lack of enforcement, the Code appears toothless. A similar rationale of an explicit acceptance by an SDO also applies to the ISO/IEC Guide 59 (2019): while its requirements go beyond those of the TBT instruments, addressing such aspects as FRAND licensing conditions and availability of appeals, its scope is limited to national bodies, which, with a few exceptions,[103] rarely develop *global* ICT standards.

## ICT Standardization beyond the TBT Agreement: Intellectual Property and Innovation

The TBT Agreement is of particular relevance when it comes to procedural guarantees and legitimacy of global ICT SDOs; yet ICT standards may also trigger Members' obligation under other WTO Agreements. Adoption of an ICT standard is often accompanied by the adoption of new mandatory security regulations that may be deemed discriminatory or unnecessary trade restrictive;[104] in addition, ICT standards may trigger national security concerns, which are being increasingly discussed in the international trade arena.

By far the most contentious debate of ICT standardization revolves around IPR protection of SEPs. While SDOs' disclosure and licensing rules are not covered by the TBT Agreement,[105] some aspects of IPR licensing may be addressed by the General Agreement on Trade-Related Aspects of Intellectual Property (TRIPS).[106] Article 44 of TRIPS allows

[102] Partiti argued that the Code covers a very broad range of SDOs. See Partiti, 'What use of an unloaded gun?'.

[103] Such exceptions would include ETSI, which is a semipublic body.

[104] For instance, Sun, 'Piercing the veil,' illustrates that Chinese proliferation of domestic standards was in the same time as security measures challenged by Western countries.

[105] They are, however, addressed in the revised ISO/IEC Guide 59.

[106] General Agreement on Trade-Related Aspects of Intellectual Property (TRIPS) 1869 UNTS 299 33 ILM 1197. Note that TRIPS may also become useful to address IPR issues other than SEPs, such as copyright protection of software or of standards documents themselves, or even trademarks for standards.

SEP holders to protect their innovation by seeking injunctions, while Article 31 enables WTO Members to authorize the use of proprietary technology when a patent-holder is unwilling to provide a license through compulsory licenses, especially if public benefit is at stake: in this case, the licensing rates are established by the State, and not during the negotiation processes among the licensee and licensor, while the possibility of judicial review of compulsory licenses remains present.[107]

However, SEP disputes are different from other patent law disputes because of the entangled issues of antitrust and contact law.[108] From this perspective, the TRIPS, and WTO law in general, has little to offer except for very few provisions on IPR protection and competition, Articles 8.2, 31.k and 40.[109] In this regard, it has been argued that Article 40.2 allows WTO Members to control SEP licensing practices through competition law in case these practices are not FRAND, but that refusal to license can only be addressed by a broad reading of Article 40 that includes contractual clauses as well as all circumstances surrounding licensing.[110] The same authors claimed that Article 8(2) of TRIPS would cover refusal to license and enforcing injunctions.

Arguably, while SEP enforcement remains the matter of national or regional competition provisions, TRIPS obligations may have a role to play when they are read flexibly. At the same time, while regional competition rules support cooperative innovation and incentivize IPR protection, they leave little space for TRIPS' narrow competition law provisions, which moreover may not be apt for the situations where IPRs constitute a part of public goods.[111] In this regard, IPR issues of ICT

107 S. Ragavan, B. Murphy and R. Dave, 'FRAND v. compulsory licensing: the lesser of the two evils' (2016) 14 *Duke Law & Technology Review* 83–120 at 84, borrowing the definition of compulsory licensing from pharmaceutical studies of P. Gorecki ("involuntary contract imposed and enforced by States").

108 This was suggested by Tsang and Lee, 'Unfriendly choice'.

109 See also M. Bakhoum and B. Conde Gallego, 'TRIPS and competition rules: from transfer of technology to innovation policy', in H. Ullrich, R. M. Hilty, M. Lamping and J. Drex (eds.), *TRIPS plus 20, MPI Studies on Intellectual Property and Competition Law* (New York: Springer, 2016), pp. 529–59.

110 Ibid., pp. 532–3 for supporting arguments. Some scholars have argued that TRIPS does not offer guidance to Members on how IPR policy should be used to permit discrimination, like in the GATT, R. Okediji, 'Legal innovation in international intellectual property relations: revisiting twenty-one years of the TRIPS agreement' (2014) 36 *University of Pennsylvania Journal of International Law* 191, 214.

111 H. Ullrich, 'Expansionist intellectual property protection and reductionist competition rules: a TRIPS perspective' (2004) 7 *Journal of International Economic Law* 401–320 at 403.

standardization are more likely to be covered in bilateral treaties,[112] while licensing rates remain determined in negotiations between licensees and licensors, or by the national courts in licensing disputes. The peril is that the latter may lead to different interpretations of FRAND and as a consequence, fragmented IPR enforcement: for instance, where China mostly applies Chinese law when dealing with implementor's third-party right to receive FRAND-license under ETSI IPR policy, the rest of the world uses French law.[113]

In a similar way, the minimum guarantees offered by the TRIPS agreement leave the door slightly ajar when it comes to FRAND interpretations. Currently, two meanings of FRAND are present in the scholarly debate: "license to all" implies that SEP needs to be licensed to all entities in the production chain, thus also on the component level; "access to all" implies that SEP owners commit to make their technology *available* through licensing. The latter naturally generates larger royalties and is preferable among SEP owners[114] while it also raises obvious access and availability concerns among implementers. The level of licensing is not mandated by law,[115] but rather subject to courts' interpretation[116] and above all, to the SDOs IPR policies, some of which have indeed adopted FRAND interpretation that favors component-level SEP licensing.[117] TRIPS' tools are thus fairly limited to address the issue of SEP licensing.

[112] See X. Wu, 'Interplay between patents and standards in the information and communication technology (ICT) sector and its relevance to the implementation of the WTO Agreements' (2017) WTO Working Paper ERSD – 2017-08; B. An, 'Intellectual property rights in information and communications technology standardization: highly profiled disputes and collaboration potentials between the United States and China' (2009) 45 *Texas International Law Journal* 175–99. See also US-China Joint Fact Sheets on the 25th, 26th and 27th U.S.-China Joint Commissions on Commerce and Trade, available at https://ustr.gov/.

[113] See Tsang and Lee, 'Unfriendly choice', providing an overview of the most salient issues and decisions.

[114] Scholars also claim that the "license to all" approach is not supported in the patent law doctrine, Layne-Farrar and Stark, 'License to all'; Borghetti et al., 'FRAND licensing levels'.

[115] See, for instance, European Commission, Communication from the Commission to the European Parliament, the Council and the European Economic and Social Committee, 'Setting out the EU approach to Standard Essential Patents' (November 29, 2017) COM (2017) 712 final.

[116] While in the EU, "Access to All" seems the prevailing approach, the US courts sometimes also followed the "license to all" interpretation.

[117] For example, IEEE.

Last but not least, trade barriers brought by ICT standards may be a result of protectionist or discriminatory standardization and innovation policies. This argument is being increasingly made by Western powers with regard to China. For instance, China's IPR systems traditionally allowed inventors some reward rather than monetization of their inventions, which was considered by the West as a lack of IPR protection. This issue appears to have been resolved with China's accession to international IPR treaties and its WTO accession protocols.[118] With China becoming an active player in ICT standardization upon the WTO accession,[119] its standardization and innovation policies continued to raise concerns, especially when its domestic standards had a clear preference for indigenous intellectual property,[120] as it was the case of WAPI, as well as different SEP licensing rules of Chinese SDOs.[121] Contrary, strict Western licensing practices may create innovation barriers for standardization latecomers as China,[122] who (used to) largely rely on foreign technology and whose companies, until recently, have been predominantly active as manufacturers.

[118] P. Pusceddu, 'Hic sunt dracones? Mapping the legal framework of China's innovation policy: standardization and IPRs' (2020) 51 *International Review of Intellectual Property and Competition Law* 559–93 at 570, referencing Yu (2004).

[119] D. Breznitz and M. Murphree, 'The rise of China in technology standards: new norms in old institutions (2013) Report, available at www.uscc.gov/sites/default/files/Research/RiseofChinainTechnologyStandards.pdf, discussing China's rapid industrial development and success in innovation technology.

[120] This was mentioned with regard to Chinese security regulation. According to the US Representative, "the Guidelines required 'tests and certification' to be conducted by state regulators and laid out product requirements that were based on design and descriptive characteristics (e.g., equipment that had intellectual property rights (IPR) owned and/or developed by Chinese-invested enterprises or 'indigenous IPR') rather than performance requirements." Sun, 'Piercing the veil', quoting Minutes of the Meeting of March 18–19, 2015, 2.16. Committee on Technical Barriers to Trade, Note by the Secretariat: Minutes of the Meeting of March 18–19, 2015, 2.65, WTO Doc. G/TBT/M/65 (May 28, 2015).

[121] See the discussion in Pusceddu, 'Hic sunt dracones', pp. 581–4. For the analysis of China's judicial policy on SEP see J. Lee, 'Implementing the FRAND standard in China' (2016) 19 *Venderbilt Journal of Entertainment & Technology Law* 37–85.

[122] Pusceddu suggests that China did not benefit from international standardization efforts because of its reliance on foreign technology and focus on the "final stage" of production where components are made abroad; and because of royalty rates that did not go down remained problems for manufacturers, decreasing profit margins, and domestic standards also had effect on negotiating power loyalties with foreign IPRs, Pusceddu, 'Hic sunt dracones', p. 577.

# 4

## The EU Regulatory Framework

### Evolution of the EU Standardization System

Involving private parties in administrative rule-making is fairly common in the EU.[1] The EU standardization system is a good example of "co-regulation" between the European and national public institutions and private technical bodies.[2] Standards play an essential role in EU policy since they ensure technical harmonization across the Member States and support the functioning of the Internal Market. Therefore, the European regulatory framework governing private standardization has an effect on national standardization policies of Member States.

To understand the current ecosystem of the EU standardization, it should be considered how the EU regulatory framework has evolved over time.[3] From the outset, European standards were specified in the patchwork of Directives, with the Low Voltage Directive of 1973 as one of the most prominent examples.[4] Yet, their complexity and detailed approach was ineffective at providing rapid technical harmonization:[5] before the introduction of the Information Directive in 1983, the European

[1] See M. Eliantonio and M. Medzmariashvili, 'Hybridity under scrutiny: how European standardization shakes the foundations of EU constitutional and internal market law' (2017) 44 *Legal Issues of Economic Integration* 323–35.

[2] Ibid., 324; see also M. Kallestrup, 'Stakeholder participation in European standardization: a mapping and an assessment of three categories of regulation' (2017) 44 *Legal Issues of Economic Integration* 381–94.

[3] For a comprehensive overview, see H. Schepel, 'New approach to New Approach: the juridification of harmonized standards in EU Law' (2013) 12 *Maastricht Journal of European and Comparative Law* 521–33; van Gestel and Micklitz, 'European integration'; J. Pelkmans, 'The new approach to technical harmonization and standardization' (1987) XXV *Journal of Common Market Studies* (3) 249–69.

[4] Council Directive of February 19, 1973 on the harmonization of the laws of Member States relating to electrical equipment designed for use within certain voltage limits, OJ 1973 No. L77/30.

[5] Schepel, *The Constitution of Private Governance*, p. 63.

Community was adopting around ten Directives a year.[6] In addition, standardization processes of those times were criticized for the lack of accountability and legitimacy, and achievement of consensus on technical content of a standard among Member States was politically challenging.[7] Meanwhile, the European markets remained balkanized by national standards and regulations, which posed major obstacles for intercommunity trade and precluded the completion of the Internal Market.[8]

The response to these inadequacies followed in 1985 with the introduction of the "New Approach," which aimed to accelerate technical harmonization at the Council level while offering sufficient flexibility for the industry.[9] The "New Approach" Directives merely cover general ("essential") requirements, such as health, safety, and consumers or environment protection, while development of harmonized technical standards that *can* be used to comply with these requirements is left to the three private European Standardization Organizations (ESOs): CEN, CENELEC, and ETSI.[10] Companies can participate in the ESOs through National Standards Organizations (NSOs),[11] which the respective Member States are obliged to notify to the Commission, which in turn publishes the list of NSOs in the OJ of the EU.[12]

However, the New Approach legislation of 1985 became outdated in due time as a consequence of the growing role of consortia standards and standards for services, as well as the advancement of the Internal Market.[13] The major update to the EU standardization system was introduced with the Regulation 1025/2012, which formulated a number

[6] Pelkmans, 'The new approach', p. 251.

[7] Schepel, *The Constitution of Private Governance*, p. 63. See also Cafaggi and Janczuk, 'Private regulation'; Pelkmans, 'The new approach'.

[8] Schepel, 'New approach to New Approach', p. 522.

[9] Council Resolution of May 7, 1985 on a New Approach to Technical Harmonisation and Standards, OJ 1985 No. C136/1.

[10] Annex I of EU Regulation 1025/2012. For the list of New Approach Directives and Regulations see www.newapproach.org/Directives/DirectiveList.asp. Note that in principle, other means to demonstrate compliance with EU law than harmonized standards also exist. See van Leeuwen, *European Standardization of Services*, p. 17.

[11] Rec. 2 and 15 of EU Regulation 1025/2012. However, companies can directly participate in ETSI.

[12] Ibid., Article 27. Note that this requirement does not require an adoption of a national legal act by a Member State that explicitly recognizes a body as an NSO, and that the Member States enjoy a wide discretion to determine their notified bodies.

[13] Services initially fell outside the scope of Directive 98/34/EC, and ICT standards were only covered by Council Decision 87/95/EEC of December 22, 1986 on standardization in the field of information technology and telecommunications. For further critique, see

of long-term objectives to ensure the effectiveness and efficiency of standards as EU policy and regulatory tools, with a view to promoting international trade and cooperation.[14] In particular, the Regulation set out an elaborative system for standardization agenda-setting,[15] addressed the importance of ICT standards for providing interoperability in single market and facilitating users' freedom of choice, and offered a procedural framework for the development of interoperability standards and their identification for referencing by the EC, which is discussed later.

While the decentralized standardization system of the New Approach was generally praised by policy-makers and the ESOs for enabling participation of a wide range of stakeholders and ensuring that the views of the industry as well as the EU institutions are represented in decision-making, the New Approach policy and its implementation have also been subjected to some critique from the scholarship, not least for its lack of throughput legitimacy.[16] To this day, the European standardization system is presented with a challenge of balancing the efficiency of private rule-making with legitimacy concerns.[17] Arguably, trust in European standardization process can be reinforced by effective participation of affected stakeholders, as well as the ex post judicial review of standards development processes.[18]

## Procedural Mechanisms of Regulation 1025/2012

### *General Procedural Requirements*

Regulation 1025/2012 (hereinafter: the Regulation) establishes procedural rules that govern EU standardization. The Regulation emphasizes that standards are private voluntary instruments.[19] Its definition of a

L. Goerke and M. Holler 'Strategic standardization in Europe: a public choice perspective' (1998) 6 *European Journal of Law and Economics* 95–112.

14 Rec. 6 of EU Regulation 1025/2012.

15 See ibid., Articles 8 and 10.

16 Senden, 'Towards a more holistic legitimacy approach', p. 36. Among others, a recent study suggested that the intentions and obligations to ensure stakeholder participation may not have materialized in a sufficient manner. Kallestrup, 'Stakeholder participation'.

17 See J. Hettne, 'Standards, barriers to trade and EU internal market rules: need for a renewed approach?' (2017) 44 *Legal Issues of Economic Integration* 409–20.

18 Eliantonio and Medzmariashvili, 'Hybridity under scrutiny'; L. Senden, 'The constitutional fit of European standardization put to the test' (2017) 44 *Legal Issues of Economic Integration* 337–52. But see P. Coccuru and M. Eliantonio, 'It is not all about judicial review: internal appeal proceedings in the European standardization process', in J. B. Auby (ed.), *The Future of Administrative Law* (Paris: LexisNexis SA, 2019), pp. 475–88.

19 Regulation 1025/2012 does not discuss the legal value of HESs standards, just noting that they are voluntary and thus not equal to legal requirements.

standard generally comprises the elements of ISO/IEC Guide 2 (2004), with the exception of consensus;[20] though, the Regulation repeatedly acknowledges consensus-building as the essence of European standardization.[21] The Regulation states that European standardization is based on the WTO standardization principles, which it refers to as "the founding principles," and which include consensus, but also coherence, openness and independence from special interests.[22] Furthermore, it highlights the importance of transparency and stakeholder participation, especially for consumers, environment and societal organizations, small and medium-sized enterprises (SMEs), and public authorities.[23] Procedural principles encapsulated in the Regulation should be respected by ESOs as well as NSOs in drafting their rules and procedures.[24]

## *ICT Standards*

The Regulation allows the Commission to identify, either following a proposal from a Member State or on its own initiative, ICT technical specifications developed by private SDOs[25] to be referenced for EU public procurement purposes, where such specifications do not conflict with European standards and have been accepted by the market, meaning that there are "operational examples of compliant implementations from different vendors."[26] The Commission takes the decision after consulting the European multi-stakeholder platform, whose evaluation and advice may also be submitted to sectoral experts.[27] The identified

20 Article 2(1) of EU Regulation 1025/2012.

21 An example is ibid., Article 10(1): "European standards and European standardisation deliverables shall be market-driven, take into account the public interest as well as the policy objectives clearly stated in the Commission's request and based on *consensus*" (emphasis added).

22 Ibid., Rec. 2.

23 See, generally, ibid., Articles 3–7, 15, and 16.

24 NSOs are members of CEN and follow CEN Guides, which in turn reflect the procedural principles of the Regulation and the WTO.

25 The Regulation defines those private SDOs as not-for-profit organizations of professionals that are not national, European, or International organizations; Annex II.3 EU Regulation 1025/2012.

26 Article 13 of EU Regulation 1025/2012. The "existing EU framework" on common technical specifications in public procurement refers to Directives 2004/17/EC, 2004/18/EC, and 2009/81/EC, and Regulation (EC, Euratom) No. 2342/2002; see Annex II of EU Regulation 1025/2012.

27 This process is also described, for instance, in the Commission Implementing Decision 2017/1358 on the identification of ICT Technical Specifications for Referencing in public procurement, OJ 2017 No. L190/16.

ICT specifications constitute "common technical specifications" referred to by the EU legislation;[28] the Decisions on the Commission to identify (a) certain ICT specification(s) are published in the OJ of the EU and can thus be challenged ex post following the procedure of Article 263 Treaty of Functioning of the EU (TFEU).

Regulation 1025/2012 further stipulates that to have their standards identified by the Commission, SDOs developing ICT standards and specifications should comply with procedural requirements of Annex II.[29] These requirements, in turn, include the familiar principles of openness, transparency, and consensus, but also refer to the qualitative characteristics of ICT standards, FRAND licensing terms for essential IPRs, and public availability of technical specifications on reasonable terms, that is, either for a reasonable fee or free of charge (note that the Regulation does not explain the meaning of "reasonable").[30] When the conditions of Annex II are not (longer) met, the Commission may decide, upon consulting with European multi-stakeholder platform on ICT standardization and sectoral experts, to modify or withdraw the identification.[31] At the time of writing, the Commission has issued eight Decisions where it identified ICT technical specifications for EU public procurement, developed by, among others, IETF, Organization for the Advancement of Structured Information Standards (OASIS), European Computer Manufacturers Association (ECMA), and World Wide Web Consortium (W3C).[32] Hence, the EU public law framework on standardization provides mechanisms to regulate standards development processes in ICT consortia, albeit only for procurement purposes.

## Standards Interpretation and Normative Power in the EU

### *Harmonized European Standards*

Amid many documents developed by the ESOs,[33] HESs are by far the most influential instrument in EU technical harmonization. The

[28] See above n. 26.
[29] EU Regulation 1025/2012, Article 13.
[30] See ibid., Annex II.
[31] Ibid., Articles 13(3) and 14. The European multi-stakeholder platform is comprised of ESOs, Member States, and relevant stakeholders.
[32] The list of the decisions is available at https://single-market-economy.ec.europa.eu/single-market/european-standards/ict-standardisation/ict-technical-specifications_en
[33] Such as guidelines and technical specifications.

development of HESs typically follows a specific process within the ESOs, requiring review and approval by NSOs,[34] and can be mandated by the Commission[35] or initiated by the ESOs' Members. References to adopted HESs are published in the OJ of the EU,[36] and the act of publication of the references can be subjected to legal review through the formal objection procedure initiated by Member States and the European Parliament and under which the Commission may decide, upon consultations with experts,[37] whether to publish or maintain a harmonized standard.[38]

In line with the principle of mutual recognition of *Casis the Dijon*,[39] the Member States are obliged to transpose HESs into their national standardization systems and to withdraw any conflicting national standards (a so-called "standstill" obligation).[40] Compliance with HESs remains voluntary, but grants presumption of conformity with the essential requirements of the New Approach Directives for the purpose of free circulation in all Member States. This implies that, while manufacturers

[34] As example, see the description of ETSI processes in Chapters 7 and 8.

[35] Article 10 of EU Regulation 1025/2012. At the same time, the Commission denies any responsibility or accountability that an endorsed standard meets the "technical requirements"; see Schepel, 'New approach to New Approach', 524. Recently, Coccuru noted a mismatch between the formal qualification of mandates and the substantial role they play in market regulation that goes beyond implementation. P. Coccuru, 'Regulating by request: on the role and status of the "standardization mandate" under the New Approach', in M. Eliantonio and C. Cauffman (eds.), *The Legitimacy of Standardization as a Regulatory Technique in the EU: A Cross-disciplinary and Multi-level Analysis* (Cheltenham and Northampton: Edward Elgar Publishing, 2020), pp. 48–63, at p. 57.

[36] Article 10(6) of EU Regulation 1025/2012. Note that under the "old" approach, publication was merely informative.

[37] Commission follows either the advisory or examination procedure, Article 11(2)(3) of EU Regulation 1025/2012; in this regard, see also Regulation No. 182/2011 of February 16, 2011, laying down the rules and general principles concerning mechanisms for control by Member States of the Commission's exercise of implementing power, OJ 2011 No. L55/14.

[38] Articles 1 and 11 of EU Regulation 1025/2012. This ex post action is, however, not often invoked by the Member States, see the list of formal objections at https://ec.europa.eu/growth/single-market/european-standards/harmonised-standards/formal-objections_en. Schepel argued that the act of publication of the references to harmonized standards is an act susceptible to legality review in direct actions; Schepel, 'New approach to New Approach', 529. The decision to publish a reference to a standard in the OJ of the EU is challengeable under Article 263 of the TFEU.

[39] Case C-120/78, *Rewe-Zentral AG* v. *Bundesmonopolverwaltung für Branntwein* [1979] ECR 649.

[40] Rec. 14 of EU Regulation 1025/2012. The obligation is further implemented in the operational framework of each of the ESOs.

may choose any other means to demonstrate conformity of their products with the essential requirements of the Directives, in practice, adherence to HESs appears a preferred option among economic operators.[41]

It is the legal puzzle of whether and how the free movements provisions apply to private standardization (and certification) activity, which the European Court of Justice (CJEU) has been challenged to resolve. In *Commission* v. *Belgium*, the Court found that a voluntary mark developed by l'Institut Belge de Normalisation (IBN), which granted presumption of conformity with legislative requirements, restricted free movement of goods within the meaning of Article 34 of the TFEU[42] The fact that IBN was found a "public body" acting in public interest and under the supervision of the Ministry of Economic Affairs rendered its actions attributable to the Belgian State, which in turn "encouraged" compliance with national marks for products that were lawfully marketed in other Member States.[43] Later on, the CJEU ruled in *Latchways* that a publication of a reference to a mandated standard, which did not concern the particular equipment and did not provide it the presumption of conformity with the EU Directive, did not accord the provisions related to that equipment the status of a HES;[44] hence, the Court concluded, these provisions did not constitute a part of EU law.[45]

In *Fra.bo*, the Court had to render the decision whether *private* (emphasis added) standardization and certification bodies monitoring compliance with technical standards can be scrutinized under the free movement provisions of EU law.[46] Deutsche Vereinigung des Gas- und Wasserfaches (DVGW) was a private, nonprofit body that developed technical standards for the water industry and certified compliance with those standards. Certification by the DVGW resulted in a presumption of conformity with the legal requirements of *AVBWasserV* (Regulation on General Conditions for Water Supply), establishing voluntary sale conditions for water supply undertakings. Fra.bo, an Italian producer of copper fitting, was denied the DVGW certification when it failed to

[41] Van Leeuwen, *European Standardization of Services*, p. 42. See also Schepel, 'New approach to New Approach', 528.

[42] Case C-227/06, *Commission* v. *Belgium* [2008] ECR I-00046.

[43] Ibid., paras. 37–9. See also Schepel, 'New approach to New Approach', 525–6.

[44] Case C-185/08, *Latchways* [2010] ECR I-99830, paras. 31–4.

[45] Ibid., para. 35.

[46] Case C-171/11, *Fra.bo SpA* v. *Deutsche Vereinigung des Gas- und Wasserfaches* [2012] 3 CMLR 38.

prove compliance with the amended DVGW standard; moreover, DVGW refused to recognize a certificate of an Italian accredited laboratory. Since in practice, almost all German consumers purchased copper fitting that were certified by the DVGW in accordance with the *AVBWasserV*, compliance with DVGW standards was the only option for the copper fitting manufacturers to market their products in Germany.[47] Accordingly, Fra.bo argued that DVGW's refusal to certify its copper fittings impeded its access to the German market. In its reasoning, the Court largely followed the opinion of the Advocate General (AG) and found that, despite being a private body, DVGW could de facto regulate market access "in the light of inter alia the legislative and regulatory context in which it operates,"[48] opening the avenues for horizontal direct effect of Article 34 of TFEU.

The CJEU's landmark decision in *James Elliott* concerned the national version of a HES for construction materials that was incorporated in a sales contract between private parties. Although acknowledging the voluntary nature of HESs, the private status of the ESOs, as well as producers' choice to demonstrate compliance with the EU Directives by other means than adhering to the HESs, the Court nevertheless ruled that, given the publication of a reference in the OJ of the EU, HESs were measures implementing or applying an act of EU law, and hence should be viewed as its part[49] and as having legal effect, which also allowed private parties to challenge HESs in a preliminary reference procedure.[50] Shortly after, the CJEU stated in *Schmitt* that although the liability of Technischer Überwachungsverein (TÜV), a German notified certification body that assesses conformity with EU requirements, towards private parties is governed by national private law, it nevertheless owns a

[47] Ibid., para. 30. See also Schepel, 'New approach to New Approach'.

[48] Ibid., para. 26. In other words, state measures that infringe free movement of goods by encouraging compliance with private standards will not become lawful by virtue of the fact that those standards are private, See also Schepel, 'New approach to New Approach', 527.

[49] See Case C-613/14, *James Elliott Construction Ltd* v. *Irish Asphalt Ltd*, paras. 32–40.

[50] Ibid., para. 47. See also A. Volpato, 'Harmonised standards before the ECJ: *James Elliott Construction*' (2017) 54 *Common Market Law Review* 591–603; K. Purnhagen, 'Voluntary "new approach" technical standards are subject to judicial scrutiny by the CJEU: the remarkable CJEU judgment "Elliott" on private standards' (2017) 2017/05 Wageningen Working Papers in Law and Governance.

duty of care, albeit a very narrow one, to end-users of the products that obtained its certification.[51]

The discussed case law reflects CJEU's consistent trend towards the constitutionalization of private industry regulation.[52] While *Fra.bo* limited the Member States' options to escape the purview of EU legislation by "subcontracting" regulatory activities to private bodies,[53] *James Elliott* attempted to clarify HESs' legal status and allowed their interpretation by the CJEU, possibly paving the way for third parties affected by these standards to obtain judicial protection; and *Schmitt* obliged notified bodies to act with all due diligence when performing conformity assessment.[54] According to some scholars, the more standards enter the realm of law, the more the Commission delegates regulatory competence to the ESOs, and should comply with the delegation principles of *Meroni*.[55] Others, in turn, suggested the lawfulness of such delegation is ensured by the existence of adequate control mechanisms.[56]

Scholars have also noted that when submitting voluntary standards to fundamental principles of EU law, the Court opened a Pandora's box of issues concerning the copyright protection of HESs:[57] if a publication of

[51] Case C-219/15, *Elisabeth Schmitt* v. *TÜV Rheinland LGA Products GmbH* [2017].

[52] See P. Verbruggen and B. van Leeuwen, 'The liability of notified bodies under the EU's New Approach' (2018) 43 *European Law Review*, 3, 394–498.

[53] Van Gestel and Micklitz ('European integration') found this reasoning convincing.

[54] Verbruggen and Van Leeuwen, 'The liability of notified bodies.'

[55] Schepel, *The Constitution of Private Governance*, pp. 225–7. In essence, *Meroni* prohibited delegation of power that is too broadly and insufficiently defined, stating that the Commission can entrust certain tasks to private law bodies provided that it only delegates those powers that it enjoys itself and that are "strictly executive" and not "discretionary"; the exercise of delegated powers is accompanied by the same guarantees as if they had been exercised directly by the Commission, such as juridical review and transparency; the delegated powers remain subject to conditions determined by the Commission and subject to its supervision, and the institutional balance between the institutions of the European Community is not distorted. See Cases 9/56 and 10/56, *Meroni & Co, Industrie Metallurgiche* v. *High Authority* [1957–1958] ECR 133.

[56] See, for instance, Senden, 'The constitutional fit'; M. Medzmariashvili, 'Delegation of rulemaking power to European standards organizations: reconsidered' (2017) 44 *Legal Issues of Economic Integration* 353–66, suggesting that European standardization can be assessed for compliance with the ESMA case law; Case C-270/12, *United Kingdom of Great Britain and Northern Ireland* v. *European Parliament and Council (ESMA)* [2014].

[57] See B. Lundqvist, 'European harmonized standards as "part of EU law": the implications of the *James Elliott* case for copyright protection and, possibly, for EU Competition Law' (2017) 44 *Legal Issues of Economic Integration* 421–36, who also argued that the *James Elliott* decision raises questions for competition law claims, and more specifically, whether ESOs are not to be considered as (association of) undertakings if standards are "law." I disagree with this claim since the Court did not change the status of ESOs.

the reference to a HES is a part of EU law, should standards then be publicly accessible? In this context, it should be noted that standards development, administration, and other related activities of the ESOs are co-financed by the EU,[58] and questions on their availability and copyrights should be discussed bearing in mind the funding mechanisms for HESs. From the three ESOs, only ETSI puts its standards in public domain.[59] While the matter on standards accessibility has been addressed by some national courts, the copyright of HESs has been recently affirmed by the General Court in *PRO and Right to Know* v. *Commission*, which considered that disclosure of HESs could undermine commercial interests of ESOs and NSOs.[60]

### *National Standards*

While Member States' national standardization frameworks and NSOs are not examined in this study,[61] some national case law is relevant for the discussion on the legal value and interpretation of private voluntary standards. The German Federal Court of Justice (Bundesgerichtshof) stated that standards developed by the Deutsches Institut für Normung (DIN), and which are referenced in a national legislative act, are excluded from copyright protection granted by the applicable German law. Such standards, the Court found, produced a certain external effect,

[58] Articles 15 and 16 of EU Regulation 1025/2012.

[59] Perhaps the reason for that is that ETSI members, being mostly large commercial firms, are prepared to pay higher membership dues to compensate for the "loss of income" from standards' selling; note that such financial models would not work for CEN and CENELEC, where only NSOs can become members and where the nature of standardization activities, and thus the companies involved via NSOs, is different.

[60] Case T-185/19, *Public.Resource.Org and Right to Know* v. *Commission*, paras. 61–73, on appeal at the moment of writing. Related, some recent copyright decisions of the CJEU increasingly harmonized the notion of a work, including potential exclusions from copyright-ability on the public interest grounds; see JRC Report, p. 51, referring to Case C-310/17, *Levola Hengelo BV.* v. *Smidle Food BV* [2018]. Accessibility of private standards and their copyrights was also addressed by CEN and CENELEC shortly after the *James Elliott* judgment was issued. CEN/CENELEC position on the consequences of the judgment of the European Court of Justice on *James Elliott Construction Limited* v. *Asphalt Limited* (2017), available at www.cencenelec.eu/news/policy_opinions/PolicyOpinions/PositionPaper_Consequences_Judgment_Elliott%20case.pdf.

[61] For further reading on this topic, see H. Schepel and J. Falke, 'Legal aspects of standardization in Member States of the EC and EFTA, volume 1' (February 25, 2000) European Commission Publications, available at https://publications.europa.eu/en/publication-detail/-/publication/9acd4259-13c6-436f-8c12-2740ccf7bb71.

and thus are "pulled" into the public domain.[62] In the Court's consideration, later approved by the Federal Constitutional Court (Bundesverfassungsgericht), public interest of free access to these standards prevailed over their copyright protection.[63]

In a similar vein, the Dutch District Court (Gerechtshof), followed by the Supreme Court of the Netherlands (Hoge Raad) had to decide on the legal status of the Nederlandse Normalisatie Instituut (NEN), a private SDO, and the accessibility of the technical standards it produced.[64] In this case, however, the Courts found that the Building Decree that referred to the particular NEN standard was not published following the procedure specified in applicable Dutch law, and hence the standard was not legally binding, meaning that NEN is entitled to charge fees for and collect copyrights from the sale of the standard.[65] The question remains whether similar considerations will be guiding the Court of Justice in its forthcoming appeal decision in the *PRO and Right to Know* v. *Commission.*

## Standardization in EU Competition Law

In the EU, antitrust concerns associated with standardization have been discussed in legal and policy documents as well as in the decisions of the EC and the CJEU. From the perspective of good governance, the procedural rules that SDOs have to abide by in order to avoid that their standards result in a collusive behaviour, constitute an interesting lens for assessing standards' public law legitimacy. At the same time, EC's and the Court's considerations on when licensing practices are abusive provide a good illustration on the European approach to SEP licensing, as well as the general context in which further analysis of SDOs' IPR policies should be situated.

### *SDOs as Vehicles for Collusion in the EU*

In the EU, collusion is prohibited by Article 101(1) of the TFEU, which forbids decisions taken by associations and agreements between undertakings that may affect intercommunity trade and have as their object or

[62] Bundesgerichtshof [BGH] (June 30, 1983), GRUR 1984.
[63] Bundesverfassungsgericht [BVerfGE] (July 29, 1998), ZUM 1998.
[64] Hoge Raad (June 22, 2012), LJN: BW0393.
[65] See the analysis in van Gestel and Micklitz, 'European integration'.

effect the distortion of competition within the Internal Market. SDOs are considered associations of undertakings since their membership consists of various companies engaged in economic activity:[66] accordingly, Article 101 of TFEU applies to decisions of SDOs, including its standards or policies,[67] even when an SDO has a status of a national body.[68] Standardization decisions are granted presumption of pro-competitiveness, and, as such, are rarely found to breach the applicable competition rules, unless a collusive practice has indeed taken place; in this sense, SDOs are typically exempted from antitrust liability provided that their processes comply with a set of principles, which is discussed further in this section.

### Decisions on Cartels

Not every investigation on cartels in standardization agreements by the Commission have led to the findings of the breach of Article 101 of TFEU; yet, they provide a good overview of which practices in SDOs would be considered anticompetitive. In one of its first investigations, *Videocassette recorders*, the Commission found a cross-licensing agreement between Sony, Philips, and other VCR producers, which prohibited parties to implement other systems or standards, to preclude introduction of better

[66] The CJEU defined undertaking as "every entity engaged in an economic activity, regardless of the legal status of the entity or the way in which it is financed"; in Case C-41/90, *Klaus Höfner and Fritz Elser* v. *Macrotron GmbH* [1991] ECR I-01979. See also opinion of AG Jacobs in Case C-67/96, *Albany International BV and Stichting Bedrijfspensioenfonds Textielindustrie* [1999] ECR I-0575. See further Case C-1/12, *Ordem dos Técnicos Oficiais de Contas* v. *Autoridade da Concorrência* [2013], finding that an "association of undertakings" within the meaning of 101 TFEU can be a trade association or even a professional body; Case C-309/99, *J.CJ. Wouters, J.W. Savelbergh, Price Waterhouse Belastingadviseurs BV and Algemene Raad van de Nederlandse Orde van Advocaten* [2002] ECR I-01577. In certain cases, an association can be held accountable instead of its individual members, Joined Cases T-217/03 and T-245/03 *Fédération nationale de la coopération bétail and viande (FNCBV) e.a.* v. *Commission* [2006] ECR II-04987.

[67] A constitution of a trade association, as well as the regulations governing its operation, can be regarded as its decision; see Case T-66/89, *Publishers Association* v. *Commission* [1992] ECR II-01995.

[68] See case *Wouters* and Summary of Commission Decision in *MasterCard*, Case COMP/ 34.579 (November 6, 2009) OJ 2009 No. C264/8. Note that legal exception of 101(3) TFEU would still apply, if the agreement contributes to improving conditions for production or distribution or promotes technical or economic progress to the benefit of consumers, meaning that consumers should have a "fair share" of the resulting benefit, and does not impose on the firms concerned indispensable restrictions for attaining the abovementioned objectives, or provide these firms with the possibility of eliminating competition in respect of a substantial part of the products at issue.

systems and, hence, negatively affect competition.[69] *IGR Stereo Television/ Salora* also revolved around licensing practices: IGR licensed its technology to German color TV manufacturers with whom it formed a patent pool,[70] and provided limited licenses to other companies only later.[71] The complaint was brought to the Commission by a company who was refused a license by IGR and hence was prevented from accessing the market. The case was dropped after IGR agreed to grant licenses as to any quantity, presumably due to the high possibility that the Commission will find licensing practices among the patent pool members collusive and excluding competitors from the market.[72]

In *Pre-Insulated Pipes Cartel*, the Commission found a standard for pre-insulated pipes to reduce product diversification and delay introduction of a new technology, which in turn enabled a price cartel and hence violated 101(1) TFEU (ex 81(1) EC Treaty).[73] The Commission also investigated the Conseil Européen de la Construction d'Appareils Domestiques (CECED), a Belgian association of manufacturers of domestic appliances operating in various Member States,[74] and found that CECED's standard for energy efficiency, with which all manufacturers and importers had to comply, fell outside the scope of 101(1) (ex. 81 (1)): despite narrowing down consumer choice and restricting competition between the parties, the agreement was found to contribute to economic and technical progress by reducing electricity consumption and hence, providing collective benefits for users and consumers by reducing the pollution. The agreement was thus exempted by virtue of fulfilment of the cumulative conditions of 101(3) (ex 81(3)).[75]

A number of landmark decisions in the domain of collusion and standards agreements was issued by the European Courts. In *SELEX*, the General Court held that Eurocontrol, an international

[69] See Commission Decision *Videocassette Recorders*, OJ 1977 No. L47/42.

[70] In patent pools, licensors typically agree to license their IPRs in a bundle. An example is AVANCI, a patent pool for the IoT, see http://avanci.com/.

[71] See B. Lundqvist, *Standardization under EU Competition Rules and US Antitrust Laws: The Rise and Limits of Self-Regulation* (Cheltenham: Edward Elgar, 2014), p. 206.

[72] Ibid., p. 212.

[73] Decision of the Commission, *Pre-Insulated Pipes Cartel* (1999) COMP IV/35.691/E.4 (October 21, 1998) OJ 1998 No. L24/1, 30.1.

[74] Manufacturers could become CECED members either by acquiring direct membership or through their membership in national trade associations.

[75] Decision of the Commission (1999) Case IV.F.1/36.718. CECED (January 24, 1999) OJ 1999 No. L187/47.

standard-setting body in the field of air traffic management,[76] did not have a market of its "standardization services," could not be considered a service provider and, accordingly, has not been engaged in an economic activity.[77] Hence, since standard-setting fell within the public task of Eurocontrol, competition law provisions did not apply.[78] In its decision, the Court distinguished between Eurocontrol's tasks in preparation and adoption of standards, and the adoption of standards by the Council of Eurocontrol,[79] which subsequently became binding for all States of the organization; it considered the latter to be a "clearly legislative activity (. . .) which directly concerns the exercise by those States of their powers of public authority"[80] and that the role of Eurocontrol is "akin to that of a minister who, at national level, prepares legislative or regulatory measures which are then adopted by the government."[81] On appeal, the CJEU found that production of standards could not be separated from their adoption and, hence, from the public task of the Eurocontrol, supporting its line of reasoning with the Convention of the Safety of Air Navigation:[82] yet, the CJEU upheld the decision of the General Court that Eurocontrol's technical standardization activities were not an economic activity and fell outside the scope of competition law.[83]

[76] Case T-155/04, *SELEX Sistemi Integrati SpA* v. *Commission of the European Communities* [2006] ECR II-04797. The European Organization for the Safety of Air Navigation (Eurocontrol) developed standards in the area of air navigation services and airspace use; the case was concerned with three areas of activities of the Eurocontrol, namely, regulation, standardization, and validation; research and development; and assistance for administration of MSs in the field of planning, specification and creation of Air Traffic Management (ATM) services. SELEX Sistemi Integrati SpA, an Italian company, challenged the inaction of the Commission against the regime of intellectual property rights for the prototypes of ATM equipment, set by Eurocontrol under the second area of its activities, which, following SELEX, created factual monopolies in the systems that become standards since the firms providing the prototypes were in an advantageous position.

[77] Case T-155/04, *SELEX*, para. 61.

[78] Ibid., paras. 59–61.

[79] The Council of Eurocontrol comprised directors of the civil aviation administration of each Member State of the organization, appointed by their respective States for the purpose of adopting technical specifications that will be binding in all those States; Case T-155/04, *SELEX*, para. 59.

[80] Case T-155/04, *SELEX*, para. 59.

[81] Ibid.

[82] Case C-113/07, *SELEX Sistemi Integrati SpA* v. *Commission of the European Communities* [2009] ECR I-02207, paras. 89–92.

[83] Ibid., para. 93. Note however, that in some earlier cases Courts rejected this type of "immunity."

On other occasions, however, the Court found a breach of antitrust provisions of private bodies developing voluntary technical standards. In early 1980, the Court held that an agreement concluded between Belgian trade associations of manufacturers and sole importers of dishwashers and washing machines was restricting parallel trade.[84] The arrangement stipulated that only those devices that comply with Belgian standards and carry a label of Communauté de l'Électricité (CEG), a Belgian not-for-profit organization, could be connected to the water supply system; yet, CEG only provided the labels to official manufacturers and importers with whom it had entered into special agreements.[85] In *Stichting Certificatie Kraanverhuurbedrijf* (SCK), a Dutch certification institution that obliged the certified companies to comply with statutory requirements regarding the management of a crane-hire firm and the use of cranes, and prohibited certified firms to subcontract their activities to noncertified firms, was found restraining parallel trade and creating barrier for market access.[86] The CJEU classified SCK as an undertaking: SCK carried out an economic activity akin to a private undertaking and, since certification was provided upon the payment, was also seeking profits.[87]

The CJEU also scrutinized a Portugal-based association for Chartered Accountants that established the system of compulsory training[88] Upon finding that the Ordem dos Técnicos Oficiais de Contas (OTOC) held a public service mission and was de facto acting in a relevant market for professional training of chartered accountants, the Court held that the rules of OTOC laid down discriminatory conditions to the detriment of

[84] Joined Cases 96/82 to 102/82, 104/82, 105/82, 108/82 and 110/82, *N V IAZ International Belgium e.a.* v. *Commission* [1983] ECR 03369.

[85] Ibid.

[86] In that specific sector, hiring cranes from subcontractors was essential to be able to meet the demand, see Schepel, *The Constitution of Private Governance*, p. 290.

[87] Joined Cases T-213/95 and T-18/96, *Stichting Certificatie Kraanverhuurbedrijf (SCK), Federatie van Nederlandse Kraanverhuurbedrijven (FNK)* v. *Commission* [1997] ECR II-01739, para. 117; see also N. Petit, 'The IEEE-SA revised patent policy and its definition of "reasonable" rates: a transatlantic antitrust divide?' (2017) 27 *Fordham Intellectual Property, Media and Entertainment Law Journal* 211–51 at 226–7; Schepel, *The Constitution of Private Governance*, p. 291.

[88] Case C-1/12, *Ordem dos Técnicos Oficiais*. The association allowed competing bodies to provide compulsory training but claimed certain courses exclusively.

its competitors and hence reflected an exclusionary agreement among the members of the organizations in breach of Article 101 of TFEU.[89]

From the procedural angle, the key decision was issued by the CJEU in *EMC Development*. A Sweden-based cement manufacturer accused the European Portland cement producers, the European Cement Association (Cembureau), and CEN of creating entry barriers for European cement market by means of an industrial standard.[90] The standard at issue was developed in a CEN Technical Committee under the mandate of the Commission and the European Free Trade Association (EFTA). The cement offered by EMC was produced with different materials and did not fit into the five main cement types stipulated in the standard; accordingly, EMC alleged to have been excluded from the relevant market. Crucially, EMC also stated that the procedure of guiding the development of the standard has been influenced by Cembureau and was neither transparent nor open, and that the standard was de facto binding. The Commission, and later the Court, dismissed the claims of EMC based on the lack of evidence for its allegations,[91] but accepted the possibility to scrutinize CEN's standard-setting against the procedural requirements of the *safe harbor*, bypassing the analyses on alleged cartelization:[92] accordingly, it is only the process of drafting a standardization agreement, not its effects, that were subject to scrutiny under competition law. This case illustrates that standards crafted within CEN could be potentially addressed under the 101 (1), despite that the earlier case law found CEN to be an ESO entrusted with general economic interest.[93] Although the Commission stated that CEN's members could be considered undertakings for the purpose of EU competition law,[94] the question remained whether, and under which circumstances, the work of a Technical Committee of an SDO should be considered as an agreement between undertakings.

[89] Ibid., para. 97. Although this case rather deals with associations establishing training rules, a parallel can be drawn with SDOs; see also Lundqvist, *Standardization under EU Competition Rules*, pp. 190–1, who suggests that following the decision in *OTOC*, SDOs connected to trade associations would be considered associations of undertakings according to 101 TFEU.

[90] Case T-432/05, *EMC Development AB* v. *European Commission* [2010] ECR II-01629.

[91] Ibid., para. 87.

[92] Ibid., paras. 94–104.

[93] Case T-4/92, *Evangelos Vardakas* v. *Commission* [1993] ECR II-00357, para. 47.

[94] Case T-432/05, *EMC Development*, para. 81.

It appears that voluntary standardization agreements can breach 101 (1) TFEU once they reduce product diversity and de facto exclude competing standards while having collusive price effects. At the same time, the Commission seems to be willing to exempt such agreements under the "efficiency defense" of 101(3) TFEU, provided that the cumulative conditions of this article are fulfilled. With regard to SDOs' liability under competition law, the CJEU has indeed accepted a public-body exception in *Eurocontrol*, but still allowed examination of CEN's processes for the purpose of establishing an antitrust violation: in this regard, the *EMC Development* case is of a particular importance since it illustrates how compliance with certain procedural principles can bring SDOs outside the scope of 101 TFEU.

### Procedural Framework of Horizontal Guidelines

Despite that agreements between competitors are generally not desirable, the Commission recognizes that certain types of horizontal cooperation between rival companies might boost the economy, increase welfare, and bring benefits for consumers. In 2001, it adopted the guidelines that apply for six types of horizontal cooperation agreements (hereinafter: the Guidelines), including standardization. The Guidelines were updated in 2011 following a series of investigations of Rambus and Qualcomm.[95]

The Guidelines (2011) describe standardization agreements as agreements with the primary objective to define technical or quality requirements with which current or future products, production processes, or methods may comply,[96] and that may affect competition on four markets, namely, product market, technology market, service market for standard-setting, and market for conformity assessment.[97] Next to recognizing standards' benefits, the Guidelines warn that standardization agreements might harm competition by reducing prices, foreclosing

[95] Guidelines on the applicability of Article 101 of the Treaty on the Functioning of the European Union to horizontal cooperation agreements (2011) C 11/1 (hereinafter: Horizontal Guidelines). It is suggested that the 2011 guidelines are less formalistic and adopt a dynamic view; see R. Whish and D. Bailey, *Competition Law* (New York: Oxford University Press, 2015), p. 645. It is also suggested that the aim of the Horizontal Guidelines was to establish a "safe harbor" for SDOs akin to the one that already existed in the US; Lundqvist, *Standardization under EU Competition Rules*, p. 197.

[96] Horizontal Guidelines, para. 257.

[97] Ibid., para. 261. Lundqvist finds these definitions rather broad and preferred the Commission to focus on narrower standards that may be problematic from a competition law perspective. Lundqvist, *Standardization under EU Competition Rules*, p. 198.

innovative technologies, and preventing effective access to the standard[98] – all three scenarios related to the issue of IPR licensing and royalty pricing. The Guidelines do not cover standards crafted as an execution of public power or professional rules;[99] neither do they appear to cover the activities of ESOs, provided that those cannot be considered undertakings or association of undertakings under Articles 101 and 102(3) of TFEU.[100] Market share held by firms is not considered when assessing the effects of standardization agreement, since it is not always feasible to establish at the beginning of standards development, whether the standard will be adopted by a large group of industry players.[101]

Similar to any agreement under the scope of Article 101 of TFEU, standardization agreements may be restrictive either by object or by effect. An example of the former is when the use of standards is aimed at preventing or delaying the introduction of new technologies on the market,[102] when the most restrictive licensing terms are disclosed prior to the adoption of a standard as a cover for jointly price fixing,[103] or when the members of the standardization group can only sell products that comply with the standard created by them,[104] – in short, when standardization is used in a discriminatory manner or as a tool for exclusion of actual or potential competitors.[105] These types of agreements do not benefit from the exceptional treatment under the Guidelines, and should be dealt with under Article 101(3).[106]

98 Horizontal Guidelines, para. 264. It should be noted that access can be restricted both with regard to a standard and the IPRs essential for its implementation.

99 Ibid., paras. 39–44 and 92.

100 Ibid., para. 258; Lundqvist suggests that a plaintiff that would like to bring an action against CEN is better off using both internal market provisions (Article 34 of TFEU) and competition law provisions (101 and 102 TFEU); Lundqvist, *Standardization under EU Competition Rules*, p. 199 (the question remains, however, how does this provision of Horizontal Guidelines square with the decision in *EMC Development*). It was also suggested that standards development of the three ESOs, if considered as exercise services of general economic interest, may under circumstances also benefit from the exception of Article 106(2) of TFEU; Mataija, *Private Regulation*, p. 243, n.109.

101 Horizontal Guidelines, para. 296. See also F. Wijckmans and F. Tuytschaever, *Vertical Agreements in EU Competition Law* (Oxford: Oxford University Press, 2011), p. 420.

102 See the decision in *Pre-Insulated Pipes Cartel*, above n. 73.

103 Horizontal Guidelines, para. 274.

104 Ibid., para. 293.

105 Ibid., para. 273. See also Wijckmans and Tuytschaever, *Vertical Agreements*, p. 419. Lundqvist refers to such agreements as "fraud" standardization agreements; Lundqvist, *Standardization under EU Competition Rules*, p. 199.

106 Horizontal Guidelines, para. 19.

The Guidelines (2011) further introduce procedural principles to which SDOs have to adhere not to breach the EU competition rules. Standards development processes would *normally* (emphasis added) fall outside the scope of 101(1), as long as they follow the four cumulative conditions of the "safe harbor" of the Guidelines, which are moreover consistent with the principles developed in the judgment of *EMC Development* v. *Commission*: unrestricted participation in standard-setting, transparent procedure for adopting the standard in question, no obligation to comply with the standard, and providing access to the standard on fair, reasonable, and nondiscriminatory terms.[107] The latter condition also encourages SDOs to implement a clear and balanced IPR policy adapted to the particular industry and to the needs of the SDO: such policy should be based on FRAND commitments, as determined by companies, subject to a transfer obligation, but should still allow patent-holders to exclude technology from licensing.[108] The failure to fulfil any of the conditions of *safe harbor* does not directly lead to a presumption of anticompetitive conduct:[109] an effect-based assessment is required to establish whether the agreement at issue falls under 101(1) TFEU, and whether it can be "saved" by the 101(3).[110]

### *Unilateral Conduct and Abuse of Power*

Abuse of dominant position that may potentially result from SEPs holder licensing practices is prohibited by Article 102 of TFEU.[111] In 2007, the Commission accused Rambus, a US-based chipmaker company, of engaging in patent ambush: the Commission asserted that Rambus was intentionally not disclosing its SEPs and patent applications in the Joint Electron Device Engineering Council (JEDEC) and claimed excessive royalties for these patents after the standard running on them was

[107] Ibid., para. 280.

[108] See JRC Report, p. 140.

[109] Horizontal Guidelines, para. 279.

[110] Ibid., para. 273; Geradin, 'The European Commission policy', 1135. See in this regard Commission Decision Ship Classification in Case 39.416 (October 14, 2009) 7796 OJ C 2/5.

[111] Certain exceptions, including the requirement of a "new product" suggested by CJEU on a number of occasions, were subject to critique in legal scholarship. See, for instance, N. Petit, 'Injunctions for FRAND-pledged SEPs: the quest for an appropriate test of abuse under Art. 102 TFEU' (2017) 9 *European Competition Journal* 677–719.

adopted, thereby breaching Article 102 of TFEU (ex. 82 TEC).[112] Rambus eventually agreed to lower its royalty rates, and the case ended with a settlement. Another investigation on excessive royalties was launched against Qualcomm, a SEP holder for the Wideband Code Division Multiple Access (WCDMA) standard,[113] accused by a number of mobile phone equipment manufacturers of breaching its FRAND commitment under ETSI IPR policy; the Commission, however, could not demonstrate that royalty rates asked by Qualcomm were indeed "exploitative" within the meaning of 102 TFEU.[114]

With regard to injunctive relief and abuse of dominance, the Commission's position has for a long time remained vague. In its decision on the merger between Google and Motorola Mobility, the Commission recognized that seeking injunctions by patent-holders who have made a FRAND commitment might be abusive, but failed to define the circumstances when this is the case, in particular, when a licensee is acting in "good faith" and is "willing" to purchase a license.[115] More guidance was provided in the investigation against Samsung Electronics and Google/Motorola (MMI), where companies that made a FRAND licensing commitment and were seeking injunctions against implementers were accused of abusing their dominant position and distorting competition on the market of mobile devices.[116] Whereas in the case of Samsung the Commission confirmed that patent-holders should be able

[112] The Commission's preliminary view was that Rambus would not have been able to charge the royalty rates as it did without the conduct leading to "patent ambush"; see Antitrust: Commission confirms sending a Statement of Objections to Rambus (2007) MEMO/07/330, available at https://ec.europa.eu/commission/presscorner/detail/en/MEMO_07_330.

[113] Press Release, 'Commission initiates formal proceedings against Qualcomm' (2007) MEMO/07/389. The complaints were filed by Broadcom, Ericsson, NEC, Nokia, Panasonic, and Texas Instruments, and were based on the understanding of FRAND commitments that essential patent-holders should not be able to exploit the extra power they have gained as a result of having technology based on their patent incorporated in the standard.

[114] See Press Release, 'Commission closes formal proceedings against Qualcomm' (2009) MEMO/09/516. Qualcomm, however, entered into a settlement with the complainants; see Geradin, 'The European Commission policy', 1132.

[115] Geradin, 'The European Commission policy', 1138. See *Google/Motorola Mobility* (2012) COMP/M.6381, available at https://ec.europa.eu/competition/mergers/cases/decisions/m6381_20120213_20310_2277480_EN.pdf. It was understood that Google wanted to acquire Motorola to gain access to its SEPs portfolio.

[116] Press Release, 'Commission opens proceedings against Samsung' (2012) IP/12/89; Press Release, 'Commission opens proceedings against Motorola' (2012) IP/12/345.

to seek injunctions when its potential licensees are unwilling to purchase a license on FRAND terms,[117] it did not come to the same conclusion for MMI,[118] illustrating its "case-by-case considerations" as regards abusive licensing practices.

The decisions of the Commission demonstrated its struggle in determining when royalties sought by patent-holder are "fair, reasonable and non-discriminatory" or "exploitative."[119] It has been suggested that the modification of the Guidelines for Horizontal Cooperation on 101 TFEU was somewhat motivated by the frustration of the Commission in the outcomes of its investigations, which did not allow it to specify any guidelines for standards development activities and licensing practices.[120]

Courts in the EU have followed the *Orange Book* line of cases, based on the ruling of the German Federal Court of Justice, which confirmed that a SEP holder requesting injunctive relief may indeed be in breach of Article 102 of TFEU.[121] The long-awaited guidance for determining when a SEP holder abuses its dominant position by seeking injunctive relief was provided by the CJEU in *Huawei* v. *ZTE*.[122] The Court found that a patent-owner who has committed to license its IPR under the FRAND terms may still seek injunctive relief after they have notified the alleged infringer by defining and specifying the violation, *and* in case when the alleged infringer has expressed its willingness to conclude a licensing agreement on FRAND terms,[123] but has not diligently responded to the offer of this agreement.[124] The Court thus proposed a procedural meaning of FRAND,[125] implying that this notion requires commitments from both SEP owners and (potential) licensees. The CJEU's rejection of the understanding of FRAND as a pricing mechanism appeared to be shared

[117] Press Release, 'Commission sends Statement of Objections to Samsung on potential misuse of mobile phone standard-essential patents' (2012) IP/12/1448.

[118] Press Release, 'Commission sends Statement of Objections to Motorola Mobility on potential misuse of mobile phone standard-essential patents' (2013) IP/13/406.

[119] This determination typically happens pursuant the CJEU decision in Case 27/76, *United Brands* v. *Commission* [1978] ECR 00207, and according to Geradin, is context specific; Geradin, 'The European Commission policy', 1133.

[120] Geradin, 'The European Commission policy', 1133.

[121] Bundesgerichtshof [BGH] (2009) 180 BGHZ 312.

[122] Case C-170/13, *Huawei Technologies Co. Ltd* v. *ZTE Corp* [2015].

[123] This agreement should be presented to that infringer as a specific, written offer for a license on such terms, identifying, in particular, the royalty and the way in which it is to be calculated.

[124] Meaning in accordance with recognized commercial practices in the field and in good faith.

[125] In contrast to a "content obligation" of licensing terms.

by CEN and CENELEC, who suggested that FRAND should be considered as a "participative instrument that seeks to foster stakeholders' *ex ante* incentives to get aboard SDOs."[126]

Despite providing a recipe to solve future SEP disputes, *Huawei* v. *ZTE* still leaves certain questions unanswered, one of them being the definition of good faith. In the recent UK decision in *Unwired Planet* v. *Huawei*, Justice Birss stated that failure to satisfy the *Huawei* v. *ZTE* requirement does not automatically lead to the finding that a patent-holder abuses its dominant position, and that the request for injunctions filed by such patent-holder should be rejected; accordingly, the Court ruled that Unwired Planet did not abuse its dominant position by prematurely issuing proceedings against Huawei, neither by claiming a "global" license, seeking injunctions, nor bundling SEPs and patents that were not essential.[127] On appeal, the Court stated that there is no obligation to satisfy the requirements of *Huawei* v. *ZTE* prior to seeking injunctive relief: rather, these conditions provide a safe harbor for SEP-holders, and failure to comply with them does not necessarily breach 102 TFUE.[128] In other post-*Huawei* judgments, the Courts were stricter in applying the *Huawei* framework: for instance, the Higher Regional Court (*Oberlandesgericht-OLG)* of *Düsseldorf* held that a SEP-holder should fulfill the requirements set forth in *Huawei* before applying for a preliminary injunction,[129] and in *NTT DoCoMo* v. *HTC*, the Court referred to the *Huawei* judgment for the rules of due conduct in SEP licensing negotiations.[130]

[126] CEN-CENELEC's position paper 'Standard essential patents', p. 14.

[127] *Unwired Planet Int Ltd and Unwired Planet LLC* v. *Huawei Technologies Co Ltd and Huawei Technologies UK Co Ltd* [2017] EWHC 711 (Pat). The Court of Appeal later confirmed that the global license offered was FRAND.

[128] *Unwired Planet Int Ltd and Unwired Planet LLC* v. *Huawei Technologies Co Ltd and Huawei Technologies UK Co Ltd* [2017] [2018] EWCA Civ 2344.

[129] *OLG Düsseldorf* (2017) I-2 U 23/17.

[130] *NTT DoCoMo* v. *HTC* Case No. 7 O 66/15.

# 5

# The US Regulatory Framework

## The US Standardization System

As opposed to the coordinated and hierarchical system of the EU, US standardization is largely based on decentralization and public–private partnership:[1] US federal policy encourages federal agencies to use private sector standards to fulfil their regulatory needs,[2] which became a common practice across different industries. US building, construction, and mechanical model codes for a long time have been representing a mixture of industry standards, semipublic codes, and public law.[3] The US Consumer Product Safety Act (CPSA) advises the Consumer Product Safety Commission to use voluntary consumer product safety standards to eliminate or reduce the risk of injury.[4] Model codes referenced in legislation are drafted by private bodies (such as the International Code Council) which, however, may only confer voting rights exclusively on governmental stakeholders; in turn, these codes refer to private standards drafted by other private associations.[5] For instance, the US Department of Housing and Urban Development (HUD) was obliged by the Manufactured Housing Construction and Safety Act of 1974 to consult private stakeholders when drafting building standards. To fulfill this condition, HUD sought recourse to private standards, but due to the abundance of the applicable industry norms, HUD was compelled to select a private body to facilitate its regulative activities.[6] Furthermore, in 2013, the US Food and Drug Administration (FDA) recognized three categories of private interoperability standards, namely, risk management

1 Mattli and Büthe, 'Setting international standards'.

2 J. L. Rubin, 'Patents, antitrust and rivalry in standard-setting' (2007) 38 *Rutgers Law Journal* 509–38 at 517.

3 Schepel, *The Constitution of Private Governance*, p. 153.

4 See Rubin, 'Patents, antitrust and rivalry', p. 517, citing 15 USC § 2056(b)(1) (2000).

5 Schepel, *The Constitution of Private Governance*, p. 155.

6 Ibid., pp. 90–1.

for connected and networked environments; interoperability standards establishing nomenclature, frameworks, and medical-device-specific communication; and cyber security standards for media devices.[7] It further listed twenty-five private standards, of which twelve belong to the IEEE 11073 set of specifications for medical device-communication, to serve as a guidance for manufacturers.[8]

The differences and similarities between the EU and US regulatory frameworks governing standardization have been extensively analyzed in the scholarship.[9] It appears that both States rely on privately driven SDOs that support their regulatory policies and, in one way or another, reference standards developed by these SDOs in their regulation; yet, whereas "incorporation by reference" of private standards in the US yields these standards a formal legal effect, HESs remain voluntary even after the reference to them is published in the OJ of the EU[10] and regardless the CJEU's ruling in *James Elliott*. Moreover, the EU Commission, at least in theory, has a power to request standards development, while US federal agencies would typically have to choose from the already existing private standards:[11] there are no "formally" recognized SDOs in the US, as opposed to the ESOs and NSOs in the EU system, and private standards are principally developed in private bodies for nongovernmental purposes. Furthermore, unlike in the EU, the standardization ecosystem of the US is not governed by a single legal instrument, but rather by a Statute document and executive policy, as well as procedural rules introduced by a private SDO fulfilling a specific function.

Despite the US and EU standardization systems bearing some similarities in relying on private standardization efforts (as opposed, for instance, to standardization systems in China or the former Soviet Union),[12] challenges arise when the US and EU use different standards to regulate the same goods or processes: the (so far, stalled) negotiations

[7] R. Schneiderman, *Modern Standardization: Case Studies at the Crossroads of Technology, Economics and Politics*, Standards Information Network (Hoboken: John Wiley & Sons, Inc., 2015), pp. 133–4 provides the full list of examples of these standards recognized by FDA.

[8] Ibid.

[9] See, predominantly, the work of Bremer, Schepel, Mattli and Büthe.

[10] Bremer, 'American and European perspectives', p. 328.

[11] Although in exceptional cases, an agency can request an SDO with which it is working to develop or update a standard; ibid., pp. 327–8.

[12] See, for instance, W. Ping, 'A brief history of standards and standardization organizations: a Chinese perspective' (2011) East-West Center Working Papers: Economic Series No. 117.

of Transatlantic Trade and Investment Partnership (TTIP),[13] as well as discussions on post-Brexit trade between the US and UK and the UK and EU, respectively, serve as a good illustration for challenges that arise due to the differences between US and EU standards.[14] Another concern relates to the fact that the US-based SDOs cannot directly participate in the ESOs' development of HESs – standards that, although voluntary, affect foreign companies' presence on the EU market;[15] meanwhile, nothing precludes EU companies from directly participating in US SDOs that develop standards to be referenced in law.[16] Ultimately, one of the main challenges of US standardization as such remains pacing the federal rule-making processes to the development and update of standards that have to respond to the changing market conditions, and as a result the existence of outdated references.[17]

## Procedural Mechanisms of the US Standardization Law and Policy

### *NTTAA*

Statutory requirements that apply to private standardization are introduced in the National Technology Transfer and Advancement Act of 1995 (NTTAA). While recognizing that industrial innovation in US depends on actions by businesses, the act emphasizes governmental cooperation with private entities and addresses a wide range of issues related to the US technical development,[18] such as governmental cooperation with private sector and the protection of IPR for technology inventions.[19]

NTTAA covers the development, adoption, or application of any standard, technical regulation, or conformity assessment procedure. The act requires governmental bodies to use voluntary consensus

[13] See Bremer, 'American and European perspectives', pp. 328–9.

[14] For instance, the discussion whether the UK will allow the import of chlorine-washed poultry meat from the US, which is currently prohibited by EU standards.

[15] While companies can join ETSI, the decision to adopt a standard as a HESs largely depends on NSOs vote (see Chapter 8); moreover, US companies would not be able to obtain membership of CEN/CENELEC, which are composed of NSOs.

[16] Bremer, 'American and European perspectives', p. 329.

[17] See E. S. Bremer, 'On the costs of private standards in public law' (2015) 61 *Kansas Law Review* 279–333.

[18] Section 2(2) of US National Technology Transfer and Advancement Act of 1995, Public Law 103–13, 110 STAT. 775 (1996) (hereinafter: NTTAA).

[19] Ibid., section 4.

standards developed by voluntary consensus standards organizations in lieu of governmental regulation for the purpose of achieving their policy objectives,[20] with "use" meaning incorporation of a standard as a whole, in part or by reference for procurement purposes, or inclusion of (a part of) a standard, or by reference in regulations.[21] In this regard, federal agencies and departments are also required to consult with SDOs and to participate in their standards development processes.[22] In case an agency refuses to follow a private consensus standard, it can use standards developed by other bodies than voluntary consensus SDOs, as long as they provide the Office of Management and Budget (OMB) with a valid explanation:[23] for instance, when the existing private standard is inconsistent with applicable law, such refusal is deemed appropriate.[24] In a similar vein, an agency that opts to use governmental standards instead of available private voluntary standards, must report the explanation to the National Institute of Standards and Technology (NIST).[25]

Despite introducing the crucial provisions in the US standardization system, the NTTAA does not explain how and when agencies should assess voluntary consensus standards for their fitness to be referenced in their regulatory documents. To address this gap, section 12(d) of the NTTAA and the related executive orders of the US Government[26] are further implemented by the federal policy in the OMB Circular A-119

[20] Ibid., sections 2(1) and 11.

[21] This is clarified in section 5(c)(i) OMB Circular No. A-119, Federal Participation in the Development and Use of Voluntary Consensus Standards and in Conformity Assessment Activities, 81 Fed. Reg. 4673 (2016) (hereinafter: OMB Circular). Moreover, the preference of US standardization system is for performance standards and in view of trade development, international standards, 5(e) of OMB Circular.

[22] See section 6 of OMB Circular.

[23] Section 15(d)(3) of NTTAA. OMB then summarizes all explanations and transmits them to the Congress.

[24] The OMB Circular also notes that standards are "impractical" when use of such standards would fail to serve agency's program needs or impose more burdens or be less useful than another standard, 5(c)(ii) OMB Circular.

[25] NIST is a nonregulatory agency of the US Department of Commerce, responsible for facilitating the implementation of federal standards policy.

[26] Those were adopted after 1998 revision of the Circular: Executive Order 12866 ('Regulatory planning and review'); Executive Order 13563 ('Improving regulation and regulatory review'); Executive Order 13609 ('Promoting international regulatory cooperation'); Executive Order 13610 ('Identifying and reducing Regulatory burdens'). These documents can be retrieved at www.archives.gov/federal-register/executive-orders.

(hereinafter: the OMB Circular), which covers standards referenced by incorporation for the purpose of public procurement.[27]

## *OMB Circular*

The OMB Circular was enacted already in 1982;[28] yet, its ambiguity provided little guidance as to how standards should be implemented by regulatory agencies.[29] The Circular was practically ignored until 1995, when NIST gained control over standardization and conformity assessment policy and, as explained earlier, mandated agencies to use voluntary consensus standards in lieu of governmental standards.

Subsequently, the Circular has undergone a number of revisions, in consultation with the relevant stakeholders:[30] among others, the updates clarified the role of federal agencies in US standardization activities, addressed the issue of national implementation of private voluntary standards and provided agencies with a certain flexibility to adopt the most suitable conformity assessment program and, where needed, to issue additional guidance for the use of standards.[31] The latest revision at the moment of writing took place in 2016 and addressed some adjustments in regulatory, standardization, and trade policy: for instance, it provided additional guidance for federal agencies serving on SDOs' boards and technical committees; set out factors to evaluate when referencing a standard in regulation; called for increased internal coordination on standards; explained how federal agencies should implement the Circular in their regulatory frameworks; and encouraged agencies to

[27] Authority to issue this Circular is based on 31 USC § 1111, which gives the OMB a broad power to establish policies for the improved management of the Executive Branch to improve regulatory and policy outcomes.

[28] OMB Circular No. A-119, Federal Participation in the Development and Use of Voluntary Consensus Standards and in Conformity Assessment Activities, 47 Fed. Reg. 49,496 (1982).

[29] See Schepel, *The Constitution of Private Governance*, p. 88, n. 49.

[30] To gather information for this revision, the OMB published a Request for Information in the Federal Register on 30 March 2012 (77 Fed. Reg. 19357) on "whether and how to supplement Circular A-119" and held a public workshop on May 15, 2012. The OMB issued a Request for Comment on a Proposed Revision of OMB Circular A-119, 'Federal participation in the development and use of voluntary consensus standards and in conformity assessment activities,' on February 11, 2014 (79 Fed. Reg. 8207). More than 80 comments were received from a wide range of stakeholders, including companies, trade associations, academics, public interest groups, SDOs, conformity assessment bodies, and individuals.

[31] Section 7 of OMB Circular.

provide a public notification when considering participation in a standards development process. With regard to the standards development processes, the updated Circular refers to openness, balance of interests, due process, appeal process, and consensus.

The OMB Circular (2016) introduced factors to be considered by agencies when deciding to reference a private standard, such as effectiveness and suitability of that standard for agency's needs, the extent to which it falls under the definition of a "voluntary consensus standard" (i.e., developed or adopted by voluntary consensus standards bodies in a voluntary consensus standards development process),[32] and whether the standard is "reasonably available"[33] – the latter, remarkably, is not echoed in Regulation 1025/2012 apart from the reference to "reasonable terms" in the case of ICT standards identified by the Commission for EU procurement.[34] Whether the standard should be implemented in the absence of any of these factors is left at the discretion of the agencies, which are also expected to collaborate with SDOs for ensuring appropriate access for stakeholders and to be able to justify the reasoning for their choice of a particular standard.[35]

It is the notion of "reasonable availability" of a standard that generated a wide-ranging discussion during the last revision process and prompted a number of questions concerning standards' accessibility in a nonregulatory context, availability for "the class of persons affected," and the necessity of a "freely available, non-technical summary."[36] While the definition of "reasonable availability" remains a matter of the Office of the Federal Register (OFR),[37] the Circular (2016) nevertheless clarified certain factors that can assist agencies in determining whether a standard is indeed reasonably available to interested parties, including: accessibility of a read-only version of a standard during the comment period; costs associated with the access to a standard and incorporated materials; the degree to which such access is required to achieve agency's policy goals;

32 Ibid., section 2(d)(e).

33 Ibid., section 5(f).

34 See Annex II of EU Regulation 1025/2012, which says that standard is reasonably available when it is offered for free or against a reasonable fee.

35 OMB Circular, p. 7.

36 This is the "reasonably available" requirement of the Freedom of Information Act (FOIA), 5 USC Sect. 552 (a) (1), as amended by Public Law No. 104-231, 110 Stat. 3048.

37 USC §552(a)(1). The statutory obligation of OFR on reasonable availability is balanced with US copyright law, US international trade obligations, and agencies' ability to substantively regulate under their authorizing statutes; see 79 Fed. Reg. 66267.

and availability of a summary explaining the content of a standard to those lacking relevant technical expertise.[38] Surprisingly, the issue of standards' copyright, while being especially pertinent in the US, did not seem to have played a significant role in deliberations on standards' availability during the revision of the Circular.

### *ANSI Essential Requirements*

The third instrument governing US standardization does not stem from Statutes or Federal policy, but from a private, not-for-profit organization: the American National Standards Institute (ANSI). ANSI does not develop its own standards, and neither does it mandate standards development; rather, ANSI's role is one of an "administrator and coordinator" of the US standardization system.[39] In this capacity, ANSI defines essential requirements for standard development that apply to US-based SDOs and to their standards.[40] By overseeing compliance with these requirements, ANSI aims to contribute to the increase in global competitiveness of US businesses and to maintain the integrity of standards developers.[41] In 1998, NIST and ANSI signed a Memorandum of Understanding (MoU) which, despite being not enforceable, clearly stressed the allocation of tasks between the two bodies: for NIST, to ensure that private standards respond to policy needs and are used by the governments, and for ANSI, to monitor that private standards are developed according to its procedural principles.[42]

ANSI's Essential Requirements target standards development processes and constitute "the minimum acceptable due process requirements for the development of consensus."[43] These due process principles include openness, lack of dominance, balance, coordination and harmonization, notification of standards development, consideration of views and objections, consensus vote, appeals, written procedures, and compliance with IPR and Antitrust policies. Only those SDOs whose governance and standards procedures are in line with ANSI's Essential

[38] Section 5(f) of OMB Circular.

[39] Bremer, 'American and European perspectives', p. 341.

[40] ANSI, 'ANSI Essential Requirements, Due Process Requirements for American National Standards' (Edition: January 2022) (hereinafter: ANSI Essential Requirements), available at https://share.ansi.org/.

[41] See 'About ANSI', available at www.ansi.org/about_ansi/overview/overview?menuid1.

[42] The new version of MoU was signed on April 29, 2019, which reaffirmed the need for coordinated approach to US standardization.

[43] Sections 1.0 ANSI Essential Requirements.

Requirements are accredited as Accredited Standards Developers (ASDs).[44] The same set of due process principles is used in accrediting private standards as American National Standards (ANSs).[45] In principle, however, an SDO does not need to be designated as an ASD for its standards to be incorporated by reference, and regulators can also implement standards that are not ANSs: ANSI's two independent accreditation processes thus either grant presumption of compliance with the Circular to SDOs, or confer legitimacy to particular standards, but cannot be seen as regulatory requirements. Some SDOs producing standards that are already well-established on the global market have even indicated they give little consideration to ANSI's accreditation of their standards.[46]

## US Voluntary Consensus Standards

US federal policy does not specify which SDOs can produce standards to be incorporated by reference into public regulation: as explained later, the legitimacy of private standards depends on the process followed during their development, rather than any kind of formal recognition of the SDO in which these processes have taken place. The applicable legal instruments define a (technical) standard as "performance-based or design-specific technical specifications and related management systems practices" (note the departure from the definition in ISO/IEC Guide 2 (2004), which does not include professional standards of personal conduct or institutional codes of ethics,[47] and largely refer to the notion of "voluntary consensus standards" developed by "voluntary consensus bodies"). A standard running on patented technologies can only be qualified as a "voluntary consensus standard" when it is easily accessible and accompanied by clear rules on disclosure and licensing

[44] See ANSI Accreditation of American National Standards Developers, available at www.ansi.org/standards_activities/domestic_programs/accreditation_as_developer/accredit.

[45] To access standards incorporated by reference in the US Code of Federal Regulations, see https://ibr.ansi.org/.

[46] Recent example is the withdrawal of ANSI accreditation of an updated version of 802.11 WLAN standard; although no official explanation has been provided on this matter, anecdotal evidence suggested that the loss of ANSI accreditation is not of importance, and that the endorsement of the new standards by ISO/IEC/JTC1 is of a greater value to that particular industry.

[47] Section 12(5) of NTTAA and para. 2(1)(2) OMB Circular.

of the proprietary components, taking into account the interests of all parties.[48]

As it is the case in the EU, copyrights of US standards referenced in law is increasingly becoming a topic of discussion. Reproduction or distribution of US standards documents is effectively prevented by their private ownership, and placing private standards referenced in law into public domain risks violating SDOs' copyright over these standards. In this regard, a relevant point to consider is that while the development of HESs may obtain a limited funding from the Commission,[49] US standardization is financed privately, with each individual SDO responsible for its funding, and the copyright being an important "source of income."[50] The US courts have on a number of occasions ruled on the issue of access to copyrighted standards referenced in regulation. These decisions attempted to strike a balance between dual policy objectives: on the one hand, the incentives of regulators to produce law and, on the other, public domain considerations on due process and free access.[51]

In *BOCA*, the disagreement arose between an author of a private building code, offered for sale against a fee, and a copier who put the code into public domain once it was embedded into a state regulation.[52] A comparable dispute took place in *CCC*, where the "Red Book," published by a private author and containing information on used car values, was valued as an alternative standard to set minimum loss payoffs.[53] In both cases, the judges were reluctant to provide a definite statement regarding the legal value of private codes, but concluded that an author loses the copyright over its standard once it was referenced in a legal act, following the established case law that judicial and legislative works are free of copyright claims.[54] In *Practice Management*, a governmental regulation instructed the Health Care Financing Administration (HCFA) to establish a uniform system for identification of physicians'

48 Para. 5(a)(iii)(v) of OMB Circular.

49 See Articles 15 and 16 of EU Regulation 1025/2012.

50 Bremer observes that SDOs are funded primarily through membership fees, but then also through copyrights and charitable contributions. See 'American and European perspectives', pp. 342–3. Note, however, that the argument on copyrights as a source of SDOs' income was rejected by the Court in *Veeck* and as well as in *ASTM* v. *PRO*.

51 L. A. Cunningham, 'Private standards in public law: copyright, lawmaking and the case of accounting' (2005) 104 *Michigan Law Review* 291–344 at 303.

52 *Bldg. Officials and Code Admin.* v. *Code Tech., Inc.*, 628 F 2d 730 (1st Cir. 1980).

53 *CCC Info. Servs. Inc.* v. *MacLean Hunter Mkt. Rep., Inc.*, 44 F 3d 61 (2d Cir. 1994).

54 E.g., *Wheaton* v. *Peters*, 33 US (8 Pet.) 591 (1834).

services used in claim forms. HCFA used the code of American Medical Association (AMA), with which it signed a contract requiring the use of AMA's system. This time, the Court granted AMA the right to claim copyright, taking into consideration the facts that standards were easily available to public, and that the opposite decision would provoke controversy about the copyrights of other private model codes and standards.[55]

The landmark decision on the issue of copyright of standards incorporated into law was issued by the US Court of Appeals in *Veeck*,[56] where the Court confirmed, similarly to the German Bundesgerichtshof, that once put into public domain, the code in question was transformed into law and hence fell outside the purview of copyright provisions.[57] After a privately drafted Southern Building Code (SBC) was adopted by two municipalities in Texas, it was published on a website by an individual, despite the explicit prohibition thereof and without specifying its author. The Southern Building Code Congress International (SBCCI), a private association that drafted the code at issue, claimed the protection of its copyright. While the District Court ruled in favor of SBCCI, the decision was quashed on appeal. In an en banc session, the US Court of Appeals stated by majority that once put into public domain, the code was transformed into law and hence fell outside the purview of copyright provisions.[58] Moreover, the Court considered the "merger doctrine" in copyright law, stating that the code became a "fact" or "idea" incapable of expression in any way except as embodied, and is therefore off copyright.[59] The Court did not accept SBCCI's argument regarding the lack of revenues as a consequence of the denial of copyrights, since the association had been active for quite some time and had an interest in promoting its codes. Despite the lack of unanimity, the appeal decision was not revised by the Supreme Court.[60]

[55] *Practice Mgmt. Info. Corp.* v. *Am. Med. Ass'n*, 121 F 3d 516 (9th Cir. 1997), amended by 133 F 3d 1140 (9th Cir. 1998).

[56] *En banc, Veeck* v. *S. Bldg. Code Cong. Int'l, Inc.*, 293 F 3d 791 (5th Cir. 2002), cert. denied 539 US 969 (2003) (hereinafter *Veeck* v. *SBCCI*).

[57] Ibid., para. 26.

[58] Ibid.

[59] Ibid., paras. 31–6.

[60] For further analysis of US case law on copyright of private standards, see Cunningham, 'Private standards'. Note that the Court explicitly stated that *Veeck* did not revolve around standards incorporated by reference (which, according to the Court, do not become law "merely because a statute refers to them"), but concerned the wholesale adoption of a model code promoted by the SDOs that drafted this code for the purpose to be used as legislation. Accordingly, the decisions and "hypothetical situations" in *CCC*

In the recent dispute *ASTM* v. *PRO*, four SDOs have initially obtained permanent injunctions against any authorized use of their incorporated standards by PublicResource.org (hereinafter: PRO), a nonprofit organization concerned with availability of governmental materials.[61] On appeal, PRO questioned the validity of SDOs' property rights over the standards in the light of prohibition to copyright US Government works.[62] To that end, it observed that US Government employees may have taken part in drafting processes of standards at issue and suggested that incorporation by reference renders private standards "a part of the law."[63] Most intriguing, however, was PRO's critique on the current standardization system, alleging that by lobbying to have their standards adopted into law and then limiting access to the standards document with copyright, SDOs ignore the right to access the text of the law.[64] The Court of Appeal restated that binding laws should be available free of charge to US citizens,[65] but was cautious in drawing any further conclusions regarding public access to copyrighted standards, merely stating that standards incorporated by reference into law are "at the outer edge" of "copyright's protective purposes."[66] The Court thus refused to address broader constitutional issues that arise from permitting private ownership of standards referenced in law, suggesting a case-by-case approach.[67]

## Standardization in US Competition Law

Similarly to the EU, standardization in the US has been extensively discussed in case law on collusion and abuse of dominance, with some landmark decisions leading to the development of procedural framework for SDOs to follow. In a like manner, SDOs in the US are typically

and *Practice Management* should be distinguished from the one in *Veeck*, since in the latter, the model code "served no other purpose than to become law." *Veeck* v. *SBCCI*, paras. 41–4.

61 *American Society for Testing & Materials* v. *Public.Resource.org, Inc.*, No. 1:13-cv-01215 (TSC), 2017 WL 473822, (DDC February 2, 2017), *amended by* No. 17-7035 (DC. Cir. 2018).

62 *ASTM* v. *PRO*, 2017 WL 473822, at 15 et seq.

63 Ibid., pp. 19–20.

64 Ibid., p. 28.

65 *ASTM* v. *PRO*, 2018 No. 17-7035, at 24, quoting *Howell* v. *Miller*, 91 F 129, 137 (6th Cir. 1898).

66 Ibid., p. 24.

67 Ibid., p. 19.

exempted from antitrust liability: their processes are granted presumption of pro-competitiveness and, as such, are rarely found to breach the applicable competition rules. Despite these similarities, when it comes to antitrust and abusive practices concerns, the US system offers interesting observations that are of the increasing relevance to global standardization.

### *SDOs as Vehicles for Collusion in the US*

#### Decisions on Cartels

Any contracts or conspiracies between two or more enterprises aiming to limit trade or commerce are prohibited under §1 of the Sherman Act.[68] Early cases included *Standard Sanitary*, where patents for process were used as a mechanism to fix prices.[69] A number of manufacturers of sanitary products agreed to develop their products following a certain process, owned and licensed to them by a "ring-leader," and subsequently agreed on prices for their products on the US market. Products that did not follow this process were effectively prohibited from being sold within the US, which naturally reduced product variety and was eventually confirmed by the Supreme Court as breaching §1 of Sherman Act. *Standard Oil* dealt with a patent pool created by several firms developing "cracking" processes – a process of heating oil under pressure in order to produce gasoline – as a response to the complexities around patents' scope and ownership; here, the Supreme Court found the patent pool beneficial, or even essential, since the license agreements ensure the division of royalties between the patent-holders.[70]

In *Macaroni*, a shortage of durum semolina was mitigated by adopting a product standard for pasta that required less durum semolina: this modification of a standard allowed manufacturers to suppress their costs and, therefore, the price of their products.[71] In *C-O Two and Household*

[68] The decisions of single economic entities fall outside the scope of this article, see *Copperweld Corp.* v. *Independence Tube Corp.*, 467 US 752.

[69] *Standards Sanitary Mfg. Co* v. *United States*, 226 US 20 (1912).

[70] *Standard Oil Co.* v. *United States*, 337 US 293 (1949). On more cases on patent pools and Sherman Act; see D. Homiller, 'Patent misuse in patent pool licensing: from national harrow to "the nine no-nos" to not likely' (2006) 5 *Duke Law and Technology Review* 1–21.

[71] *National Macaroni Manufacturers Association, et al.* v. *Federal Trade Commission*, No. 14713 (1965).

*Radiators*, creating a narrow standard that reduced product differentiation was found collusive.[72] In *Radiant Burners*, SDO members decided not to certify a specific burner: without this certification, however, gas companies, who also happened to be members of this SDO, refused to provide gas. This conduct was found to constitute an antitrust violation since the intent of SDOs' members was to exclude competition.[73] Hence, already from early on, the Court assigned a high value for products' choice and differentiation and considered the intent behind an agreement among SDOs' members.

The US courts have also found practices that aimed to exclude companies from a standard to violate the Sherman Act and confirmed that antitrust liability can be attributed both to SDOs' members as well as to the SDOs. A remarkable decision in this context was issued in ASME v. *Hydrolevel*, where the Supreme Court found that SDOs can be held liable for the acts of their agents' misuse of standard-setting processes with an anticompetitive objective, even if those SDOs have never ratified, authorized, or derived any benefit from the activity of the latter. Hydrolevel, a water boiler manufacturer and a new successful player on the market, suspected that some undertakings that were members of the American Society of Mechanical Engineers (ASME), a consensus based SDO developing standards for mechanical devices, manipulated an interpretation of ASME's Code, which was adopted as a regulatory requirement in most US States. The companies' officials, who were also serving as volunteers in ASME's committees, requested a dedicated subcommittee to interpret whether Hydrolevel's processes were compliant with the ASME's Boiler Code; the interpretation was indeed provided by the chair of the committee, affiliated with one of Hydrolevel's competitors, in the form of an "unofficial response," and subsequently used by companies to "warn" potential Hydrolevel customers about its alleged noncompliance with the ASME Boiler Code, which resulted in Hydrolevel's loss of its customer base. While the conspiracy case against the individuals involved ended with a settlement, the Supreme Court ultimately rejected ASME's claim that it cannot be held responsible for the actions of its volunteers, since the ASME officials, the "agents," have acted under the "apparent authority" of the ASME, "the principal."[74]

72 *C-O-Two Fire Equip.* v. *United States*, 197 F 2d (1952), *United States* v. *Am Radiator and Standard Sanitary Corp.* 433 F 2d 174 (1971).

73 *Radiant Burners, Inc.* v. *Peoples Gas Co.*, 364 US 656 (1961).

74 *American Society of Mechanical Engineers* v. *Hydrolevel Corporation*, 456 US 556 (1982).

In another landmark case, *Allied Tube and Conduit Corp* vs. *Indian Head Inc.*, the standards development process of the National Fire Protection Association (NFPA) was brought under the scrutiny of antitrust law.[75] The NFPA was a private SDO developing fire protection standards that were subsequently adopted as state law and codified in the National Electric Code. Within the NFPA, a standard was selected by the means of voting. Allied Tube, a manufacturer of plastic electrical conduit in the new Code, proposed to include that type of conduit into the 1981 Code and initially got approval by an NFPA panel; later, some of the NFPA members agreed to introduce new members to the SDO with a purpose to defeat the proposal – as a result, the proposal was overthrown with the help of 230 new members. The Supreme Court found such conduct to represent unreasonable restrains on trade and violation of the Sherman Act, and stated that, to be considered pro-competitive, private standard-setting programs should be based on the merits of objective expert judgment and follow procedures that prevent standards development processes from being biased by members with economic interests in stifling competition. Remarkably, the Court also held that "statutory adoption of private standard does not determine whether that private entity's conduct is immune from the antitrust laws."[76]

On a number of occasions, the conduct of SDO's members was found not to violate the provisions of the Sherman Act. For instance, when the Open Software Foundation (OSF), an SDO entrusted with developing an alternative UNIX operating system (OFT-1),[77] did not select an expensive and complex software offered by a security software developer Adamaxx to be included in the standard, both the District Court and the Circuit Court agreed that under the rule of reason and on the facts, Adamaxx's loss was not caused by the conduct of the SDO; hence the OSF was not found to be excluding competitors and creating monopsony. In the famous *Golden Bridge* line of cases, lawsuits were filed against members of the 3rd Generation Partnership Project (3GPP) who allegedly restricted the 3G standard in such a way that the essential technology of the plaintiff could no longer be included in the standard,

[75] *Allied Tube* v. *Indian Head, Inc.*, 486 US 492 (1988).

[76] The defendant claimed the so-called Noerr–Pennington protection, which rendered concentrated effort to restrain or monopolize trade by petitioning government officials immune from antitrust laws, since the standard was implemented as law; see *Eastern Railroad Presidents Conference* v. *Noerr Motor Freight, Inc.*, 365 US 127, 135 (1961).

[77] *Adamaxx* v. *Open Software Foundation*, No. 97-1807 (1998). The standard ended up being unsuccessful.

which resulted in lost revenues due to the delisting of SEPs.[78] Despite the submitted evidence of members' discussions outside the Technical Committees, the District Court did not establish conspiracy: the decision to remove the plaintiff's technology from a standard was taken at a meeting that Golden Bridge Technology Inc. did not attend, and it was approved without objections of the Working Group members.

It appears that to avoid antitrust liability under §1 of the Sherman Act, SDOs should prevent their processes to be dominated by companies with anticompetitive intent, while also guaranteeing sufficient balance that can be achieved through inclusive, transparent, and consensus-based processes. These procedural requirements were also at stake in *TruePosition* v. *Ericsson*,[79] where TruePosition claimed that its technology was excluded from being adopted into a standard by conspiracy of competitors who held leadership positions in the SDO.

## Procedural Framework

In the US, R&D activities benefit from the so-called "rules of reason" treatment of the National Cooperative Research and Production Act of 1993 (NCRPA),[80] and are found illegal only when "their effect is unreasonably trade restrictive."[81] In 2004, as a result of case law, NCRPA was amended by the Standards Development Organizations Advancement Act of 2004 (SDOAA),[82] which extended the protection of US antitrust laws to SDOs by expanding the scope of the rule of reason to private standards development organizations.[83] Pursuant to this provision, the conduct of these organizations should be judged based on its

[78] See, as an example, *Golden Bridge Technology Inc.* v. *Motorola, Inc.*, 547 F 3d 266 (Fed. Cir. 2008).

[79] See the case study in Chapter 10.

[80] Pursuant to Lundqvist, the NCRPA disincentivizes private plaintiffs and antitrust enforcement agencies to bring to the court companies operating in R&D; Lundqvist, *Standardization under EU Competition Rules*, p. 149.

[81] The agreements on market sharing or price fixing are considered per se illegal; other agreements that may be covered by Sherman act must be analyzed under the rule of reason, see *Addyston Pipe and Steel Co.* v. *United States*, 175 US 211 (1899). Interestingly, the IEEE Business Review Letter of 2007 indicates that the rule of reason treatment will be applied to joint negotiations of licensing terms in the standard-setting context; Lundqvist, *Standardization under EU Competition Rules*, p. 181.

[82] Standards Development Organization Advancement Act of 2004 (2004), Public Law 108–237, 188 Stat. 661 (2002) (hereinafter: SDOAA (2004)).

[83] Section 102(8) of SDOAA (2004). Although private developers of standards used by government seemed to lack antitrust protection, in practice, SDOs were using the NCRPA even before the amendment since the definition of "research" was very wide

reasonableness, taking into account all relevant factors affecting competition with regard to their antitrust liability. The act aimed to address matters related to inclusion of proprietary technology in private voluntary standards, such as the disclosure of IPRs and proposed licensing terms by patents-holders.[84]

The act defines standards development activity as "any action taken by an SDO organization for the purpose of developing, promulgating, revising, amending, reissuing, interpreting, or otherwise maintaining a voluntary consensus standard, or using such standard in conformity assessment activities, *including actions relating to the intellectual property policies of the standards development organization*" (emphasis added).[85] This definition is remarkable because it clearly addresses the policy-making of SDOs, albeit only in the context of IPR policies.[86] The SDOAA (2004) excludes from the definition of "standards development activities" any practices of information exchange, price-fixing, or market-sharing[87] (presumably due to their clear anticompetitive intention). The act further provides that the policies and procedures of an SDO must fulfil the set of due process requirements, such as openness, balance of interests, due process, an appeals process, and consensus, which should be incorporated in a manner consistent with the OMB Circular.[88] The wording of the SDOAA (2004) suggests that an organization that does not comply with the mentioned principles, is not considered an SDO within the meaning of the SDOAA, and, hence, cannot benefit from the rule of reason treatment.

### *Unilateral Conduct and Abuse of Power in the US*

The Antitrust Division of the Department of Justice (DoJ) addressed the issue of SEP disclosure in its Business Review Letter to VMEbus International Trade Association (VITA),[89] where it analyzed VITA's

and could cover activities of SDOs; Lundqvist, *Standardization under EU Competition Rules*, p. 151. Note that the SDOAA did not extend to the conduct of SDOs' members.

84 See Rubin, 'Patents, antitrust and rivalry'.

85 Section 103(7) of SDOAA (2004).

86 Although this might also be viewed as a possibility to exclude IPR agreements from antitrust laws; Lundqvist, *Standardization under EU Competition Rules*, p. 153.

87 Section 103(c) of SDOAA (2004).

88 Ibid., section 103(8).

89 When asking for a Business Review Letter (BRL), firms or SDOs can ask the Antitrust Division of the US Justice Department if the proposed modifications or joint ventures

proposed Patent Policy requiring Members of standardization groups to state minimum royalties and the most restrictive additional terms for essential patent claims, and to allow royalty-free licensing of essential patents in case a patent-owner fails to disclose it or to declare the most restrictive licensing terms.[90] To that end, the DoJ recalled the necessity to preserve competition and to avoid unreasonable patent licensing terms, and recognized that disputes over IPR licensing can delay adoption and implementation of a standard.[91] By the same token, the DoJ welcomed modifications of the IEEE Patent Policy in 2007,[92] which allowed public disclosure and commitment to most restrictive licensing terms, including maximum royalty rates, and stated that the commitments demonstrated in the Letters of Assurance (LoA)[93] were binding for future patent-holders and their (nonmember) affiliates, unless specifically excluded. The subsequent modifications of the Institute's Patent Policy in 2015, which, inter alia, recommended a method of calculation of FRAND royalty rates and significantly limited the possibilities of SEP holders to seek injunctive relief, was likewise approved by the Antitrust Division.[94]

The US Federal Trade Commission (FTC) conducted a great share of investigations related to monopolization as a result of licensing practices under § 2 of the Sherman Act and § 5 of the FTC Act, prohibiting unfair or deceptive competition practices. For instance, the FTC alleged that Dell was concealing its rights for technologies to be included in the VL-bus standard, prepared by the Video Electronics Standards Association (VESA), during the process of standards development, and subsequently claiming its patented rights from standards implementers.[95] The FTC

would constitute a violation of US antitrust laws. The DoJ is not bound by the letters and may still proceed with investigations in the future.

90 DoJ, Response to Vmebus International Trade Association (VITA)'s request for business review letter (October 30, 2006), available at www.justice.gov/atr/response-vmebus-international-trade-association-vitas-request-business-review-letter. The BRL considered VITA policy a sensible effort to address standard-setting challenges.

91 Ibid.

92 DoJ, Response to the Institute of Electrical and Electronics Engineers, Inc.'s request for business review letter (April 30, 2007), available at www.justice.gov/atr/response-institute-electrical-and-electronics-engineers-incs-request-business-review-letter.

93 An LoA is a document stating the submitter's position with respect to ownership, enforcement, or licensing of a (potential) SEP; see section 6.1 of IEEE-SA Standards Board Bylaws.

94 Business Review Letter to the Institute of Electrical and Electronics Engineers (February 2, 2015), available at www.justice.gov/atr/response-institute-electrical-and-electronics-engineers-incorporated.

95 Dell Computer Corp., 121 FTC 616, 618 (1996).

established that since VESA favored standards that do not embed any proprietary technology, it would have implemented a different nonproprietary design if Dell had timely disclosed its patents.[96] The case ended with a settlement prohibiting Dell to enforce its SEP for the VL-bus standard and restricting it from claiming its patented rights for any patents included in a standard if it intentionally failed to disclose those.[97] Similarly, the FTC accused RE Union Oil Company of California (Unocal) of not disclosing its pending applications for patents that could be essential for the implementation of the emission standards adopted by the California Air Resources Board (CARB), and by this means monopolizing the production and supply of gasoline under the given standard.[98]

The next one in line in patent ambush case law was the *Rambus* case, where the FTC, similar to the European Commission, accused Rambus Incorporated of not disclosing its essential technologies in standard-setting processes of JEDEC and even evading questions concerning its patent portfolio or patents that might be relevant for the proposed standard.[99] The FTC found that Rambus' actions were deceptive in the context of a duty of good faith arising from JEDEC's policies, and constrained Rambus' royalties.[100] Equivalent allegations have been made against Qualcomm's failure to disclose its allegedly "reasonably

[96] Press Release, 'Dell Computer settles FTC charges' (November 2, 1995), available at www.ftc.gov/news-events/press-releases/1995/11/dell-computer-settles-ftc-charges.

[97] Ibid.

[98] See the documents available at www.ftc.gov/enforcement/cases-proceedings/0110214/unionoil-company-california-matter. Remarkably, the FTC did not agree with the claim that since CARB was a state agency, its actions could be immunized under the Noerr–Pennington doctrine, and suggested that false petitioning involving misrepresentation in governmental communications loses this protection when "petitioning occurs outside the political area, the misrepresentation is deliberate, factually verifiable and central to the outcome of the proceedings of case, and it is possible to demonstrate and remedy this effect without undermining the integrity of the deceived governmental entity"; see Press Release, 'FTC reinstates complaint of unfair methods of competition against Unocal' (July 7, 2004), available at www.ftc.gov/news-events/press-releases/2004/07/ftc-reinstates-complaint-unfair-methods-competition-against-unocal.

[99] FTC, 'FTC Issues complaint against Rambus, Inc. Deception of standard-setting organization violated federal law' (June 19, 2002), available at www.ftc.gov/news-events/press-releases/2002/06/ftc-issues-complaint-against-rambus-inc.

[100] See FTC Docket No. 9302 Opinion of the Commission in the Matter of Rambus Inc. (August 2, 2006). However, the DC Circuit found that there was not enough evidence to prove that a different technology would have been selected had Rambus disclosed its patents and, interestingly, that the actions of Rambus invited competitors to enter the market and compete; see US Court of Appeals of DC Circuit, No. 07-1086, *Rambus Incorporated* v. *Federal Trade Commission* (April 22, 2008).

necessary"[101] patents in JVT: Qualcomm's conduct was found inconsistent with the expectations of disclosure among the JVT's members and with an affirmative duty of the SDO's policy to disclose relevant patents, with a consequence that its patents were declared unenforceable.[102] Remarkably, both Rambus and Qualcomm claimed the IPR Policies of the SDOs to be unclear regarding the disclosure obligation. Subsequent investigations against Google/MMI ended in settlement, preventing these companies from seeking injunctions against licensees willing to enter FRAND licensing agreement,[103] unless the licensees refuse to engage in negotiation process, introducing the specific procedures purposed at protecting the interests of potential licensees willing to negotiate on FRAND terms.[104]

A landmark decision on injunctive relief was issued by the US Supreme Court in *eBay*.[105] Prior to this judgment, liability-rule protection for patented technologies was subject to FRAND commitments undertaken in SDOs.[106] In *eBay*, the Court held that injunctive relief cannot be awarded to the patent-holder merely as a consequence of a patent infringement, unless the patent-holder demonstrates that they have: (1) suffered an irreparable injury; (2) that the available legal remedies are inadequate to compensate for that injury; (3) that injunctions are necessary to balance the hardships between the patent-holders and the infringer; (4) and that public interest would not be disserved by a permanent injunction: in other words, the Court used a traditional four-factor test to determine whether an injunction should be issued. On this occasion, some have argued that patent-holders should not be awarded

[101] United States Courts of Appeals for the Federal Circuit, *Qualcomm Inc.* v. *Broadcom Corp.* (March 21, 2007).

[102] Ibid.

[103] Press Release, 'Google agrees to change its business practices to resolve FTC competition concerns in the markets for devices like smart phones, games and tablets, and in online search landmark agreements will give competitors access to standard-essential patents; advertisers will get more flexibility to use rival search engines' (January 3, 2013), available at www.ftc.gov/news-events/press-releases/2013/01/google-agrees-change-its-business-practices-resolve-ftc.

[104] See Geradin, 'The European Commission policy'.

[105] *eBay Inc.* v. *MercExchange, LLC*, 547 US 388 (2006).

[106] For a discussion of the legal background to generate such a liability rule, see D. H. Ginsburg, T. M. Owings and J. D. Wright, 'Enjoining injunctions: the case against antitrust liability for standard essential patent holders who seek injunctions' (2014) 14 *The Antitrust Source* 1–7.

injunctive relief, since they are likely to have access to other effective remedies for infringements.[107]

The US Courts have also ruled on calculation of FRAND royalties: in the dispute between Microsoft and Motorola on royalties for WLAN and video compression technology standard, the District Court for the Western District of Washington stated that FRAND royalties should reflect SDOs' goal of promoting the widespread adoption of a standard and address the risks of patent holdup and royalty stacking, while ensuring that the patent-holder is remunerated not based on the economic value of patented technology, but for the value associated with the incorporation of that technology into a standard.[108] In *TCL* v. *Ericsson*, a long-standing licensing dispute on SEPs related to 2G, 3G, and 4G specifications, the District Court for the Central District of California calculated FRAND-based royalties by using both the "top-down" approach and comparing licenses of "similarly situated" companies. The Court also noted that differences in royalty rates offered to potential licensees are not justified by differences in sale volumes alone, giving its interpretation to the "nondiscriminatory" element of FRAND commitment.[109]

[107] See, for instance, R. Hesse, Remarks as prepared for the Global Competition Review (GCR) Live IP & Antitrust USA Conference, 'A year in the life of the joint DOJ-PTO Policy Statement on Remedies for F/RAND Encumbered Standards-Essential Patents' (March 25, 2014), available at www.justice.gov/atr/file/517771/download; who refers to the decision in *Innovatio IP Ventures, LLC* Patent Litig., 921 F. Supp. 2d 903 (ND Ill. 2013) and notes that since *eBay* does not apply to the International Trade Commission (ITC), which can still issue exclusion order, there is potential divergence between how federal courts and the ITC remedy infringements of FRAND.

[108] *Microsoft Corp.* v. *Motorola Inc.*, 2:10-cv-01823-JLR, 871 F. Supp. 2d 1089 (WD Wash. 2012).

[109] *TCL Comm'n* v. *Ericsson*, C.A. No. 14-CV-341 (C.D. Cal. December 21, 2017).

# 6

# Procedural Principles for Standardization

While there are differences and similarities in how SDOs, and in particular SDOs in the ICT sector, are treated in WTO, EU, and US law, each regulatory framework generally appears to maintain a similar set of procedural requirements for SDOs to adhere to. The definition of these requirements, as well as their precision and elaborateness sometimes differ per framework. At the same time, it is not uncommon for the legal instruments to reference one another: for example, SDOAA (2004) resorts to the principles of the OMB Circular,[1] and Regulation 1025/2011 cites the WTO principles for standardization. Procedural requirements of these frameworks are thus inevitably interlinked and necessitate a holistic analysis that will distil the relevant principles from the applicable legal instruments and examine their fitness for the ecosystem of ICT standardization.

## Historical Background

Governance of standard-setting processes was relevant already at the outset of Western standardization in the nineteenth century. In Europe, technical committees where standards were originally developed, were designed to balance the membership of producers, users, consumers, and nonaffiliate participants, and to reach consensus on the technical documents.[2] The standardization processes in these committees aimed to consider all voices before taking the decision, and in a way resembled "deliberative democracy"; from outside, however, the process remained rather technocratic, with expert knowledge being a prerequisite to be included onto the committees.[3] One of the first mentioning of a

[1] Interestingly, unlike the US instruments, two EU instruments do not refer to each other.

[2] J. Yates and C. N. Murphy, *Engineering Rules: Global Standard Setting since 1880* (Baltimore: John Hopkins University Press, 2019), p. 9.

[3] Ibid.

comprehensive set of standardization principles in Europe was reported in 1917 and pertained to the work of the Engineering Standards Committee (ESC), the predecessor of the BSI: these principles included representation of all interested parties; voluntary adoption of standards and voluntary service on technical committees; clear demand for standardization; practical, engineering, and commercial orientation; and regular standards revision.[4] DIN added the principles of consistency and scientific integrity of the standardization process, which also meant that all interested stakeholders should be involved.[5]

In turn, the US embraced the principles of voluntary consensus standardization as a response to industry's reluctance to otherwise adopt nongovernmental standards: to address this weakness, technical committees and societies emerged from a mixture of technical, institutional, and cultural forces.[6] Since support of a strong network of manufacturers and buyers was crucial for such voluntary standards to survive, technical committees accepted engineers and managers form all interested parties.[7] In the beginning of the twentieth century, procedural principles for standards development have been codified by a number of organizations: the International Association for Testing Materials (IATM), the predecessor of the American Society for Testing and Materials (ASTM), was governed by the principle of balance, including balancing technical and economic consideration;[8] the American Standards Association (ASA) emphasized the principle of consensus.[9] Subsequently, the US evolution of private standardization seemed to shift SDOs towards an "OpenStand" movement in certain standardization sectors,[10] while the concept of openness remained ambiguous.[11] On both sides of the Atlantic, the

[4] Ibid., pp. 60–2.

[5] Ibid.

[6] A. L. Russel, *Open Standards and the Digital Age: History, Ideology, and Networks* (New York: Cambridge University Press, 2014), p. 43.

[7] Ibid.

[8] Yates and Murphy, *Engineering Rules*, pp. 60–2.

[9] Russel, *Open Standards and the Digital Age*, p. 279.

[10] The movement gained prominence in the internet and web standardization, where it refers either to the process of standards creation or to the royalty-free SDO IPR policies. C. B. Biddle, 'No standards for standards: understanding the ICT standards-development ecosystem', in J. L. Contreras (ed.), *The Cambridge Handbook of Technical Standardization Law: Competition, Antitrust and Patents* (Cambridge: Cambridge University Press, 2018), p. 21. Due to the limited scope of application and lack of legal basis, the OpenStand principles are not further discussed in this book.

[11] Russel, *Open Standards and the Digital Age*, p. 279, suggesting that by the time the importance of open systems was realized by internet engineers, openness was attributed

requirements of due process and consideration of all views mainly aimed to prevent dominance in standardization processes as well as to ensure that a standard is not adopted over the objections of stakeholders.[12] These procedural principles were taken up by other national SDOs and were institutionalized with the further evolvement of NSOs and increased globalization of standards development. Actors establishing the initial principles of due process were a rather small community of Western engineers:[13] modern standardization, however, involves a broader range of actors, and the rules governing standardization are also prescribed by lawyers and politicians.

Against this backdrop, this section examines the procedural principles introduced in the regulatory frameworks, to which it will collectively refer as "*due process*" *principles*. While previous studies of standardization processes analyzed each procedural framework separately, this research follows a different approach, and aims to review the principles holistically and in the context of ICT standardization. As a starting point, this section takes the principles of the WTO framework, referenced in both the US and EU, and considers how these principles are implemented in the national and competition law frameworks, discussing also those principles that do not stem from the TBT instruments.

## Analyzing Due Process Principles for Standards Development

### *Transparency*

In a multilateral trading system, transparency facilitates harmonization and coherence of technical requirements across the WTO Members. The general provision on transparency in standardization activities, Article 2.9 of the TBT Agreement, is implemented by the TBT Committee Decision (2000), which specifies steps to be taken by ISBs to achieve greater transparency, such as publishing of work programs,[14] notifying standardization activities, allowing access to the relevant information *at*

with political, economic, technical, and cultural meaning, and linking the openness in standardization with the concept of "openness" in US politics.

12 Yates and Murphy, *Engineering Rules*, pp. 60–2; Russel, *Open Standards and the Digital Age*, p. 56.

13 See historical overview of the main actors in Yates and Murphy, *Engineering Rules*.

14 The Seventh Triennial Review elaborates on this requirement; see Committee on Technical Barriers to Trade, Seventh Triennial Review of the Operation and Implementation of the Agreement on Technical Barriers to Trade Under Article 15.4 (November 6, 2015) WTO Doc. G/TBT/37, para. 4. See also the parallel requirement for

*least* to the interested parties, and providing opportunities to comment on standards' drafts (note that no clarification as to which parties are to be considered as "interested" is provided).[15] When publishing their working programs or (draft) standards, ISBs should consider the technical means available in different countries.[16] ISO/IEC Guide 59 (2019) further specifies that when national bodies develop standards or contribute to international standardization work, they should provide sufficient and updated information and maintain appropriately documented procedures.[17] Together with the draft standards, these documents should be freely available for any *stakeholder* (meaning, according to the Guide 59 (2019), all those that can affect, be affected, or perceive to be affected by the particular standardization activity); all other draft documents should be received by *participants* (those involved in standards development.[18]

The Code of Good Practice clarifies that a copy of a draft standard should be provided in a nondiscriminatory manner to any interested party requesting it (and not only to "all Members of an ISB" as it is the case with international bodies),[19] and that an "adequate period of time" for submitting comments amounts to at least sixty days.[20] A notice of the period for commenting should ideally state whether a standard deviates from the relevant international standard;[21] the necessity of this deviation shall be explained in responses to the comments of those SDOs that accepted the Code of Good Practice.[22] Furthermore, the working program of an SDO should be published on SDOs' website (and, for ISBs, the websites of the ISO/IEC Information Center) at least every six months,[23] and a standard should be promptly published upon its adoption.[24] In recent years, a number of steps have been taken by the TBT Committee to facilitate Members' implementation of the principle of transparency: examples include strengthening of the TBT Notification

standards bodies in the Code of Good Practice Annex 3(J) of TBT Agreement and Article 4.2.6 of ISO/IEC Guide 59 (2019).

15 Annex 4, para. B (4) of TBT Committee Decision (2000).
16 Ibid., Annex 4, para. B (3).
17 Articles 4.2.1, 4.2.2 and 4.2.5 of ISO/IEC Guide 59 (2019).
18 Ibid., Articles 3.5, 3.7 and 4.2.4.
19 Annex 3(M) and (P) of TBT Agreement.
20 Ibid., Annex 3(L).
21 Ibid.
22 Ibid., Annex 3(N).
23 Ibid., Annex 3(J). See further Seventh Triennial Review (2015), para. 4.
24 Annex 3(O) of TBT Agreement.

Submission System (TBT NSS), exchanging regional experiences, and improving the functioning of TBT enquiry points.[25]

Transparency also sits at the center of procedural requirements stipulated by the EU. Regulation 1025/2012 requires ESOs and NSOs to ensure transparency of their standards and standards development processes by using publicly available working programs that contain information on preparation and amendment of standards; exchanging draft documents; and providing interested parties with opportunities for commenting on prospective deliverables,[26] in fact, linking transparency to institutional cooperation among ESOs and NSOs. In this regard, ESOs and NSOs are encouraged to provide online user-friendly mechanisms to submit comments, as well as to enhance the access to their activities by supporting virtual meetings or web-conferencing.[27] ESOs should also annually report to the Commission on a number of issues, including representation of stakeholders and cooperation among NSOs and ESOs.[28] Annex II of the Regulation (2012) fine-tunes the principle of transparency for ICT standards and provides that SDOs should document all information on technical discussions, announce new standardization activity through suitable and accessible means, seek participation of all relevant stakeholders,[29] and ensure that comments of interested parties are considered and addressed.[30] Horizontal Guidelines (2011) further mention that standardization platforms should implement procedures informing stakeholders in "good time" of ongoing, finalized, and future standardization work at each stage of standards development.[31]

Similar to the TBT framework, where the role of "notifications hub" is entrusted to the ISO and the WTO TBT facility, Regulation 1025/2012 provides that notifications of NSOs and informal SDOs whose standards may be used by the Commission for procurement purposes should be submitted to the ESOs.[32] Yet, where Regulation 1025/2012 obliges

[25] Committee on Technical Barriers to Trade, Eighth Triennial Review of the Operation and Implementation of the Agreement on Technical Barriers to Trade under Article 15.4 (November 9, 2018) WTO Doc. G/TBT/41, paras. 6.1 and 7.

[26] Articles 3 and 4 of EU Regulation 1025/2012.

[27] Ibid., Rec. 18.

[28] Ibid., Article 24.

[29] It has been suggested that "stakeholders" can be business or professional associations, consumers, States, and NGOs; van Leeuwen, *European Standardization of Services*, p. 19.

[30] Annex II. 3(c) of EU Regulation 1025/2012.

[31] Horizontal Guidelines (2011), para. 282.

[32] In practice, that implies that NSOs would need to notify the WTO TBT facility, ISO and ESOs.

SDOs to make their work programs publicly available,[33] TBT Committee Decision does not speak in terms of "public availability," but rather, "easy accessibility" of information regarding SDOs' current work programs.

In the US regulatory framework, transparency applies both to federal agencies, which should announce their participation in standardization activities related to the issues of national priority or (international) regulation,[34] and to SDOs, which should notify their work on current and new standards and make written procedures available to all stakeholders.[35] In a similar vein, requirements to notify all parties affected by the particular standardization activity and to allow access to information are laid down in the SDOAA (2004).[36] Other elements of transparency are encapsulated in the ANSI's principle of "openness" and include providing information on parties' affiliation and notifying stakeholders of particular development activities.[37]

### *Openness and Participation*

Related to transparency is the principle of participation or openness. The TBT Committee Decision (2000) provides that open and unrestricted participation in international standardization should be guaranteed at all levels of standard-setting (namely, proposals of new work items, technical discussions, submission of comments, standards review, voting, standards adoption, and dissemination)[38] and *policy development* (emphasis added).[39] However, pursuant to the wording of the Decision, the requirement to ensure that participation is also *meaningful*[40]

[33] Article 3.3 of EU Regulation 1025/2012.

[34] Section 6(e) of OMB Circular.

[35] Sections 1.5, 1.9 and 2.5 of ANSI Essential Requirements (2022). Note that ANSI refers directly to notification requirements and not to the notion of transparency. Specific procedures apply to project initiation notifications, including notifying ANSI and providing public review.

[36] Section 102 of SDOAA (2004).

[37] Section 2.1 of ANSI Essential Requirements (2022).

[38] Note that these stages are defined differently by ISO/IEC Guide 59 (2019): proposal and acceptance of new work items; technical discussion on proposal; submission of comments on drafts; review of existing standards; resolution of comments and approval of standards and availability of approved standards, Article 4.3.1 of ISO/IEC Guide 59 (2019).

[39] Annex 4, para. C (6) of TBT Committee Decision (2000).

[40] In terms of administrative law requirements, this can be equated with "decisional" participation, or participation that allows to change the outcome of the decision-making processes.

(emphasis added) applies only to standards development.[41] In turn, ISO/IEC Guide 59 (2019) limits the scope of openness to "all stages of the standards development process," noting that such participation should be on a nondiscriminatory basis to all stakeholders.[42] It is then up to national bodies to facilitate inclusive participation of all stakeholders, also those who are potentially underrepresented, without imposing undue membership barriers, as well as to ensure availability of documents and procedures necessary for participation.[43] The Code of Good Practice further specified that participation of SDOs that have signed the Code in international standardization efforts should preferably occur through one delegation per WTO Member.[44]

In the EU standardization ecosystem, participation is built on openness, equality, and meaningful opportunities to express one's position and have it considered. Regulation 1025/2012 stipulates that ESOs should ensure effective participation of all affected stakeholders, particularly those representing social interests or a particular group;[45] public authorities; and medium-sized enterprises,[46] both at the policy development level and at various stages of standards development (i.e., standardization proposal, technical deliberations, submission of comments, and revision processes).[47] The word "effective" may suggest that the degree of participation sought by the Regulation implies actual involvement in decision-making; at the same time, the Regulation (2012) clarifies that "effective participation" does not entail that stakeholders be granted voting rights for (all) standardization activities/standardization phases, unless those rights are provided by the procedural framework of ESOs[48] (to compare, ANSI states that *unreasonable* restriction of voting rights precludes participation.)[49] In the case of ICT standards, Annex II of the Regulation (2012) highlights with regard to participation that technical specifications should be developed based on open decision-making, which is accessible to all interested parties in the market affected by

41 Annex 4, para. C (7) of TBT Committee Decision (2000).
42 Article 4.3.1 of ISO/IEC Guide 59 (2019).
43 Ibid., Articles 4.3.2, 4.3.3, 4.3.4, and 4.3.5.
44 Annex 3(G) of TBT Agreement.
45 Rec. 17 and 24 of EU Regulation 1025/2012.
46 Ibid., Articles 5, 6, and 7. Participation of underrepresented stakeholders is also mentioned by Article 4.3.3 of ISO/IEC Guide 59 (2019).
47 Article 5(1) of EU Regulation 1025/2012.
48 Ibid., Rec. 23.
49 Sections 1.1 and 2.1 of ANSI Essential Requirements (2022).

those specifications.[50] Naturally, where ESOs operate on the basis of national delegation, the duty to involve all relevant actors lies upon NSOs.[51] Horizontal Guidelines (2011) add to the EU regulatory framework that SDOs should implement the principle of participation via objective and nondiscriminatory distribution of voting rights, in particular as regards to the processes of technology selection.[52] Opportunities to take part in standards development should be granted to all competitors in the relevant market(s) and – where the work of SDO concerns de facto industry standard – also to third parties.

Pursuant to the OMB Circular (2016), standards development processes should be open to interested parties and provide them with meaningful opportunities to participate on a nondiscriminatory basis.[53] Similar to Regulation 1025/2012, the Circular (2016) addresses participation of governmental actors, noting that the engagement of agencies in activities of SDOs does not imply their endorsement of SDOs' decisions.[54] At the same time, agency representatives should be able to participate in all relevant discussions of SDOs on an equal basis with other members, including voting and serving in official capacities, unless precluded by law or the agency itself.[55] In the earlier version of the Circular, the principle of openness was explained as "providing meaningful opportunities to participate *at all stages* of standards development."[56] During the revision of the OMB Circular, however, many commenters voiced concerns that the providing participation "at all stages" may burden the work of SDOs while, as a practical matter, this requirement was already implemented by the principle of transparency. Accordingly, the sentence was replaced by "providing meaningful opportunities to participate *on a non-discriminatory basis*"[57] (note that the language of the EU suggests "effective participation" of "all affected stakeholders," and does not as such mention nondiscrimination).

[50] Article 5 and Annex II. 3(a) of EU Regulation 1025/2012.

[51] Ibid., Articles 6 and 7.

[52] Horizontal Guidelines (2011), para. 281.

[53] Section 2(e)(j) of OMB Circular.

[54] Ibid., section 6(d).

[55] Ibid.

[56] Which mirrors the principle of "openness" of the TBT Committee Decision. Note also the similarities with the wording of Article 4.3.1 of ISO/IEC Guide 59 (2019).

[57] OMB Circular, at p. 9. Note that the "all stages" requirement is still present in ISO/IEC Guide 59, alongside with the requirement to participate on a nondiscriminatory basis; Article 4.3.1 of ISO/IEC Guide 59 (2019).

In turn, ANSI's explanation of participation encapsulates the principle of transparency, while clarifying that participation in standards development and approval processes should be open for all directly and materially affected stakeholders (which is closer to the wording of the EU Regulation), without undue financial barriers or unreasonably restricted voting membership.[58] SDOAA (2004) is limited to the requirement that all procedural principles, including openness, should be applied also to all SDOs' standardization activities and "actions relating to the IPR policies."[59]

It comes as no surprise that both US and EU frameworks address governmental agencies' participation in (national) SDOs: after all, standards may be used for regulatory and policy purposes at both sides of the Atlantic, so keeping governments informed of and engaged in industry activity is advantageous both for the public and private sector. Neither do the restrictions imposed on voting rights seem unreasonable: in a narrow, specialized technical field, increased participation may dissipate the effectiveness of technical processes, cause breakdowns in experts' negotiations,[60] or unnecessarily prolong technical deliberations, which in turn threatens the effectiveness of a standard. What is astonishing is that none of the frameworks explain what should be understood under the term "policy development" – even though the TBT Committee Decision and Regulation 1025/2012 accurately define standards development stages. And while SDOAA (2004) seems to limit its scope to SDOs' IPR policies, it is unclear whether those are covered by the TBT Committee Decision, especially given the fact that the TBT Agreement is silent on the intellectual property issues related to standards. Likewise, any requirements for standards' accessibility and understandability, an important component of their throughput legitimacy,[61] in the context of openness, are also absent from the regulatory frameworks.

### *Consensus, Impartiality, and Balance*

Consensus is the cornerstone of private voluntary standardization. As stipulated in ISO/IEC Guide 2 (2004), a standard is by definition

[58] Sections 1.1 and 2.1 of ANSI Essential Requirements (2022).
[59] Section 103(1)(7) SDOAA (2004).
[60] Stasavage, 'Open-door or closed-door?', p. 50.
[61] Senden, 'Towards a more holistic legitimacy approach', p. 35.

established by consensus,[62] which the Guide defines as a "general agreement characterized by the absence of sustained opposition to substantial issues by any important part of the concerned interests and by a process that involves seeking to take into account the views of all parties concerned and to reconcile any conflicting arguments," but that "does not imply unanimity."[63] Some regulatory frameworks, however, employ consensus together with the requirements of impartiality or even balance, purposed at avoiding dominance of particular (group of) interests;[64] "balance of interests" is then different from "integration of interests," which rather falls under the principle of openness.

The principle of consensus is crucial for defining a standard and establishing the coverage of the TBT Agreement.[65] When referring to consensus-based standards, the TBT Committee Decision (2000) further develops the requirement of meaningful opportunities, emphasizing that standards development processes should not privilege or favor particular interests, and that consensus procedures should seek to consider the views of all parties concerned and reconcile any conflicting arguments.[66] In this context, all standards development processes should guarantee impartiality.[67] The fact that impartiality and consensuses are merged into one principle invites an assumption that for international standardization, consensus only serves as a safeguard of impartiality during the preparation of standards. In addition, due attention has to be paid to the difference in the wording: whereas impartiality "*should be* accorded," consensus process "should *seek to take into account* the views of all parties."[68]

[62] Article 3.2 of ISO/IEC Guide 2 (2004).

[63] Ibid., Article 1.7.

[64] The author is aware that there are different views with regard to the concept of balance and dominance in SDOs: for instance, the JRC Report suggests that consensus can impede balance. In its recent intervention, the DoJ stated that consensus decision of an SDO with unbalanced membership may fail to produce a balance of interests. See *NSS Labs, Inc.* v. *Crowdstrike, Inc.*, Case No. 3:18-cv-05711, Statement of Interest of the United States (ND Cal., filed June 26, 2019). See also J. L. Contreras, 'Understanding "balance" requirement for standards-development organizations' (2019) 2 *CPI Antitrust Chronicle* 1–16.

[65] See Chapter 3.

[66] TBT Committee Decision (2000), Annex 4, para. D (8).

[67] Ibid. para. D (9).

[68] Compare Annex 4, paras. D (8) and (9) of TBT Committee Decision (2000). Perhaps this suggests an implicit awareness of the Committee that the consensus-based process is not always attainable.

ISO/IEC Guide 59 (2019) stipulates that impartiality should be accorded with respect to the access to participation in work, submission of comments on drafts, considerations of views and comments, decision-making through consensus, obtaining information and documents, availability of drafts and approved standards, adopting ISO/IEC standards as regional or national standard, and standards' revision.[69] It further elaborates that national bodies should conduct their work in a consensual and impartial manner, meaning that no party is favored over another and no stakeholder (category) dominates the processes,[70] and should prefer consensus over voting and document its standpoints and decisions.[71] To contribute to the requirement of balance of interests, Guide 59 (2019) suggests categorization of stakeholders and participants according to the broad area of interests, and assessing the relevance of these categories in the context of standards development projects.[72] The governance structure of national bodies should support neutrality, independency, and impartiality regarding specific interests of the participants, and should invite its participants to build consensus: to that end, the Guide offers some suggestions on how NSO leadership, while acting impartially in the discussion and the normative work on standards,[73] should deal with objections or "sustained opposition" which, the Guide notes, cannot be interpreted as a right to veto; interestingly, Guide 59 (2019) specifically notes the effort-based character of this requirement: "the obligation to address the sustained opposition does not imply an obligation to successfully resolve it."[74] With regard to behavioral independency, national bodies should, among other things, allow their governing bodies and staff to behave independently from those financing standardization projects:[75] these requirements render the updated ISO/IEC Guide 59 (2019) the only procedural instrument so far that addresses the independence and impartiality of leadership positions.

The Code of Good Practice only refers to consensus in the context of "coherence," suggesting SDOs within the territory of a Member make

[69] Article 4.4.1 of ISO/IEC Guide 59 (2019).

[70] Ibid., Article 4.4.2.

[71] Ibid., Article 4.4.4(c)(d). Note that the latter also concerns the requirement of transparency.

[72] Since not all categories are relevant to all standards projects, Article 4.4.5 of ISO/IEC Guide 59 (2019).

[73] Ibid.

[74] Articles 4.4.3 and 4.4.4(b) of ISO/IEC Guide 59 (2019).

[75] Ibid., Article 4.4.6.

*every effort* to achieve a national consensus on standards they develop.[76] As in the Committee Decision, the principle of consensus is formulated as a "best effort" requirement, rather than an obligation.

Regulation 1025/2012 highlights the importance to have collaborative and consensus-driven decision-making processes that do not favor any particular stakeholder. Consensus is only defined in the context of ICT standards as not implying unanimity, but an achievement of the general agreement by seeking to take into account the views of all parties concerned and to reconcile conflicting arguments; consensus is typically reached when there is an absence of sustained opposition to substantial issues by affected stakeholders.[77] In this regard, impartiality for ICT standards should be viewed in the light of scientific technological development: standards should be neutral and stable and should not distort the market or impede competition and innovation.[78] The principle of balance is mentioned as a goal of participation of all relevant categories of interested parties, rather than a separate principle.[79]

As noted earlier, the US framework endorses standards that are based on consensus, which already appears from NTTAA's and Circular's references to "voluntary consensus standards" and "voluntary consensus standards bodies." The OMB Circular (2016) defines consensus as a general agreement, but not necessarily unanimity, and notes that consensus-building implies consideration of comments and objections in a fair, impartial, open, and transparent process.[80] ANSI adds that in order to comply with the essential requirement of consensus, an effort should be made to resolve all expressed disagreements and that the evidence of consensus should be documented,[81] and clarifies that procedures on how consensus should be determined is a matter of SDOs' governance. The Circular further requires SDOs to preserve standards development processes that are balanced, provide a meaningful engagement from a broad range of parties, and ensure that no single interest dominates the decision-making.[82] This terminology is rather simplified as opposed to "balance of interests" or "balance of representation" in the

[76] Annex 3(H) of the TBT Agreement.

[77] This definition of consensus is mentioned with regard to ICT standards; see Annex II, 3 (b) of EU Regulation 1025/2012.

[78] Annex II (4)(e) of EU Regulation 1025/2012.

[79] Ibid., Annex II (3)(c)(iii).

[80] Section 2(e)(v) of OMB Circular.

[81] Sections 1.7, 2.6, and 2.7 of ANSI Essential Requirements (2022).

[82] Section 2(e)(ii) of OMB Circular.

earlier versions of the Circular, as well as in the ANSI Essential Requirements (2019) or the SDOAA (2004), and probably aims to avoid confusion and allow certain flexibility to determine balance during standards development procedures.[83]

ANSI concurs that standards development processes should (strive to) have a balance between different interest categories. The criteria for balance provide that for SDOs establishing safety-related standards, no single interest category may constitute more than 1/3 of the membership, whereas for SDOs dealing with other types of standards, no single interest category may constitute a majority of the membership.[84] Moreover, interest categories should be discretely defined by SDOs and cover all materially affected parties.[85] ANSI also emphasizes lack of dominance by any single interest category, individual, or organization, meaning exclusion of other considerations due to the leverage, strength, or representation of a dominant stakeholder (group).[86] In general, no test for dominance is required, except when the dominance is claimed in writing by a directly and materially affected party.[87]

### *Effectiveness and Relevance*

Under the TBT Committee Decision, the principles of effectiveness and relevance provide positive and negative obligations for ISBs. Positive obligations imply that standards should respond to regulatory and market needs, be paced to scientific and technological development, and, ideally, be performance-based; the latter is echoed in the Code of Good Practice and thus also applies to SDOs that are not ISBs within the meaning of the TBT Agreement.[88] ISO/IEC Guide 59 (2019) adds that standards developed by national bodies should also contribute to advancing trade in the broadest geographical and economic contexts, and focus on user-friendliness.[89] As to negative obligations, standards should not distort the global market, affect fair competition, give preference to certain countries' technical requirements, or impede innovation and

[83] See OMB Circular, at p. 9.
[84] Sections 1.3 and 2.3 of ANSI Essential Requirements (2022).
[85] Ibid., section 2.3.
[86] Ibid., section 1.1.
[87] Ibid., section 2.2.
[88] Annex 4, para. D (11) of TBT Committee Decision (2000) and Annex 3(I) of TBT Agreement.
[89] Articles 4.5.6 and 4.5.7 of ISO/IEC Guide 59 (2019).

technological development, the latter also required from non-ISBs SDOs.[90] In order for their standards to be effective and relevant, ISBs should take into account the requirements of the market, the state of scientific development, and implement procedures for identifying and reviewing standards that are no longer necessary.[91] The fact that these two principles are merged together again opens avenues for assumptions: for instance, the wording of the TBT Committee Decision may suggest that ineffective international standards should also be considered per se irrelevant, or that all relevant standards are effective. The Appellate Body in *EC-Sardines* held that an international standard should be regarded as ineffective and inappropriate for application when it does not accomplish the legitimate objective pursued ("ineffective") and is not specifically suitable for the fulfilment of those legitimate objectives ("inappropriate").[92]

Regulation 1025/2012 notes in Recital 9 that an effective and efficient standardization system requires a flexible and transparent platform for consensus-building between all participants, and that this platform should be financially viable, in a way linking effectiveness with ESOs' financing. It further addresses the principle of relevance in the context of ICT standardization: ICT specification should respond to the needs of the markets as well as to the regulatory requirements,[93] and in this matter are also linked to the principle of coherence. They should further ensure neutrality and stability by being scientifically driven and performance-oriented, but also allowing competition and innovation.[94] Moreover, ICT standards should be of sufficient quality to enable the development of competing implementations and not to be "hidden or controlled" by anyone other than the SDO that established them.[95] Once adopted, ICT standards should remain subject to ongoing support and maintenance, and be publicly available for implementation and use against a reasonable fee, if necessary.[96] Proprietary components essential for

[90] Annex 4, para. D (10) of TBT Committee Decision (2000) and Annex 3(E) of TBT Agreement.

[91] Similar requirement is echoed in Articles 4.5.1 and 4.5.5 of ISO/IEC Guide 59 (2019).

[92] *EC-Sardines*, paras. 259–91. It has also been argued that the difference between effectiveness and appropriateness lies in the fact that the former bears upon the results of the means employed, whereas the latter relates to the nature of the means employed. See Partiti, 'What use of an unloaded gun?', p. 853.

[93] Annex II, 4(d) of EU Regulation 1025/2012.

[94] Ibid., Annex II, 4(e).

[95] Ibid., Annex II, 4(f).

[96] Ibid., Annex II, 4(b).

implementation of these standards should be licensed on FRAND-basis: this also includes licensing without compensation.

To ensure that standards maintain their relevance, the OMB Circular (2016) requires agencies to utilize the retrospective periodic review mechanism,[97] and urges them to collaborate with SDOs in order to consider updates and alternatives to existing standards.[98] As such, ANSI does not address standards' relevance, but mentions coordination and harmonization as tools to resolve potential conflicts between and among existing and future ANSs.[99]

The striking absence of any further elaboration on efficiency and relevance by US and EU frameworks may be explained by the assumption that standards that do not respond to the needs of the market and the society are most likely not to be used by the industry or to be endorsed by governmental agencies as policy tools. In fact, deviation from ineffective and irrelevant standards is not prohibited in these regulatory systems, although may occur at some costs.

### *Coherence and Coordination*

Another principle that facilitates development of effective standards is coherence. Coherence ensures optimal allocation of SDOs' resources, avoids duplications in SDOs' activities, and prevents possible contradiction among standards. To eliminate the existence of conflicting international standards, the TBT Committee Decision (2000) emphasizes the importance of coordination and cooperation between relevant international bodies.[100] In a similar vein, SDOs within the territory of one Member shall strive to achieve a "national consensus" on standards they produce and to avoid duplication and overlap between their work and the work of relevant ISBs.[101] ISO/IEC Guide 59 (2019) introduces the

[97] Those mechanisms are defined in Exec. Order No. 13563, 76 Fed. Reg. 3821 (January 18, 2011) and Exec. Order No. 13610, 81 Fed. Reg. 4213 (May 2, 2010).

[98] See OMB Circular, p. 8.

[99] Sections 1.4 and 2.4 of ANSI Essential Requirements (2022).

[100] Annex 4(D) of TBT Committee Decision (2000). Although it might be suggested that the principle of coherence does not refer to standard and standard-setting processes within a single ISB (i.e., Delimatsis, 'Global standard-setting 2.0', p. 317), it nevertheless guides the policies and communication of that ISB and might affect its decisions in relationship with other organizations.

[101] Annex 3(H) of TBT Agreement. For national bodies developing international standards, see also Articles 4.6.2 and 4.6.4 of ISO/IEC Guide 59 (2019).

requirement of voluntary coordination to comply with within each national body, as well as among national bodies within each country or region.[102] With regard to national standards, Guide 59 (2019) encourages NSOs to adopt flexible policies and procedures to support effective coordination and cooperation with regard to development of national standards,[103] and notes that involvement of public bodies and officials is essential when standards are adopted to support legislation.[104]

Coherence is especially crucial in the EU regulatory framework, since EU standardization does not only influence harmonization of technical requirements, but also consistency in EU policy-making. Coherence in European standardization system is ensured by the so-called "standstill" obligation, which prohibits NSOs to adopt or maintain national standards that contradict their European equivalents.[105] In view of standards relevance to the market, Regulation 1025/2012 also supports regular information exchange between NSOs, ESOs, European stakeholder organizations and the Commission when designing annual standardization programs.[106] In a similar vein, ICT technical specifications should cover domains that are not (yet) subject to European technical harmonization,[107] while remaining "relevant enough" to be implemented by different vendors.

ANSI mentions coordination and harmonization as tools to resolve potential conflicts between and among existing and future ANSs (and thus not within SDOs' areas and scope of work),[108] defining a "conflict" as a situation where the terms of one standard are incompatible with the terms of the other standard and preclude proper implementation of the latter.[109] Such situations should be resolved in "good faith," requiring substantial, thorough, and comprehensive *efforts* (emphasis added) to harmonize the prospective and existing ANSs, and the evidence of compliance with this requirement should be documented.[110] To avoid

[102] Ibid., Article 4.6.1.
[103] Ibid., Article 4.6.6.
[104] Ibid., Article 4.6.7.
[105] Articles 3.5 and 3.6 of EU Regulation 1025/2012.
[106] Ibid., Rec. 27.
[107] Ibid., Annex II, 2.
[108] Sections 1.4 and 2.4 of ANSI Essential Requirements (2022). This conflict is also mentioned in Article 4.6.5 of ISO/IEC Guide 59 (2019).
[109] Section 2.4.1 of ANSI Essential Requirements (2022).
[110] Ibid., section 2.4.2.

duplication of technical requirements and maintain coherence in US standardization environment, Federal, State and local bodies should coordinate with standardization activities of the private sector.[111]

### *Concerns of Developing Countries or "Weaker Parties"*

The fact that effective participation of developing countries is encapsulated in a separate principle in the TBT Committee Decision (2000),[112] and not dealt with under the principle of openness akin to US and EU frameworks addressing the involvement of weaker parties,[113] is no accident, given the mandate of the WTO. Under the TBT Committee Decision (2000), this principle consists of both passive and active elements: it prohibits de facto exclusion of developing countries,[114] and calls upon providing technical assistance for improving their participation – which is echoed in the relevant provisions of the TBT Agreement.[115] Involvement of potentially underrepresented stakeholders and providing access to the relevant information, as well as ensuring that standards contribute to broad geographical context, is also promoted among national bodies by ISO/IEC Guide 59 (2019).[116]

It should be noted, however, that even when set forth by a specific provision, increased involvement of developing countries may have similar flaws as broad participation in general: Western companies often admit fearing the "race to the bottom" and decrease in quality of international standards as a consequence of active involvement of developing countries in SDOs' decision-making. On a positive side of the ledger, participation in global standardization fora provides developing industry with a steep learning curve and in the long run may, eventually, facilitate expansion of multilateral trade.

[111] Section 12(b) of NTTAA 1995.

[112] Annex 4, para. E (13) of TBT Committee Decision.

[113] In this regard, the JRC Report concluded that the interests of underrepresented groups are best served when public authorities look out for the public interest within the current regulatory scheme, following and deepening the previously mentioned procedural and safe harbor approaches; see the JRC Report, p. 17.

[114] It is suggested that this requirement is defined in a negative manner; Delimatsis, 'Global standard-setting 2.0', p. 318.

[115] Article 12 of TBT Agreement.

[116] Articles 4.3, 4.5.6, and 4.7 of ISO/IEC Guide 59 (2019).

### *Appeal and Review*

The OMB Circular (2016) provides that SDOs should incorporate processes for handling procedural appeals.[117] ANSI elaborates that such processes should offer "identifiable, realistic, and readily available appeals mechanism for the impartial handling of procedural appeals regarding any action or inaction,"[118] and shall be available to all parties concerned without imposing an undue burden on them, and consideration of appeals shall be fair and unbiased and fully address the expressed concerns.[119] SDOAA (2004) further stipulates that SDOs should ensure that appeals can be filled by those parties who oppose SDOs' decisions.[120]

The fact that neither the EU nor the WTO framework requires SDOs to maintain appeal or review processes is quite astonishing. Regulation 1025/2012 mentions technical review only in the context of ICT specifications,[121] which leaves the door ajar for SDOs to decide whether they should provide appeal and review procedures for the decision-making processes leading to the adoption of a standard. Indeed, appeal procedures are present in EU standardization through the procedural mechanisms of the three ESOs;[122] yet, the fact that ANSI obliges all SDOs to comply with its Essential Requirements for accreditation purposes encourages a large part of US-based SDOs to introduce appeal and review processes that accommodate stakeholders' procedural and material concerns into their operational framework, which arguably is not the case for SDOs based in the EU. In turn, the updated version of ISO/IEC Guide 59 (2019) suggests that national bodies should implement procedures for responding to enquiries, hearing complaints, and handling appeals that arise from their standardization processes and implementation of the Code of Good Practice;[123] yet, since the Guide does not

[117] Section 2(e)(iv) of OMB Circular.

[118] Section 1.8 of ANSI Essential Requirements (2022).

[119] Ibid., section 2.8.

[120] Section 102(5)(F) SDOAA (2004).

[121] Annex II(4)(a) of EU Regulation 1025/2012.

[122] However, an analysis of CEN/CENELEC appeal procedures reveals lack of transparency of appeal processes. Coccuru and Eliantonio, 'It is not all about judicial review'. Some authors note that while SDOs' appeal processes are not designed to replace judicial review, they are instrumental to the legality of EU standardization processes.

[123] Presumably from the terminology, it means the TBT Code of Good Practice. But the document provides as example the Procedures for the technical work in ISO/IEC Directives Part 1. See Article 5.12 of ISO/IEC Guide 59 (2019).

replace or interpret the TBT framework, this requirement is of little use for SDOs implementing the TBT Code of Good Practice.

### *Access to Standards on Fair, Reasonable, and Nondiscriminatory Terms*

Availability of standards documents was discussed under the principle of transparency; nevertheless, some standardization frameworks explicitly address access to proprietary elements incorporated into a standard or technical specification. More often than not, the applicable instruments require SDOs to implement a patent policy that is based on F/RAND licensing commitments.[124] Regulation 1025/2012 explains that the FRAND principle also covers royalty-free licensing requirement.[125] OMB Circular (2016) clarifies that RAND licensing obligations[126] extend to "implementers of the standard" and not to "all interested parties," unlike what was stipulated in its earlier versions. The SDOAA (2004) itself does not contain a specific F/RAND provision (this requirement is introduced in the Circular to which the SDOAA refers), but states that its principles apply to actions related to the IPR policies of SDOs.

The Horizontal Guidelines (2011) suggests that SDOs should have a clear and balanced IPR policy, which would be adjusted for the needs of particular industry and organization in question,[127] and which requires a commitment from patent-holders to disclose their essential intellectual property and license their technology on FRAND terms.[128] In addition, the IPR policy should oblige the owners of technologies (potentially) essential for standards implementation, to disclose their patents in good faith, by this means allowing the standards development group to make an informed choice.[129] This disclosure obligation is based on "reasonable endeavors" of standards development participants to identify the

[124] See Contreras, 'An empirical study'.

[125] Annex II, 4(c) of EU Regulation 1025/2012.

[126] Which the Circular explains as "a term of art in the rulemaking context"; OMB Circular, at p. 9.

[127] Horizontal Guidelines (2011), para. 284.

[128] Ibid., para. 285. This commitment, which is of a contractual nature, should be given prior to the adoption of the standard, and shall bind undertakings to which essential patents might later be transferred.

[129] Ibid., para. 286. Needless to say, these conditions do not apply for SDOs with royalty-free standards policy.

essential IPR reading on the prospect standard, and, as such, does not require firms to conduct an onerous research. The assessment whether the licensing terms are indeed "fair and reasonable" should be based on considerations whether those fees bear a reasonable relationship to the economic value of the intellectual property.[130] While the Guidelines suggest that the FRAND commitment aims to ensure the accessibility of the essential technology to the standard users on fair, reasonable, and nondiscriminatory conditions,[131] many have claimed that the actual purpose of the FRAND commitment was to prevent a "holdup" situation, or even to preclude a patent-holder from seeking injunctions in case of infringement.[132]

While ISO/IEC Guide 59 (2019) provides that patent solutions may be included in a standard if justifiable for technical reasons and licenses are negotiated under FRAND, whenever the patent-holder is located,[133] inclusion and licensing of proprietary technologies into standards is not addressed by the TBT Agreement, although concerns related to intellectual property sometimes arise at TBT Committee meetings. One of such concerns related to intellectual property implemented in China's guidelines for secure IT risk control mechanism in banking sector.[134] Another, and perhaps the most famous, example is the discussion on WAPI, a Chinese homegrown encryption standard for WLAN developed as a counterpart of IEEE's 802.11 standard: as discussed in Chapter 3, one of the many issues that caused the discontent of Western WTO Member was the lack of FRAND obligations for proprietary algorithms on which WAPI specifications were running.

## Fitness of the Procedural Frameworks for ICT Standardization

While standards development processes are addressed in all frameworks, ICT standards bodies and, consequently, the standards they produce may

[130] Ibid., para. 289.
[131] Ibid., para. 287.
[132] P. Chappatte, 'FRAND commitments: the case for antitrust intervention' (2009) 5 *European Competition Journal* 319–46 at 331; such reasoning links to the investigations of the Commission in *Rambus* and *Qualcomm*.
[133] Article 4.5.8 of ISO/IEC Guide 59 (2019). Note that Guide 59 is the only document so far that describes the commitment globally.
[134] Committee on Technical Barriers to Trade, Minutes of the Meeting of March 18–19, 2015, WTO Doc. G/TBT/M/65 (May 28, 2015), para. 2.2.2.2.

encounter some coverage problems. As noted in Chapter 3, it is complicated to curb ICT SDOs under the requirements for ISBs under the TBT Agreement and, while the TBT Code of Good Practice possesses sufficient tools to scrutinize their processes, it is practically not used by the Member States. In principle, TBT requirements are implemented both in the EU and US. In the EU, however, the ESOs have a wide discretion in defining, implementing, and enforcing procedural rules of Regulation 1025/2012. In the US, procedural requirements may be passed on to private SDOs and consortia through ANSI accreditation; yet not all SDOs that produce global ICT standards seek this recognition. At the same time, extraterritorial application of US and EU competition laws would allow these frameworks to cover a broader geographical and institutional scope of SDOs, especially given that the applicable competition law tools do not require any formal acceptance by SDOs or any reference to their standards by governmental authorities. Yet the competition law requirements are rather limited, especially in the EU, and while they address the arising concerns of IPR policies, they leave aside such an important governance feature as judicial review.

Two caveats are at order in this analysis. Firstly, many procedural instruments examined in this book are not binding and, although their wide usage by courts[135] and the regulators provides them with a normative power, adherence to their principles ultimately depends on their enforcement. Secondly, while participation of governmental stakeholders in private standards bodies arguably contributes to their public law legitimacy in the EU and US, this is not the case with the WTO, where the Secretariat does not partake in the meetings of technical experts (which US agencies are encouraged to do) or enjoy a Counsellor or observer status in private SDOs, nor proposes standardization projects (which is the Commission's prerogative in the ESOs). This does not take away the fact that already by participating in private standardization activity, regulators can be the watchdog of due process in SDOs on the national level, albeit by them contributing to standards development on an equal footing with other stakeholders.

[135] At the same time, in liability cases, courts in EU and US tend to refer to good governance principles only as auxiliary arguments, see P. Verbruggen, 'Good governance of private standardization and the role of tort law' (2019) 2 *European Review of Private Law* 319–52 at 349.

### *Relevance of the Principles*

The procedural principles for standardization may differ in their definition, but to some extent, they are also intertwined. Transparency underpins openness, since effective participation is impossible without access to the relevant information; transparency also underpins coherence, allowing SDOs to coordinate their work programs and ensuring efficient allocation of standards development projects; consensus and balanced procedures that allow for the resolution of objections facilitate consent within the industry and thus ensure that standards are relevant, effective, and widely accepted. From the other view, however, the principles sometimes seem contradictory: for instance, openness can undermine the principle of balance,[136] and consensus is by definition associated with exclusion.[137]

The question arises whether and to which extent can these principles be adhered to by all SDOs operating in the ICT sector. Compliance with the principles is especially questionable for industry consortia: these informal SDOs can be expected to lack transparency, as it is defined by the applicable procedural principles,[138] and openness, since most of them can be assumed to prefer being a closed group of technical experts and not to publish information relevant to their ongoing and future standards development.[139] Moreover, increased openness of standards development committees is generally presumed to cause delays, which in turn are significant indirect costs of standardization of technologies;[140] at the same time, it is also believed to improve the outcomes of standardization processes.[141]

Likewise, consortia may fall short on impartiality and balance: W3C is infamously considered a "benevolent dictatorship" where the Director

[136] JRC Report, p. 14.

[137] Russel, *Open Standards and the Digital Age*, p. 19.

[138] For instance, SDOs such as VXI bus and the Open Geospatial Consortium, while providing information on their recent products or sometimes even putting their standards into public domain, do not publish their work program, which is required under the notion of transparency.

[139] This assumption was in part confirmed by the interviews with experts.

[140] In this regard, see R. Mazzoleni and R. R. Nelson, 'The benefits and costs of strong patent protection: a contribution to the current debate' (1998) 27 *Research Policy* 273–84.

[141] Simcoe, 'Standard setting committees', on the example of IETF.

has the ultimate decision-making power.[142] Whether consensus is always beneficial, let alone feasible, is likely to depend on SDOs' operational field and scope of activities: development of web standards, for instance, is mostly driven by technical excellence, rather than consensus.[143] Coherence is almost an oxymoron in R&D-intensive SDOs: most widely accepted ICT standards were subject to fierce competition from other standardization initiatives in the early stages of their development and were selected by the market due to their technical features, costs, or compatibility with other technologies.[144] Finally, appeal and review are strikingly absent from a number of regulatory frameworks, most notably from the TBT instruments, with ISO/IEC Guide 59 (2019) limiting the requirements of maintaining appeal procedures to NSOs.

### *Due Process as Good Governance*

Whereas from public law perspective the discussed principles constrain SDOs governance, from the viewpoint of private law, they represent procedural rights granted to SDOs' participants, and which they can claim against other participants or against SDOs. At the same time, in the context of global governance, the regulatory frameworks are expected to fine-tune the broader "good governance" principles to the field of standardization and, where applicable, to ICT standards development. While this is marginally the case (for instance, with regard to transparency, some frameworks indeed state which information should be provided), some theoretical concepts of global regulation, that is, "all affected principle," do not seem to materialize through the analyzed regulatory regimes: even when referring to "affected stakeholders,"[145] the frameworks do not clarify the threshold to determine when a stakeholder is "affected" (the exception would be the updated ISO/IEC Guide 59 (2019), which defines such terms as "stakeholder" and "participant").[146] Moreover, availability of review and appeal mechanisms, while being the leading principle in global governance scholarship, is not implemented in most regulatory frameworks.

[142] See J. L. Contreras, 'A tale of two layers: patents, standardization and the internet' (2016) 93 *Denver Law Review* 853–95 at 874–5, n. 102.

[143] J. Way, 'A brief history of HTML5' (December 6, 2011), quoting Ian Hickson, available at https://code.tutsplus.com/articles/a-brief-history-of-html5--net-23064.

[144] See also Chapter 11.

[145] That is, EU Regulation 1025/2012.

[146] Article 3.5 of ISO/IEC Guide 59 (2019).

It should be noted that procedural safeguards of global governance provide mechanisms to hold non-State regulators accountably and by this means, to compensate for democratic deficit of global regulation. In this context, it remains questionable whether standardization is, and should be considered, a democratic process: arguably, the principles were designed to prevent dominance and ensure technical excellence, rather than provide SDOs' committees with democratic scrutiny, and have evolved into procedural requirements that SDOs have to follow to escape certain liability. At the same time, with the evolution of standardization from purely technical exercise to a modus of global governance, its democratic deficit can no longer be ignored.

## SYNOPSIS

While ICT standardization is evolving, its regulation in public law appears to lag on many points. This becomes particularly apparent from international trade law, where the shortcomings of the TBT Agreement and limited and even strategic enforcement of its procedural instruments by WTO Members leaves little space for consideration of challenges to the global trade that arise from ICT standards. Interestingly, nothing in the TBT negotiations history precludes the coverage of private standards, such as ICT standards, by TBT obligations,[147] but such flexible reading of the TBT Agreement and broad interpretation of its definitions may be met with reluctance by many Members, leaving the Dispute Settlement Bodies no other option than to engage in case-by-case interpretation of the terms "recognized body" and "international standards."

Less problematic appears the addressing of ICT standards on national and regional levels, where they fall under the broader scope of legislation and have become a part and parcel of national policies as well as their regulatory export.[148] But also these frameworks are not unproblematic: the EU standardization system has received criticism from policy-makers and scholars alike for limiting representation of public interests, lacking accountability and meaningful opportunities for transparency and

[147] Rather, it is single-actor standards for their own use that were excluded in the first phase, see Du, *The Regulation*, p. 32.

[148] See M. Cantero Gamito, 'Europeanization through standardization: ICT and telecommunications' (2018) 37 *Yearbook of European Law* 395–423.

participation, and limiting access to dispute resolution of ESOs.[149] If even ESOs have flaws when it comes to participation, transparency, and voluntarism,[150] the principles incorporated into the Horizontal Guidelines (2011), how can less formal organizations be expected to adhere to these requirements?

At the same time, recent case law and policy discussion on the national levels demonstrate just how politized standardization has become as a part of national industrial policy. Within the past ten years, the US approach to SEP licensing has taken a U-turn at least twice,[151] and the debate on the level of FRAND licensing remains open at both sides of the Atlantic, with the European Commission maintaining a "no one size fits all" approach[152] and the US case law fluctuating between component and end-product device level. Furthermore, the availability and competitiveness of national champions in the semiconductor industry pertain considerations of national security, challenging the appropriateness of the degree of governmental involvement in ICT standardization.

The differences in the treatment of SDO governance in the EU and US can be explained historically: in ESOs and NSOs, governance requirements were initially directed towards technical qualities, while consensus and balance were more prominent in the US SDOs. This does not take away the fact that prevention of dominance and ensuring that standards are not adopted over objections has been a leading consideration at both sides of the Atlantic. It may be speculated that it is after lawyers have joined the purely technical processes, as a reaction to increasing legal and regulatory complexity of ICT standards, that the governance principles started to evolve from purely technical to administrative and included such requirements as judicial review and interest representation. While the EU approach is believed to be more constitutional, and the US one more procedural, both regulatory frameworks shift the responsibility to

149 European Commission, 'An EU strategy on standardization. Setting global standards in support of a resilient, green and digital EU Single Market', COM (2022) 31; Senden, 'Towards a more holistic legitimacy approach' p. 40; C. Cauffman and M. Gébrardy, 'Competition law as a tool to ensure the legitimacy of standard-setting by European standardisation organisations', in M. Eliantonio and C. Cauffman (eds.), *The Legitimacy of Standardization as a Regulatory Technique in the EU: A Cross-disciplinary and Multi-level Analysis* (Cheltenham and Northampton: Edward Elgar Publishing, 2020), pp. 64–90 at p.84.

150 Ibid., p. 87.

151 See the DoJ's 2015 Business Review Letter to IEEE, as well as its 2020 supplement.

152 EC Communication on SEP (2017).

monitor compliance with the procedural principles to the designated SDOs. The public law legitimacy of ICT standardization is thus provided by (semi)-private bodies.

With regard to procedural guarantees, certain aspects appear strikingly absent from the regulatory frameworks. First and foremost is the lack of consideration regarding the copyright of private standards. While some clarity could have been offered by the principle of transparency and the requirement of "reasonable availability" of standards, implemented in the WTO and US frameworks, the threshold for reasonable availability remains opaque. ISO/IEC Guide 2 (2004) provides that standards' *public* (emphasis added) availability is "... presumed to constitute acknowledged rules of technology ...,"[153] which may suggest that standards that are not publicly available should not, in principle, be endorsed as industry rules. This does not seem to be the case in the US standardization system, which allows incorporation of standards that are not placed into the public domain. The OMB Circular (2016) explicitly refused to provide any concrete definition of the "reasonably available" requirement, referring to the OFR, but offered some guidance by mentioning which aspects should be viewed as facilitating such availability, including access to standards' summary and read-only versions.

Furthermore, the considerations regarding SDO's governance processes are also absent: the frameworks do not clarify whether the principles apply to *all* activities of SDOs, or only to technical development of standards. Such clarification has so far only been provided by the ANSI, whose due process requirements apply only to the development of ANSs;[154] yet, the design of SDOs' rules has become increasingly important in standardization ecology. In the absence of a clear regulatory framework, SDOs arguably have a wider discretion when designing their governance rules rather than when developing their standards: a standard can then be drafted following procedures that were developed in opaque and closed processes that did not represent industry consensus. While the role of the SDO leadership has been addressed in the recently updated ISO/IEC Guide 59 (2019), the Guide's scope is rather limited, since it applies only to standards development processes, and only to national bodies.

[153] Article 3.2.1 of ISO/IEC Guide 2 (2004).

[154] "These requirements apply to activities related to the *development* of consensus for approval, revision, reaffirmation, and withdrawal of *American National Standards* (ANS)" (emphasis added), section 1.0 ANSI Essential Requirements (20122).

In this context, due process principles represent a set of institutional norms that are "best effort" practices[155] and that ultimately aim to ensure that SDOs' processes are not dominated by a single group of actors, and whose interpretation is flexible. Arguably, by employing vague and ambiguous terms, the procedural frameworks provide SDOs with room for maneuver to adjust their governance to specialized technical activities in the industry field and the regulatory environment in which they operate. In the light of this "convenient vagueness," these best effort practices allow for SDOs to escape antitrust liability, develop standards to be referenced in national regulations, or to benefit from increased public law legitimacy. In abstracto, these principles have little meaning and require further concretization by SDOs.

[155] Procedural principles for standardization as "best effort" have been discussed in the context of the WTO; see M. Du and F. Deng, 'International standards as global public goods in the world trading system' (2016) 43 *Legal Issues of Economic Integration* 113–44 at 134–5; and by Mataija, who views them as "quasi-administrative law" for SDOs; see Mataija, 'Leveraging trade law', 311.

# PART III

## Governance Architecture and Decision-Making Process of SDOs

Informal regulatory systems have their own substantive rules that their members should follow; establish their own procedures to solve potential conflicts; and maintain their own enforcement mechanisms, often relying on contract law, organizational law, or reputation (e.g., "blaming and shaming").[1] Incentives to comply with the set of rules are provided by the organizations' membership requirements as well as their ability to exclude noncompliant parties. To be resilient, specialized organizations do not only have to serve their membership, but also satisfy external requirements of their institutional environment, which implies that they should develop goals and actions that may not be part of their internal technical mission.[2] Often, their self-monitoring and self-enforcement arrangements are somehow facilitated by national legislation;[3] however, organizations that supply weak due process, and where the demand for

1 See, among many others, E. Stringham, 'The extralegal development of securities trading in seventeenth-century Amsterdam' (2003) 43 *The Quarterly Review of Economics and Finance* 321–44; L. Bernstein, 'Private commercial law in the cotton industry: creating cooperation through rules, norms and institutions' (2001) 99 *Michigan Law Review* 1724–90; Bernstein, 'Opting out of the legal system', suggesting that stakeholders that have been long involved in the diamond business would not dispute basic concepts of acceptable business practices. Similar suggestions appear from the literature on transnational private regulation: e-commerce, for instance, does not only use legal sanctions such as termination of account to "punish" those not compliant with the platform's rules, but also reputational sanctions imposed by peers and that based on platform regulation; F. Cafaggi, 'The many features of transnational private rule-making: unexplored relationships between custom, jura mercatorum and global private regulation' (2015) 36 *University of Pennsylvania Journal of International Law* 875–938 at 906, who also warns that in transnational private regulation, conflicts do not only concern application but also validity of the rules.

2 See J. W. Meyer and B. Rowan, 'Institutional organizations: formal structure as myth and ceremony' (1977) 83 *American Journal of Sociology* 340–63, who explain decoupling of organizations' external tasks from internal activities.

3 Ostrom provides an example of fishers in Alanya employing a "rotation system," which was accepted by governmental officials; Ostrom, *Governing the Commons*, p. 20.

an institutional change is weak, are likely to favor sustained regulatory capture.[4]

Against this backdrop, there are only a few studies that have addressed institutional governance and procedural rules of standardization institutions.[5] As such, SDOs' decision-making follows the rules determined in their operational frameworks, which in turn may depend on many factors: for instance, their State of incorporation,[6] technical nature of their activities (e.g., the degree and intensity of testing needed prior to standards adoption), and the industry preferences.[7]

This study understands under "decision-making" not only those decisions that are technical and reflect the main functions of SDOs, that is, inclusion of technology or approval of a standard, but also those that are of an administrative or policy nature and that support the functioning of SDOs, that is, admission to membership, resolution of disputes, or modifications of operational rules.[8] This book argues that both "levels" of decision-making, namely, policy and standards development, are equally important: while SDOs are indeed technical organizations, their technical work would not be possible without nontechnical decisions taken by their governance bodies.

Members and participants of SDOs take decisions collectively during the interactions in technical committees and governance bodies. It is these decisions that create standardization ecosystem and ultimately impact society. By affecting the interplay between various actors, SDOs' decision-making mechanisms influence standardization costs, which in turn affects the advancement of new technologies and their future acceptance by the market.[9] For SDOs operating in the ICT sector, IPR

[4] Mattli and Woods, 'In whose benefit?', p. 5.

[5] See, for instance, the JRC Report; R. Werle, 'Institutional aspects of standardization – jurisdictional conflicts and the choice of standardization organizations' (2001) 8 *Journal of European Public Policy* 392–410.

[6] For instance, SDOs established in the US are likely to follow *Robert's Rules of Order*; H. M. Robert and S. C. Robert, *Robert's Rules of Order Newly Revised*, 11th ed. (Boston: Da Capo Press, 2011).

[7] See also Abbott and Snidal, 'International "standards"', p. 346.

[8] The JRC Report, which also analyzes governance and standards development processes of SDOs, suggests that SDOs' governance can be analyzed as an "interaction between relatively autonomous organizations and its stakeholder base" or as a "form of decision-making by heterogeneous groups of actors participating in organizations with specific rules and procedures for making decisions as a group"; see the JRC Report, p. 84.

[9] Werle, 'Institutional aspects', p. 406, discusses the process of data networking standard by Xerox in CCITT.

policies are of a particular importance since they may affect the degree of stakeholder participation in these SDOs and consequently, the R&D embedded in their standards.[10]

As member-driven organizations, SDOs should ensure that their operational rules first and foremost satisfy their stakeholders, which, in the case of ICT sector, are predominantly commercial industry players. As a supplier of private governance, however, SDOs should also ensure, as a minimum, that their rules provide sufficient opportunities for those stakeholders that are not included in their decision-making to indirectly participate in – and challenge the outcomes of – their processes.[11] Arguably, whether the balance between epistemic decision-making and addressing democratic deficit can be achieved depends on the extent to which SDOs implement the established procedural principles for standardization in their operational frameworks.[12]

Earlier scholarship suggested that SDOs have a similar institutional pattern and largely mimic each other's processes.[13] The resemblance of operational rules and institutional structures arguably explains the rarity of "jurisdictional" conflicts between formal ("traditional") and private SDOs,[14] despite the considerable overlap of their work. Recent research, however, observed that membership and operational rules of technological SDOs are determined endogenously as a result of institutional competition;[15] and concluded that there is a considerable heterogeneity in SDOs governance.[16]

Despite their voluntary nature, standardization through SDOs is accompanied by various forms of sanctions. Naturally, when a standard is made mandatory through regulatory endorsement, companies that do not comply with it may be boycotted or denied certification.[17] By the same token, companies that choose not to comply with a standard that is made mandatory through market forces risk being excluded from this market. These sanctions, however, are not imposed by the SDOs

[10] Chiao et al., 'The rules'.
[11] See Chapter 2 for supporting arguments.
[12] See Chapter 3 for supporting arguments.
[13] Werle, 'Standards', p. 17.
[14] Werle, 'Institutional aspects', p. 400. This lack of "jurisdictional" disputes may, however, as well be the consequence of SDOs' common "weaknesses," such as limited resources and small administration; ibid., p. 401.
[15] Spulber, 'Innovation economics'
[16] The JRC Report, p. 43.
[17] See Brunsson et al., 'Dynamics of standardization', p. 625.

themselves, but rather by the third parties, such as auditors, certifiers, or market players. It may be assumed, however, that SDOs have some kind of sanctioning mechanisms in place to penalize their members and participants when those do not comply with the SDOs operational rules, such as requirements of IPR policies or working procedures of technical committees.

Whether SDOs operational frameworks indeed reflect the established procedural principles, provide affected stakeholders with sufficient opportunities to participate in SDOs' decision-making, and self-enforce compliance with the operational rules should be verified by a thorough examination of SDOs' institutional architecture. To that end, the following chapters offer a systematic, detailed analysis of the governance and standards development processes of seven prominent SDOs developing ICT standards.

## The Choice of Organizations

The SDOs examined in this book were selected based on their overall relevance in ICT standardization, significance of their technologies, and awareness of their standards among nontechnical actors, as well as their different institutional settings.

The ITU was established in 1865 as a Western initiative to ensure interoperability between telegraph networks,[18] and became a specialized ICT UN body in 1949. The main tasks of ITU include allocating the global radio spectrum and developing global telecommunication standards – "Recommendations." It presents an interesting example for our study since its intergovernmental and quasi-regulatory character is complemented by market-driven forces: while, arguably, the ITU governance model started losing its relevance due to telecoms liberalization and the development of internet standards,[19] as well as the failure to effectively integrate private stakeholders in its decision-making framework,[20] it still managed to survive through these technical revolutions as the oldest global ICT forum. The ITU administration thus enjoys certain legitimacy, but at the same time is challenged by the emergence of more flexible,

[18] J. Shanin, 'The European Union's performance in the International Telecommunications Union' (2011) 33 *Journal of European Integration* 683–98 at 685.

[19] S. Hoffmann, D. Lazanski and E. Taylor, 'Standardising the splinternet: how China's technical standards could fragment the Internet' (2020) 5 *Journal of Cyber Policy* 239–64.

[20] Hinricher, 'Law-making of the International Telecommunications Union (ITU)'.

private SDOs or SDOs that are tailored to a specific industry. At the moment of writing, ITU membership counts 193 States and more than 900 companies.

The ETSI was established in 1988 by the European Conference of Postal and Telecommunications Administrations (CEPT)[21] as a not-for-profit association under French law,[22] with an intention to create a European ICT standards body.[23] ETSI develops global standards and specifications[24] in such fields as internet technologies, mobile telecommunication, and cellular networks,[25] for example, the General Packet Radio Service (GPRS),[26] and the Global System for Mobile Telecommunication (GSM).[27] As one of the three ESOs,[28] ETSI can be considered a semipublic organization; unlike other ESOs, ETSI's standards are available free of charge.[29] ETSI thus performs an important normative function within the EU, while also having a wide-reaching influence on the international telecommunications market.[30] ETSI cooperates with global SDOs and

21 CEPT was formed in 1959 as a coordinating body for European postal and telecommunication services. For further information, see https://cept.org/cept/.

22 Article 1 of ETSI Statutes, Version approved by a Specially Convened Meeting of the ETSI General Assembly (December 1, 2021). ETSI operational framework is codified in ETSI Directives, Version 44 (December 2021), available at https://portal.etsi.org/Resources/ETSI-Directives.

23 'The convergence of the telecommunications, media and information technology sectors, and the implications for regulation', (1999) COM (1999) 108 final available at http://aei.pitt.edu/983/1/telecom_convergence_gp_follow_COM_99_108.pdf.

24 Apart from standards, ETSI also develops technical specifications, reports and guides, see Annex E.1.1, E.2.1, and 2.2 and 2.3.

25 'Vision, mission and long term strategy', available at www.etsi.org/about/what-we-do/vision-mission-strategy. According to its website, ETSI published between 2.000 and 2.500 standards each year; see www.etsi.org/standards.

26 This standard enables data connection for 2G and 3G cellular services; see www.etsi.org/technologies-clusters/technologies/mobile/gprs.

27 Which enables cellular communication networks; see www.etsi.org/technologies-clusters/technologies/mobile/gsm.

28 Annex I of EU Regulation 1025/2012.

29 Annex 6 of ETSI Rules of Procedure, Version approved by a Specially Convened Meeting of the ETSI General Assembly (December 1, 2021). The copyright of the standards belongs to ETSI; Article 3.2.1 of ETSI Guide on Intellectual Property Rights (IPRs), Version adopted by Board #133 (June 10, 2021).

30 Article 3 of ETSI Statutes. In this regard, ETSI members should also support the promotion of ETSI documents as the basis of worldwide recommendations standards within ITU and JTC1, Article 13.8 of ETSI Rules of Procedure. See also 'ETSI long-term strategy 2016–2021', available at www.etsi.org/images/files/Brochures/ETSI_LTS%20Brochure_WEB.pdf stating that ETSI's aims is to be an enabler of global standards.

other legal entities through a Cooperation Agreement.[31] At the moment of writing, ETSI counts more 900 members from over 60 counties.

Together with six other national and regional SDOs,[32] ETSI is a founding organizational partner of the 3GPP, established in the 1990s a consortium of telecommunications standard development bodies responsible for the development and maintenance of technical specifications for 3G, 4G, and 5G cellular telecommunications technology.[33] These specifications are later transposed into standards by the partner-SDOs and form the basis of member contributions to ITU. Despite its intended global reach,[34] 3GPP was born out of Western governance traditions, and is driven by market actors rather than governments.[35] 3GPP membership counts more than 700 companies.

The IEEE was established in 1963 as a private, nonprofit organization.[36] IEEE is headquartered in New York and currently counts more than 422,000 members from nearly 160 countries. It carries out scientific and educational work in the field of electrical engineering and ICT.[37] The Institute serves as an overarching organization for a large number of voluntary associated groups dedicated to specific scientific interests or geographical areas,[38] and which have their own administrative and management settings.[39] Standardization activities are undertaken in the IEEE Standards Association (hereinafter: IEEE-SA)[40] – a private

[31] Article 1.8.1.1 of ETSI Technical Working Procedures, Version adopted by Board #134 (October 18, 2021). Note that the relationship between ETSI and ITU is different than the one of CEN/ISO and CENELEC/IEC. While being members of ETSI, NSOs may not acquire the membership of ITU, unless they are a part of a governmental body.

[32] ATIS, ARIB, TTC, TTA, CCSA, and TSDSI.

[33] ETSI's GSM specifications served as a basis for 3GPP's work on 3G.

[34] 3GPP-04/12/1998, '3GPP partnership project description'.

[35] R. Nanni, 'The "China" question in mobile Internet standard-making: insights from expert interviews' (2021) 45 *Telecommunications Policy* 1–12.

[36] See IEEE Certificate of Incorporation (1993), available at www.ieee.org/documents/01-05-1993_Certificate_of_Incorporation.pdf.

[37] Article 1, section 2 of IEEE Constitution. IEEE Constitution and Bylaws (January 1, 2022) are available at www-ieee-org.proxy.library.uu.nl/about/corporate/governance/index.html.

[38] This means that IEEE operate according to a so-called "dual complementary regional and technical structure." Next to the Standards Association (IEEE-SA), the IEEE coordinates the work of Educational Activities Board (EAB), Publication Services and Products Board (PSPB), Member and Geographic Activities Board (MGAB), and Technical Activities Board (TAB).

[39] Section I-107 of IEEE Bylaws. The Major Boards are the Committees of IEEE within the meaning of the New York Not-for-Profit Corporation Law.

[40] Section I-303.6 of IEEE Bylaws.

professional association accredited by ANSI.[41] Although hierarchically linked to the Institute's governing bodies, this specialized Major Board of the Institute enjoys a high degree of independency in its technical work.[42] The most prominent IEEE standards are the set of specifications for Wi-Fi chipsets, which enabled interconnection of electronic technologies via wireless telecommunications. IEEE standards can be implemented by other organizations with which IEEE has signed a reciprocal agreement or MoU.[43]

The Internet Engineering Task Force (IETF) is a "loosely self-organized group of people who contribute to the engineering and evolution of Internet technologies."[44] IETF has no membership and is not incorporated in any jurisdiction, and its work is supported by a small secretariat is located in the US. For decades, IETF has been the principal SDO developing and maintaining voluntary internet standards and specifications, having an important role in defining internet governance. IETF standardization is generally based on engineering excellence rather than policy and business considerations,[45] and is guided by the IETF's key principle "We reject kings, presidents and voting. We believe in rough consensus and running code."[46] Standardization efforts within IETF typically result in a publicly available Request for Comments (RFC);[47] RFCs that are normative documents become standards once approved by the IETF.[48] IETF governance rules are specified in the Best Current Practices (BCP). To ensure the smooth functioning of internet standardization, IETF maintains informal liaisons with other SDOs, such as W3C and IEEE.[49]

41 ANSI, 'Accredited Standards Developers' (January 10, 2022), available at https://share.ansi.org/Shared%20Documents/Standards%20Activities/American%20National%20Standards/ANSI%20Accredited%20Standards%20Developers/JAN2022ASD.pdf.

42 Article 7 of IEEE-SA Operations Manual (December 2021). IEEE-SA operational framework is available at https://standards.ieee.org/about/policies/index.html.

43 Article 7 of IEEE-SA Operations Manual.

44 See IETF, 'The Tao of IETF: a novice's guide to the internet engineering task force', P. Hoffman (ed.) (2019), available at www.ietf.org/tao.html.

45 'IETF Standards Process', available at www.ietf.org/about/standards-process.html.

46 See 'The Tao of IETF', referring to the quote of David Clark.

47 The rationale behind the term "Request for Comments" is the constantly changing technical system of the internet, and the need to constantly update technical documents managing it.

48 Section 6 of 'The Tao of IETF'. Other RFCs are informational (e.g., D. Thaler, 'What makes for a successful protocol' (July 2008), available at https://tools.ietf.org/html/rfc5218; experimental or historic.

49 The nature of these liaisons is rather informal, since they are not established by an agreement between SDOs but take place in Working Groups; see section 8 of 'The Tao of

The W3C was founded in 1994 as a response to slow and inflexible IETF processes.[50] The consortium represents a nonhierarchical cooperation between universities and research facilities and does not have a typical organizational structure. W3C is managed by a joint agreement among four "host" institutions, namely, Massachusetts Institute of Technology, European Research Consortium for Informatics and Mathematics (ERCIM), Keio University (KEIO), and Beihang University (BEIHANG),[51] and has regional offices to facilitate administration. W3C standards take the form of Recommendations; most prominent examples are XML, HTML5, web design protocols, and web applications, which ensure functionality and accessibility of the web on a global scale.[52] In its process, W3C adheres to a set of Open Standards Principles of the modern paradigm for standards.[53] Like IETF, W3C has a strong sense of community among standardization participants, but although the membership is involved in W3C process, the ultimate decision-maker is the Director. W3C counts more than 450 Members.

The Bluetooth Special Interest Group (SIG) is an industry consortium incorporated in Kirkland, Washington,[54] and dedicated to the development of specifications for wireless connectivity solutions and low-power wireless connectivity technologies.[55] Next to drafting normative documents, Bluetooth SIG establishes testing tools programs and qualification rules and procedures for its Members to demonstrate the compliance of their products with Bluetooth specifications.[56] The consortium was formed by five companies in 1998, and its first specification (Bluetooth

IETF'. As suggested by an expert, "If there is somebody who participates in both organizations, it is a sign that both organizations have overlapping activities; if not it is a good sign that they do not." Interview with an expert from an SDO, January 12, 2018. For more information, see 'Liaisons', available at www.ietf.org/liaison.

[50] See A. L. Russel, 'Constructing legitimacy: the W3C's patent policy', in L. DeNardis (ed.), *Opening Standards: The Global Politics of Interoperability* (Cambridge, MA: MIT Press, 2011), pp. 159–76.

[51] 'Facts about W3C', available at www.w3.org/Consortium/facts.html.

[52] See 'W3C Standards', available at www.w3.org/standards/.

[53] The Agreement between W3C and Open Standard was signed on August 29, 2012.

[54] See Fourth Amended and Restated Certificate of Incorporation of Bluetooth SIG, Inc.; and section 2.1 of Bylaws of Bluetooth SIG, Inc. (May 17, 2019) (hereinafter: Bluetooth SIG Bylaws), available at www.bluetooth.com/about-us/governing-documents/. The Bluetooth SIG operational rules are available at www.bluetooth.com/membership-working-groups/membership-types-levels/membership-agreements.

[55] Allegedly, one of the reasons why Bluetooth SIG was created as a new organization as a response to dissatisfactions in ETSI, Interview with an industry expert, April 18, 2018.

[56] Sections 2.2 and 2.3 of Bluetooth SIG Bylaws.

1.0) was realized in 1999. Since that time, the consortium membership has grown to more 20,000 entities, and Bluetooth products are widely used by the global community.[57]

## Methodology

The operational frameworks of the seven SDOs were analyzed in a desk study by reviewing the SDOs' documentation that is publicly available on their websites, including their statutes, bylaws, rules of procedure, and other governance documents, as well as additional information made available on their website, such as the description of standardization processes.

This analysis distinguishes between two decision-making processes in SDOs: governance rules and policies (Chapter 7) and developing of technical standards (Chapter 8).[58] The SDOs' governance features that were examined in Chapter 7 are the membership and funding models, governance bodies, dispute resolution, policy drafting, and IPR policies. Technical processes of SDOs' examined in Chapter 8 were divided into three stages: proposal of standardization projects, technical deliberations in SDOs' committees, and approval of standards.[59]

While addressing similarities and differences between the governance and procedural elements of the seven organizations is inevitable in such institutional analyses, the ultimate aim of this study is *not* to compare these SDOs: such comparison would not be meaningful given the differences in SDOs' institutional setting, historical background, and operational field. Nor does this study aim to suggest whether a certain SDO should be held liable under the applicable regulatory frameworks. Instead, Chapter 9 provides evaluation of SDOs governance and technical processes in the context of due process principles, which points to

[57] According to the Bluetooth SIG website, there are currently more than 8.2 billion users of Bluetooth specifications, and Bluetooth is recognized by 92 percent of consumers.

[58] This distinction was introduced by David and Shurmer, who argued that such conceptualization reflects a "technological idealism," meaning that the decisions of engineers should be based on merit rather than strategic considerations. P. A. David and M. Shurmer, 'Formal standard-setting for global telecommunications and information services: towards an institutional regime transformation?' (1996) 20 *Telecommunications Policy* 789–815.

[59] Some regulatory frameworks (i.e., WTO and EU law), as well as the operational frameworks of SDOs, maintain their own standards development stages; the division in three stages, which are present in every SDO, was used for the sake of coherence.

the diversity of the ecosystem and, having a rather explorative purpose, aims to facilitate understanding of institutional aspects of current ICT standardization.

There are a number of caveats that concern this descriptive analysis of SDOs' governance and procedures. Firstly, the descriptive study is somewhat asymmetric due to the difference in the amount of information that SDOs make publicly available; moreover, operational rules of some SDOs may be more thorough and complex than those of others. Secondly, SDOs' procedures are often amended: while most of these changes are editorial and unsubstantial, some appear important for the SDOs' functioning.[60] This study thus describes the state of affairs at the moment of writing.

[60] Examples are IEEE SASB bylaws changes regarding IPR policies, and update of Bluetooth SIG Bylaws.

# 7

# Policy-Making in SDOs

SDOs' core activities are technical processes that revolve around the development, approval, and maintenance of standards and technical specifications. These technical processes are enabled by a set of rules – "policies" – that state requirements for SDO members and participants. The nontechnical administrative rules are often portrayed in the shadow of standardization processes and started to get scholarly attention only recently;[1] yet, they are instrumental for the functioning of SDOs, and create expectations among standards developers and standards users: they hold SDOs together, provide organizational structure, and create a unique institutional environment, and by this means affect the content of standards. Like the rules for technical deliberations and standards approval, SDO policies emerged as a result of industry preferences, regulatory landscape, and cultural traditions pertaining to the specific industries, and hence reflect not only engineering, but also commercial and political issues; however, they also should not be seen in isolation from technical rules, discussed in Chapter 8.

## SDO Membership

Whom do SDOs allow to partake in their processes, whether governance or technical, is essential for understanding their functioning. ITU *voting* members are UN Member States,[2] represented by governmental agencies, but private entities and scientific or industrial organizations are encouraged to join ITU by becoming members of one of the ITU sectors:[3]

[1] For example, JRC Report.

[2] Article 2 of ITU Constitution; non-UN Members can become members when supported by 2/3 of the ITU membership.

[3] Braun and Koenig, 'The international regulatory framework of EC telecommunications law', p. 21, see also Articles 2 and 4 of ITU Constitution.

the Radiocommunication Sector (ITU-R), the Telecommunication Standardization Sector (ITU-T), and the Telecommunication Development Sector (ITU-D), each having its own governance. Except for international telecommunications or standards organizations, the sector membership request of the entities should be approved by the Member State concerned,[4] which points towards ITU's governments-driven character.

ETSI membership categories are NSOs, recognized by their governments as national standard-setting bodies; governmental bodies, such as administrations responsible for electronic communications;[5] and private entities, including network operators, service providers, and manufacturers.[6] Companies can join ETSI with multiple entities (i.e., from different countries),[7] which has been criticized by the European Commission.[8] Demonstrated interest in ETSI's activities and acceptance of ETSI Directives is required to obtain its membership.[9] The status of full ETSI Members is only granted to affiliates located within the geographical area of the CEPT; others can join as associate Members[10] or – if they fulfil membership conditions but opt for limited participation – as observers.[11] Full Members are entitled to participate in the meetings of the General Assembly *and* Technical Bodies and have a right to vote in all matters, except for the cases in which the weighted national majority applies;[12] associate Members generally have the same rights as full Members, but with stricter voting limitations;[13] observers are neither entitled to vote in the governance-related matters, nor can they attend

[4] Article 19 of ITU Convention.

[5] See Annex 1.1 of ETSI Rules of Procedure.

[6] Article 6.1 and 6.3 of ETSI Statutes; Annex 1, Article 1 of ETSI Rules of Procedure. Those members can participate individually or grouped in National or European Organizations (i.e., group of manufacturers).

[7] This is evident from the list of current members; see 'ETSI members around the world', available at www.etsi.org/membership/members.

[8] 'An EU strategy on standardization' COM (2022).

[9] Article 6.3 of ETSI Statutes.

[10] Ibid., Articles 6.4 and 6.5; Articles 1.2.2 and 1.2.3 of ETSI Rules of Procedure.

[11] Article 6.6 ETSI Statutes; Article 1.2.4 of ETSI Rules of Procedure. Companies or NSOs may opt for observership when they are located outside CEPT countries and want to maintain a formal relationship in ETSI but have no capacity or mandate to participate in ETSI's technical work.

[12] Article 1.2.2 of ETSI Rules of Procedure.

[13] Ibid., Article 1.2.3; Article 1.4 of ETSI Technical Working Procedures.

standards development meetings,[14] and their membership fees are relatively lower than those of full and associate Members.[15] Applications to ETSI membership are examined and approved by consensus by the General Assembly.[16] Membership can be terminated by dissolution, abolition, resignation of the organization, or its expulsion by the General Assembly for nonpayment of contributions or substantial breach of other membership obligations – the latter is unspecified by the applicable provisions.[17]

3GPP members[18] are seven organizational partners – SDOs with national or regional recognition and compatible IPR policies[19] – market representation partners,[20] and, with the approval of organizational partners, individual members, legal entities that are members of (one of the) seven SDOs.[21] 3GPP partners operate at the governance level, and are responsible, that is, for 3GPP scope, creating of governance bodies, and conducting procedural appeals, as well as for terminating individual membership;[22] individual members contribute to the work of technical committees. 3GPP has two observers, SDOs from Australia and the US, and seven Guests (an individual member for a limited time), who may participate in standardization meetings on a limited basis: for instance, observers cannot submit changes to standards documents or hold leadership positions.[23]

IEEE membership is open to individuals and offers a variety of grades and categories depending on the applicant's professional and personal

[14] Unless exceptions are made and justified by legitimate interests, Article 1.4, ETSI Technical Working Procedures.

[15] Article 1.2.4 of ETSI Rules of Procedure. Interestingly, ETSI Statutes require to refer to observers as "members," unless the context indicates otherwise; see Article 6.2 of ETSI Statutes.

[16] Article 7.4.2 of ETSI Statutes; Article 1.4.3 of ETSI Rules of Procedure; pursuant to Article 1.3.2 of ETSI Rules of Procedure, the Director-General has an advisory function.

[17] Article 8 of ETSI Statutes.

[18] Membership categories are described in Article 4 of 3GPP Working Procedures (April 29, 2021), available at www.3gpp.org/ftp/Information/Working_Procedures/3GPP_WP.pdf, and are: partners, individual members, ITU representatives, observers, and guests. Note that ITU representatives have a specific membership status.

[19] Article 1.2 of 3GPP Partnership Agreement (December 4, 1998), available at www.3gpp.org/ftp/Inbox/2008_web_files/3gppagre.pdf; Article 6 of 3GPP Working Procedures. New partners can join when approved by organizational partners, Article 6 of 3GPP Partnership Agreement.

[20] Articles 1.3 and 4 of 3GPP Partnership Agreement; Article 7 of 3GPP Working Procedures.

[21] Article 8 of 3GPP Working Procedures.

[22] Ibid., Article 9.

[23] Ibid., Article 10.

circumstances,[24] and which are decided upon by the Admission and Advancement Committee.[25] In turn, IEEE-SA is largely comprised of entities, although its membership is also available to individuals.[26] Although the latter do not necessarily have to be affiliated with the IEEE, their prior membership of the Institute is encouraged by the lower participation fees.[27] All IEEE-SA members can vote in an unlimited number of standardization processes.[28] Members can be suspended or expelled from the IEEE-SA by the Board of Governors (BoG) upon approval of two-thirds of the BoG's voting members.[29] IEEE-SA Working Groups may further establish their own rules on acquiring, but also losing, membership and voting rights.[30]

IETF has no formal membership, and its work relies on volunteers joining the Working Groups. Every interested individual can join IETF activities by signing up to its Working Groups' mailing list, or by attending – less frequent – in-person meetings.[31] Joining IETF Working Groups by attending implies acceptance of IETF rules, including its IPR policy. Most contributors to IETF standards are engineers and field experts, who participate in their personal capacity, even when affiliated with or employed by an entity.[32]

W3C members are entities represented by nominated experts in Working and Interest Groups,[33] and who are approved by the Advisory

[24] Section I-100 of IEEE Bylaws. IEEE has following Membership grades: Honorary Member, Fellow, Senior Member, Member, Associate Member, Graduate Student and Student; and following membership categories: Electronic Membership, Life Members, Minimum Income, Permanently Disabled, Retired or Unemployed. IEEE Bylaws further specify the requirements for each category. Every category has its own conditions, rights, and privileges.

[25] Ibid., section I-106.6.

[26] Ibid., section I-403; in general, they are divided into three categories: individuals, not-for-profit enterprises, and for-profit enterprises.

[27] 57 US $ in comparison with 256 US $ for external parties; see Article 6.2 of IEEE-SA Operations Manual.

[28] Article 6.3.1 of IEEE-SA Operations Manual. Naturally, individual members vote in individual-based processes, while entities vote in in entity-based processes.

[29] Article 6.4.1 of IEEE-SA Operations Manual.

[30] In 802.11, for instance, participants were for a long time able to lose all voting rights "in one go," as it appears from the minutes of 802.11 Working Group's meetings.

[31] However, what was mentioned during the meetings also must be mentioned on the mailing lists. Interview with an expert from a cyber police authority, January 11, 2018.

[32] See 'Getting started in the IETF', available at http://ietf.org/newcomers.html.

[33] Clause 3.1 of World Wide Web Consortium Process Document, C. M. Nevile (ed.) (March 2017), available online at www.w3.org/2017/Process-20170301/ (hereinafter: W3C Process Document).

Committee.[34] All W3C members enjoy equal benefits, including a seat in the Advisory Committee, access to restricted information, opportunities to initiate a Member Submission process, and the possibility for their representatives to take part in W3C technical processes.[35] Different rights and obligations apply to the four host organizations, which are expected to provide vendor-neutral technical and administrative leadership and take an active role in the establishment of the Advisory Committee. Participation of civil society in W3C activities is possible through Community and Business Groups, which unlike Working Groups, are open to nonmembers, but also via specifications reviews, contributions of use cases, tests, and implementation feedback. Individuals may join W3C forum either as Affiliate Members or as "invited experts" upon the approval or invitation by the Working Group Chair.[36]

Bluetooth SIG membership is open to entities, and distinguishes between three classes: Promoters,[37] Associate Members, and Adopter Members. Promoters have voting power and are entitled to appoint a representative to the Board of Directors.[38] Adopter Members may implement the specifications and may participate in certain committees of the Bluetooth SIG.[39] Adopter Members that are promoted to Associate Members can access information from the Working Groups and committees, and certain subclasses of Associate Members also have voting power in these bodies.[40] Each Member has the right to access Bluetooth specifications, to participate in the Bluetooth Qualification Program and Testing Tools Program, and to license trademarks. Membership applications are approved by the Board of Directors; the Promoter members of this body may unanimously decide to suspend or terminate membership

[34] See Code of Ethics and Professional Conduct (2015) and the disclosure requirements as defined in Clause 6 of the W3C Patent Policy, D. J. Weitzner (ed.) (February 2004), available online at www.w3.org/Consortium/Patent-Policy-20040205/#sec-Disclosure (hereinafter: W3C Patent Policy).

[35] Clause 5 of the Draft International World Wide Web Consortium Member Agreement (2021).

[36] Clause 3.4 of W3C Process Document (2017).

[37] Initially, only seven founding companies were granted the status of Promoters – namely, Ericsson AB, Intel Corporation, Lenovo (Singapore) Pte. Ltd., Microsoft Corporation, Apple Inc., Nokia Corporation, and Toshiba Corporation, but other companies may be granted Promoter Membership upon the unanimous consent of then-current Promoters, section 4.4(a) of Bluetooth SIG Bylaws (2019).

[38] Ibid., section 4.1 and 4.3(a).

[39] Ibid., section 4.3(c).

[40] Ibid., section 4.3(b).

in case a Member has committed a material and serious violation of consortium's legal documents or has engaged in a conduct harmful for the purposes and the interest of the SIG.[41] Omission to pay membership dues does not necessarily lead to termination, but to demotion to a less influential membership category.[42]

By and large, industry membership, mostly commercial companies, or research facilities, appears to be dominating in (almost) all SDOs (Table 7.1). Governmental stakeholders have a specific status in ITU and ETSI (when it comes to ENs); their participation in other SDOs, while not prevented by operational rules, is rather rare, as it appears from their membership lists, and occurs on an equal footing with the rest of the members. Participation opportunities for nontechnical stakeholders are provided through possibilities to observe in technical committees (yet, typically at the discretion of a chair), or through stakeholder consultations, public review (IEEE, ETSI), or testing procedures (Bluetooth SIG).

Furthermore, technical knowledge and interest in the particular operational fields are necessary requirements to be eligible for SDOs membership. In all examined SDOs, signing a membership agreement or joining the Working Groups (IETF) implies acceptance of SDO rules, including IPR policies. Membership allocation typically affects membership fees, rights, and duties, especially in consortia. Almost all SDOs allow companies to join with multiple entities, with each entity maintaining its membership rights: W3C and Bluetooth SIG maintain specific requirements for members associations[43] and Affiliates, respectively.[44] Importantly, regardless of whether participation is individual-based (IETF, and to some extent IEEE), or entity-based, as in the majority of SDOs, experts are required to disclose their affiliation; members of some SDOs' governance bodies are required to act in private capacity and have fiduciary duty to the SDO (i.e., IEEE-SA, ETSI Board).[45]

[41] Ibid., section 4.6.

[42] Ibid., section 4.4.

[43] Clause 2.1.2 of W3C Process Document (2017).

[44] Any entity directly or indirectly controlled by a Bluetooth SIG Member is considered its Affiliate and is entitled to the same rights and restrictions as the Member; Member and Affiliate have one vote. Section 4.9 of Bluetooth SIG Bylaws (2019).

[45] To the contrary, members of other ETSI governance bodies owe fiduciary duty towards their employers.

*Table 7.1. Comparison among members and membership types*

| SDOs | Members | Membership types | Contributors to standards development |
|---|---|---|---|
| ITU | Governmental agencies of UN Member States, companies, scientific and industrial organizations, telecommunications organizations, SDOs | UN Member States and Sectoral Members | In principle all Members, UN Member States have voting power in the Plenipotentiary Conference |
| ETSI | NSOs, network operators, service provides, manufacturers, users, research bodies, administrations, governmental bodies | Full (CEPT countries); associates and observers (non-voting) | Full and associate members (via representatives) |
| 3GPP | Regional SDOs and their (company) members | Organizational partners, market representation partners, individual members, observers and guests | Individual members (legal entities) |
| IEEE-SA | Individual experts/professionals, commercial entities, trade associations, governmental agencies | Individual or corporate | Individuals and entities (via representatives), no prior membership required |
| IETF | No formal membership, individuals wishing to contribute join the mailing lists of working groups | N.A. | Software engineers, individuals affiliated with network operators and networking hard- and software vendors, academics, representatives of computer and trade press |
| W3C | Organizations, in some cases also individual experts | Four host organizations (non-members); entity-members; member consortium; affiliate members (individual experts) | Organizations via representatives; individuals |
| Bluetooth SIG | Firms, corporations, or other legal entities with a demonstrated interest in the activities of the consortium | Promoters (voting members), Associate Members and Adopter Members | Associate Members and Promoters in Working Groups, and all membership in Expert or Study Groups. |

## SDO Financing

While income generation is not the purpose of SDOs,[46] they nevertheless require funding to support their administrative and technical activities; in some cases, this also includes remunerations for SDO staff and officers, although such administrative and leadership positions are largely voluntary. ITU and ETSI[47] benefit directly from governmental funding due to their mandates;[48] but governments may also contribute to the funding of private SDOs via grants, joint programs, and research support.[49] SDOs may also raise revenues through research grants, sponsorship, donations, and through royalties from intellectual property and the sales of standards documents (e.g., IEEE).[50] Furthermore, SDOs' activities and meetings are financed by membership fees.

Membership dues in ITU are allocated per unit classes, established by the ITU Council, and approved by the Plenipotentiary Conference,[51] and depends on members' geographical and institutional background.[52] Developing countries are allowed to pay the lowest membership fee, while a minimum unit class of contribution is required for Sector Members, except entities located in developing countries.[53] ETSI's membership fees for full and associate members are identical; they are proportional to the number of class units of contribution applicable to every membership category.[54] Microenterprises, SMEs, public research bodies, and user associations are subject to reduced annual membership fees.[55] IEEE membership dues vary according to the membership class, but

[46] At the same time, increased income, at least in theory, can ensure sustainability of an institution, involvement of all stakeholders, and better-quality standards. See also the ASTM argument in *ASTM* v. *PRO*.

[47] The funding from the EC and EFTA amounts to 15–20 percent of the ETSI budget; see 'Funding ETSI', available at www.etsi.org/about/what-we-are/funding.

[48] US-government financing of IETF activities has ceased upon the increased commercialization of the internet.

[49] Bremer, 'American and European perspectives', pp. 342–3.

[50] Note that is generally the case for those SDOs that offer their standards for sale, including CEN/CENELEC, IEC, and ISO.

[51] See next section for the explanation of ITU governance bodies.

[52] Article 7 and Article 33 of ITU Convention. Rules and procedures applied for selection and approval of unit classes by Member States, see Articles 28bis, 28(3), 28(3).

[53] Article 33 of ITU Convention.

[54] See Annex 2 of ETSI Rules of Procedure for the determination of contributions.

[55] Interestingly, trade associations are "effectively" considered SMEs; see Clause 2 of ETSI, Guidelines for the Implementation of Annex 2 of the Rules of Procedure, Version adopted by General Assembly #58 (November 30, 2011).

IEEE-SA operated on an expense-neutral basis to IEEE. Like IEEE-SA, IETF management bodies maintain separate funding mechanisms; its Secretariat, for instance, is financially supported by the IASA, which derives its revenues from IETF meetings and the Internet Society (ISOC) funding.[56] In W3C, membership fees depend on stakeholders' revenues and type and location of its headquarters;[57] its finances are managed by the host organizations.[58] Bluetooth SIG members do not derive any financial benefit from standardization activities, and membership fees are used to support its testing, promotion, and operational expenses.[59]

## SDOs' Governance Bodies

While this section cannot extensively discuss the structure and composition of *all* SDO governance bodies – committees responsible for SDO management and administration – it attempts to highlight the most important issues.

The governance bodies of ITU are the Plenipotentiary Conference, the ITU Council, the World Conference on International Telecommunications, three ITU Sectors (where most technical activities are carried out), and the Secretariat.[60] Each ITU Sector has its own boards, conferences, and assemblies, which may establish working methods and procedures for the management of the respective Sector. The main ITU policy-making body, the Plenipotentiary Conference, consists of ITU Member States and is held every four years; it discusses diplomatic and administrative aspects of ITU's work; adopts the General Rules of conferences, assemblies, and meetings; and elects SDO leadership.[61] The ITU Council acts as a governing body between Plenipotentiary Conferences; it consists of different Working and Expert Groups. Council members are elected by the Plenipotentiary Conference among individuals appointed by the Member States;[62] Council seats are divided between five

56 Section 2.2.1 of 'The Tao of IETF'.

57 Clause 2 of Draft International W3C Member Agreement (2021).

58 H. Halpin, 'The crisis of standardizing DRM: the case of W3C encrypted media extensions' (2017) in *Proceedings of the 7th International Conference, SPACE 2017*, Goa, India, December 13–17.

59 Section 4.5 of Bluetooth SIG Bylaws (2019).

60 Article 7 of ITU Constitution.

61 Ibid., Articles 8 and 32.

62 Article 4(5) of ITU Convention.

geographical regions, and the number of Council Members is determined by the Plenipotentiary Conference every four years but cannot exceed 25 percent of ITU Member States.[63] The Council elects its own leadership, taking into account rotation between the regions. The ITU has a heavily involved Secretariat with a large number of staff;[64] it is directed by the Secretary General, who acts as ITU's legal representative,[65] who is assisted by the deputy and the ITU Coordination Committee, which also represents ITU in international organizations.[66]

ETSI's main bodies are the General Assembly, the Board, the Technical Organization, Special Committees, Industry Specification Groups, and a Secretariat.[67] The General Assembly is the highest authority of the Institute, and is comprised of representatives of all Members and Counsellors of EC and EFTA,[68] preceded by a Chairman who is elected from full ETSI members. The General Assembly adopts ETSI's procedural rules and binding resolutions;[69] it also appoints the Board, which consists of representatives of full Members[70] who act in their individual capacity.[71] The Board elects the Director-General, ETSI's legal representative,[72] assisted by the Secretariat, which is also entrusted with logistical and operational tasks.[73] Technical work takes place in ETSI's Technical Organization, which in turn encompasses three types of Technical Bodies with different scope of activities: an ETSI Project, Technical Committee, and ETSI Partnership Project.[74] Technical Bodies further establish their Working Groups and decide on the rules governing their activities. The General Assembly may intervene in the work of the Technical Organization by modifying its structure or setting

[63] Articles 9(1a), 10, and 61 of ITU Constitution; Article 4 of ITU Convention.
[64] Shanin, 'The European Union's performance', p. 686.
[65] Article 11 of ITU Constitution.
[66] Article 6 of ITU Convention.
[67] Article 10 of ETSI Statutes; Article 2 of ETSI Rules of Procedure.
[68] Article 11 of ETSI Statutes.
[69] Ibid.; see Article 3 of ETSI Rules of Procedure for the full list of the General Assembly's functions.
[70] Article 13 of ETSI Statutes; Article 5 of ETSI Rules of Procedure. Although both full and associate members may nominate the candidates, only those affiliated with full members can get elected.
[71] Annex 7.2 of ETSI Rules of Procedure.
[72] Article 15 of ETSI Statutes; Article 8 of ETSI Rules of Procedure.
[73] Article 16 of ETSI Statutes; Article 9 of ETSI Rules of Procedure.
[74] Article 14 of ETSI Statutes; Article 6 of ETSI Rules of Procedure. Article 1 of ETSI Technical Working Procedures. Technical Bodies are established by the General Assembly or the Board.

up Special Committees[75] and Special Task Forces with a limited duration.[76]

3GPP consist of the Project Coordination Group (PCG) and three Technical Specification Groups (TSGs) covering different work areas – Radio Access Network, Services & Systems Aspects, and Core Network & Terminals. The PCG is the highest decision-making body of 3GPP, which is responsible for the SDO's overall management, leadership appointment, handling of technical and procedural appeals, and final adoption of the work item;[77] it is composed of representative of organizational and market partners, and TSGs chairs and vice chairs as ex officio members, and a maximum of three ITU representatives and one representative of each observer.[78] TSGs prepare, approve, and maintain technical specifications and reports, handle technical appeals from individual members, and provide technical coordination.[79] Next to partners, TSGs are also open to individual members, observers, and guests.[80] TSGs further break their work into "goals" and "features," to be broken down into building blocks and work tasks and assigned to a specific Working Group where the technical work on standards is conducted.[81]

The governing bodies of IEEE are the Board of Directors and the Assembly. The Board of Directors counts thirty-one directors who represent various interests and are elected either by the IEEE voting members or the Assembly;[82] it is the highest authority of the institution and deals with the matter of fundamental importance: for instance, it may propose amendments for IEEE Constitution, approve assessments of IEEE members,[83] and sanction those members whose conducts violate

[75] Article 3.4 of ETSI Rules of Procedure.

[76] Ibid. Special Task Forces are established to fulfil specific tasks in support of the standardization activities, and in general follow the same rules as Technical Committees. After approval and adoption of the deliverables by the Technical Body, the Special Task Force cease to exist, unless decided otherwise.

[77] Articles 14 and 42 of 3GPP Working Procedures.

[78] Ibid., Article 15.

[79] Ibid., Article 20.

[80] Ibid., Article 21.

[81] Ibid., Article 11; Article 2.2 of 3GPP Partnership Agreement; J. Baron and K. Gupta, 'Unpacking 3GPP Standards' (2018) 27 *Journal of Economics and Management Strategy* 433–61.

[82] Article XIX section 4 of IEEE Constitution.

[83] Section I-301 of IEEE Bylaws. For that decision to be taken, 2/3 favorable votes of the Board of Directors is required.

IEEE rules or are seriously prejudicial to the SDO.[84] Responsible to the Board of Directors,[85] IEEE-SA is chaired by its own President, elected for a term of two years.[86] The main governing body of IEEE-SA is the BoG[87] which adopts policies governing standardization activities and makes recommendation on matters related to standard-setting to the Board of Directors.[88] The BoG is comprised of fifteen members elected every two years by IEEE voting members who also hold the membership of IEEE-SA: its composition should reflect technical and global standards interests of the IEEE, and should also be balanced with regard to the interests involved in IEEE-SA activities.[89] The BoG annually appoints the Standards Board (SASB), which consists of minimum eighteen and maximum twenty-six individuals possessing the membership of both IEEE and the IEEE-SA.[90] The SASB coordinates standards development work, approves new projects, and reviews them against the requirements of consensus, due process, openness, and balance.[91] The activities of the SASB are divided between several committees, whose members are appointed for a one-year term by the Chair of the Standards Board (Table 7.2). As an overarching requirement, individuals in standing committees should possess the membership of the IEEE-SA and act in accordance with the IEEE and the IEEE-SA legal framework,[92] including the fiduciary duty to the Institute.

One of the main bodies dealing with the technical work of the IETF is the Internet Engineering Steering Group (IESG), which serves as a

[84] Article I-110.1 of IEEE Bylaws. No further specification is provided with regard to the term "seriously prejudicial."

[85] Section I-303 of IEEE Bylaws. Matters delegated to organizations units by means of IEEE Bylaws require approval of the governing body of that unit and subsequent review and approval of the Board of Directors prior to their implementation.

[86] Article 4.2.2 of IEEE-SA Operations Manual (February 2022). The three-year rotation scheme is similar to that of the IEEE President.

[87] Ibid., Article 4.2.1.

[88] Article 4 of IEEE-SA Operations Manual.

[89] No individual IEEE Society or council, or government, or industry should be over-represented in the structure of the IEEE-SA BoG; see Article 4.2.1 of IEEE-SA Operations Manual.

[90] Ibid., Article 5.1.2; Article 4.1 of IEEE-SA Standard Board Bylaws (February 2022). Next to that, SASB may also include nonvoting participants, like liaison representatives or members emeriti. Members of the IEEE-SA Standards Board may serve up to three consecutive one-year terms; Article 5.1.2.2 of IEEE-SA Operations Manual.

[91] Article 5.1 of IEEE-SA Operations Manual. Further explanation as regards these principles is not provided.

[92] Article 4.2 of IEEE-SA Standards Board Bylaws.

Table 7.2. *Structure of IEEE-SA committees*

| Name of committee | Number of members | Tasks |
|---|---|---|
| ProCom | Minimum six, no ex officio | Recommends modifications to the IEEE-SA governing documents |
| NesCom | Ten to fifteen members of various technical divisions, of which at least four voting members of IEEE-SA SASB; six ex officio | Reviews whether proposed standardization projects comply with the IEEE requirements |
| RevCom | Twelve to fifteen, at least three voting members of IEEE-SA SASB; no ex officio | Evaluates and recommends (dis)approval of new or amended standards |
| AudCom | At least five, five current or former members of IEEE-SA SASB; no ex officio | Provides oversight of Sponsors' activities in standards-development procedures |
| PatCom | Four to six voting members of IEEE-SA SASB *or* IEEE-SA BoG; one IEEE Standards staff designated by the Managing Director of Standards Activities; ex officio. | Reviews standard-setting processes regarding the use of patented technologies; provides overview for the use of patents and patent information in the IEEE standards; delivers nonbinding recommendations for defining of IPR policy |

"management group" of IETF and bears direct responsibility for the progress of the standardization project, including final approval of specifications as Internet Standards. IESG is comprised of the IETF Chair and the Area Directors (AD), randomly selected by the Nominating Committee (NomCom) from a pool of volunteers and approved by the Internet Architecture Board (IAB) for a term of two years, each of them responsible for an area of a specific focus of IETF work.[93] ADs may assume a liaison role within other organizations when it comes to the

[93] Section 2.2.2 of 'The Tao of IETF'. It is also possible that multiple ADs are responsible for one area.

matter of technical cooperation.[94] Each area of IETF activities[95] is comprised of multiple Working Groups, whose coordination also falls under the responsibility of the ADs. In turn, each Working Group is chaired by one or more volunteer who manages its work an ensures that the necessary deadlines are met.[96]

Long-range coordination of IETF activities is entrusted to the IAB,[97] which reviews new IETF Working Groups as regards their architectural consistency and integrity, oversees the IETF liaisons, appoints the IETF Chair and approves IESG candidates.[98] IAB also serves as an appeal board for complaints of improper standard-setting process and for appeals against IESG and the IETF Administrative Oversight Committee (IAOC).[99] IAB members do not represent their affiliations, and neither do they owe fiduciary duty of loyalty or care to any governance body.[100] IAB is comprised of twelve full members selected for a two-year term by the NomCom and approved by the ISOC Board, and nonvoting IETF Chair.[101] In turn, the NomCom is composed of a nonvoting chair, appointed by the President of the ISOC; two or three liaisons from IESG, IAB, and ISOC; and an advisor, who is typically a previous NomCom chair, as well as ten members randomly selected from eligible IETF volunteers who have attended a minimum three of the last five IETF meetings.[102] The administrative structure of the IETF Working Groups, IESG, IAB, and Internet Research Task Force (IRTF) is provided by the IETF Administrative Support Activity (IASA),[103] whose scope is

94 Ibid.

95 For the full description of areas, see http://ietf.org/iesg/area.html.

96 See 'Working groups', available at www.ietf.org/wg/. A full list of active IETF Working Groups can be found at http://datatracker.ietf.org/wg/.

97 'Charter of the Internet Architecture Board (IAB)', B. Carpenter (ed.) (May 2000) RCF28050, available at https://tools.ietf.org/html/rfc2850; 'Internet Architecture Board: overview', available at www.iab.org/about/iab-overview/. The partnership between IAB and IETF was, however, tested by the tensions between OSI and TCP/IP, where the different approaches to architecture and organizational structure resulted in "constitutional crisis" that forced IETF participants to revisit their procedural beliefs. See A. Russel, '"Rough consensus and running code" and the internet-OSI standard wars' (2006) 28 *IEEE Annals of the History of Computing* 48–61.

98 Section 2 of the 'Charter of the Internet Architecture Board (IAB)' (2000).

99 Ibid.

100 Ibid., section 1.

101 Ibid.

102 See 'IAB, IESG, and IAOC selection, confirmation, and recall process: operation of the nominating and recall committees', M. Kucherawy (ed.), (January 2015) RFC 7437, available at https://datatracker.ietf.org/doc/rfc7437/?include_text=1.

103 'Structure of the IETF Administrative Support Activity (IASA)', R. Austein (ed.) (April 2005) BCP 101, available at https://tools.ietf.org/html/rfc4071.

established by the IAOC[104] The IAOC is composed of volunteers selected directly or indirectly by the IETF community and ex officio members from ISOC and IETF leadership.[105]

The highest governance body of the W3C, the W3C Team, is composed of the CEO, W3C paid staff and fellows (employed by W3C Members), and the Director, who has the ultimate decision-making power.[106] Director's tasks include assessing whether consensus has been reached within the W3C community, appointing group chairs, and adjudicating as "tie-breaker" for Group decision appeals. The other three hosts supply a Deputy Director, responsible before the Director for the activities within the ERCIM, KEIO, and BEIHANG.[107] W3C members are represented in the Advisory Board,[108] which reviews charter proposals, recommendations, and process documents; and is chaired by a person appointed by the Team, typically the CEO.[109] The Team is obliged to update the Advisory Committee as regards the membership modifications and the overview of the W3C finances. The W3C Team is furthermore assisted by the Advisory Board on issues of strategy, management, process, legal matters, and conflict resolution; the Advisory Board also manages the evolution of the Process Document and provides support in the disagreements between the Members by hearing a Submission Appeal.[110] It is comprised of nine participants elected by the Advisory Committee for a term of two years, and a Chair, appointed by the Team.[111] Technical issues around web architecture are managed by the Technical Architecture Group (TAG), whose tasks include interpretation and clarification of web architecture principles and coordinating cross-technology developments within and outside W3C.[112] The TAG consists of eight participants, of which three are appointed by the Director, and five elected by the Advisory Committee, for a term of two years; each of the TAG members has one vote.[113]

[104] Section 2.2.1 of 'The Tao of IETF'.
[105] See 'IAB, IESG, and IAOC selection, confirmation, and recall process'.
[106] Clause 2.2 of W3C Process Document (2017).
[107] Clause 4 of Draft International W3C Member Agreement (2021).
[108] Clause 2.3.1 of W3C Process Document (2017).
[109] Ibid., Clause 2.2.
[110] The later occurs in cases unrelated to web architecture; Ibid., Clause 2.3.
[111] Ibid.
[112] Ibid., Clause 2.4.
[113] Ibid.

The governing body of the Bluetooth SIG is the Board of Directors,[114] responsible for the final adoption of all Bluetooth specifications, the oversight and the final approval of Qualification Program and Testing Tool Program, and the establishment of all committees and Working Groups,[115] as well as appointment of the SIG's leadership.[116] It is composed of one representative appointed by each Promoter for an unlimited time,[117] and up to four Associate Member Directors (AMD) serving a two-year term,[118] appointed by the unanimous approval of the Promoter Members.[119] Directors typically are not remunerated for their services to the consortium,[120] but financial compensation may be provided by the Members who appointed the Directors.[121] Each Member can appoint individuals to observe the meetings of the Board of Directors.[122] Other bodies that support the work of the Bluetooth SIG are the Bluetooth Qualification Review Board (BQRB);[123] the Bluetooth Test and Interoperability Group (BTI),[124] responsible for the qualification and testing programs; and the Bluetooth Architectural Review Board (BARB), providing the architectural oversight of the specifications and supporting the Working Groups and consisting of one member appointed by each Promoter.[125] The Chairmen of these bodies are selected by the 4/5 votes of the Board of Directors, to whom these bodies are also accountable.

There are three types of groups entrusted with technical activities of the SIG: Working Groups are responsible for the development and modification of Bluetooth specifications and are open to Associate Members and Promoters; Expert Groups provide expertise and

[114] Section 6.1 of Bluetooth SIG Bylaws (2019).
[115] Ibid., section 6.7.
[116] Ibid., section 7.1.
[117] Representatives are typically employees of Member-entities.
[118] The access to the minutes of board meetings is restricted.
[119] Section 6.3 of Bluetooth SIG Bylaws (2019). As it is the case for the Promoter-members, such individual should be an employee of the Associate Members.
[120] However, a reasonable fee may be paid to Directors for attending regular and special meetings of the Board of Directors and performing their duties.
[121] Section 6.7 of Bluetooth SIG Bylaws (2019).
[122] Ibid., section 6.18.
[123] Ibid., section 8.5 (a).
[124] Ibid., section 8.5 (b).
[125] Ibid., section 8.5 (c).

guidance to the Working Groups, and are open to all members; Study Groups develop guidelines to enable new usage models, and are open to all members. To contribute to the Working Group, an eligible Member has to apply online for the group's membership and to comply with the requirements of the Working Group's Charter.

SDOs' governance and management bodies function as a complex network that provides ecosystem for technical activities and support the functioning of their technical committees and working groups. The analyzed SDOs demonstrate some institutional similarities: for instance, the distinction between the bodies responsible for SDOs management and those dealing with technical activities; leadership appointment or election; participation of ex officio members without voting power in the governance bodies (i.e., ITU, IEEE, and multiple IETF(-related) bodies). The highest authorities of some SDOs are composed of the entire membership of that SDO, as in case of the General Assembly in ETSI. More often, however, the "membership" of governance bodies is limited to certain types or categories of SDO members/participants. For example, the W3C Advisory Committee is comprised of all W3C members, but the crucial role in W3C governance is played by the W3C Team and, ultimately, the Director. In the ITU, the Plenipotentiary Conference is composed of Member States, which are then presumed to represent the interest of the private sector – the Sector Members – at the policy-making level.

## Decision-Making in Policy Drafting

SDOs' operational frameworks need to reflect the regulatory landscape and the preference of SDO stakeholders; otherwise, SDOs risk breaking the applicable regulatory requirements or losing their relevance as standard setters. Hence, whenever any of these or other factors external to SDO governance are changing, the operational rules can be expected to change accordingly. Similar to processes of developing a standard, SDOs would have specific requirements as to actors authorized to modify their policies, as well as procedures to be followed for drafting and updating SDOs' rules, which may differ from their usual decision-making procedures.

ITU governance rules are codified in the Constitution, Convention, Administrative Regulation, and the Resolutions; they can be modified by the Plenipotentiary Conference (thus, the ITU Member States).

Amendments to the Constitution and Convention can be proposed by any Member State; the quorum to consider the proposal is more than one half of the delegations at the Plenipotentiary Conference; and to adopt the amendments to the Constitution – at least 2/3 of the voting members of the Plenipotentiary Conference (more than a half for the Convention).[126] Resolutions that further specify ITU procedures are typically adopted in a consensus-based process, which is also how the Plenipotentiary Conference takes its other decisions. The ITU Council adopts its own rules and procedures.[127] Policies and processes of each Sector are drafted by this Sector's assembly composed of Member States and Sector Members. ITU-T Study and Working Groups operate following the procedures established by the World Telecommunications Standardization Assembly.

ETSI Directives are drafted by the General Assembly. When amending the Statutes and the Rules of Procedure, the General Assembly should take decisions by qualified majority voting; the quorum for Statutes' modification is at least 75 percent of the total weighted votes cast in favor, and for the Rules of Procedure, at least 71 percent.[128] Although both full and associate Members have a right to vote in the General Assembly, only the ballots of full Members are considered when determining the quorum.[129]

Interestingly, while ideally consensus based,[130] the General Assembly uses different procedures for the issues pertaining ETSI's governance. The Weighted National Voting is used for decisions pertaining to European Standards, amendments of legal framework, and disputes arising from the application of the Rules of Procedure;[131] votes are cast by the NSOs.[132] Membership issues and matters related to policy or regulatory documents intended to be used in the EU are handled by the Weighted Individual Voting by *full* ETSI Members. In other situations, the Weighted Individual Voting by *both full and associate*

126 Article 55 of ITU Constitution; Article 42 of ITU Convention.

127 Article 4 Sub 10 of ITU Convention.

128 Article 18 of ETSI Statutes; Article 19 of ETSI Rules of Procedure.

129 Article 11.1 of ETSI Rules of Procedure.

130 Ibid., Article 11.1.1.

131 Ibid., Article 11.2.1.

132 The allocation of weighted national votes is introduced in Annex 3 of ETSI Rules of Procedure; Members having the most votes are Germany, UK, France, and Italy, while Montenegro is a member with the least votes.

*Members* is used.[133] Under the mentioned procedures, a decision is approved by 71 percent of positive ballots. The voting quorum for the General Assembly is at least 50 percent of the total number of weighted votes of *full* members; abstentions of or submitting failures to not count as a vote.[134] Minority rights should be protected during the voting procedures:[135] however, the regulatory provisions of the ETSI leave obscure the concept of "minority," and do not specify which rights should be protected and how.

3GPP's Partnership Agreement can be modified by consensus of organizational partners[136] and its working procedures by consensus of the Project Coordination Group (organizational and market partners).[137] Consensus is the typical decision-making process of the Project Coordination Group; however, if consensus cannot be reached, the chair can resort to voting, with 50 percent of the total number of organizational partners being a quorum,[138] and 71 percent of favorable votes a tiebreaker. The Technical Specification Groups and Working Groups should also endeavor to reach consensus; if consensus cannot be achieved, chairs can establish tentative working agreements,[139] or resort to voting, with a quorum of 30 percent of total number of voting members.[140]

IEEE's Constitution is amended in the balloting process of all IEEE voting members, while its Bylaws by the Board of Directors,[141] both with an approval quorum of 2/3.[142] IEEE-SA Standards Board Bylaws, which provide policies for management and creation of IEEE standards, are maintained by IEEE-SA SASB or its standing committees;[143] amendments are adopted upon the favorable votes of 2/3 of the voting IEEE-SASB members[144] *and* the approval by the BoG.[145] Working procedures

133 Annex 4 of ETSI Rules of Procedure.
134 Ibid., Article 12.1; for voting for standards approval by correspondence, this minimum should be reached by a specific date.
135 Ibid., Article 11.1.4.
136 Article 5 of 3GPP Partnership Agreement.
137 Article 60 of 3GPP Working Procedures.
138 Ibid., Article 19.
139 Ibid., Article 25 and Annex G.
140 Ibid., Article 26; see also Article 35 for voting lists.
141 Article III section 3 of IEEE Constitution.
142 Ibid., Article II section 2.
143 For instance, PatCom is consulted for modifications of IPR policy.
144 Article 8 of IEEE-SA Standards Board Bylaws.
145 Article 4.1.1 of IEEE-SA Operations Manual.

of the SASB are governed by the IEEE-SA SASB Operations Manual: SASB members or standing committees may propose modifications to this document to the Standards Board Secretary; however, only ProCom is entitled to review the SASB Operations Manual, and the final approval of any modifications should be sought by the IEEE-SA SASB.[146] The IEEE-SA Operations Manual contains rules for IEEE-SA governance bodies, and is created and modified by the IEEE-SA BoG.

The decision-making processes also differ per governance body. The IEEE Assembly, the Board of Directors (BoD), and any other IEEE Major Board or its committees decides the majority voting of those present at time of the vote; approval of a BoD action without a meeting requires a unanimous consent of BoD.[147] Approval or status modification of IEEE standards[148] and the formulation of a new Sponsor requires favorable votes of at least 75 percent of the SASB voting members.[149] IEEE-SA Study and Working Groups establish their own operational rules, as long as they comply with the requirements of fair and open participation, due process, consideration of technical alternatives, and such transparency obligations as publishing meeting agenda and making the minutes of meeting available. The Policies and Procedures (P&P) of all Working Groups should be approved by their Sponsor. Study and Working Groups take decisions based on consensus. In case majority voting is required, it is up to the committees to define "majority"; IEEE-SA Study Group Guidelines recommend a minimum of five persons for individual-based groups, and a minimum of three entities for entity-based groups, but the ultimate determination of the voting quorum is left to the Sponsor.[150]

IETF rules for policy drafting are decided by consensus in dedicated Working Groups and are subsequently published as BCP RFCs. IETF IPR policy is expected to represent the consensus of the IETF community, and, therefore, is subject to public review and approval by the IESG.[151]

[146] Article 9.1 of IEEE Standards Board Operations Manual (January 2022).

[147] Section I-300.4 of IEEE Bylaws.

[148] For example, from "active" to "inactive" status.

[149] Article 5.1 of IEEE-SA Standards Board Bylaws.

[150] 'IEEE-SA study group guidelines', available at https://standards.ieee.org/develop/corpchan/studygrp.pdf.

[151] See, for instance, the 2017 IPR Policy, stating, "This document is a product of the Internet Engineering Task Force (IETF). It represents the consensus of the IETF community. It has received public review and has been approved for publication by the Internet Engineering Steering Group (IESG)." 'Intellectual property rights in IETF technology', S. Bradner and L. Contreras (eds.), (May 2017) BCP 79, available at www.rfc-editor.org/rfc/rfc8179.txt (hereinafter: IETF IPR Policy).

IETF governance bodies establish their own decision-making mechanisms and quora: for instance, IAOC decides by consensus with voting as an alternative;[152] IAB and IESG prefer unanimity, but allow consensus, with IAB seeking an agreement of least seven full members and allowing a dissent of a maximum of two; and IESG seeks the agreement of the chair and ADs.[153] NomCom voting mechanism is established by its chair.[154] Working Groups do not maintain "hard rules" for decision-making, and entrust the decision on whether consensus has been reached by their chair.

The W3C Process Document, containing rules for W3C Working Groups and governance bodies, is developed by the Advisory Board' Process Task Force in the Revising W3C Process Community Group and is subsequently reviewed by the W3C Membership.[155] W3C Working Groups should strive to achieve consensus during the meetings, with chairs playing important roles in consensus-reaching; but voting is also listed as an option for resolving substantial issues or taking a process decision.[156] Formal voting procedures and quora are specified in the Working Group charters, and Working Groups should set minimum threshold of support to avoid decisions to be taken with many abstentions.[157]

The Bylaws of Bluetooth SIG may only be amended by unanimous approval of the Promoters.[158] The rules of procedure are usually described in the committees' or Working Groups' charters, subject to approval by 4/5 of the entire Board of Directors.[159] The Working Group Process Document is approved with 4/5 votes of the entire Board of Directors. The Specification Management Process Document (SMPD) defines the processes that should be followed for developing new specifications or updating the existing ones.[160] Although it is unclear from the

152 Section 4.2 of IAOC Administrative Procedures (February 15, 2016), available at https://iaoc.ietf.org/policy-procedures.html.

153 See Charter of the Internet Architecture Board (IAB) (2000).

154 'Update to RFC 3777 to clarify nominating committee eligibility of IETF leadership', B. Leiba (ed.) (January 2013) RCP 6859, available at https://tools.ietf.org/html/rfc6859.

155 For the evolution of the document, see the marked comparison available at www.w3.org/2017/Process-20170301/diff-20150901.html.

156 Clause 3.3 of W3C Process Document (2017).

157 Ibid.

158 Article XVI of Bluetooth SIG Bylaws (2019).

159 Ibid., section. 8.3.

160 Note that Bylaws and Membership Agreements take precedence over conflicting elements in these documents and the SMPD. Section 1.1 of Bluetooth SIG Bylaws (2019).

document which committee is in charge of its amendments, the BARB appears a contact point for any questions regarding SMPD.[161] The Board of Directors decides by majority voting, unless the legal framework of the SIG provides otherwise.[162] However, the approval of certain actions, including the appointment of the AMDs, the approval of new membership subclass, or adoption of a document establishing substantive or procedural rights for multiple committees requires unanimous consent of the Promoter Members of the Board of Directors.[163] Approval of any changes to the Working Groups' processes and the annual budget, as well as vetoing of Working Group actions, requires 4/5 votes of the *entire* Board of Directors.[164]

Policy drafting processes thus vary across SDOs.[165] Perhaps somewhat contra-intuitively, operational rules of some "formalized" SDOs, that is, ETSI and IEEE-SA, are amended more frequently than those of some informal institutions or consortia, that is, IETF and W3C[166] (even though the updates are generally marginal).

A striking phenomenon is that despite their differences, as a contrast to their consensus-based standardization processes, almost all SDOs (3GPP being an exception) appear to not pursue consensus in their policy-making. Likewise, with the exception of ETSI, policy amendments are typically drafted and approved by specific committees, rather than the whole membership. In ITU, only Member States are allowed to take decisions related to its governance; it can be argued, however, that the Member States take on board the interest of their Sector Members, thereby bringing "national consensus" to the Plenipotentiary Conference. Some SDOs do not directly involve the entire membership

[161] It remains unclear, however, how are the contributors to the document are appointed/ selected.

[162] Section 6.14 of Bluetooth SIG Bylaws (2019).

[163] Ibid., section 6.19.

[164] Ibid.

[165] The JRC Report, having studied a larger example of SDOs, notes that the processes differ with respect to individuals participating in policy development: some SDOs are membership driven, while others expect individuals to have fiduciary duty to the SDO, and are more leadership driven. JRC Report, p. 13.

[166] For a long time, standardization activities within IETF were governed by the IPR Policy that dates to 2005; the policy has been amended only in 2017; in turn, the W3C IPR Policy was established in 2004. The operational framework of IEEE-SA, 3GPP, and ETSI has been amended once or even twice a year. Bluetooth SIG implemented important changes to its Bylaws and Process Document, modifying the Bluetooth specifications approval process.

in their policy-making, but allow their members to review (and comment on) amendments to their governing documents (i.e., W3C, IEEE-SA, and to a certain extent, IETF, where the process is identical to standards development). Furthermore, SDOs generally allow their specialized committees and Working Groups to adopt their own procedural and even membership rules, which sometimes require the approval of a governing body. In this regard, Working Groups chairs are left with great decisional discretion on meeting conduct and consensus-seeking.

The differences between membership types and categories are apparent from the voting allocation within SDOs' bodies. In ETSI, an entity or NSO with higher membership fees will have more voting units; ETSI is the only SDO in our sample that does not follow the "one member, one vote" principle. IEEE voting members can elect the Institute's officials and determine the composition of its governing bodies, whereas IEEE-SA members vote only in the standardization activities, which, at first glance, questions their representation at the higher hierarchical levels. The Bluetooth SIG grants voting rights only to the permanent group of Promoters, who also nominate the Board of Directors and approve the accession of new Promoters to the SDO, in fact confirming the close nature of the decision-making group.

## Appeal and Dispute Resolution

Like other types of international disputes, disagreements between Member States that relate to interpretation of the ITU's regulatory framework are preferably resolved through negotiations, diplomatic channels, or as prescribed in the treaties among these Members, or any other mutually agreed method;[167] if none of these methods is used, Member States party to the optional protocol on the compulsory settlement of disputes should resort to arbitration.[168] Appeals procedures for the decisions of ITU bodies and officers are typically handled by the Board of the relevant Sectors, or by the relevant bodies, depending on the decisions concerned.[169] At the plenary meetings, any Member State

[167] Article 56 of ITU Constitution and Article 41 of ITU Convention.

[168] Optional Protocol on the Compulsory Settlement of Disputes Relating to the Constitution of the International Telecommunication Union, to the Convention of the International Telecommunication Union and to the Administrative Regulations (December 22, 1992).

[169] For example, Article 10 of ITU Convention for Radio Regulations Board regarding frequency assignment.

delegation may appeal against the chairman's ruling, which, however, stands unless a majority of the delegations present and voting are against it.[170]

Disagreements between ETSI Members should likewise be resolved bilaterally: if this fails, the Members concerned can ask the General Assembly to offer a friendly mediation, for instance, by other Members and/or the Secretariat. Decisions of the Technical Organization can be directly appealed to the Board and the General Assembly.[171] Escalated disputes are litigated under French law, unless the parties concerned agree differently;[172] IPR disputes where a patent has been granted and there is no agreement between the parties involved are dealt with by the national courts of law.[173] In case of disputes between a Member(s) and ETSI, parties should exhaust all appeals procedures available under the Institute's legal framework prior to initiating legal proceedings under French law.[174] Members commencing proceedings against the ETSI are also obliged to reimburse the SDO's expenses in connection with the dispute (i.e., attorneys, investigation costs, and expert fees).[175]

Appeals on procedural matters from individual 3GPP members are first handled by the PCG and, subsequently, by the organizational partners; in turn, appeals on technical matters are handled by the relevant Technical Specifications Group and only then by the PCG.[176] The PCG also considers objections of individual members regarding the decisions of Working Group chairs, or claims of bias in the Working Group leadership, after these have been voiced within the relevant group.[177] Similar to the ETSI, 3GPP requires individual members to exhaust all internal appeal possibilities prior to commencing any legal proceedings against 3GPP's decisions, leadership, staff, or organizational partner(s).[178]

[170] Article 20.3 of ITU General Rules of Conferences, Assemblies and Meetings of the Union.

[171] Article 14 of ETSI Statutes.

[172] Article 18 of ETSI Rules of Procedure.

[173] Article 4.3 of ETSI Guide on IPRs.

[174] Article 18.1 of ETSI Rules of Procedure.

[175] Ibid., Article 18.2. This rather discouraging factor for litigation was implemented into ETSI framework after *TruePosition* v. *Ericsson*.

[176] Article 29 of 3GPP Working Procedures.

[177] Ibid.

[178] Ibid., Article 59A, also Article 9 of 3GPP Partnership Agreement.

Stakeholders directly and materially affected by IEEE standards may, upon the exhaustion of the appeals procedures of any relevant subordinate committee or body, appeal procedural actions or inactions to the IEEE-SA SASB. An SASB Appeal Panel is comprised of a chair and two other members not involved in the dispute or affected by the decision at issue.[179] Final decisions of the SASB Appeal Panel can be appealed to the BoG, which is also entitled to handle appeals against its own actions and inactions.[180] A BoG Appeal Panel is comprised of three voting members of the IEEE-SA BoG not involved in the dispute or affected by the decision at issue.[181] Both SASB and the BoG deal exclusively with procedural appeals; matters around technical decisions, including making a technical comment during balloting period, are resolved at or below the Sponsor level following the procedures of the relevant committee and the Sponsor.[182]

Decision or inactions of the IAOC or IESG may be appealed to the IAB and, subsequently, to the ISOC Board of Trustees by any member of the IETF community.[183] Disputes within the NomCom are preferably resolved within this committee for the reason of confidentiality. When it does not seem to be possible, a written request should be submitted to the ISOC President,[184] who appoints an arbiter to investigate the issue and, in consultation with the principal parties, decides on the resolution. Decisions of IETF Working Group chairs can be appealed to the AD, and subsequently to the IESG. If the Working Group disagrees with the resolution provided by the IESG, an appeal can be filed by the IAB.[185]

Any issues arising in W3C Working Groups should be resolved through a dialogue. Members disagreeing with the decisions (including those that were taken by voting), should file a formal objection with the Working Group's chair.[186] All objections raised within the Working Groups must be reported to the Director and publicly

[179] See Article 5.8 of IEEE-SA Standards Board Operations Manual (January 2019).
[180] Ibid., Article 5.8.9.
[181] Article 4.4 of IEEE-SA Operations Manual.
[182] Article 5.2 of IEEE-SA Standards Board Bylaws.
[183] Section 2.2.3 of 'The Tao of IETF'.
[184] See 'IAB, IESG, and IAOC selection, confirmation, and recall process'.
[185] For this reason, the IAB chair and the liaison from the IAB do not participate in the IESG appeals; see 'An IESG Charter', H. Alvestrand (ed.) (February 2004) RFC 3710, available at http://ietf.org/rfc/rfc3710.txt.
[186] Clause 3.5 of W3C Process Document (2017).

documented.[187] When a group of participants believe that their concerns, either technical or procedural, are not being taken into account by the Working Group, they may initiate a Group Decision Appeal to the Director asking him to confirm or deny the decision.[188] The Advisory Committee may also file an appeal for certain decisions of the Director,[189] and Advisory Committee members may initiate an appeal against or for W3C decisions taken following Advisory Committee review, that is, creation and modification of working groups or the maturity level of Recommendations (Advisory Committee Appeal). The appeal request should be filed within three weeks of the decision by sending a request to the Team and should be supported by at least 5 percent of the Advisory Committee participants.[190] Once this quorum is reached, the Team organizes an appeal vote to approve or reject the contested decision. Matters that cannot be resolved through the dialogue or internal appeals procedure are settled by the Commercial Rules of Arbitration of the American Arbitration Association (for members incorporated in the US) or by the Rules of Conciliation and Arbitration of the International Chamber of Commerce (for members incorporated outside the US).[191]

Bluetooth SIG does not maintain a formal appeal procedure. Disputes arising from the Membership Agreement are decided exclusively by the state and federal courts of New York.[192]

It appears that SDOs largely prefer the disputes within them to be resolved bilaterally among the concerned parties, or within the relevant technical or governance bodies; formal appeals function as a "last resort facility." Furthermore, while all SDOs encourage diplomatic methods of dispute resolution, there is a strong preference for internal appeals procedures over arbitration by third parties or litigation, especially in ETSI and 3GPP. While reasonable from SDOs' viewpoint, this questions the independence of the SDOs appeal bodies and officers, who, despite

[187] Ibid., Clause 3.3.2. When the Chair believes that the Group has duly considered the legitimate concerns of dissenters as far as is possible and reasonable, the group should continue its work despite the existence of such objections.

[188] Clause 3.5 of W3C Process Document (2017).

[189] Ibid., Clause 7.2; although this rarely happens in practice, see Halpin, 'The crisis of standardizing DRM'.

[190] Clause 7.2 of W3C Process Document (2017).

[191] Clause 19 of Draft International W3C Member Agreement (2021).

[192] Section 10(c) of Bluetooth SIG Membership Agreement (Version 3.0, May 2017).

precautions in the operational frameworks, may end up handling appeals against the decisions in which they have been closely involved. In consortia, stakeholders with significant institutional power have the ultimate say in the appeal decisions: this is apparent for W3C and even for 3GPP.

## IPR Policies

IPR issues are essential in ICT standardization and, perhaps for that reason, SDOs policies governing disclosure and licensing of SEPs, as well as opportunities to seek injunctions against implementers, have been examined in detail by several academic studies.[193] Rules on whether and how proprietary technologies can be embedded into a standard have a significant role in attracting contributors to an SDO,[194] and provide SDO stakeholders with important procedural guarantees. Moreover, SDOs are required to maintain such rules to comply with the antitrust and competition requirements.[195]

Although an SDO may be dealing with different IPR questions, including copyright and trademark of their standards, this study only focuses on policies related to SEPs. The reference to "IPR policies" is thus somewhat inaccurate, but follows the common approach pursued in the field. Furthermore, although IPR policies are critical to the technical deliberations taking place in SDOs' committees and working groups, this study examines IPR policies as a part of SDOs' governance rules rather than standards development processes. That said, like other operational rules, IPR policies should be viewed in the context of SDOs institutional settings, their membership, and standards they create.

Together with ISO and IEC, ITU-T and ITU-R follow the ISO/IEC/ITU Common Patent Policy, which states that a patent fully or partly embodied into an ITU Recommendation must be accessible to everybody without undue restrictions but leave the detailed arrangements regarding licensing or royalties to the parties. While early disclosure is encouraged, the SDOs are not involved in evaluations of patent relevance or essentiality, or in settling SEP-related disputes. Implementation of the common

193 For example, R. Bekkers and A. Updegrove, *A Study of IPR Policies and Practices of a Representative Group of Standards Setting Organizations Worldwide*, updated version (Washington DC: National Academies of Science, 2013).

194 See P. Delimatsis, O. Kanevskaia and Z. G. Verghese, 'Strategic behaviour in standards development organizations in times of crisis' (2021) 2 *Texas Intellectual Property Law Journal* 127–85.

195 See Chapters 4 and 5.

patent policy is facilitated by the Guidelines for Implementation of the Common Patent Policy for ITU-T/ITU-R/ISO/IEC,[196] which restates the importance of early disclosure and that SDOs are not required to do provide patent searches. The Chairmen of the ITU Technical Standardization Bureau are required to ask for knowledge of patents during the meetings.[197] A patent-holder should file to ITU-T or ITU-R boards a licensing declaration form – a written statement – identifying whether they are willing to license their patents free of charge, on a nondiscriminatory basis and reasonable terms and conditions, or not willing to license at any of these conditions at all.[198] A specific ITU Patent Statement and Licensing Declaration form was introduced in 1990, the same year the Guidelines were first published; these documents were revised almost every year since then until 2007, when the revisions started being less frequent.[199] As of 2006, each revision was approved by the IPR Ad Hoc Group.

ETSI's IPR Policy was established by the General Assembly in 1993 as a response to increasing concerns of patent holdups.[200] The IPR Policy has been investigated by the Commission in 1994 and 2005, which led to its modifications.[201] In 2007, the policy was revised to permit, however not require, ex ante disclosure of the maximum royalty rates. ETSI IPR Policy is commitment based, requiring each Member to make *reasonable endeavors* to notify the ETSI on the essential IPRs.[202] The term "reasonable endeavors" is rather ambiguous: pursuant to the DG Competition, it

[196] IEC/ISO/ITU, Guidelines for Implementation of the Common Patent Policy for ITU-T/ ITU-R/ISO/IEC (November 2, 2018), available at www.itu.int/dms_pub/itu-t/oth/04/04/ T04040000010005PDFE.pdf.

[197] Ibid., Clause 5.

[198] Clause 2, Common Patent Policy for ITU-T/ITU-R/ISO/IEC (2006), available at www .itu.int/en/ITU-T/ipr/Pages/policy.aspx.

[199] See Record of revisions to the Patent Policy, the Forms and the Guidelines, available at www.itu.int/en/ITU-T/ipr/Pages/revpatent.aspx.

[200] R. Bekkers and J. West, 'IPR standardization policies and strategic patenting in UMTS' (2008) in *Proceedings of 25th DRUID Celebration Conference*, Copenhagen, June 17–20, 2008, pp. 5–6; M. Dolmans, 'Standards for standards' (2002) 26 *Fordham International Law Journal* 163–208 at 181. See also ETSI Guide on IPRs. An overview of landmark events, including modifications of IPR policy, is available at www.etsi.org/about/what-we-are/landmarks.

[201] The first revision resulted in the fact that the adopted policy also required patent disclosure and broad FRAND licensing, while the second revision addressed the Commission's concerns that disclosure obligation is too weak; see Dolmans, 'Standards for standards'.

[202] Article 4 of ETSI Intellectual Property Rights Policy, ETSI Rules of Procedures (December 1, 2021) Annex 6.

refers to the disclosure obligation, as it cannot be reasonably expected from an ETSI Member to identify potential IPR holders in the standardization process that Member is not a part of.[203] Indeed, neither ETSI nor its Members are obliged to conduct IPR searches.[204] "Reasonable endeavors" thus focuses on the steps taken to reveal the SEP and the IPRs by its holders, their activities, and the knowledge of Members' representatives. For instance, each meeting of a Working Group must commence with a call for the IPRs.[205] The disclosure requirement is particularly applicable to a Member submitting a technical proposal on a working item, who should inform about any of their IPRs that *might* be essential if the proposal is adopted. The obligation is deemed to be fulfilled if a Member belongs to a Patent Family of ETSI.

ETSI's IPR Policy is based on the FRAND principle. Any discussion within Working Groups on the meaning of "fair" and "reasonable," or which address the essentiality and validity of patents, constitutes an anticompetitive conduct and is prohibited,[206] as further explained in the Guidelines for Antitrust Compliance.[207] Any denial of licensing should be explained in written and sent for consideration by the Director-General. When the licenses are not available, the General Assembly should explore whether there is a viable alternative, which would satisfy the ETSI requirement and would not be blocked by the IPRs. In case such a technology does not exist, it is up to the Director-General to take appropriate measures, which will commonly result in asking the SEP holder to reconsider their position.[208] The denial to license is not explicitly named as a breach of the IPR Policy, and thus Members not complying with the FRAND commitment cannot be subject to expulsion. In contrast, a situation when it can be demonstrated that an ETSI Member has deliberately withheld the disclosure significantly beyond what could be expected from normal consideration of "timeless" ("intentional delay") is considered as a breach of the IPR Policy and can be sanctioned by the General Assembly.[209]

203 Article 4.6.3.1 of ETSI Guide on IPRs.
204 Article 4.2 of ETSI IPR Policy.
205 Article 2.1.1 of ETSI Guide on IPRs.
206 Even when such a discussion concerns availability of IPR on royalty-free bases since, technically, it still refers to the price.
207 ETSI Guidelines for Antitrust Compliance, version adopted by Board on January 29, 2011.
208 Article 8 of ETSI IPR Policy.
209 Article 2 of ETSI Guide on IPRs.

Individual Members of 3GPP are bound by the IPR policy of their respective Organizational Partner,[210] to which they should declare, at the earliest opportunity, technologies that they believe are (potentially) essential to a 3GPP standard. IPR policies of 3GPP organizational partners are rather similar and are based on FRAND licensing requirement.[211] Neither 3GPP nor the organizational partners perform an IPR search. TSG and Working Group chairmen are required to make a call for IPRs, as well as a statement relating to antitrust and competition law, during each meeting.

The first IEEE IPR policy introduced FRAND requirement and permitted SEP holders to ex ante disclose their licensing terms.[212] A SEP holder disclosing a potentially essential patent should submit to the IEEE a Letter of Assurance (LoA) stating their intentions and (a) assure that they will license its SEP to implementers of the standard (i.e., for a reasonable royalty, at the holder's election, royalty-free), (b) assure that they will not enforce its SEP against implementers, (c) state that they do not have SEPs, or (d) decline to provide assurance.[213] The vagueness in FRAND commitment and the inability to make a cost-benefit comparison when deciding on the inclusion of patented technologies in a standard led to the policy revision in 2007. The proposed modifications established the requirement of ex ante disclosure of maximum royalty rates and licensing terms, stipulated the irrevocability of patent-holders' assurance, and clarified the binding effect of the assurance on the submitter's affiliates.[214] After obtaining a favorable BRL from the Antitrust Division of the US DoJ,[215] the new policy was approved by the IEEE governing bodies and became enforceable in May 2007.

In practice, however, the policy proved to be unsuccessful in achievement of its goals: not only did it fuel the discussion on the meaning of "reasonable rate" and "unfair discrimination," which is suggested to

[210] Article 55 of 3GPP Working Procedures.

[211] See also Article 3 of 3GPP Partnership Agreement.

[212] See Contreras, 'An empirical study', p. 13.

[213] Article 6.1 of IEEE-SA Standard Board Bylaws.

[214] IEEE-SA Request for Business Review Letter to the US Department of Justice, Antitrust Division, November 29, 2006, available at www.justice.gov/sites/default/files/atr/legacy/2014/01/28/302148.pdf.

[215] DoJ, Response to the Institute of Electrical and Electronics Engineers, Inc.'s request for business review letter (April 30, 2007).

provoke diverse interpretation of the policy,[216] but it also proved to be ineffective as only two LoAs accepting to disclose maximum rates were received by the IEEE-SA.[217] In 2015, IEEE IPR policy was revised again: this time, amendments were more extensive and preliminarily sought to mitigate the alleged concerns of patent holdup and royalty stacking. In its request to the DoJ to provide a BRL, the IEEE-SA submitted four modifications[218] it intended to implement in the new policy. While two of the proposed modifications – prohibition for Submitters of LoAs[219] that have been determined complete and posted on the IEEE-SA website ("Accepted LoAs") to seek, or seek to enforce, injunctions (or "Prohibitive Order") against implementers unless those fail to participate in, or to comply with the outcome of an adjudication by the appropriate authorities;[220] and permission for patent-holders to require reciprocity in licensing *only* with regard to the patents that are essential to a single standard, and *only* when the reciprocity relates to an SEP(s) – introduce explicit changes to the Policy, two other points are believed to take the form of clarifications:[221] the option to determine the "reasonable rate" based on the value of the relevant functionality of the smallest saleable patent practicing unit (SSPPU)[222]-compliant implementations of the SEP; and clarification that IPRs shall be licensed for "any Compliant Implementation," meaning any product or service that conforms to any mandatory or optional portion of a normative clause of an IEEE Standard.[223] Also this policy was a subject to fierce critique by scholars,

216 The Policy was considered as "overly ambitious"; see K. Karachalios, 'Fundamental uncertainty at the intersection between patents and standards' (November/December 2015) *The Patent Lawyer* 33–5.

217 See Petit, 'The IEEE-SA revised patent policy', p. 216.

218 Those are sometimes termed by IEEE as "clarifications" highlighting that no major changes were made and suggesting that the more specific obligations of the version after 2015 also apply to commitments made before 2015; some, however, refer to "changes" or "revisions" to highlight the departure of the new Policy from practice.

219 Note that according to the language of IEEE Patent Policy, "Submitter" is an individual or an organization providing an LoA, who may not necessarily be the SEP holder.

220 The reason that policy provides is that there is sufficient compensation for Accepted LoAs.

221 Although this is disputed by many SEPs holders.

222 See D. Kappos and (The Honorable) P. R. Michel, 'The smallest salable patent-practicing unit: observations on its origins, development, and future' (2018) 32 *Berkley Technology Law Journal* 1433–56, explaining the Court's rulings on SSPPU.

223 M. A. Lindsay, Business review letter request to Assistant Attorney General, W. J. Baer (September 30, 2014), available at www.justice.gov/sites/default/files/atr/legacy/2015/02/17/311483.pdf.

governmental agencies, and other SDOs, not least for its departure from the common industry practice.[224]

IEEE-SA Working Groups are explicitly prohibited to discuss the status or substance of ongoing or threatened litigation on the matters of IPRs, essentiality, or validity of patent claims or specific license terms or IPRs other than those mentioned in the accepted LoAs.[225] Additionally, IEEE Antitrust and Competition Policy provides nonbinding guidelines to prevent its activities from becoming anticompetitive arrangements.[226] Each Working Group meeting commences with a statement concerning the IEEE-SA IPR policy and a call to identify or disclose SEPs; refusal to license on the IPR policy terms is typically followed by a dialogue between SEP holder and the Working Group (chair), intending to reveal the reason of denial, and the absence of LoA is carefully considered during the standards' approval process.

IETF generally encourages the use of nonpatented technology, and Working Groups prefer technologies without IPR claims, or those that can be licensed on royalty-free basis.[227] That said, IETF acknowledges that superior technology may outweigh technologies accompanied by free licensing or fewer IPR claims, and, as other SDOs, introduces the rules governing IPRs inclusion in IETF standards. Provisions regarding the IPRs were mentioned for the first time in 1992 in IETF's first formal IPR Policy, adopted as RFC 1310 and largely mirroring the language of ANSI's IPR Policy.[228] The policy was instigated by the changing landscape of standardization and growing commercialization of the internet.[229] In 1994, the policy was strengthened with the requirements for patent-holders to grant an royalty-free license to ISOC, as well as to license their technologies to those implementing IETF standards on RAND or royalty-free basis.[230] Yet, the IPR policy became relevant only in 1995, when Motorola refused to commit to license its patents for PPP

224 See Chapter 10.

225 Article 6.2 of IEEE-SA Standards Board Bylaws.

226 IEEE SA Antitrust and Competition Policy, available at http://standards.ieee.org/develop/policies/antitrust.pdf.

227 Section 6.4.5 of 'The Tao of IETF'. The Tao introduces the IBM license for RFC 1822 as an example of successful royalty-free licensing.

228 Contreras, 'A tale of two layers', p. 870.

229 Ibid.

230 Section 5.6 of 'The internet standards process – revision 2', C. Huitema and P. Gross (eds.) (March 1994) RFC 1602, available at www.rfc-editor.org/rfc/pdfrfc/rfc1602.txt.pdf.

Compression Control Protocol, which led to disagreement in the Working Group; Motorola eventually agreed to license its technology on RAND terms, but only after the standard containing patent claims was already published.[231]

IETF IPR Policy was revised the following year, and this time, it only contained a disclosure obligation.[232] The Policy established the three basic principles of IPR claims, namely, that IETF (a) does not have an obligation to determine the validity of IPR claims; (b) can decide to use technologies for which IPR disclosures have been made; and that (c) all contributors and participants must disclose the existence of any IPR that they believe (may) cover the technology under discussions, without requiring prior patent search. The disclosure should be made as soon as it is reasonably possible after the document is published as an Internet Draft or an RFC.[233] This approach was maintained in the subsequent modifications of March 2005,[234] which brought clarity into the ambiguities regarding the disclosure obligation, and in April 2007, adding a clarification of third-party disclosure.[235] Under this policy, participants were free to choose their own format for disclosure and may include any additional information regarding their licensing intentions, such as ex ante disclosure of licensing terms.[236] In May 2017, IETF adopted a new IPR policy that, inter alia, modified some definitions, changed the focus to "participants" rather than "contributors," explained that IETF disclosures can be made by anyone (also outside IETF community), and added procedures for adopting the IPR rules to non-IETF stream documents.[237]

The first version of the W3C IPR policy was drafted in 1999 and included both disclosure and licensing commitments, which required W3C members to license their SEPs to all implementers on royalty-free and RAND terms. This policy was not applauded by the group of open-source software developers, who feared that the W3C process would be

[231] Contreras, 'A tale of two layers', p. 870.

[232] Section 10.3 of 'The internet standards process – revision 3', S. Bradner (ed.) (October 1996) RFC 2026, available at https://tools.ietf.org/html/rfc2026.

[233] Ibid.

[234] 'Intellectual property rights in IETF technology', S. Bradner (ed.) (March 2005) RFC 3979, available at https://tools.ietf.org/html/rfc3979.

[235] 'Clarification of the third-party disclosure procedure in RFC 3979', T. Narten (ed.) (April 2007) RFC 4879, available at https://tools.ietf.org/html/rfc4879.

[236] Contreras calls this policy an "informal" ex ante approach; Contreras, 'An empirical study', p. 18.

[237] See Section 13 of IETF IPR Policy (2017).

"hijacked" by companies wishing to monetize their patents.[238] The new policy was proposed in 2002 and was merely built on royalty-free licensing commitment; the final version of 2004 included an exception that allowed incorporation of proprietary technologies in W3C standards after a positive assessment of a "Patent Advisory Group" (PAG), comprised of all working group members and the W3C Chair.[239] The general principle, however, is that the W3C does not approve Recommendations based on essential claims that are not available on royalty-free terms.[240]

In the course of standards development, W3C may issue disclosure request to any party that is deemed to have knowledge of essential claims.[241] When receiving a disclosure request, an individual in a Member organization has to make a disclosure statement regarding the knowledge of a patent. The disclosure obligation is satisfied if the patent-holder commits to royalty-free licensing and is hence very limited and only necessary when a member does not wish to license on royalty-free terms. Although the policy is incorporated as a part of the Process Document and hence binds all W3C members, the royalty-free commitment is only compulsory when their representatives join a Working Group, meaning that the W3C membership alone does not give rise to the royalty-free licensing obligations under the IPR policy.[242]

When resigning from a Working Group within ninety days after the polishing of the first public draft, a member is exempted from all licensing commitments that arose from participation in that group; in case of a later resignation, the licensing commitment remains binding. Members may exclude essential claims within sixty days after leaving a Working Group, which, however, does not affect their disclosure obligations.[243] Specific essential claims may also be excluded from royalty-free licensing requirement if the participant refuses to license specific claims no later than 150 days after the publication of the first public working draft and specifically discloses the claims subject to this exclusion.[244]

[238] Contreras, 'A tale of two layers', p. 877. W3C received nearly 2,500 public comments on the draft policy, most of which opposed it.

[239] This process, however, has not been often invoked. See Contreras, 'A tale of two layers', p. 878, discussing the cases of Voice XML and Eolas.

[240] Clause 2 of W3C Patent Policy, D. J. Weitzner (ed.) (February 5, 2004), available at www.w3.org/Consortium/Patent-Policy-20040205/.

[241] Clause 6 of W3C Patent Policy (2004).

[242] Ibid., Clause 3.2.

[243] Ibid., Clause 4.

[244] Ibid.

Once becoming a member of Bluetooth SIG, companies also sign the Bluetooth Patent/Copyright License Agreement,[245] by which all members and their affiliates grant each other a "nonexclusive, royalty-free, perpetual, irrevocable, non-transferable, non-sublicensable, worldwide license under its Necessary Claims" for the use, distribution, and sale of Compliant Portions.[246] The term "necessary claims" refers to claims of a patent or patent application owned by a member that will be necessarily infringed by implementing Bluetooth Specifications, and such an infringement cannot be avoided in the absence of any *technically reasonable* alternatives.[247] In case of disputes arising from patent infringement by a member of the SIG, and when such disputes are not defensive based on a patent infringement claim or suit by such a member, the latter is entitled to change the license grant from a royalty-free license to a reasonable royalty license and to collect such royalty retroactively.[248]

Almost all IPR policies provide a definition of the concept of "essentiality" that revolves around technical features (ETSI) and lack of suitable commercial or technical alternatives (IEEE, W3C, Bluetooth SIG);[249] however, not all examined SDOs engage in evaluating essentiality, and neither do they get involved in IPR-related disputes. Remarkably, apart from IEEE-SA, the SDOs do not provide any definition or pricing mechanisms for FRAND. Furthermore, the SDOs do not *oblige* patent-holders to license their technologies on FRAND/royalty-free terms in the sense that refusal to license does not formally lead to a "sanction" in the form of a fine or expulsion from membership: yet, a patent-holder that does not comply with licensing rules may face other consequences, such as exclusion of its technology from a standard, or reputational

245 Bluetooth Patent/Copyright License Agreement (July 8, 2016), available at www.bluetooth.com/wp-content/uploads/2019/03/PCLA-ESign-Version-Version-11.pdf.

246 Ibid., section 5(b). Within the meaning of the Licensing Agreement, 'Compliant Portion' implies those specific portions of products (hardware, software, or combinations thereof) that: (i) implement and are compliant with the actual Bluetooth Specification and/or Foundation Specification, whichever the case may be; (ii) are qualified pursuant to the Bluetooth Qualification Process; (iii) are within the bounds of the Scope; and (iv) meet the requirements set forth in the Compliance Requirements, see ibid., section 1(j).

247 Ibid., section 1(o).

248 Ibid., section 5(b).

249 Note that essentiality is not mentioned in IETF, which defines IPRs as a patent, utility model, or similar right that may cover a technology implementing an IETF specification, section 1(j) and (k) of IETF IPR Policy.

damage.[250] In this regard, ETSI's IPR Policy provides that in case a FRAND-based license is not available, the General Assembly should seek a feasible alternative, which may even lead to designing around the patent. Within the IEEE-SA, a negative LoA can bear consequences for a technology's inclusion into a standard; yet no actions are required from the SASB or its committees.[251] A failure to disclose the relevant IPR in standards development of IETF may prevent a stakeholder from any further participation in IETF's standards development with respect to the technologies whose disclosure was omitted. In all SDOs, the role of the chairs is crucial to ensure timely disclosure of SEPs in Working Groups.

The recent study on SDOs governance revealed that SDOs IPR policies are based on a so-called "Baseline Policy," which serves as a "safe harbor" approach. Such Baseline Policy contains the general requirement of patent disclosure and licensing and is deemed compatible with the legal rules.[252] Some SDOs limit their IPR policies to this Baseline Policy (e.g., ITU-T), others implement the Baseline Policy with committal choices, such as royalty-free licensing requirements (W3C, Bluetooth SIG) or interpretation of FRAND terms and restriction to seeking injunctions (IEEE-SA); or noncommittal choices, where IPR policies offer different modes or optional choices and allow divergent interpretation, for instance, regarding the meaning of FRAND or the extent of licensing obligations at the company level (ETSI, IETF).[253] At the same time, IETF, W3C, and Bluetooth SIG express a strong preference for nonpatented contributions and royalty-free licensing schemes, while such preferences are not expressed in ETSI and IEEE-SA policies.

[250] See also P. Larouche and. F. Schuett, 'Repeated interactions in standard setting' (2018) 28 *Journal of Economics and Management Strategy* 488–509.

[251] PatCom only requests LoAs when those are not provided.

[252] JRC Report, p. 129.

[253] Ibid., p. 151. Consent of members is important for committal choices, while noncommittal choices are rather subject to market discipline. Committal choices are also made by leadership-driven SDOs, and noncommittal choices by membership-driven SDOs.

# 8

# Standards Development in SDOs

While interesting from the institutional perspective, SDOs' policies ultimately serve to support technical work performed by experts in working groups and committees. The main activity of SDOs is the development and adoption of technical standards (although some organizations from our sample, i.e., ITU and IEEE, have a broader scope). SDO standards development processes are thus at the crossroads between technical and governance rules and should be considered in the particular institutional context. This chapter proceeds with a systematic analysis of these rules, which it divides in three stages: drafting and submitting a standard's proposal; technical drafting of a standard; and the standard's approval.[1]

## Proposal of Standardization Activities

Standardization work in ITU-T can be initiated by ITU Member States or "authorized entities" submitting a Question to the relevant Study Group.[2]

ETSI endues its Members, the EC and EFTA, with the right to propose standardization projects.[3] Such new item proposals should be supported by at least four ETSI full and/or associate members, who are also expected to actively participate in standards development.[4] Every ETSI work item is provided with a Rapporteur, a person serving as a prime contact point for technical matters and work progress, who also bears

[1] ETSI divides standardization processes into different milestones: adoption of the working item by a Technical Body; designing the early standard draft; designing the stable draft; submitting draft for approval; approval by a Working Group; and, at last, approval by the Technical Body/ETSI membership. Article 1.6.4.1, ETSI Technical Working Procedures.

[2] WTSA-08 - Resolution 1 - Rules of procedures of the ITU Telecommunication Standardization Sector (ITU) (November 28–29, 2012), section 7.

[3] 'How does ETSI make standards', available at www.etsi.org/standards/standards-making.

[4] Article 1.6.2 of ETSI Technical Working Procedures.

management and coordination tasks.[5] Once prepared, the ETSI work item is subject to approval by the relevant Technical Body. A standardization proposal is adopted if 71 percent of the votes are in favor. If that quorum is not achieved, the proposal can still be approved if the percentage supporting votes of full members reaches 71.[6]

Proposal of work items for 3GPP occurs in one of the Technical Specifications Groups and should be approved at the TSG plenary. Proposals can be initiated by any member but must gain the support of minimum four Individual Members who also agree to actively contribute to the development processes.[7]

Once a need for an IEEE standard is established, interested parties join their forces in (potential) Study Groups.[8] During this phase, they draft a Project Authorization Request (PAR), a highly detailed legal document stating the reasons and intentions of the related standardization project. Each Study Group operates under the supervision of a Sponsor organization, typically an IEEE Committee, which determines technical content of standardization project and bears responsibility for a standardization project dedicated to it.[9] Upon its completion, the PAR is examined by the NesCom, RevCom, and AudCom, each reviewing the proposed project against certain (procedural) requirements of the IEEE-SA. Technical work on standards development starts directly after the formal approval of the PAR by the IEEE-SA SASB.[10]

In IETF, an RFC may be proposed by virtually anyone through posting in the mailing list, regardless of whether the document is intended to be informative or normative, and whether the RFC takes form of an individual submission to the IETF, or a project that should be considered within a Working Group.[11] In the case of the latter, a Working Group is

[5] Ibid., Articles 1.6.2 and 1.6.4. One of the tasks of the Rapporteur is to investigate whether any relevant use requirement documents exist.

[6] Ibid., Article 1.7.1.

[7] Article 39 of 3GPP Working Procedures.

[8] Although the Working Groups are formed after the proposal is approved, parties can already start working in so-called Study Groups, which form the potential basis of the future Working Groups. 'The standards development lifecycle', available at https://standards.ieee.org/develop/index.html.

[9] Article 5.2.2 of IEEE-SA Standards Board Bylaws; Article 5.1 of IEEE-SA Standards Board Operations Manual.

[10] Article 5.2 of IEEE-SA Standards Board Operations Manual. An extension is possible upon the Sponsor's request and the subsequent authorization from the NesCom.

[11] Section 4.2 of 'The Tao of IETF'.

initiated either by an AD or by a (group of) individual(s) after obtaining consent of the AD(s).

W3C standardization work is initiated by a representative(s) of one or more Member Organizations filing a submission request to the Director.[12] To evolve into a comprehensive standardization item, the topic should generate enough interest among the W3C Members, the Team, and the general public; the latter are invited to participate in Workshops related to the issues that are of interest to the W3C community.[13] Once the suggested topic gains enough interest, the Director proposes the development of one or more new Interest/Working Group charters describing the group's mission, procedural rules and expectations, and deadlines as regards the group's deliverables; the charters are approved by the Advisory Committee.[14] The Director then approves the establishment of (a) group(s) and therewith authorizes the technical work on a particular standardization project: from that moment onwards, every W3C member may join the Working Group, provided that this member commitments to license their patents to the Working Group's charter.[15]

Any Bluetooth SIG member can suggest development of a specification by submitting a New Work Proposal (NWP) for approval by the Board of Directors.[16] Upon its approval, the Board assigns the NWP to a Study/Working Group, which drafts the Functional Requirements Document (FRD).[17] The BARB reviews the functional requirements, problem statement, Working Group's charter, and its scope of work.[18] Once the FRD and the charter are approved by the BARB, the core technical work on standardization project commences.

Initiating of standardization processes thus requires support of SDOs' members (even in IETF, where it materializes through individuals' involvement with the proposal that was posted in the mailing list), and,

[12] Clause 10 of W3C Process Document (2017).

[13] Workshops are run with open invitations to determine whether there is a right momentum for standardization; see Halpin, 'The crisis of standardizing DRM', p. 4.

[14] Clause 5.2.6 of W3C Process Document (2017).

[15] Because the standard does not exist yet, commitments can only be made to the charter.

[16] See 'Submit an idea for specification', available at www.bluetooth.com/specifications/submit-an-idea-for-a-specification.

[17] Section 3.2 of Bluetooth Specification Management Process Document (SMPD) (December 29, 2020), available at https://manuals.plus/sig/specification-management-process-document-smpd.

[18] Section 8.5(b) of Bluetooth SIG Bylaws (2019); Section 3.4 of SMPD (2020).

typically, an approval of a governance body. Hence, even before a standards project is formally launched, there should be a pool of relevant actors willing to contribute to it. For this reason, already the first stage of standards development is characterized by a significant amount of lobbying, financial research, and technical work since it also sets the course of the standardization project and determines the relevant stakeholders.

## Technical Work on Standards

Upon acceptance by the ITU-T Study Group, standardization proposals become Study Questions and are assigned to the relevant Working Group and, subsequently, to a Technical Body within it. Study and Working Groups consist of experts nominated by Member States and Sector Members; a team of experts working on a Study Question is referred to as a "rapporteurs group."

ETSI standardization work occurs in the Technical Bodies of the Technical Organizations. Technical documents are drafted in Technical or Special Committee by individual experts who represent the ETSI Members of their affiliation. Each Member can nominate only one expert to take part in the meetings. To support standardization work, ETSI may open a call for expertise.[19] Every meeting of a Technical Body or a Working Group should start with a call for IPRs by the Chairman.[20]

Technical work on 3GPP specifications is carried out by the Working Groups, where members submit technical contributions addressing various issues to be discussed among the Working Group members during the meetings. Competing solutions are usually discussed in a consensus-building procedure or put to majority voting. An author may be required to resubmit their contribution if a stakeholder makes objections regarding the inclusion of this contribution into a technical specification.[21]

The structure and composition of IEEE Working Groups usually mimic those of the Study Group drafting the PAR. Each Working Group is tailor-made for a specific standardization project, and is

[19] See, for instance, call for proposal for Specialist Task Forces, available at https://portal.etsi.org/stf/OpenCallForExperts.

[20] Article 2.3.2 of ETSI Guide on IPRs.

[21] See Baron and Gupta, 'Unpacking 3GPP Standards'.

composed of either individuals or representatives from entities.[22] Participation in Working Groups is open to anyone with the relevant technical expertise, knowledge, and dedicated interest in the project.[23] Individuals nominated to participate in the Working Group meetings on behalf of an entity are obliged to declare to be the sole experts representing the interests of their organization prior to the balloting.[24] The Working Groups should ensure broad and balanced representation of all parties interested in standardization projects, and to encourage global engagement by approaching the members of the IEEE for their interest and expertise and issuing a call for participation. The Working Group chairs are appointed by the Sponsor or selected by the Working Group.[25]

Most of the IETF's detailed technical work is carried out via the Working Groups' mailing lists. Although the lists and the discussions are not moderated, messages sent to the announcement lists should be approved by the IETF Secretariat and a small number of IETF leaders.[26] Occasionally, Working Groups may meet face-to-face, and the costs associated with conducting the meetings are borne by the attendees or the corporate hosts of the meeting, complemented with additional funding from the IASA.[27] Decisions of the Working Groups must be taken by a "rough consensus,"[28] meaning that a large majority of Working Group participants must agree with the decision and that strongly held objections are debated until proved wrong. Decisions reached during a face-to-face meeting must also gain consensus on a mailing list.[29] Once the technical discussions are finalized and upon the decision of the Working Group Chair, it is submitted to the Working Group Last Call.

[22] When developed according to the entity method, individuals are nominated by the entities of their affiliation.

[23] 'Standards development lifecycle', n. 8.

[24] Article 5.4.1.1 of IEEE-SA Standards Board Operations Manual.

[25] In the case the standard is developed by virtue of an individual-based method, the Chair and Vice-Chairpersons should be affiliated with both IEEE and the IEEE-SA.

[26] Section 2.3 of 'The Tao of IETF'.

[27] The meetings of IETF take place in North America, Europe, and Asia, approximately once a year in each region. So far, IETF has conducted about eighty face-to-face meetings.

[28] The rationale behind it is that, in the absence of formal membership, decisions, in principle, cannot be taken by formal voting.

[29] This ensures that those who were not able to attend the meeting can still share their viewpoints; Section 3.2 of IETF Working Group Guidelines and Procedures, S. Bradner (ed.) (September 1998) RFC 2418, available at https://datatracker.ietf.org/doc/html/rfc2418.

Technical deliverables of the W3C are produced by the Working Groups, whereas Interest Groups aim to gather stakeholders willing to exchange their ideas and to evaluate potential web technologies and policies.[30] Both types of groups share similar characteristics and have to comply with the same set of requirements.[31] Member's representatives may join the groups at any time of their existence, but each organization may be represented only by one participant. Working Groups typically consist of no more than fifteen experts, and are open to three types of participants: the representatives of Members, Invited Experts, and representatives of the Team, who also aid to the group's proper integration within the SDO; Interest Groups where the only participation requirement is subscription to the mailing list, may also include public participants.[32] To join a Working Group or an Interest Group, an individual Member representative must be nominated by the Advisory Committee representative of their organization.[33] Working Group activities initially result in the First Public Working Draft, which should be made available to other W3C groups and to the general public.[34] The document may be reviewed by other Working Groups for the period of six months. Subsequently, the Working Group is expected to publish a revised Working draft, implementing the suggested modifications, or indicating the reasons for the lack of any substantial changes.[35] After the necessary changes have been implemented, the proposed specification gains the status of Candidate Recommendation.[36]

Once the technical work is commenced in Bluetooth SIG, the coverage of the FRD is defined in the Draft Improvement Proposal Document (DIPD), which is submitted to the Associates and Promoters upon the review and the approval of the BARB.[37] When the document evolves into the Final Improvement Proposal Document (FIPD) and locks down all mandatory/optional features per the functional requirement, it is subject

[30] Clause 5 W3C Process Document (2017).
[31] Ibid., Clause 5.1.
[32] Ibid., Clause 5.2.1.
[33] Ibid., Clauses 5.2.1.1 and 5.2.1.2.
[34] Ibid., Clauses 6.1.2 and 6.3.1.
[35] The latest Working Draft published within ninety days of the First Public Working Draft is termed the "Reference Draft"; see ibid., Clauses 5.2.6 and 6.1.2.
[36] Ibid., Clauses 6.1.2 and 6.4.
[37] See Section 4 SMPD (2020).

to the review and approval of the BTI and the BARB.[38] When this stage is completed, the document gains the status of Prototyping Specification and undergoes the Specification Validation (Interoperability Testing, IOP): during this stage, the Working Groups develop test plans that are subsequently reviewed by the BARB and the BTI.[39] Upon their approval, the Formal IOP Testing by all Members begins.

Technical work of SDOs is carried out in tailored Working Groups, which often operate according to their own processes and even allow external stakeholders to participate in their activities. In IETF and W3C, these processes usually occur through mailing lists. Given that the main technical decisions, including incorporation of proprietary technologies, are taken in the Working Groups, it is crucial for the Working and Study Groups to prevent the possible conflict of interests and bias: in this regard, the roles of Working Group chairs are crucial in all SDOs. Chairs reserve potential disagreements, determine when consensus is achieved and when voting should occur and are responsible for making progress in the drafting process. SDOs expect Working Group chairs to act in personal capacity and according to the highest standards of integrity. Another mechanism that SDOs use at this stage is requiring a stakeholder to be represented only by one expert; this, however, is not the case in more "formal" SDOs such as ITU and ETSI, or in 3GPP.

## Standards' Approval

Unless it falls into specific domains, for example, numbering or addressing, ITU Recommendations are approved in a fast-track "alternative approval process" (AAP):[40] after a draft Recommendation is considered mature and consent of the relevant Study Group is obtained, it is opened for online comments for both Member States *and* Sector Members for the period of four weeks. This is in contrast to the Traditional Approval Process (TAP), where formal consultations with Member States were sought prior to the draft's approval by the Study Group. A Recommendation is approved by consensus in case no substantial comments have been received; otherwise, the comments are sent back

[38] Section 8.8 of Bluetooth SIG Bylaws (2019).

[39] Section 4.3.1 of SMPD (2020).

[40] WTSA-08 Resolution 1 – Rules of procedures of the ITU Telecommunication Standardization Sector (ITU) (November 28–29, 2012), section 8.

to the experts for further consideration, followed by an Additional Review Process.[41]

ETSI approval processes vary according to the type of deliverable, but every ETSI document is firstly approved by the Working Group in charge of its creation. Guides and ETSI standards are approved by the whole ETSI membership by the Weighted Individual Voting;[42] and are approved for use within *Europe* if at least 71 percent of the weighted votes casted by full members are positive.[43] When drafted in cooperation with other SDOs, a document is subject to the Two-step Approval Procedure, whereby a Public Enquiry and Weighted National Vote are conducted separately.[44]

European standards are approved in the Weighted National Voting Procedure.[45] During the Public Enquiry stage, NSOs undertake national consultations and deliver their comments and national position. The rules and management of this process is left to the NSOs. NSOs then can vote in favor or against the adoption of the draft or opt for an abstention. Once the balloting has been conducted, the votes of the EU and the EFTA countries are counted separately: the results of this exercise determine whether the standard will be adopted in those countries.[46] If outcomes are positive, they should be followed by the endorsement of the standard in other States whose NSOs voted in its favor.[47] A negative vote should be accompanied by an explanation, which should be delivered and reviewed by the Technical Body. A draft that has been significantly modified during one of the approval stages might be subjected to another Public Enquiry or even balloting on national position in the General Assembly.[48] In case no technical comments have been received by the closing date of Public Enquiry, the process continues with the Weighted National Voting.[49]

3GPP technical specifications are first approved by the relevant Working Group; at this stage, the documents may still require some

[41] 'Standards approval', available at www.itu.int/en/ITU-T/about/Pages/approval.aspx.
[42] Article 14 of ETSI Rules of Procedure.
[43] Ibid.
[44] Article 2.2.1 of ETSI Technical Working Procedures.
[45] Articles 13.4 and 13.5 ETSI Rules of Procedure.
[46] Ibid., Article 13.5.3.
[47] Ibid., Article 13.5.3.
[48] Ibid., Articles 13.4 and 13.5.
[49] In case the vote actually fails, but it would not fail when only EU countries are voting, the standard will still be adopted but not enforced in other CEPT countries.

technical work or even undergo significant changes. Specifications that are sufficiently stable are approved by consensus by the relevant Technical Specifications Group, which then also takes control over the document.[50] Specifications approved in 3GPP are directly endorsed by the organizational partners.

Once consensus is achieved in IEEE Working Groups, and the Sponsor has decided that the draft standard is sufficiently mature, the working document moves to the phase of the Sponsor balloting. The Sponsor balloting group is formed by the Sponsor and, similar to Working Groups, can be individual- or entity-based.[51] Participation in Sponsor balloting is not conditional about the membership of the relevant Working Group: however, nonmembers of the IEEE-SA are required to pay a per-ballot fee to be eligible for balloting. Together with casting the vote, group members can provide comments when approving or disapproving a draft; reasons should be provided in the case of casting a negative vote.[52] Sponsor balloting may not be dominated by any companies or individuals, and no interest category can comprise over one-third of the balloting group.[53]A standard is approved in Sponsor balloting if the voting results in consensus, meaning that 75 percent of the group has to cast the vote and 75 percent of those votes have to be in favor, *and* that all technical or editorial comments submitted with the votes are responded to.[54] The ballot fails if 30 percent of the balloting group members abstain. Together with the initiation of the consensus ballot, a draft standard opens for a sixty-day IEEE-SA Public Review Process, providing an opportunity for any interested party to comment on the draft that is being reviewed in the consensus process and obtain responses from the Working Group.[55] A draft standard is then submitted to the IEEE-SA SASB for its final approval.[56] The SASB establishes, based on decision of the RevCom, whether the final draft still falls under the scope of the PAR and whether the applicable procedural rules have been respected throughout the process of standards development.[57]

[50] Article 44 of 3GPP Working Procedures.
[51] Article 5.4 of IEEE-SA Standards Board Operations Manual.
[52] Ibid., Article 5.4.3.2.
[53] Ibid., Article 5.4.1.
[54] Ibid., Articles 5.4.3.3 and 5.4.3.5.
[55] Ibid., Article 5.4.5.
[56] Article 5.2.4 of IEEE-SA Standards Board Bylaws.
[57] Article 4.2.3 of IEEE-SA Standards Board Operations Manual. See also 'How is final approval obtained', available at http://standards.ieee.org/develop/finalapp.html.

Upon achieving consensus within the IETF Working Group, the document is submitted for consideration by the IESG. The IESG announces an IETF-wide Last Call, which takes at least two weeks for drafts coming from Working Groups, and four weeks for individual submissions.[58] The IESG subsequently determines whether the document satisfies the applicable criteria, and its technical quality and clarity is consistent with that expected for the maturity level. Procedures for this stage are defined by the IESG, and typically involve a prior review by the responsible AD. After the approval of the IESG, the draft becomes a standards-track RFC, and is published upon necessary editing/revision. The adoption process of the BCP is similar to that of the RFC, with a difference that once the document is approved by the IESG, it is immediately published without editing.[59]

In W3C, a document that evolves into a Candidate Recommendation, the Director initiates its publication for other W3C groups and for the public and launches the Advisory Committee review. This phase can be categorized as a "Last Call Working Draft," and may also be subject to the call for exclusion as provided in the W3C Patent Policy.[60] Hence, the ultimate decision is taken by the Director, and is subsequently ratified and voted on by the W3C Advisory Committee.[61] In case of any substantial changes, a Working Group must seek the Director's approval to publish a revised Candidate Recommendation.[62] In the following step, a draft becomes a Proposed Recommendation, which should be reviewed by the Advisory Committee within at least twenty-eight days after its publication and at least ten days after the end of the last Exclusion Opportunity.[63] If any substantive changes are made to the Proposed Recommendation, the specification returns to the Working Group as a Candidate Recommendation or a Working Draft. In case of no significant modifications, the W3C should take a decision whether the document can evolve into a W3C Recommendation.[64]

In Bluetooth SIG, the results of Formal IOP Testing are successful when three independent passes are achieved per test case in the approved

[58] 'The Tao of IETF', section 6.4.

[59] See Section 3.2 of IETF Working Group Guidelines and Procedures (1998).

[60] Clause 6.1.2 of W3C Process Document (2017); Clause 4 of W3C Patent Policy (2004).

[61] Halpin, 'The crisis of standardizing DRM', p. 4.

[62] Since substantive changes will generally require a new Exclusion Opportunity as stipulated in clause 4 of the W3C Patent Policy.

[63] Clauses 6.1.2 and 6.5 of W3C Process Document (2017).

[64] Ibid., Clause 6.6.

IOP test plan for the core feature/Generic Attributes-based service,[65] and two independent passes achieved per test case in the approved IOP test plan for profiles.[66] Upon the completion of the testing, and the approval of the Board of Directors, the Working Group generates a Draft Bluetooth Specification for a "Member Review" process, which is subject to a sixty-day review by all Members, unless the Board of Directors unanimously approve to shorten this period to forty-five days.[67] A final version ("Voting Draft") is presented to the Board of Directors after the Member Review is completed; all Members should be notified of the Voting Draft at least fourteen days before the Board of Directors approves the Final Draft ("Adoption Date").[68] A specification is adopted when it gains 4/5 approval of the Board of Directors.[69]

In all SDOs, the documents' stability and "maturity," sometimes established through testing, are essential for moving forward in the approval process. Even when a draft reaches the voting phase, there is still opportunity to submit comments, and explanations are sought for negative vote, suggesting that a standard remains flexible even at the final stages of its development. Furthermore, standards are approved by a different group of actors than those involved in their drafting. In some SDOs, final approval is sought by the main governing body (i.e., ITU, IEEE-SA, W3C); while in others, standards drafts are open for a public review (IEEE-SA, W3C, and, to some extent, IETF), or for members/community-wide review (IETF, ETSI for harmonized standards). Bluetooth SIG recently implemented the Member Review process, replacing the approval by Adoption Committee. While this change in the operational framework is welcomed from the perspective of stakeholder

65 The Generic Attributes defines a hierarchical data structure that is exposed to connected Bluetooth with low energy devices.

66 Section 4.3.1 of SMPD (2020).

67 Section 9.3(a) of Bluetooth SIG Bylaws (2019). This was different before 2019, when the review period amounted to forty-five days (section 9.2 of Bluetooth SIG Bylaws (2012), on file with the author).

68 Section 9.3(b) of Bluetooth SIG Bylaws (2019).

69 Before 2019, approval needed to be gained by the Adoption Committee, which consisted of the Directors and chairpersons appointed by each Associate Member of the Working Group responsible for the specification at issue (section 8.9 of Bluetooth SIG Bylaws (2012), on file with the author). During the balloting, all members of the Adoption Committee who were not the members of the Board of Directors collectively had one vote. Such a vote is also ratified by a vote of a majority of the entire Board of Directors, which takes place within one week of the Adoption Meeting. Each Adoption Committee was tailored to the specification and ceased to exist upon the conclusion of the voting (section 9.2 of Bluetooth SIG Bylaws (2012), on file with the author).

participation, the Member Review process does not appear to require that Members comments be per se addressed or resolved, leaving the Board of Directors as the only body entitled to modify the standard.

SDOs' standardization work is not finished with standards' adoption: many SDOs also provide assistance with standards' implementation and ensure that their standards still respond to the market needs by maintaining review and withdrawal processes.

# 9

# Procedural Safeguards in SDOs

Despite some striking similarities, the operational framework of each SDO is unique in the sense that it fits the specific engineering and cultural setting. The governance architecture of these SDOs is a result of their historical purpose, complex interactions among their members, and institutional changes introduced to their processes and operational scope as a consequence of market and technology developments or even, in case of ITU, ETSI, and IETF, as a result of national politics of (multiple) State(s) (Table 9.1).

Although standards crafted within these SDOs are crucial for the functioning of many ICT systems, their regulatory impact may differ. ITU and ETSI champion the list of SDOs exerting normative pull, since their standards are implemented into national or regional regulatory requirements. 3GPP standards are often implemented on a national or regional level through their partner organizations, creating compliance pull for national industries. Standardization activities of IEEE-SA derive their normative force from the specifics of the US legal environment for standardization, as well as the endorsement of some IEEE standards by ISO/IEC/JTC1.[1] At first glance, the regulatory importance of standards developed in IETF, W3C, and Bluetooth SIG is less obvious; yet, many of their standards have also been adopted by ISO.[2] Most importantly, however, the studied SDOs contribute to the governance regime of ICT standardization by providing written rules that should be followed to ensure interoperability between products and services.

[1] Arguably, accreditation by ANSI also provides these standards with certain legitimacy and may encourage their incorporation into the US legislation; yet, as discussed in Chapter 5, incorporation by reference of US private voluntary standards is not conditional upon ANSI's accreditation.

[2] Some authors suggest that many consortia members therefore serve a "double duty," working in consortia's technical committees as well as in the committees of formal SDOs ratifying standards of these consortia. Schneiderman, *Modern Standardization*, p. 10.

Table 9.1. *Comparison of SDOs' governance, standards development, and dispute settlement*

| SDO | ITU | ETSI | 3GPP | IEEE-SA | IETF | W3C | Bluetooth SIG |
|---|---|---|---|---|---|---|---|
| **Body/ies responsible for standards approval** | **Relevant Study/ Working Group** | **General Assembly** | **Relevant TSG** | **SASB** (advised by **Standing Committees**), after sponsor balloting and public review | **IESG**, after an IETF-wide Last Call (for RFCs) | **Advisory Committee;** ultimate approval by Director | **Board of Directors** with 4/5 quorum, upon completion of Member Review |
| **Members of standards-approving body/ies** | ITU-T Sector Members | All full and associate members by weighted individual voting<br>For EN: the votes of National Delegations count (weighted national voting procedure) | 3GPP Partners, individual members, observers, guests | **SASB** members appointed by **the BoG;** | IETF Chair, the Area Directors (AD) randomly selected by the **Nominating Committee** and approved by the **IAB** | W3C Member organizations, Director elected by five host members | All Promoters and max four Associate Member Directors (AMD) |

| **Body/ies responsible to develop and update rules, procedures, and policies** | **Plenipotentiary Conference** | **General Assembly** | **Organizational Partners** (for 3GPP PA); **Project Coordination Group** | **SASB, Standing Committees and BoG** (depending on the document) | **IESG,** after an IETF-wide Last Call (for BCPs) | **The Advisory Board's** Process Task Force in the Revising W3C Process Community Group; approved by the W3C Membership; ultimate approval by Director | **Board of Directors** by unanimous consent |
|---|---|---|---|---|---|---|---|
| **Members of the policy-making body/ies** | Member States | All full and associate members; voting by qualified majority | Organizational and market partners, TSGs chairs and vice-chairs, ITU representatives; observers | **BoG** – members electedby IEEE voting members; **SASB**-appointed by the BoG; **Standing Committees** – members appointed by SASB chair (voting by majority) | IETF Chair, the Area Directors (AD) randomly selected by the **Nominating Committee** and approved by the **IAB** | **Advisory Board:** elected by **Advisory Committee** (all W3C Members); ultimate approval by Director | All Promoters and max Associate Member Directors (AMD) |

Table 9.1. (*cont.*)

| SDO | ITU | ETSI | 3GPP | IEEE-SA | IETF | W3C | Bluetooth SIG |
|---|---|---|---|---|---|---|---|
| **Dispute settlement and appeal body/ies** | Arbitration or Sector Boards | **General Assembly** assists in finding mediators (typically other ETSI Members or the Secretariat) Decisions of Technical Organization appealed **to the Board and General Assembly** | **PCG and organizational partners** (procedural); **TSGs and PCG** (technical) | **SASB;** final appeals handled by **BoG** | **IAB** | **Advisory Board,** after Working Group Chair and Domain Leader are unsuccessful | N.A. |
| **Members of the dispute settlement and appeal body/ies** | Sector Boards: elected by the Plenipotentiary Conference | Mediators: appointed by the **General Assembly**/ selected by parties in conflict | PCG: partners, TSG chairs, ITU members and observers TSGs: partners, individual members, observers, guests | SASB appeal – **SASB** members appointed by the SASB Chair; BoG appeal – three voting members of the **IEEE-SA BoG** | Twelve full members randomly selected by **NomCom** and approved by the ISOC Board; IETF chair serves as ex officio | Elected by **Advisory Committee** (all W3C Members) | N.A. |

## Adherence to Due Process Requirements of the Regulatory Frameworks

SDOs' scrutiny under the relevant regulatory frameworks and their procedural requirements would not be accurate nor desirable: in fact, the very nature of ICT standards precludes such an analysis. While ICT standards may indeed be developed by a single SDO with one set of rules, these standards, or their parts, are often referenced, adopted, or endorsed by other SDOs, which in turn may operate according to a different set of rules or enjoy a different level of acceptance among industry stakeholders and governments. Likewise, ICT standards should adapt to the requirements of markets, technology, and society, which render them subject to rapid modifications. Procedures used during the endorsement or amendments of these standards are endogenous to SDOs governance and vary accordingly; similarly, the regulatory effects a standard may have after its endorsement or modification may fluctuate. Given this rather unstable environment in which ICT standards function, SDOs developing them may in principle be curbed by multiple regulatory frameworks, or by none of them at all. For this reason, the governance rules of SDOs should be reviewed in the context of the due process principles for standardization in a *holistic* manner. Pondering the question of applicability of the different regulatory frameworks to the analyzed SDOs is nevertheless a useful exercise, since these frameworks ultimately grant a certain level of legitimacy to standards or exempt SDOs from antitrust liability.

Due to its ongoing collaboration with ISO/IEC and the WTO, ITU is assumed to be bound by the requirements of the TBT Code of Good Practice, although it should be noted that there is no formal record of ITU accepting the Code. The Code is, however, formally accepted by ETSI.[3] Although there are no formal records of the Code acceptance by IETF or W3C, these SDOs have previously indicated to comply with the criteria of the Code.[4] Furthermore, while it may be argued that IEEE-SA

[3] For list of SDOs that have accepted the Code of Good Practice, see https://tbtcode.iso.org/sites/wto-tbt/list-of-standardizing-bodies.html. Also, since ETSI is the national body, it is covered by ISO/IEC Guide 59 (2019).

[4] See the IAB reply to the European ICT questionnaire, 'Impact assessment study on the "standardization package." Request for information from forums and consortiums', available at www.iab.org/wp-content/IAB-uploads/2011/03/2010-02-05-IAB-Response-Euro-ICT-Questionnaire.pdf; 'WTO TBT Standards Code criteria applied to W3C', I. D. Daniel (ed.) (July 12, 2009), available at www.w3.org/2009/07wto-std-crit.html, which notes, however, that it is unclear if "W3C, or any other international non-governmental

should comply with the provisions of the Code by virtue of its accreditation by the ANSI,[5] this assumption is not confirmed in the Code itself: rather, IEEE-SA pledges its compliance with "WTO criteria for international SDOs" in its various documents.[6]

SDOs' coverage by the provisions of the WTO TBT Committee Decision depends on whether they can be considered ISBs, which, following the rather convoluted narrative of the WTO jurisprudence, implies that the SDOs should offer their membership to at least all WTO Members, who should also recognize standardization activities of these SDOs. Being an UN agency and an observer in the TBT Committee, ITU is most likely to pass this test. The other analyzed SDOs, however, even though driven by private actors, in principle do not pose any restrictions on the governmental authorities of all WTO Members to join their standardization activities either as decision-makers or as observers. Moreover, the fact that standards developed in the seven SDOs are globally used by both private and governmental actors in their routine activities suggests their wider recognition: apart from the broad market adoption, the "recognition" of these standards is also exemplified by their endorsement by the ISO. Hence, ETSI, 3GPP, IEEE-SA, IETF, W3C, and Bluetooth SIG should be considered ISBs in the context of the WTO to the extent that they comply with the six procedural principles TBT Committee Decisions, and especially openness to all WTO Members: the problem arises, however, as to whether these requirements are enforceable.

With regard to the national regulatory frameworks, Regulation 1025/2012 evidently applies to ETSI, as one of the ESOs. Being the developers of ICT standards that are "not national, European or international," the other SDOs may fall under the scope of Annex II of the Regulation as long as their standards are identified by the Commission for procurement purposes: while this is the case for IETF and W3C, standards and specifications developed by IEEE-SA and Bluetooth SIG have so far not

body" fits the criteria of the TBT Agreement, Annex 3 (B), since it is located within the territory of not one but many Members. Indeed, while for the purpose of the Annex the place of an SDOs' incorporation, or its secretariat location, would presumably facilitate identifying the WTO Member responsible for this SDO's acceptance of the Code, this would be challenging for an SDO that functions through cooperation of a number of universities.

5 As it was claimed in the dispute on IEEE 2015 IPR Policy Update.

6 See, for instance, the e-mail of S. Tatiner of May 21, 2012, available at https://standards.ieee.org/content/dam/ieee-standards/standards/web/documents/other/reldoc_NARA.pdf.

been referenced in the Commission's Decisions.[7] By the same token, the OMB Circular (2016) will apply to standards referenced in US law, and ANSI Essential Requirements to those SDOs that have obtained or seek to obtain ANSI's accreditation (from the current sample of SDOs, this concerns only IEEE-SA). Accordingly, private SDOs may, in principle, fall under the scope of the national regulatory framework as long as their standards are somehow endorsed in national regulation. The narrative may be different for ITU which, due to its intergovernmental status, may already enjoy certain national recognition for its standards.

Lastly, given the extraterritorial application of EU and US national competition law provisions, and the fact that most SDOs are largely private and produce standards that are globally adopted, it may be assumed that these SDOs fall within the scope of the applicable EU and US competition rules, namely, the Horizontal Guidelines (2011) and the SDOAA (2004). This is evidenced by many past and pending cases against the analyzed SDOs in the domain of competition and antitrust on both sides of the Atlantic.[8] Again, a situation may be somewhat different for ITU, which, despite its standards work being largely driven by the industry actors, remains a public body.

However, even if not covered by any of the regulatory frameworks, SDOs still have to comply with the set of procedural principles. Indeed, adherence to these principles grants SDOs certain legitimacy, for instance, under trade law or competition law; but this study argues that the role of due process principles in technical standardization is broader than demonstrating compliance with legal rules. The procedural principles serve as good governance mechanisms to ensure that SDOs take decisions that are balanced by considering the views of those affected by these decisions, and prevent dominance and exclusion in standards development, as well as offering accountability towards stakeholders.

## Procedural Principles for Standardization

### *Transparency*

Transparency in SDOs revolves around providing information and access. Requirements of transparency include publishing work programs;

[7] See 'ICT technical specifications', available at https://single-market-economy.ec.europa.eu/single-market/european-standards/ict-standardisation/ict-technical-specifications_en. At the same time, the EC most certainly uses Wi-Fi and Bluetooth standards in its daily work.

[8] See Chapters 4 and 5. See also the overview of cases by Contreras, 'A tale of two layers', 882–95.

notifying standardization activities and interested stakeholders; allowing interested parties to access information about standardization processes and to comment on standards' drafts; distributing the final version of a standard; and providing an adequate period of time for submitting comments.

All studied SDOs provide access to their governing documents via their websites free of charge; likewise, standards and specifications of most SDOs – apart from IEEE-SA – can also be retrieved from their websites or from the website of their working groups at no cost.[9] IEEE-SA publishes extensive information about the meetings of its working groups (the agenda, reports, and minutes),[10] while W3C and IETF provide access to the discussions on mailing lists.[11] Furthermore, ITU, ETSI, and 3GPP publish their work programs;[12] the other SDOs inform about their ongoing and future standardization activities through newsletters, updates, and work plans published on their websites. (Bluetooth is an exception since its annual report is available only for Members.) Furthermore, while all SDOs maintain tools to inform interested members or stakeholders about standardization activities (i.e., through liaisons or call for expertise), ETSI is obliged to notify its development projects on harmonized European standards. Technical bodies of some SDOs are sometimes required to notify other governance bodies of a planned or completed standardization activity (i.e., IEEE-SA, Bluetooth SIG). Finally, all SDOs allow for a possibility to comment on the draft standards through various mechanisms, that is, public enquiry (ETSI), public or community-wide review (IEEE-SA, IETF), members-consultation (W3C), or testing (Bluetooth SIG).

Each SDO further maintains its own mechanisms that contribute to transparency. Those include disclosure of affiliation and/or knowledge of essential technologies at the beginning of the working groups meetings (all SDOs); public availability of voting result (ETSI, IEEE-SA, IETF, and

[9] See, for instance, 'Active IETF working groups', available at https://datatracker.ietf.org/wg/. 'Web platform WG specifications', available at www.w3.org/WebPlatform/WG/PubStatus#HTML_specifications.

[10] E.g., 'Summary reports and minutes of 802.11 WG sessions', available at www.ieee802.org/11/Reports/index.html.

[11] However, access to the minutes of the meetings of W3C Advisory Committee is restricted to members only; in a similar vein, ETSI and Bluetooth SIG make the minutes available only for members.

[12] 'ITU-T work programme' database, available at www.itu.int/itu-t/workprog/wp_search.aspx; 'ETSI work programme', available at www.etsi.org/media-library/work-programme-and-annual-reports; '3GPP work programme', available at www.3gpp.org/DynaReport/GanttChart-Level-2.htm.

W3C), availability of working group charters (IETF and W3C), and public working drafts (IETF, W3C).[13] In this regard, some SDOs are more transparent with regard to the decision-making processes in their standards development meetings rather than governance meetings (i.e., IEEE-SA; IETF; W3C),[14] and some may also distinguish between active and passive provision of information, offering the requested documents only upon request.

### *Openness and Participation*

Openness and participation imply opportunities to contribute to standardization work, either by participating in technical committees or by commenting on standards drafts. Such opportunities should enable interested stakeholders to voice their disagreements with decisions taken during the meetings and by this means, prevent exclusion from the processes, but they may as well relate to objective distribution of voting rights.[15]

Restrictions on membership in the SDOs examined in this study, or on participation in their technical processes, do not appear unreasonable given the operational field and institutional setting of these organizations. The SDOs are open to a large spectrum of stakeholders, but some may be claimed to be more open by accepting also individual participants or observers irrespective of their affiliation; especially IETF seems to offer a high degree of openness since its standardization activities are easy to join. W3C and Bluetooth SIG assign some members more rights than others, which is also typical for specialized consortia.[16] ETSI has voting rights limitations when it comes the approval of harmonized standards, which may be explained by the fact that, despite its global role, ETSI remains an SDO producing HESs; ETSI also distributes its voting rights

[13] In some of SDOs, a draft standard can be obtained against a fee (IEEE-SA). The JRC Report noted two reasons why some SDOs may refuse to provide a public draft of their standards: preventing nonmembers from using the draft to obtain patents that would be asserted against SDO members and avoiding sending inaccurate signals to the marketplace regarding the content of final standards (this applied to DVB, VITA, and JEDEC). The JRC Report, p. 118.

[14] Ibid.; the fact that individual votes in the governing bodies of these SDOs are not disclosed counterbalances potential conflict of interests.

[15] The JRC Report suggests that openness takes two forms: openness to membership and ability to participate in standardization work. It notes that all SDOs it examined permit all interested parties to participate, while their membership appears more limited, and that participation in governance processes is limited to members. JRC Report, p. 117.

[16] Delcamp and Leiponen, 'Innovating standards', p. 38.

according to the size and turnover of its members. Some SDOs contribute to openness by issuing a call for participation among their members (i.e., IEEE-SA), or offer guidelines and training on how to participate in their technical discussions (i.e., IETF, W3C). In principle, standards development meetings, and sometimes even meetings of governing bodies of all SDOs, are open for observers, although occasionally upon a payment of a fee (ETSI), but permission of the Chair to attend the meeting is usually required.

Furthermore, some SDOs clearly differentiate between their members when it comes to strategic and nontechnical decision-making; this is self-evident in consortia, but also in 3GPP and ITU. When examining the composition of SDO governance bodies, it also appears that SDO officials are often rotating between different committees and governance bodies (i.e., IEEE-SA), or serve as ex officio members in different nontechnical committees. From one side, this ensures that only those with sufficient knowledge and experience are entitled to participate in governance decisions; from the other side, it creates a closed group of individuals who are in charge of SDOs' governance. While restrictions on the membership of SDO governance bodies limit SDO openness and decisional participation, they can be justified by an assumption that organizations should be governed by those with significant expertise in their operational field.

Participation in SDOs may take a different turn in the aftermath of COVID-19 measures, shifting attention from physical participation and requiring the amendments of SDOs' operational frameworks.[17] However, moving their discussions online is likely to affect SDOs' financing, including membership fees, and hence also SDOs' "income" to support their activities: potentially, this could lead to introducing "participation fees" in online meetings that would otherwise be free of charge.

### *Consensus, Impartiality, and Balance*

The requirement of balanced, impartial, and consensus-based standards development aims to avoid bias in SDOs' technical committees and prevent a situation when a standard is adopted over a strong opposition.[18]

[17] Akin to the "Crisis Annex 1" in 3GPP Working Procedures, activated by the PCG in May 2020.

[18] Although the US Supreme Court held in a case on software copyright (see *MGM Studios, Inc.* v. *Grokster, Ltd.*, 545 US 913 (2005)) that "time and market forces often provide equilibrium in balancing interests," this balance should not be taken for granted in SDOs' technical committees.

Similar to openness, consensus prevents exclusion from the process, which arguably, leads to better results.[19] The meaning of consensus differs per SDO, but always implies an absence of opposition and resolution of comments. In ITU, consensus refers to the interests of nation-states;[20] 3GPP and ETSI definitions of consensus largely mimic those of ISO/IEC;[21] 3GPP moreover encourages "informal" methods of reaching consensus on all issues. IEEE-SA, consensus is achieved when those concerned with the scope of the standard have reached a substantial agreement, which means more than a simple majority, but not necessarily unanimity, and that all views and objections have been considered and efforts have been made towards their resolution;[22] in W3C, consensus is achieved when a substantial number of group participants support the decision and nobody dissents by registering a *Formal Objection*;[23] in IETF Working Groups, consensus means that "very large majority" agrees with the decisions, and may be achieved through "humming" (although some of its governing bodies, i.e. IAB and IESG, may decide by unanimity).[24] Bluetooth SIG does not support consensus, but rather operates according to 4/5 voting quorum; one may, however, suggest that industry consensus is achieved through testing prior to the adoption of Bluetooth specifications.

While working groups of some SDOs may have consensus quorum, in all SDOs it is the working group chairs who are entrusted to determine whether consensus is achieved and can decide to resort to other

[19] Some studies have noted that in ITU, IPR policy consensus was important for resolving IPR disputes and did better than voting, since it gave leverage to firms to include their IPR as a standard and helped excluding unimportant technologies and open debate, so that superior technologies emerge; see Greenstein and Rysman, 'Coordination costs and standard setting'. Another study suggests that, in certain institutional settings, i.e., organizations with adequate continuity and enough long-time members to take a decision, "rough consensus" can be a more powerful mechanism than majority voting; J. F. Nickerson and M. zur Muelen, 'The ecology of standards processes: insights from internet standards making' (2006) 20 *MIS Quarterly, Special Issue on Standards Making* 467–88 at 476. In other types of organizations of economic governance, different scholars suggested that unanimous decision-making produces better outcomes, and frequency of voting matters. D. Mueller, *Public Choice III* (Cambridge: Cambridge University Press, 2003); A. A. Alchian and H. Demsetz, 'Production, information costs and economic organizations' (1972) 62 *American Economic Review* 777–95.

[20] Whereas ISO and IEC are preliminary concerned with consensus among domestic industry actors. Yates and Murphy, *Engineering Rules*.

[21] Annex A of 3GPP Working Procedures.

[22] Article 2.1 of IEEE-SA Standard Board Bylaws.

[23] See Clause 3.3 of W3C Process Document (2017).

[24] See section 4.2 of 'The Tao of IETF'.

decision-making mechanisms, be it voting or, as in 3GPP, providing interim solutions in the form of "Working Agreements" that can be challenged by the working group members.

Next to consensus, SDOs employ different mechanisms to ensure that their processes are balanced. US-based SDOs are expected to attach particular attention to balanced stakeholder representation, due to the relevant ANSI requirement. Some SDOs set certain participation or composition quorum for technical committees or voting groups (i.e., ETSI, IEEE-SA), others have rules that ensure balance in their governance bodies (ETSI, IETF, W3C); or focus on "regional" balance (i.e., ITU) or balance of commercial stakeholders (i.e., 3GPP). It remains unclear whether the rules of Bluetooth SIG actually pursue balanced decision-making, since requirements of impartiality, consensus, or balance are not mentioned in its operational framework. However, all SDOs in a way maintain an obligation to provide reasons for stakeholders' comments or objections, which ultimately ensures that the processes do not get stalled, and proposals are not blocked without valid justifications. (Note that reason-giving is as such not mentioned in the regulatory frameworks governing SDOs, while it is an important requirement in the context of private governance.)

It remains questionable whether SDOs that allow companies to join with multiple affiliates are truly balanced. By the same token, it is unclear whether the requirement for individual participants to represent their own views, rather than those of the entity of their affiliation, really works in the real-life setting.[25] Moreover, SDOs' mechanisms to ensure balance relate to representation of interests of *market players*: indeed, participation rules of SDOs require technical knowledge as a precondition to membership or participation in their activities – and rightly so. However, the increased societal and legal impact of ICT standards implies that the notion of "affected" stakeholders should be broader than those active on the market. To illustrate, internet protocols, while being extremely technical, have a large impact on society and human life, and arguably should take into account human rights.[26] But even when limited

[25] This would depend on many variables that are difficult, if not impossible, to measure, such as employees' loyalty to the company, personalities of individuals, etc.

[26] Arguably, engineers define human rights more narrowly than lawyers: for instance, engineers see privacy breach as a technical attack undermining trust in networks. See C. Cath and L. Floridi, 'The design of internet architecture by the Internet Engineering Task Force (IETF) and human rights' (2017) 23 *Science and Engineering Ethics* 449–68, who argue that IETF should follow the approach that enables human rights through protocols.

to commercial interests, stakeholders with greater expertise and financial means, typically large IPR holders and users, will tend to invest more in the process and have more weightage in SDOs.[27]

### *Effectiveness and Relevance*

The requirement for standards to be effective and relevant to market's demands relates to long-term technical considerations in SDOs as well as the (maintenance of) standards' quality. Standards' effectiveness and relevance are achieved through such processes as updating technical documents, conducting market research, and pacing standardization activities to current technical and societal needs. Procedures for reviewing, amending, and withdrawing of standards are present in all examined SDOs;[28] all SDOs also require that their work be based on engineering and technical decisions, rather than political and commercial considerations.[29] Yet, technical standardization remains a political exercise with a lot of tensions between conflicting interests, some of which may be dealt with in a hidden way.[30] In this context, some SDOs have a clear division among technical and management bodies, arguably avoiding experts being distracted from technical work by administrative issues. Before launching a new standardization project, most SDOs require that there is sufficient support from their members and the industry, which spares technical and human efforts from being devoted to an activity that is not relevant for the industry. Effectiveness and relevance are also ensured by the requirement to produce standards that are clear and complete for implementation.

### *Coherence and Coordination*

To ensure coherence in their processes, all SDOs typically have liaison agreements, MoU, or partnerships with other SDOs or international organizations.[31] Especially in ICT standardization, SDOs must cooperate and coordinate their work to ensure consistency of networks and systems:

[27] See Gandal and Régibeau, 'Standard-setting organizations', pp. 394–433.

[28] For instance, ETSI standards are reviewed at least once in five years, while IEEE standards, in ten years.

[29] For instance, IETF governance bodies were established as noncommercial organizations that valued technical capability over economic returns; see Nickerson and zur Muelen, 'The ecology of standards processes'.

[30] See Cafaggi, 'The many features' on accounting standard-setting.

[31] For example, Article 60 of ITU Constitution.

standardization of IoT technologies is a clear example of this collaboration. Sometimes coordination is almost inevitable due to the endorsement of standards by another SDO: for instance, while 3GPP specifications often form the basis of ITU Recommendations, they are put through ITU by 3GPP organizational partners/national ITU members and following national processes.[32] Members and participants are generally allowed, and sometimes even encouraged,[33] to attend the meetings of their partner organizations, in most cases, again, with prior approval of the chairs.

### *Concerns of Developing Countries or "Weaker Parties"*

ITU is by far the only SDO that actively promotes assistance to developing countries through its constitutional provisions,[34] resolutions,[35] and ITU-D – the Development Sector – but also through the requirements pertaining to the composition of its governance bodies that requires representation of different regions. IETF and W3C address the needs of developing countries to access global networks, as well as participate in the creation of internet and web standards, by conducting training and workshops to educate experts.[36] Meetings of these SDOs take place all over the world, which enables participation of experts from developing countries. Recently, assistance to developing countries also became an agenda item in the ETSI.[37] However, without a strong mandate from an SDO or related procedural requirements, it is unclear whether these initiatives are sufficient in the context of the relevant WTO requirement. Indeed, companies or governmental agencies from developing countries are not precluded from joining all SDOs on an equal basis with those from the developed world (perhaps except ETSI for certain voting

[32] Article 51 of 3GPP Working Procedures establishes procedures for submissions of 3GPP results to ITU.

[33] ITU officials, for instance, can participate in the 3GPP PCG meetings.

[34] Article 1(b) of ITU Constitution.

[35] For example, Resolution 30 (Rev. Dubai, 2018) Special measures for least developed countries, small island developing states, landlocked developing countries, and countries with economies in transition.

[36] See S. Boyera, 'The mobile web in developing countries: the next step', available at www.w3.org/2006/12/digital_divide/public.html; J. Arkko, 'Diversity' (April 2013) available at www.ietf.org/blog/diversity/.

[37] See 'IoT, 5G, security and privacy focus on the 20th Global Standards Collaboration Meeting', available at www.etsi.org/newsroom/news/1087-2016-04-news-iot-5g-security-and-privacy-focus-of-the-20th-global-standards-collaboration-meeting?.

quorum); in practice, however, technical committees of SDOs are presumably led by the developed countries.[38]

### *Appeal and Review*

While this principle concerns availability of mechanisms for challenging or reviewing decisions taken by SDOs' technical or governance bodies, it also encompasses the processes around dispute resolution, such as availability of appeal procedures, establishment of appeal bodies and availability of appeal decisions, and, in that sense, also contributes to transparency. Within SDOs, disputes can arise either between members of a working group or between members of working groups and governance bodies. Earlier studies have observed that market participants thoroughly assess how an SDO resolves disputes, including to whom it assigns authority in dispute resolution and whether these assignments result in biases.[39]

All SDOs but Bluetooth SIG have appeal bodies and maintain procedures on how appeals are conducted, including the timeline to issue the decision or confirm the receipt of an appeal brief. Some SDOs publish appeals documents and decisions (IEEE-SA; IETF; W3C). Appeals in most SDOs are handled by the appointed members of governing bodies; however, in W3C, the ultimate decision in appeal procedures lies with the Director, while ETSI aims to involve the whole membership in the General Assembly. IETF has different dispute resolution systems for different governance bodies. Furthermore, governance bodies of some SDOs are also entitled to verify whether all procedural guarantees have been satisfied during the decision-making processes in other bodies (IEEE-SA; IETF).

It has been suggested that, despite their availability, internal appeals of SDOs are not often used, and that parties prefer to settle before the formal appeal decision is issued.[40] Information available on the SDOs' websites indeed supports that claim: decisions of appeal boards are rather uncommon. This is perhaps due to the community-like nature of

[38] J. Baron and O. Kanevskaia, 'Global Competition for Leadership Positions in Standards Development Organizations" (March 2021), available at SSRN: http://dx.doi.org/10.2139/ssrn.3818143.

[39] Greenstein and Rysman, 'Coordination costs and standard setting'.

[40] Coccuru and Eliantonio, 'It is not all about judicial review', regarding CEN/CENELEC, p. 484.

standardization committees, where disagreements are preferably resolved through conversations rather than formal proceedings. Nevertheless, the structures of SDOs' appeal mechanisms raise some significant issues, such as access to appeal procedures by *outsiders* to SDOs that are affected by their decisions[41] and independence of appeal boards, which may be comprised of officials that are indirectly involved in the decision-making of the bodies against which the appeal is sought.

Availability of internal appeal may, however, not be enough to ensure procedural guarantees. While private expertise is needed for adequate decisions on complex technical issues, such methods of dispute resolution often lack legal expertise and risk essential due process rights being ignored;[42] moreover, SDOs' dispute settlement bodies cannot impose adequate corrective or reparative remedies,[43] which moreover are usually limited to SDOs' members. These shortcomings may be compensated by a recourse to litigation, which will also allow external parties to challenge SDOs' decisions that affect them.[44] SDOs, however, appear reluctant to support litigation:[45] the reasons for it may be high litigation costs and time constraints, as well as the jeopardy of legal intervention into technical decisions.

[41] Ibid., on the fact that in CEN/CENELEC, participation in standards development is a precondition for launching appeals (a measure implemented to, arguably, preclude specious and abusive uses of the procedure).

[42] Delimatsis, 'The Future of transnational self-regulation', p. 66. In a similar vein, eBay realized that its own alternative enforcement system is not reliable without enforcement treat behind its community system and the coercive power of government. See J. Goldsmith and T. Wu, *Who Controls the Internet? Illusions of a Borderless World* (Oxford: Oxford University Press, 2006), p. 136.

[43] In this regard, see P. Cane, 'Administrative law as regulation', in C. Parker, C. Scott, N. Lacey and J. Braithwaite (eds.), *Regulating Law* (Oxford: Oxford University Press, 2004), p. 221.

[44] In the case of ETSI developing HESs, it may also be relied on the "control function" of the Commission, which has a power to set the agenda, mandate standards and marginally review the work of SDOs. Coccuru and Eliantonio, 'It is not all about judicial review', p. 479.

[45] While one SDO that falls outside the scope of this study makes recourse to mandatory arbitration (DVB), this process has never been used in practice (remarks on a SDOs' governance workshop, Brussels, March 2018). Litigation on IPR issues occurs outside the SDOs and is between the stakeholders. In this regard, Contreras demonstrated that interoperability standards' litigations often revolve around similar standards and similar actors, while it is not the case for internet standards; and that standards policies that de-emphasize patent monetization have led to fewer litigations; see Contreras, 'A tale of two layers'.

### Access on Fair, Reasonable, and Nondiscriminatory Terms

While some SDOs favor licensing policies that are based on royalty-free requirements, all SDOs seem to support the minimum requirements of the "Baseline Policy" from the applicable regulatory provisions.

### SDOs' Internal Procedural Principles

It should be noted that each of the SDOs maintains its own procedural principles on which it builds its standardization activities. To illustrate, ETSI emphasizes openness, meaning that its decision-making should be accessible to all interested parties; consensus, meaning that decision-making processes do not favor any particular stakeholder; transparency, requiring archiving all information on technical discussions, public announcement of new standardization activities, seeking of participation of interested parties to achieve balance, and considerations and response to comments. Furthermore, ETSI standards should meet the requirements of maintenance, illustrated by an ongoing support of published standards; public availability of standards;[46] FRAND-based IPR policy, possibly without monetary compensation; effectiveness and relevance for the market needs; neutrality and stability; and quality.[47] These principles echo the requirements of Annex II of Regulation 1025/2012, which is not surprising due to the ETSI's role as an ESO.

To ensure fairness and good standards practice, as well as to protect itself from liability, IEEE-SA follows due process, meaning having visible standards developing procedures and following them; openness, ensuring that all interested parties can participate actively in the standards development process; consensus, which defines the percentage of balloting group vote to approve a draft of a standard; balance, ensuring that the balloting group includes all interested parties and avoids dominance; and right of appeal, allowing anyone to appeal a standards development decision at any point.[48] These principles are closely related to the Essential Requirements of ANSI which, again, may be expected due to IEEE's accreditation by ANSI.

[46] Note that the requirement is worded to indicate that public availability also means *use* on reasonable terms (including for a reasonable fee).

[47] See 'Standards making', available at www.etsi.org/standards/standards-making.

[48] See 'Develop standards', https://standards.ieee.org/develop/develop-standards/govern.html.

IETF and W3C support the OpenStand movement,[49] referring either to the open process of standards creation or to the royalty-free IPR policies.[50] OpenStand principles include appeal opportunities, clear procedures for review, and fairness (note that the latter, as such, is absent from the regulatory frameworks); they also emphasize absence of dominance, referring to broad consensus, transparency in terms of public consultations, availability of documents, and balance.[51] With regard to participation requirements, OpenStand mentions that processes should be open to all parties that are interested and *informed* (emphasis added); this wording allows for an assumption that even open standards processes can exclude certain stakeholders, in this case those who are "uninformed" (note that no threshold is offered to qualify as an "informed" stakeholder). Also, these principles gain their own interpretation in SDOs.[52]

To some extent, the rules of SDOs indeed address the shortcomings of the regulatory frameworks, at least for their specific standardization activity. SDOs devote close attention to balance, although it does not always entail a balance of interests, but rather a balance to prevent dominance. Some SDOs also address procedural guarantees in governance bodies, although the differences between standards development and "policy development" processes are notable, in some organizations less than in the others.

## SYNOPSIS

SDOs' processes follow certain patterns, but only to some extent; their heterogeneity can be explained by historical, cultural, and political factors. SDOs have to adhere to both internal (imposed by their operational frameworks) and external (imposed by the applicable regulatory

[49] See 'Leading global standards organizations endorse "OpenStand" principles that drive innovation and borderless commerce' (August 2012), available at www.ietf.org/blog/leading-global-standards-organizations-endorse-openstand-principles-drive-innovation-and-borderless-commerce/; The Agreement between W3C and Open Standard was signed on August 29, 2012.

[50] Biddle, 'No standards for standards', p. 21 and https://open-stand.org/.

[51] See 'Infographic: The 5 Core Principles of OpenStand' available at https://open-stand.org/.

[52] See 'W3C self-evaluation of OpenStand principles', available at www.w3.org/2012/08/open-stand-w3c.html. Earlier studies concluded in this regard that IETF and W3C are becoming increasingly similar in the sense that they are open and provide support with implementation; see C. Vincent and J. Camp, 'Looking to the internet for models of governance' (2004) 6 *Ethics and Information Technology* 161–73.

frameworks) procedural principles. The latter serve as a meta-regulation, introducing best practices for good standardization governance and providing SDOs with accountability mechanisms; in turn, SDOs enjoy a high degree of self-regulation by setting and managing their own rules and processes, and ensuring that these rules are enforced through procedural mechanisms that they provide. Not only do they have flexibility to implement the due process requirements in a way that suits their unique operational scope and membership,[53] but also to determine what these requirements mean, defining such terms as "consensus," "openness," and "balance" in their procedural rules. SDOs' procedural legitimacy thus underpins their public law legitimacy, but also goes beyond it.

When designing their rules, SDOs have to strike a balance between processes that are self-disciplinary and ensure sufficient procedural guarantees and processes that are attractive for the majority of stakeholders and provide for sufficient quality and smooth implementation of their standards.[54] It may be expected that strictly defined processes, while aiming at balanced and inclusive decision-making, could be viewed by many industry actors as burdensome or unnecessarily bureaucratic.[55] In this context, and given the evolving standardization ecosystem, due process mechanisms of SDOs may not be sufficient to ensure good governance and representation of all interests in their decision-making.[56] Moreover, the effectiveness of each rule will be obsolete without its effective enforcement. For these reasons, while governmental agencies should in principle trust SDOs internal rules, an external review of their decisions is necessary to ensure procedural safeguards of standardization processes.[57]

[53] As noted by Ostrom, a set of rules used in one physical environment may have different consequences when used in a different environment; Ostrom, *Governing the Commons*, p. 23. Hence, rules that work for one SDO may not have the same effect in a different SDO.

[54] See Wiegmann et al., 'Multi-mode standardization'.

[55] After all, this was one of the main reasons behind the creation of W3C and Bluetooth SIG. See also Simcoe, 'Standard setting committees', observing that consensus-driven decision in standardization committees take longer, although they do guarantee better-quality decisions.

[56] See also Mattli and Woods, 'In whose benefit?', p. 15.

[57] Schepel observes that while the US private system implies self-discipline of private bodies, questions related to due process, i.e., consensus, would be posed by courts to governmental agencies referencing the standards, and not the SDO. See Schepel, *The Constitution of Private Governance*, p. 284.

In epistemic rule-making, such external review may be provided by the proclamation of a "special expertise topping other expertise," which also has coordinative function.[58] In practice, this would imply introducing a "meta SDO" that would serve as a guardian of due process in standardization. It is, however, unlikely that such a body would be effective, and its decisions enforceable. Firstly, it would not be possible to render compliance with its rules mandatory: to the contrary, as observed from the history of SDOs, such a stricter approach will fuel the emergence of new SDOs with even looser procedural norms, which will only exacerbate the issue. Even such "meta" bodies as ISO and ANSI are still considered voluntary within standardization ecosystems. Legally, acceptance of the rules of a hypothetical standardization body can only be ensured through a governmental regulation adopted in every national law (due to the global impact of ICT standards), or through private law (i.e., contracts between companies or between companies and SDOs).

Secondly, such a body would still be comprised of industry experts, and arguably would not compensate for democratic deficit in SDOs' governance regime. Conversely, having a "meta" SDO composed of nontechnical experts, while contributing to democratic legitimacy of the SDO, is likely to undermine its epistemic legitimacy.

Another option may be a review by regulatory agencies. Arguably, governments already possess sufficient mechanisms to control ICT standardization,[59] especially when such standards are incorporated in US regulation or identified by the European Commission for public procurement. To ensure due process, regulatory agencies may intervene in private standardization through hierarchical means, for instance, by imposing stricter rules in their national laws, encouraging stakeholders to conduct their technical work in particular organizations, or sponsoring certain technical solution.[60] Yet, while intervention by political bodies may in principle promote democracy and balance, in technical

[58] See, in this regard, Shapiro, '"Deliberative," "independent" technocracy', p. 343, who mentions this as a past British civil service tradition of the "administrative class."

[59] Goldsmith and Wu (*Who Controls the Internet?*) explain how governments can exercise control over free speech on the internet by providing example of the famous *Yahoo! Case, Yahoo!, Inc.* v. *La Ligue Contre Le Racisme*, 169 F. Supp. 2d 1181 (ND Cal. 2001). Lessig suggested that governments may be more successful than private parties in designing internet codes that serve to the interest of users; see Lessig, *Codes and Other Laws*.

[60] For instance, a code of good practice/trust for cloud standardization has allegedly failed due to the refusal of private parties to standardize through the formal processes, which included the support of the European Commission.

decision-making at the transnational level, governmental interference will likely be viewed as attempts of nation-states "to gain national advantage at the expense of the members of transnational regime."[61]

Ultimately, procedural safeguards may be ensured by increased judicial review of SDOs' processes. While providing accountability to private regulatory regimes,[62] judicial review may also minimize the risk of standards developers being unduly influenced by regulators when the latter serve as controllers.[63] The peril of increased juridification, however, is traversing the technical nature of SDOs' processes, which in turn may also discourage SDOs' work due to the increased chance of their liability;[64] this is particularly evident from SDOs' reluctance to discuss their decision-making in courts.[65]

[61] Shapiro, '"Deliberative," "independent" technocracy', 349. In this regard, Russel also observes that aggressive regulators and policy-makers involved in standardization may have an agenda to promote national industrial or innovation policies; see A. Russel, 'Standardization history: a review essay with an eye to the future', in S. Bolin (ed.), *The Standards Edge: Future Generations* (Ann Arbor: Sheridan Press, 2005), pp. 247–60.

[62] Cafaggi, 'A comparative analysis'.

[63] See Cane, 'Administrative law as regulation', who also notes that public functionalities, like private actors, are motivated by self-interest.

[64] These fears have been expressed as an aftermath of the Courts' decisions in *TruePosition v. Ericsson* and *James Elliot* cases.

[65] Schepel doubts whether judicial review, public authority voices, and other mechanisms of public decision-making can promote socially responsive institutions of deliberation in private bodies, and suggests that such mechanisms would disrupt social structure of communication and perverse effects of litigation; Schepel, *The Constitution of Private Governance*, p. 257.

# PART IV

## Due Process in ICT Standardization
### *From Theory to Practice*

That fact that SDOs may respond differently to the regulatory and industry pressures when developing and modifying their institutional architecture is evidenced by the heterogeneity of their governance models and their evolution over time. But ICT standards are not defined only by legal and institutional forces; in fact, standardization processes largely remain the work of experts who follow the repertoire of rules prepared by SDOs. Standards provide technical infrastructure at the global level; they are futile unless deemed useful by the industry applying them. Following the same logic, SDOs provide methods for standards development, which would be futile unless followed in practice. Unlike rules mandated by the regulatory agencies, rules stemming from private authorities are deemed less effective due to the lack of enforcement as well as the availability of regulatory alternatives: this places SDOs in a competitive relationship, adding supplementary pressures to design their governance rules in a way that is accepted by their industrial "demos."

A typical legal and institutional analysis of (private) regulatory processes often fails to factor in the scientific, technical, and individual incentives. To understand the ecology of ICT standardization, one should cut through the layers of regulation and consider its practical application.

From the perspective of legitimacy, the question remains whether increasing due process in SDOs can improve the quality of ICT standards they produce and, ultimately, substitute for the lack of democratic input. Scholarship on global and private governance suggests that safeguarding participation and transparency of non-State regulation, and offering review opportunities for private decision-makers, leads to increased legitimacy and positively affects the uptake of regulation. In other words, increased input and throughput legitimacy of SDOs should also increase their output legitimacy. Establishing whether such formula applies to ICT standardization requires technical knowledge and understanding of the functioning of ICT standards and is a matter of case-by-case analysis. However, some insights on implementation of due process principles and legitimacy of ICT standards can be provided by studying the practice of ICT standardization.

Against this backdrop, this part of the book evaluates theoretical findings of the previous chapters in a qualitative empirical study of SDO governance, performed through interviews and case studies.

## Methodology

### *Interview Format*

The qualitative empirical study was performed through conducting semistructured interviews with experts who had considerable experience in ICT standardization, aiming to reveal *how due process principles for ICT standardization are implemented in practice.* An open-ended interview format fitted the explorative nature of this study since it enables asking respondents both about the facts of a particular matter and about their opinion, allowing them to propose their own insights and suggest other sources of evidence.[1] A standardized interview script was developed based on the findings of the descriptive study on SDOs' operational frameworks, and was later adapted for each expert.

The potential interviewees were identified based on their affiliation – predominantly, leading multinational tech companies that are large stakeholders in ICT standardization, and which were categorized either as "patent-intensive companies," whose business models were largely built on innovation and patent monetization, or as "user companies" (i.e., media companies, device manufacturers, etc.). Further categorization proved less suitable, since each SDO maintains different membership and participants categories, making a coherent categorization of interviewed stakeholders problematic. Other subjects approached for an interview were affiliated with consultancies, governmental organizations, and global and regional SDOs, not necessarily limited to the analyzed SDOs. Some affiliates of private companies approached were also appointed, or have been appointed in past, as members of SDOs' governance bodies.

Furthermore, potential interviewees were identified based on their experience with and knowledge of governance and technical processes in different SDOs: for instance, individuals who hold or held leadership

[1] R. K. Yin, *Case Study Research: Design and Methods*, 3rd ed. (Thousand Oaks, CA: Sage Publications, 2003), p. 89.

positions in SDOs' governance bodies; individuals who are or have been involved in (ongoing) standardization activities; or individuals who are or have been involved with standardization management, strategy, or policy of their employer. While the selection criteria were not as such constrained to the individuals' experience with the analyzed SDOs, many experts have indicated to have been involved in the processes in at least three of these SDOs.

In total, fifty-two individuals have been contacted with an invitation for an interview. From them, four individuals have been first informally approached at the conferences and events that the author attended and have later received an e-mail with an interview request. Eleven individuals have been first approached via LinkedIn Messaging and InMails with a short explanation of the study and an invitation for an interview: five individuals have responded positively to this invitation and have then received an e-mail with a detailed explanation of the study, as well as the interview questions. Three individuals have been suggested by other experts during the interviews and have also received an invitation for an interview by e-mail. Thirty-four interview subjects have been approached directly by e-mail.

From fifty-two individuals, interviews have been conducted with twenty-six experts and twenty-four of these interviews were used in this study. From twenty-six experts with whom the interviews have not been conducted, six initially indicated to have interest in the study and agreed to be interviewed, but could not participate due to time constraints, referred to another expert, or did not reply to follow-up e-mails; five disagreed to be interviewed, noting lack of time, expertise in the subject matter, or interest in the study as their reasons; and fifteen provided no response at all (Tables PIV.1 and PIV.2).

Table PIV.1 *Number of respondents and nonrespondents for the interviews*

| Total individuals contacted | 52 |
|---|---|
| Total interviewed | 26 |
| Agreed to participate, but no follow-up (experts did not say "no") | 6 |
| Disagreed to participate (experts said "no") | 5 |
| No response | 15 |

Table PIV.2. *Demographics of interview subjects approached*

| Experts contacted | 52 |
|---|---|
| Private companies | 26 |
| Consultancies/small research bodies | 5 |
| Governmental bodies | 3 |
| Global SDOs | 12 |
| National SDOs | 6 |

A substantial majority of contacted experts were affiliated with Western companies, SDOs, and (non)governmental actors based either in the US or EU. This is not surprising given the fact ICT standardization is largely carried out by Western stakeholders in SDOs based in the US and the EU. To provide a more comprehensive view, participation of non-Western companies was sought: affiliates of six leading Asian tech companies involved in the different layers of ICT standardization have been approached with an invitation to participate in the study, of which two have been interviewed, two agreed to participate but did not follow up on further e-mails, one declined, and one did not respond. All individuals approached were based in Western branches of the companies.

### *Respondents' Demographics*

Respondents had experience in multiple industries: many were involved in standardization at different abstraction layers, had wide experience with IPR strategy and licensing policies of their company, or contributed to the development of internet and web protocols. The respondents were also of a mixed professional background, including policy advisors, management strategists, (ICT) engineers, and lawyers. Most of the respondents had an extensive experience with working for multiple private companies, SDOs' secretariats or (non)governmental bodies, where they held different leadership positions. All individuals have been involved – either directly or as observers – in multiple standards development and governance processes. All respondents were interviewed in private capacity, which was agreed with them prior to the interview: hence, the respondents did not only reflect on the practices of their current employers, but also shared their own experiences and observations.

Table PIV.3 illustrates the demographics of the twenty-four respondents whose interviews were used in this study.

Table PIV.3. *Respondents' demographics*

| Total subjects interviewed | 24 |
|---|---|
| Patent-intensive company | 8 |
| User company | 4 |
| SDO staff member | 5 |
| Consultancy/research body | 4 |
| Governmental body | 1 |

### *Methods of Approaching Respondents and Conducting and Processing Interviews*

Potential interviewees were approached from December 2017 to April 2018. The interviews were conducted between January 2018 and July 2018. Experts were approached by e-mail explaining the nature of purpose of the study, introducing the researcher, and asking for their participation; the e-mail also provided assurance that no references would be made to the interviewee's affiliation.[2] In case of positive responses, the potential interviewees were sent the list of questions to be asked during the interviews.

Some of the questions on the list were asked to all interviewees ("general questions"): such questions related to the advantages of SDOs where they participate; barriers for (effective) participation in standardization work; differences between SDOs' standards development processes and governance processes; SDOs' dispute resolution processes; procedural guarantees; and effectiveness of SDOs' standards. Other questions were tailored to a specific SDO, standard or a case study, depending on the interviewee's affiliation and experience ("specific questions"). Since the interviews took the form of "guided conversations," experts' responses were sometimes open-ended. Based on their answers, experts have also been asked follow-up questions. Some interviewees provided feedback to rephrase the questions or indicated that they preferred not to

[2] As interviews were scheduled before GDPR came into effect, no consent form was distributed at this stage of the empirical research.

Table PIV.4. *Interview methods*

| Total interviews | 24 |
|---|---|
| Interviewed in person | 5 |
| Interviewed via Skype/phone | 17 |
| Provided written answers to interview questions | 2 |

answer some questions – both conditions have been respected in the course of the interviews.

The interviews were conducted either in person or through various means of telecommunication (i.e., Skype, WebEx, phone calls) (Table PIV.4). For those interviews where the experts granted an explicit permission to make recordings, transcripts of the conversations were made and sent to the experts for their approval; for other interviews, the interviewer was taking notes during the interviewing process. Some experts, noting lack of time, preferred to answer interview questions per e-mail, but also offered insights and suggestions that went beyond the questions, and were available to provide further comments and clarifications. All interviews were conducted in English.

All written documents that resulted from the interviews were stored in compliance with the applicable legal rules. The answers to the questions were subsequently grouped under separate topics and analyzed in a coherent text that follows the narrative of this study. Answers that related to the three case studies on procedural dispute were analyzed in the context of the desk study. The excerpts from the interviews used in this study have been shared with the experts in order to confirm that their statements have not been misinterpreted.

### *Qualitative Case Studies on Disputes in SDOs*

Case studies of SDO disputes preliminarily aimed to reveal *what can be learned from disputes on SDOs' procedures with regard to implementation of due process principles for standardization.* The case studies were mostly performed by desk research using the following sources: relevant case law, organizational documents placed in public domains, archival records available on SDOs' websites (i.e., minutes of the meetings, text of proceedings, e-mail correspondence), official statements of companies involved in the disputes, and previous (academic) case studies. Where possible, the desk study was supplemented by the answers to semistructured interview questions provided by individuals who have been involved in the disputes or have profound knowledge of the events. These questions formed part of the "specific questions" and were sometimes asked as follow-up questions during the interviews.

Since not all relevant documents were made equally available for all three case studies, the representation of views risked being unbalanced.[3] This shortcoming was attempted to be mitigated by reaching out to different stakeholders and formulating questions in an objective manner, without taking any position based on the desk study research or previous studies in the field.

## Limitations and Caveats

The majority of experts interviewed in the context of this study are affiliated with leading ICT commercial enterprises; only a few contributors are linked to smaller-scaled companies, governmental agencies, or SDOs' secretariats. Hence, it should be admitted that the results of this study are rather limited and do not necessarily represent an equal share of all standardization interests. This limitation can be explained by the following: firstly, most stakeholders in ICT standardization are indeed large private companies, which also explains the choice of stakeholders approached for the interviews; secondly, due to the limitations imposed by the research design of the study, it was practically impossible to identify and approach *all* relevant stakeholders in ICT standardization. Hence, the conclusions derived from these interviews, even if taking a form of anecdotal evidence, should be viewed in the light of this limitation.

The second limitation relates to the demographic homogeneity of the interview subjects: all interviewed individuals were affiliated Western-based companies, or Western branches of Asian companies, SDOs, or governments. This limitation can be explained by the fact that the ICT sector is still largely driven by Western companies from the US and EU, and Western-based SDOs. It should be noted that the research questions that guided qualitative empirical studies took no account of nationality, country of residence, or gender of interviewed experts.

[3] As noted by Yin, case studies in general may lack rigor and, as any type of qualitative research, do not allow to make any generalizations (Yin, *Case Study Research*, p. 9).

Third, although the interviews sought the insights of various parties, not all approached stakeholders agreed to participate: for this reason, the case studies do not represent the views of all parties, and there is an inequality between the number of interviewed companies termed as "patent-intensive" and "user."

Fourth, open-ended interview questions, while having a benefit of not restricting the interview subjects to the scripted list of questions and allowing them to choose the conservation format, may have also resulted in somewhat unbalanced findings. This especially concerns responses submitted per e-mail, since it limited the opportunities to ask follow-up questions during the interviews.[4] Moreover, some experts preferred to cover multiple questions in one response, or not to follow the questions' script at all; in a similar vein, most interviewed experts preferred not to be recorded, which eliminated the possibility of sending transcripts for verification.

Last, due account should be taken of the fact that experts participated in the study in their private capacity. Their contributions were based on their particular experience and may also include their own opinion, which may not always correspond to the position prevailing in the industry or even the company of their affiliation. At the same time, account should be taken of certain preferences in experts' views resulting from their affiliation. Depending on experts' background or the industry in which they are involved, their interpretation of such concepts as transparency, openness, and consensus may differ.

Despite the mentioned caveats, the findings of this empirical study contribute to the analysis of procedural guarantees in SDOs by offering a different, practical perspective on complex legal issues.

[4] Experts were, however, available to answer any follow-up questions, or to clarify their answers, by e-mail.

# 10

# Case Studies on Dispute Resolution in SDOs

Resolution of disputes between SDOs' stakeholders, or between an SDO and its members, is one of the most contentious issues discussed in the context of procedural guarantees. While the scholarship on global governance and private regulation suggests that dispute resolution mechanisms of private regulators are to benefit from legal expertise and increased due process offered by nontechnological actors outside an SDO, such "external" review is not particularly welcomed by SDOs and their stakeholders and may be considered an unnecessary intervention in technical processes. In this context, it is of particular relevance to study how some of the procedural disputes that arose within ICT SDOs have been resolved and what was the effect, if any, of these disputes on the standardization ecosystem.

The word "dispute" here does not assume a negative connotation and does not only refer to litigation or arbitration processes. Rather, dispute should be understood as challenges and disagreements between SDOs' stakeholders. Such disputes are common in all standards development processes, and arguably improve the ultimate quality of standards by offering additional checks and reviews. Hence, a large number of appeal and review proceedings that have taken place, or are still ongoing, in many SDOs qualify as disputes in the context this research. This study thus aims to reflect how the disputes are resolved either by SDOs' leadership (i.e., chairs, governance bodies) or, when disagreements are escalated, by "external" actors (i.e., courts).

This chapter discusses three disputes where stakeholders challenged rules and processes of three levels of SDOs' governance: standards development processes, policy drafting processes, and appeal processes. As such, the three disputes differ in their subject matter and were resolved by different bodies. In the first case study, an SDO was a defendant in a court case on antitrust liability and exclusion of technologies. In the second one, an SDO's policy-making processes were claimed to be unbalanced and excluding interested stakeholders; the dispute was handled by the SDO's dispute resolution bodies, and its operational rules were ultimately scrutinized by an organization charged with its accreditation as a national standards body. In the third case study, the approval of a standard by an SDO's leadership was challenged on appeal to its membership. And while the lack of procedural guarantees was not the only claim raised in these three disputes, the arguments presented by the parties, and the ultimate decisions of the dispute resolution authorities, bear important consequences for the standardization ecosystem.

The case studies do not aim to offer a detailed reconstruction of dispute resolution processes, and neither do they aim to judge the appropriateness of parties' arguments or the outcomes of the disputes. Nor does this chapter aim to compare the disputes, acknowledging their institutional and material differences. Rather, the three disputes should be viewed within the context of procedural guarantees in SDOs, in which they reflect current discussions and challenges in the standardization ecosystem.

## Collusion and Due Process in Standards Development: TruePosition vs Ericsson, ALU, Qualcomm, ETSI, and 3GPP

The *TruePosition* case is remarkable for sparking the discussion on clarity and binding effect of SDOs' working procedures and on potential abuse of power by working groups' chairs.[1] TruePosition, a developer of technology for determining callers' location by emergency responders,[2] accused three large companies, Qualcomm, Ericsson, and Alcatel-Lucent USA (ALU) ("Corporate Defendants") as well as two SDOs, 3GPP and ETSI, of obstructing TruePosition's superior positioning technology from the inclusion into the Long-Term Evolution (LTE) standard with the purpose of promoting the rival technology of uncertain quality developed by the Corporate Defendants.[3]

TruePosition's location technology, Uplink-Time Difference of Arrival (UTDOA), was the successor of its Uplink Time of Arrival (UL-TOA), which did not make it into the 2G specifications due to the market

1 The latter, according to the TruePosition's arguments, is an "extraordinary powerful position"; as noted by one of the interviewees, this position is mostly filled by large companies leading a particular standardization activity, Interview with an industry expert, January 25, 2018.

2 Such technology is used in cell phones, for instance, when dialing 911.

3 *TruePosition, Inc.* v. *LM Ericsson Tel. Co.* (January 6, 2012), No. 11-4574, 2012 WL 33075 (E.D. Pa. January 6, 2012).

preference of the alternative Enhanced Observed Time Difference (E-OTD) developed by Ericsson.[4] However, Ericsson's technology did not meet the regulatory requirements of the Federal Communications Commission (FCC) regarding location accuracy.[5] The UTDOA was then developed by TruePosition as a "work-around" solution compliant with FCC's demands, which was standardized into 2G and 3G releases as of 2004.[6] According to TruePosition, UTDOA was unique in using location measurement units (LMUs), equipment located at multiple cell towers, for collecting timing information that was necessary to determine a mobile handset's location;[7] other technologies, including Ericsson's Observed Time Difference of Arrival (OTDOA), were less advantageous since they depended on the handset to perform the calculation.[8]

In its complaint filed in 2011, TruePosition asserted that the decision not to adopt UTDOA into the LTE standard violated § 1 of the Sherman Act (conspiracy) and, with regard to Ericsson and ALU, also § 2 of the Sherman Act (monopolization);[9] the Amended Complaint filed in 2012 only alleged combination conspiracy in violation of § 1 of the Sherman Act.[10] Interestingly, while the LTE standard containing 4G technology has been developed by 3GPP and not ETSI, the latter faced similar accusations by being an organizational partner of 3GPP and providing administrative support for the standards development

[4] TruePosition believed that this was due to the fact that market of that time was dominated by radio access network (RAN) vendors, but no conspiracy claims were filed against those decisions in the time when 2G releases were developed. *TruePosition, Inc.* v. *LM Ericsson Tel. Co.* (August 12, 2012), No. 11-4574, 2012 WL 3584626 (E.D. Pa. Aug. 21, 2012), at 15–16.

[5] Ibid., p. 17.

[6] Ibid., pp. 17–18.

[7] Ibid., p. 15. The location was ultimately determined by measuring the difference in the time they receive a signal sent over a cellular network in the ordinary course from the handset.

[8] Ibid., Complaint *TruePosition Inc.* v. *LM Ericsson Telephone Company, Qualcomm Inc., Alcatel-Lucent. S.A., Third Generation Partnership Project and European Telecommunications Standards Institute*, filed on July 20, 2011, Case 2:11-cv-04574-RK, at 20–3.

[9] Ibid.

[10] The Amended Complaint was filed in February 2012 to the District Court for the Eastern District of Pennsylvania. The Court, referring to the earlier case law (i.e., *Golden Bridge Tech., Inc.* v. *Motorola, Inc.*, 547 F 3d 266, 273 (5th Cir. 2008) (quoting *Consol. Metal Prods., Inc.* v. *Am. Petroleum Inst.*, 846 F 2d 284, 294 (5th Cir. 1998)), which stated that exclusions of some products are in the nature of SDOs activities do not constitute antitrust violations, found that TruePosition failed to provide evidence of a conspiracy against UTDOA between the Defendants.

meetings where alleged anticompetitive conducts have taken place.[11] The Corporate Defendants, in turn, argued that TruePosition failed to prove that it suffered from an antitrust injury; ETSI furthermore asserted the lack of jurisdiction of the US courts.[12]

In essence, TruePosition submitted that the affiliates of Qualcomm, Ericsson, and ALU held key functions in the relevant committees and collaboratively manipulated the 3GPP processes with a result of inclusion of their own technologies into specifications, eliminating competition from TruePosition's technologies,[13] and that 3GPP and ETSI facilitated conspiracy by failing to perform their tasks of monitoring and enforcing compliance with 3GPP rules, despite having witnessed the alleged conduct during the meetings as well as having been notified of anticompetitive conduct by TruePosition.[14] The Claimant invoked a number of conducts it deemed anticompetitive, which all took place within RAN Plenary meetings or TSG Working Groups, including: chairmen's acceptance of proposals that were prepared privately by the Corporate Defendants and that were intentionally submitted after the deadline without providing for any possibilities of review and response, in violation of due process safeguards of 3GPP; the chairman's (affiliated with Ericsson) rejection of TruePosition and AT&T's requests to consider UTDOA technology for inclusion into specifications; and the fact that UTDOA technology was submitted to rigorous restrictions that were not imposed on OTDOA, despite TruePosition's successful demonstration and testing of the technology and even though this decision led to an inevitable delay of standardization processes.[15]

[11] *TruePosition, Inc.* v. *LM Ericsson Tel.* (January 6, 2012) at 17. ETSI was dismissed from the action on August 10, 2012.

[12] Ibid., at 18.

[13] The specification at issue was 2008 Work Item Release 9 and 3GPP Standards. OTDOA technology required specialized hardware and software of the type manufactured by Qualcomm in every handset, as well as RAN equipment of the type manufactured by Ericsson and ALU. TruePosition alleged that Ericsson and Qualcomm each hold patents that are essential to the implementation of OTDOA. *TruePosition, Inc.* v. *LM Ericsson Tel.* (August 21, 2012) at 15.

[14] TruePosition submitted that exclusion from the standard guarantees company's commercial failure and is likely to lead to absolute foreclosure from the market and that uncertainties as regards the implementation of UTDOA in LTE will also harm the selling of this technology for 2G and 3G. See Complaint filed by TruePosition on July 20, 2011.

[15] Ibid. Some experts interviewed for this research believed that the chair position, even when the chairman is not a staff member, does not represent the decision of ETSI, since chairmen are elected and have to comply with ETSI rules under their own liability. Interview with an expert from an SDO, April 4, 2018.

TruePosition insisted that neither Ericsson nor ALU had previously succeeded in opposing UTDOA independently, meaning that they needed to coordinate their efforts to preclude TruePosition's technology from being adopted into the LTE standard. Together with Qualcomm, the three companies "wielded sufficient power in the marketplace to avoid serious commercial repercussions from a major customer that they could not, otherwise, face acting alone."[16] Such unfairly gained competitive advantage, according to TruePosition, stems from conspiracy. The Court found that the allegations against the *Corporate Defendants* (emphasis added) were plausible both on the grounds of agreement on conspiracy and unreasonable restriction on trade – the two elements of § 1 of the Sherman Act.[17] Accordingly, TruePosition's allegation of antitrust injury was deemed proven.

In the meantime, 3GPP responded with counterclaims, alleging, among other things, that TruePosition breached its contractual obligations toward the SDO under 3GPP Working Procedures.[18] More specifically, 3GPP rules stated that TruePosition should have followed objection and appeal processes by discussing their position with the Working Group's chairman and brought the issue to the Project Coordination Group.[19] The SDO insisted that compliance with these provisions was crucial to ensure a fair and impartial standards development process that is based on technical merits; without the recourse to its appeal procedures, 3GPP cannot reverse or modify decisions of its Study and Working Groups.[20] 3GPP furthermore submitted that by filling a lawsuit, TruePosition undermined the standardization process since it attempted to include technology through juridical intervention rather than a technical merits procedure.[21]

TruePosition, however, maintained that breach of contract could not be claimed by 3GPP since the Working Procedures did not constitute a contract, and hence were nonbinding.[22] The Court agreed with this statement and found that albeit the provisions being material and

[16] *TruePosition, Inc.* v. *LM Ericsson Tel.* (August 21, 2012) at 23.

[17] Ibid., at 41.

[18] *TruePosition, Inc.* v. *LM Ericsson Tel. Co.* (October 9, 2012) 977 F. Supp. 2d 462 (E.D. Pa. 2013). While the Counterclaims were filed on four Counts, this study only addresses Count I.

[19] Ibid., p. 468.

[20] Ibid.

[21] Ibid.

[22] Ibid.

essential and implying parties' obligations and entitlements, the terms of the rules of procedure were too indefinite to be enforceable: in other words, the language of the articles was ambiguous regarding parties' obligations, since they did not define which actions would constitute a breach of those provisions and which sanctions will be imposed in case of violation.[23]

The case ended with a settlement,[24] leaving many questions unexplored, such as whether and when can an SDO be accused of conspiring with its members by not intervening in their anticompetitive behavior. For ETSI, the settlement was necessary due to the increased costs of litigation,[25] which also fueled uncertainties among its stakeholders regarding the membership fees and consequences for the members in case ETSI would have been found liable.[26] Although the case is not believed to have drastically affected ETSI's or 3GPP's operational rules,[27] some changes to ETSI Directives related the costs of litigation with ETSI were implemented.[28] To ensure that ETSI cannot be held liable for chairmen's decisions, antitrust training for chairs and vice chairs were put in place.[29] Overall, this case illustrates the need for clear and enforceable working procedures to safeguard SDOs from antitrust liability, as well as SDOs' tendency to resolve the disputes internally, rather than in courts.

[23] Ibid., pp. 470–3, citing "To be enforceable, an agreement must be certain about 'the nature and extent of its obligation[s].'" *Shell's Disposal & Recycling, Inc.* v. *City of Lancaster*, 504 F App'x 194, 202 (3rd Cir. 2012) (quoting *Am. Eagle Outfitters*, 584 F.3d at 585). "That requirement does not mean that the presence of any interpretive ambiguity renders an agreement unenforceable." Ibid. (citing *Am. Eagle Outfitters*, 584 F.3d at 585). "Rather, a contract fails for indefiniteness when it is 'impossible to understand' what the parties agreed to because the essential terms are ambiguous or poorly defined." Ibid. (*Am. Eagle Outfitters*, 584 F.3d at 585).

[24] Press Release, 'TruePosition and Ericsson settle Antitrust litigation' (July 31, 2014), available at www.ericsson.com/en/press-releases/2014/7/trueposition-and-ericsson-settle-antitrust-litigation.

[25] Interview with an expert from an SDO, April 4, 2018.

[26] Interview with an industry expert, January 23, 2018.

[27] Interview with an expert from an SDO, April 4, 2018.

[28] Interview with an industry expert, January 23, 2018. (Article 18.1 of ETSI Rules of Procedure.) A couple of years later, a proposal to delete this provision was successfully opposed by SMEs and the EC; see 'SME friendly dispute resolution in standardization at risk' (May 4, 2016), available at www.digitalsme.eu/sme-friendly-dispute-resolution-standardisation-risk/.

[29] Interview with an industry expert, January 15, 2018, on file with the author; Interview with an expert from an SDO, April 4, 2018.

## Collusion and Due Process in Governance Processes: "Innovators" vs "Implementers" in IEEE-SA

Procedural controversies related to modification processes of SDOs' rules, namely, the IPR Policy, arose in IEEE-SA.[30] Unlike the TruePosition case, dispute on IEEE-SA's IPR Policy Update was not subjected to litigation; instead, companies used IEEE's internal appeal procedures and, once those were exhausted, sought the decision of ANSI Executive Council (ExSC). The aftermath of IPR Policy Update raises an important procedural question: do SDOs' governance processes have to offer the same procedural safeguards as required from SDOs' standards development processes?

Among a number of modifications to IEEE IPR policy,[31] the 2015 IPR Policy Update was especially criticized for its departure from common practice.[32] Discussions on IPR Policy amendments were carried out by the Ad Hoc committee, that was appointed specifically for this purpose by IEEE-SA PatCom during its meeting in March 2013.[33] The committee was composed of seven 2013 PatCom members, an upcoming 2014–2015 PatCom member, a 2014–2015 PatCom nonvoting member, one IEEE staff member, and two nonvoting members of the 2016 BoG (the secretary and the administrator).[34] Within the following fifteen months, a draft of the Policy Update was put together by a subcommittee of the Ad Hoc. Given that neither the minutes of the Ad Hoc committee's meetings nor those of the subcommittee were made publicly available, the course of the discussions and the rationale behind the decisions taken at those

[30] This case study is based on an earlier article by Zingales and Kanevskaia, 'The IEEE-SA patent policy update'.

[31] See Chapter 7.

[32] IEEE is claimed to be the first SDO regulating FRAND royalties and referring to commercial essentiality. See J. G. Sidak, 'The antitrust division's devaluation of standard-essential patents' (2015) 48 *The Georgetown Law Journal Online* 48–73 at 59. Similar changes to patent policy were not accepted in ETSI or ITU due to the lack of consensus among the SDOs' membership, Interview with an industry expert, January 15, 2018; Interview with an industry expert, January 16, 2018; Interview with an industry expert, January 17, 2018.

[33] PatCom Meeting Minutes of March 4, 2013, available at http://standards.ieee.org/about/sasb/patcom/0313mins.pdf.

[34] As it appeared from the author's conversations with different parties, while those opposing the 2015 IPR Policy Update claimed that there was no open call for experts to participate in amendment processes, IEEE staff members asserted that there were sufficient opportunities to join the process. The author does not possess any documentation that proves or disproves either of the statements.

meetings remain unknown; allegedly, this accountability gap was filled by the presentation of reports at the PatCom meetings and the IEEE-SA Patent Forum.[35]

Once approved by the Ad Hoc committee, the draft was submitted for an online public review. This process was followed for each of the four drafts produced by the Ad Hoc, and generated a total of 680 comments, of which 547 were responded to by the Ad Hoc. The fourth and the last version incorporated some of the suggested modifications.[36] It needs to be mentioned that all members of IEEE committees have a fiduciary duty towards the SDO and act in their private capacity; nevertheless, it was believed by the opponents of the policy[37] that affiliation of PatCom and Ad Hoc committee members had played a significant role in the final approval of the revised policy by PatCom in June 2014. This process of simple majority voting resulted in a favorable vote from three individuals who were also members of the Ad Hoc committee affiliated with companies known as the driving forces behind policy modifications.[38] The negative votes came from the two individuals who were not part of the committee and have opposed the changes during the commenting process. The Chair, also the member of the Ad Hoc, abstained.

The draft IPR policy was subsequently submitted for consideration to the IEEE-SA SASB, which discussed the proposed Policy Update in its open session held in August 2014. The SASB accepted PatCom's report in a secret balloting process, eventually approving the new Policy with fourteen votes in favor and five votes against.[39] In December 2014, the draft was also accepted by the BoG with nine votes in favor, three against, and one recusing.[40] Subsequently, and allegedly to gain more

[35] Lindsay, Business review letter request, at pp. 13–15.

[36] See M. A. Lindsay and K. Karachalios, 'Updating a patent policy: the IEE experience' (2015) 3 *CPI Antitrust Chronicle* 1–6 at 4.

[37] This was suggested in a number of interviews, but also in some scholarly articles. See, for instance, R. Hoffinger, 'The 2015 DOJ IEEE business review letter: the triumph of industrial policy preferences over law and evidence' (2015) 3 *CPI Antitrust Chronicle* 1–24.

[38] See PatCom Meeting Minutes of June 10, 2014, available at http://standards.ieee.org/about/sasb/patcom/0614patmins.pdf.

[39] Unlike the minutes of the PatCom meetings, the minutes of the SASB meetings do not reveal the identity of individuals behind every vote. Such a form of paper balloting should therefore be considered "secret balloting." IEEE-SA Standards Board Meeting Minutes of August 20–21, 2014, available at http://standards.ieee.org/about/sasb/0814sasbmin.pdf.

[40] See IEEE-SA Board of Governors Resolution of December 2014, available at https://standards.ieee.org/about/bog/resolutions.html; IEEE Standards Association Board of Governors (BoG) Meeting Minutes of December 5, 2014.

legitimacy,[41] a further approval was sought and obtained from the Board of Directors at a meeting in February 2014.[42]

It appears thus that while the Policy Update was contested at the "lower" level of the process, it managed to reach sufficient support at the "higher" level by the BoG (75 percent in favor, which also complies with the IEEE-SA benchmark of consensus for standards approval) and the Board of Directors.[43] The procedural questions thus remain at the "lower" level with Ad Hoc committee, PatCom, and SASB.[44]

In August 2014, an appeal was filed by a number of stakeholders disadvantaged by the substantive and procedural aspects of the updated Patent Policy before the BoG.[45] In their complaint, a group comprised of Qualcomm Incorporated, Alcatel-Lucent USA Incorporated, Fraunhofer-Gesellschaft e.V., InterDigital Incorporated, Nokia Corporation, Nokia Solutions and Networks Oy, Panasonic Corporation, and SanDisk Corporation asserted that the Policy was not drafted by all interested stakeholders and that the process that led to its adoption ran afoul with the principle of consensus, which requires a substantial agreement reached between directly and materially affected interest groups and implies a consideration of all diverging views and objections.[46] The appeal was rejected by the BoG on the ground that it was not related to an inaction of the SASB, since the decision of SASB to hold a joint meeting with the PatCom constituted an "action" and should have been appealed within thirty days following its notification (the appeal at issue was filed within sixty days as an "inaction").[47] Even if the appeal had been filed timely, the BoG Appeal Panel found that the "inaction" had

[41] Interview with an industry expert, February 13, 2018; Industry expert's answers to the questionnaire, received April 27, 2018.

[42] See Lindsay and Karachalios, 'Updating a patent policy', p. 4.

[43] Recall that the Board of Directors is a democratically elected body of IEEE, which represents various interests.

[44] This approval by high-level bodies was also contested. As one expert suggested, the BoG believed that the decision will eventually benefit the broader community, but since BoG is not comprised of commercial actors, its judgment of "right" and "wrong" in commercial space is questionable. Interview with an industry expert, January 15, 2018. It has also been suggested that IEEE did not follow a correct process by relying on voting, which resulted in IEEE's departure from FRAND principles, and that the role of staff in this decision should have been more limited. Interview with an industry expert, June 13, 2018.

[45] Appellants' Appeal Brief of August 11, 2014.

[46] Ibid.

[47] Section 5.8.3 of IEEE-SA Standards Board Operations Manual.

already been remedied by the voting on draft policy approval within the SASB.[48]

A second appeal, this time related to the SASB approval of draft policy modifications, was filed before the BoG in September 2014,[49] but was again unsuccessful: the BoG Appeal Panel found that the arguments did not demonstrate how the appellants were adversely affected by a standard or by a lack of action in the IEEE standardization process and rejected the appeal on the ground of failure to establish a prima facie case.[50]

A year later, another appeal was filed to the ANSI ExSC by Alcatel-Lucent, Ericsson, and Qualcomm, this time related to ANSI's reaccreditation of IEEE as an ASD.[51] The appeal was rejected by the ANSI ExSc Panel for the reason that ANSI Essential Requirements, compliance with which serves as a basis for the ASD accreditation, did not apply to the SDOs' governance processes,[52] meaning that SDOs are free to draft their policies in a process that is not necessarily open and consensus based.[53]

How did the process of IPR Policy Update affect the industry? While some proponents of the new IPR Policy maintain that the implemented changes were necessary for the type of standardization activity that IEEE

48 IEEE-SA BoG Appeal Officers Decision, September 18, 2014.

49 Appellants' Appeal Brief of September 18, 2014.

50 See IEEE-SA BoG Appeal Officers Decision, October 22, 2014; Section 5.4 of the IEEE-SA Standards Board Bylaws.

51 For explanation on ANSI accreditation, see Chapter 5.

52 ANSI Executive Standards Council, Summary Decision, February 25, 2016, on file with author. It is worth noting that the ANSI Intellectual Property Right Policy Committee was asked to vote on compliance of the proposed IEEE Patent Policy with the ANSI Patent Policy. The results of this balloting (fifteen votes in favor of compliance, ten votes against, and eleven abstained) arguably indicate a considerable degree of doubt between the members of the ANSI IPR Policy Committee.

53 Recently, ANSI withdrew accreditation of two 802.11 standards developed under the updated IPR Policy. In the absence of any official statement from the ANSI, a suggestion that the reason behind ANSI's refusal to accredit the new standards relates to the terms of the 2015 Patent Policy, or negative LoAs, remains speculative. See ANSI Standards Action (March 1, 2019) Vol. 50 (9), available at https://share.ansi.org/Shared%20Documents/Standards%20Action/2019-PDFs/SAV5009.pdf, at 15; L. Nylen 'Electrical Engineer Institute's new Wi-Fi measures won't get American national standards designation' (March 2019) *MLex*, available at https://mlexmarketinsight.com/insights-center/editors-picks/antitrust/cross-jurisdiction/electrical-engineer-institutes-new-wifi-measures-wont-get-american-national-standard-designation. At the same time, the fact that the new Wi-Fi standards did not get accredited by ANSI did not appear to affect the industry, so far.

is involved in, they nevertheless agree that such changes would not work for all SDOs, noting that IPR policies are not static, but evolving.[54] Moreover, they seem to share ANSI's view that each SDO should modify standardization policies in the way it deems appropriate.[55] Those on the other side of the spectrum indicated joining IEEE projects with extra caution,[56] for instance, by reducing their participation and by submitting negative LoAs.[57] The amendment of IEEE-SA's IPR Policy also reflected on other SDOs: allegedly, in 2014 IEEE wanted to join ETSI as a partner in OneM2M, but the cooperation could not take place since IEEE's amended IPR Policy was not compatible with ETSI's.[58] Moreover, the question remains how did the Policy Update affect the output quality of IEEE standardization: so far, the scholarship has not been conclusive on this matter, highlighting that the low number of positive LoAs creates uncertainties for implementers, but also that IEEE standardization activity is thriving.[59]

The main takeaway from this case study is that, even in such a complex institutional setting as the one of IEEE, policies that are designed in a nonconsensus manner are likely to result in division among the membership and, sooner or later, affect an SDO's standardization activity. Similar to the *TruePosition* case, procedural complaints included "inaction" – failure of an SDO to ensure compliance with its procedural rules. At the same time, many stakeholders tend to oppose nontechnical

[54] Interview with an industry expert, February 13, 2018; Industry expert's answers to the questionnaire, received April 27, 2018. They also suggested that the process of IPR Policy Update followed applicable standardization rules.

[55] Interview with an industry expert, February 13, 2018; in this regard, see also G. Ohana, 'Diversity in standards development: a response to Katznelson' (2015) in *Proceedings of IEEE 9th International Conference on Standardization and Innovation in Information Technology (SIIT)*.

[56] Interview with an industry expert, January 23, 2018.

[57] Interview with an industry expert, June 13, 2018.

[58] Interview with an industry expert, January 17, 2018.

[59] See K. Gupta and G. Effraimidis, 'IEEE patent policy revisions: an empirical examination of impact' (2019) 64 *The Antitrust Bulletin* 151–71; R. Katznelson, 'Perilous deviations from FRAND harmony: operational pitfalls of the 2015 IEEE patent policy' (2015) in *Proceedings of IEEE 9th International Conference on Standardization and Innovation in Information Technology (SIIT)*; T. Pohlmann, 'Empirical study on patenting and standardization activity in IEEE' (March 2017) IPlytics GmbH, available at https://asoft20107.accrisoft.com/atfrand/clientuploads/news/IPlytics_2017_Patenting%20and%20standardization%20activities%20at%20IEEE.pdf; K. Mallinson, 'Development of innovative new standards jeopardised by IEEE patent policy' (September 2017), available at www.4ipcouncil.com/application/files/6015/0479/2147/Mallinson_IEEE_LOA_report.pdf.

interference in technical processes by the secretariats and SDOs' staff members. It seems, thus, that the intervention and "disciplining" from SDOs' officials is still desirable once it is suspected that stakeholders do not adhere to SDOs' internal rules.

### "Dictatorship" in Approval and Appeal Processes: Researchers and Civil Society vs Browser Vendors and Content Providers in W3C

Another procedural dispute took place in W3C and, similar to the *TruePosition* case and disagreements on IEEE-SA Policy Update, revolved around openness and consensus of SDOs' processes. The dispute in W3C is, however, unique in the sense that it questioned the very appropriateness of the SDO's rules, namely, whether one person can have a final say in approving a Recommendation for web standards.[60] This, in turn, sparked a broader discussion on whether, and to what extent, technical processes should be influenced by political and societal considerations.

The dispute concerned standardization of Digital Rights Management (DRM) system by means of adopting Encrypted Media Extensions (EME) as a W3C Recommendation. In brief, DRMs administer information access by prohibiting unauthorized use of content[61] in a way allowing companies to influence hardware and software user behavior.[62] Due to this questionable nature, there have been no official standards for DRMs; however, DRMs could be integrated in web browsers via extensions in HTML5 specifications.[63]

Opponents of DRMs suggested that DRM standardization in W3C runs afoul of the SDO's main principle of open web that is available for all users, and may moreover risk legal consequences for W3C members.[64]

60 This has even been called a "crisis" for the W3C, and it was suggested that the future of the SDO is at stake. See Halpin, 'The crisis of standardizing DRM'.

61 D. L. Burk and T. L. Gillespie, 'Autonomy and morality in DRM and anti-circumvention law' (2006) 4 *TripleC* 239–4.

62 Examples are region-encoded video games or protocols that are designed to prevent users from reselling or illegally sharing that movie or preventing from recording live stream. The copyright-restricted publications are prevented from playing on a user's computer unless the user pays to access it first. See M. S. Daubs, 'HTML5, Digital Rights Management (DRM) and the rhetoric of openness' (2017) 3 *Journal of Media Critiques* 77–94.

63 Ibid.

64 For the list of objections, see Halpin, 'The crisis of standardizing DRM'; C. Doctorow, 'Boring, complex and important: a recipe for the web's dire future' (September 21, 2017) *Wired*, available at www.wired.co.uk/article/w3c-eff-open-standards-web-cory-doctorow.

In turn, media companies and browser-owners were convinced that standardizing DRMs via W3C will guarantee security and accessibility while balancing the rights of content creators, providers, and users.[65] Moreover, they found that standardization of DRMs would allow W3C to regain control over a practice that has already been widely adopted and implemented by the industry.[66]

The discussion on whether to standardize DRMs in W3C lasted for nearly a decade; eventually, it was Microsoft, Google, and Netflix, which joined W3C relatively recently, that, in 2012, submitted a joint proposal to W3C HTML Working Group, where they suggested development of EME that enable displaying DRM-protected content on browsers without the use of plug-ins. Soon after, the first DRM working group was created, where the technical work continued as an unofficial task force, upon approval by a chair (affiliated with Microsoft).[67] In 2013, standardization moved to the HTML Media Extensions Working Group led by browser vendors and DRM producers: the group's composition naturally caused frustration among the DRM opposition.[68]

As the work matured, various W3C members and societal actors started to raise their concerns.[69] One of the fiercest opponents, the Electronic Frontier Foundation (EFF), suggested adopting a "covenant,"

[65] The rationale for accessibility was that more individuals could engage in web without the fear of lawsuits, and that the web needs to be extensible to include access to protected content without depending on third parties' plug-in. See 'W3C publishes Encrypted Media Extensions (EME) as a W3C Recommendation' (September 18, 2017), available at www.w3.org/2017/09/pressrelease-eme-recommendation.html.en.

[66] As it was suggested by experts, the functionality was already there, and the EME specification just remove functions into browsers, moving the functionality around. Moreover, W3C represented a more independent forum; allegedly, if the standard was not approved in W3C, it would have been still developed in other SDOs with a less transparent process. Interview with an industry expert, April 4, 2018.

[67] See Halpin, 'The crisis of standardizing DRM'.

[68] The JustNet Coalition has called EME a form of "digital colonialism," and claimed that EME excludes those in the Global South who are struggling for access to information at the expense of a few North American and European corporations. See 'Open letter from Just Net Coalition to Sir Tim Berners-Lee seeking his urgent intervention to stop acceptance of Encrypted Media Extensions as a W3C standard' (April 12, 2017), available at https://itforchange.net/sites/default/files/JNCs-Open-Letter-to-Sir-Tim-Berners-Lee.pdf.

[69] See, for instance, D. O'Brien, 'Lowering your standards: DRM and the future of the W3C' (October 2, 2013), available at www.eff.org/deeplinks/2013/10/lowering-your-standards.

with which W3C members would be able to make a legally binding commitment not to prosecute security researchers investigating EME-related DRM systems, and hence "protect" them from liability under the Digital Millennium Copyright Act (DCMA). However, the vote on the covenant has never taken place; instead, W3C merely observed lack of consensus within the membership regarding the issue.[70] EME was published as a proposed Recommendation in March 2017,[71] and promoted to the W3C Recommendation in July 2017 by the decision of the W3C Director, which was taken following the procedure defined in the W3C Process Document.[72]

The decision of the Director was promptly appealed by the opposing members, who stated that the overruling of formal objections to EME by the Director was improper since the W3C membership had not been consulted on negotiation of a covenant to protect EME's users against anticircumvention regulation.[73] On appeal, the decision to publish the Recommendation was upheld by 58.4 percent of membership (108 members voted in favor, 57 opposed, and 20 abstained) which, despite the positive result for EME proponents, marks a departure from consensus.[74] Upon the adoption of the Recommendation, a number of (now former) W3C members, including EFF, announced their withdrawal

[70] See e-mail of Cory Doctorow (July 21, 2017), available at https://lists.w3.org/Archives/Public/public-html-media/2017Jul/0008.html and of Phillippe le Hégaret (March 16, 2017), available at https://lists.w3.org/Archives/Public/public-html-media/2017Mar/0016.html. It was suggested by the interviewed expert that while the proposal of EFF remained the same, despite suggestions to improve, the compromises of the W3C sufficiently addressed controversies around privacy and security. Interview with an industry expert, April 4, 2018.

[71] E-mail of Phillippe le Hégaret (March 16, 2017), available at https://lists.w3.org/Archives/Public/public-html-media/2017Mar/0016.html.

[72] E-mail of Philippe Le Hégaret (July 6, 2017), available at https://lists.w3.org/Archives/Public/public-html-media/2017Jul/0002.html.

[73] "In the absence of a call for consensus on a covenant, it was improper for the Director to overrule the widespread members' objections and declare EME fit to be published as a W3C Recommendation," https://lists.w3.org/Archives/Public/public-html-media/2017Jul/0005.html. See the e-mail of Cory Doctorow (July 21, 2017) and the e-mail of H. Halpin (July 7, 2017), available at https://lists.w3.org/Archives/Public/public-html-media/2017Jul/0003.html.

[74] 'W3C publishes Encrypted Media Extensions (EME) as a W3C Recommendation' (September 18, 2017). Apparently, it was clear from the very beginning that the Recommendation would not get approved, hence the decision of the Director was necessary. Interview an industry expert, April 4, 2018. On a side note, the procedure of appeal has never before been invoked by the W3C.

from the SDO for the reason of their "collapse of confidence in the W3C process."[75]

The dispute around EME's adoption inspired a broader debate on standardization processes and, more specifically, whether W3C should limit its discussions to merely technical issues, or also include political considerations. Clearly, DRM's supporters found that W3C is not an appropriate forum for social or political debates; the opponents meanwhile maintained that the EME Recommendation does not represent consensus of web community, but rather paves the way for web domination by a selected group of media companies.[76] This poses the question whether current practices for web standardization still hold in the modern society where the technical aspects of web standardization are becoming intertwined with broader political issues.

## Observations and Takeaways

Although fairly different, the three examined disputes revolve around similar procedural issues, namely, openness, consensus, and balance of interests in SDOs' processes. In the case of *TruePosition*, standards development processes were deemed unfair and excluding due to the alleged hijacking by a group of stakeholders; the amendment process for IEEE-SA IPR Policy which, following the taxonomy of this research, is a part of SDOs' governance processes, was claimed to lack openness and consensus and, hence, safeguard the interest of only a part of IEEE membership; the approval of EME Recommendation and the subsequent appeal process were suggested to depart from industry consensus on a topic that is of a great importance for civil society.

In all three cases, the alleged exclusion from a process was underlined by different reasons: inclusion of competing technology into a standard, promoting interests of a particular group within an SDO, and accelerating standards adoption (or, as suggested by some experts, ensuring that the standard is adopted at all). In all three cases, disadvantaged stakeholders asserted that lack of openness and consensus have adverse effects on SDOs' technical performance: adoption of inferior technology, reluctance of innovators to contribute to standards development, and negative impact on user experience. Remarkably, those opposing the three developments noted dissatisfaction with the leadership, either questioning the

[75] That is, Doctorow, 'Boring, complex and important'.
[76] Daubs, 'HTML5, Digital Rights Management (DRM) and the rhetoric of openness'.

neutrality of the chair, or invoking the failure of the members of the governance body (or the Director) to take into account the opposing views. Ultimately, in all three cases, SDOs' members were concerned that the absence of open and consensus-based processes can trigger SDOs' liability and will have consequences for future disputes in which these SDOs may be involved.[77] Hence, maintaining good procedures that follow applicable best practices principles of standardization can shield SDOs form undesired liability claims.

It is true that the complexity of the technical discussions in SDOs' working groups may compel SDOs' decision-makers to limit openness and consensus-building: after all, any multistakeholder discussion requires compromises and sometimes, difficult choices. At the same time, it should not be neglected that by providing technical interoperability or access, some standards serve as public goods and affect a community that is much wider than SDOs' membership or industry representatives: such principles as balance, openness, and consensus, even when presented as "best effort" requirements, are the crucial elements of legitimation of such standards under any legal framework and ensure that standards are adopted and used by the global community.

[77] See the e-mail of Cory Doctorow (July 21, 2017); Interview with an expert from an SDO, January 19, 2018 (IEEE-SA); Interview with an industry expert, January 23, 2018 (ETSI).

# 11

# Tendencies and Best Practices in the Industry

## Experience with SDOs' Governance

### *Differences between SDOs*

The experts have frequently addressed the differences between various institutional models of SDOs, arising, among others, from the specifics of the dimension in which SDOs operate. For instance, in the healthcare sector, which is also heavily regulated, a large share of standards is concerned with safety and essential performance of medical devices, which is not the case with the ICT, where interoperability plays a crucial role.[1] Innovations in healthcare are often not standardized, and companies prefer to use their inventions as a competitive differentiator, which renders the issue of SEPs less essential than it is in the domain of ICT.[2] However, the standardization activities of the two sectors are closely linked: to illustrate, medical body area networks require base specifications for technological interoperability, such as protocols and formats, to enable transfer of medical data via ICT vehicles.[3] Moreover, since the syntax and semantics should be modeled after the reality of clinical concepts, both ICT engineers and clinicians who share their experience with interaction patterns are involved in standardization work.[4] Healthcare standards thus evolve as they adopt the latest ICT technologies.

[1] Interview with an industry expert, January 25, 2018.

[2] The expert clarified that due to fact that the regulatory requirements tend to focus on "what" and not on "how," there are hardly any patents in standardization of medical dvices and healthcare IT. Interview with an industry expert, January 25, 2018.

[3] Such base specifications create reference architecture and are typically used in combination to cover the needs for user-cases: examples include IEEE 802.15.16, but also Digital Imaging Communication (DICOM), used for imaging by X-ray and ultrasound. Interview with an industry expert, January 25, 2018.

[4] The dynamics and interactions between different parts of these systems is crucial and must closely fit the clinical work. Put simply, it is a "mix of engineers who have a good comprehension of the clinical practice, and clinicians who have a good comprehension of technology." Interview with an industry expert, January 25, 2018.

Experts also highlighted the difference between international and European SDOs: since there is no obligation to adopt ISO standards as national standards, NSOs supposedly enjoy more freedom in the international fora.[5] Some experience IEC and CEN/CENELEC as being more prone to seeking industry advice, whereas ISO was claimed to show more tendency to rely on the judgment of NSOs' leaders; this may be explained by ISO's extremely broad, multisectoral scope, which sometimes hinders communication with stakeholders, as well as by historical factors.[6] With regard to the ESOs, it appears that a great number of innovative companies still prefer ETSI's participation model over CEN/CENELEC delegation principle.[7] The suggested advantages of ETSI were its openness, free availability, and global use of its standards, and a well-functioning IPR policy,[8] which was suggested not be the best one but certainly the one "that works."[9] From the perspective of smaller companies, however, ETSI was found to have slower, and more political, processes due to the large number of members who are willing to lead a standard.[10]

On the difference between formal and informal SDOs, it was noted that consortia are not common outside the ICT, which, in turn, also questions the relevance of formal organizations in the ICT standardization.[11] Consortia were suggested as preferring governance rules that are decided by consensus or voting,[12] as opposed to the political and top-down rules of ISO.[13] In this context, the differences in SDOs' decision-making were explained by their activities: in the GSM Association, decisions are primarily driven by mobile operators whose interests the SDO was established to serve.[14]

[5] Interview with an expert from an NSO, January 19, 2018.
[6] Interview with an industry expert, January 25, 2018.
[7] Interview with an industry expert, January 23, 2018.
[8] Interview with an expert from an SDO, April 4, 2018, on file with the author; in relation to IPR policy: Interview with an industry expert, January 16, 2018, on file with the author; Interview with an industry expert, January 17, 2018.
[9] Interview with an industry expert, February 7, 2018.
[10] Interview with an industry expert, February 21, 2018.
[11] Interview with an expert from an NSO, January 19, 2018.
[12] Interview with an industry expert, April 4, 2018. Note that this experience of the expert is striking with the common understanding of consortia as being led by a handful of firms, and formal SDOs – consensus driven.
[13] Interview an industry expert, April 4, 2018.
[14] Interview with an industry expert, January 15, 2018.

Some sectors rely on both formal and informal standards. In the area of forensic cyber standardization, all forensic laboratories support processes that follow the relevant ISO standards, and also rely on the implementation guidelines of the European Agency for Cybersecurity (ENISA).[15] However, the standard language used to ensure that forensic tools export data in a harmonized way, the Cyber-investigation Analysis Standard Expression (CASE), is developed by the forensic community and is largely led by companies and practitioners, who take their decisions by voting.[16]

By and large, it was acknowledged that a "one size fits all" approach for SDOs' governance models and procedures does not exist, even for organizations operating in the same industry subset. Every SDO follows a unique set of rules, tailored for its specific purposes and membership, and none of the existing governance models should be considered "better" or "worse."[17] For example, not all SDOs rely on the widely accepted definition of an open standard,[18] and business models for IPR licensing often differ per company.[19] Stakeholders' experience with SDOs largely depends on technology and market context, but also on the business goals of corporate stakeholders and even on the conduct of individuals participating in standardization work.[20] Standardization of telecommunications, for instance, generally requires a broad approach and a larger stakeholder pool, but some specifications, such as the USB, were claimed to be better developed in narrower groups.[21] Likewise, while FRAND licensing often forms the crux of telecoms standardization, a similar IPR model in upper-layer standardization was believed to disturb the technical work of committees, since it prevented stakeholders from focusing on performance benefits.[22]

[15] Interview with experts from cyber police authority, January 11, 2018, on file with the author. While the guidelines are voluntary, they work similar to the HESs.

[16] Interview with experts from cyber police authority, January 11, 2018.

[17] Industry expert's answers to the questionnaire, received April 27, 2018.

[18] Interview with an industry expert, June 13, 2018.

[19] Interview with an expert from an NSO, January 19, 2018.

[20] Interview with an industry expert, January 25, 2018.

[21] Industry expert's answers to the questionnaire, received April 27, 2018.

[22] Interview with an industry expert, February 19, 2018. Interview an industry expert, April 4, 2018.

### *Switching between Existing Standardization Platforms and Creating New Ones*

Due to the abundance of SDOs, their institutional variety, and voluntary membership, a scenario where participants that are not satisfied with the governance or technical activity in one SDO switch to another forum seems plausible. Such practice, however, was not observed in the recent study on SDOs' governance; rather, it was suggested that stakeholders are more likely to "step out of the room" and carry out particular standardization activities elsewhere, without terminating their SDO membership.[23] Often, such "externally" developed standards will be reintroduced in the SDO, for instance, via a fast-track process, to further resume standardization activities.

For example, in mid-2000, W3C members decided to abandon the development of HTML mark up specifications and focus on its XML-based equivalent with stricter mark up syntax rules, the XHTML, instead.[24] The work on HTML5 specifications continued in the Web Hypertext Application Technology Working Group (WHATWG), a consortia created by Apple, Mozilla, and Opera in 2004.[25] Unlike the case with W3C, WHATWG processes were not based on consensus;[26] moreover, where W3C required companies to provide royalty-free licenses for patent claims covering its specifications, WHATWG offered less strict patent protection.

Once it became clear that the XHTML standard could not replace HTML due to technical reasons,[27] W3C decided to resume the work on

[23] JRC Report, p. 68.

[24] See 'HTML5: a vocabulary and associated APIs for HTML and XHTML' (2014) W3C Recommendation of October 28, 2014, available at www.w3.org/TR/2014/REC-html5-20141028/introduction.html#history-0.

[25] These companies did not share the position of W3C membership; a proposal by Mozilla and Opera at a W3C workshop in 2004 where the companies suggested to continue the work on HTML did not gain sufficient votes. R. Tabarés-Gutiérrez, 'Taking a glance at the history of HTML5', in K. Jacobs and K. Blind (eds.), *EURAS Proceedings 2017. Digitalization: Challenge and Opportunity for Standardisation* (Aachen: Verlaghaus Mainz GmbH, 2017), pp. T351–66.

[26] Allegedly, the formation of WHATWG was also a reaction on the "slow progress without concrete results" of W3C, and not only on its decision to switch to XML.

[27] XHTML only allowed the employment of entirely new technologies and lacked backwards compatibility with older versions of HTML, while the HTML5 specifications supported both code syntaxes and allowed multimedia elements. Most importantly, the standard did not work well on Explorer, which was a major browser at that time, and was causing inconvenience for web developers. See also S. E. Madnick, 'The misguided silver

HTML:[28] WHATWG specifications were put through the W3C process, and HTML5 was adopted by W3C in 2009.[29] Yet, since browser vendors were concerned that the W3C process was too slow for HTML5, two new procedures were adopted to accelerate standardization processes: firstly, a system for creating W3C Community Groups for standardization activities became fully automized; secondly, HTML Extensions could not be defined without rechartering the Working Groups.[30]

Indeed, experts mentioned the option to "vote with the feet" when disagreeing with SDOs' processes, as well as the possibility that participants may be driven away by market forces.[31] In this context, procedural principles may come into play due to the existence of competing alternative platforms where stakeholders' positions, otherwise ignored, will be heard.[32] An example described a situation when many IEEE members were skeptical about the potential for adoption of the Apple-driven FireWire IEEE 1394 because of royalty demands of one of the contributors; consequently, an alternative set of specifications based on reciprocal royalty-free licensing, driven by Intel and others, was developed as a USB standard in a much narrower group, and subsequently widely adopted by the industry.[33] According to experts' opinion, competition in 3GPP currently takes place between proposals made by companies participating in the working groups of SDOs, rather than between parallel standards

bullet: what XML will and will NOT do to help information integration' (2001) Sloan Working Paper 4185-01, available at http://ebusiness.mit.edu/research/papers.html.

28 Tabarés-Gutiérrez, 'Taking a glance'.

29 Halpin, 'The crisis of standardizing DRM', p. 5.

30 Ibid., p. 14. However, in 2011, the groups separated once again, this time because the differences in the objectives pursued: while the WHATWG viewed HTML5 as a "Living Standard" subject to constant amendment, the W3C favored a more stable design and focused on standardization of semantic web technologies, which in turn was deemed irrelevant by browser vendors.

31 Interview with an industry expert, January 23, 2018; Interview with an industry expert, January 25, 2018; Interview with an industry expert, February 13, 2018; Industry expert's answers to the questionnaire, received April 27, 2018.

32 Interview with an industry expert, February 13, 2018.

33 Industry expert's answers to the questionnaire, received April 27, 2018. The expert noted that next to the royalty-free policy, other factors such as capability of the technology and its longevity also came into play; moreover, there were other standards such as HTTP that would never have gained such rapid and widespread adoption if engineers were faced with questionable costs.

developed by different SDOs,[34] and standards' evolution is moved to the new releases of technical specifications,[35] and not to the rival initiatives.

Some experts suggested that parallel standardization activity in other organizations is complementary rather than alternative.[36] For example, a group of 3GPP members established MulteFire Alliance to speed up standardization of LTE specifications for an unlicensed spectrum, since the work within 3GPP was affected by the hesitation of the operators who often lacked interest in specifying LTE.[37] In a longer run, however, MulteFire aims to bring standardization work back to 3GPP,[38] which indicates that this strategy should be considered as "stepping out of the room" rather than "voting with the feet."

It appears that standards drivers are more likely to create a new SDO for a particular standardization activity, rather than bringing a standardization project to another institution. As such, new organizations are created when envisaged technical work does not fit within any of the existent SDOs, or as a reaction to their misperformance.[39] Establishment of a new SDO requires a lot of effort to be put in designing their processes and ensuring that the organization has clear terms of reference, follows the broader WTO principles, and does not create antitrust problems;[40] moreover, an organization's operational rules should be designed in a way that, from the outset, they do not allow the work of this organization to be hijacked by a particular interest group.[41] Although the rules of such new organizations are initially written by a few founding

[34] Interview with an industry expert, February 1, 2018.

[35] Ibid.

[36] Interview with an industry expert, January 16, 2018.

[37] Interview with an industry expert, January 15, 2018; Interview with an industry expert, February 1, 2018; Interview with an industry expert, February 7, 2018. The experts explained that in such a consensus-based organization like 3GPP, unlicensed spectrum is not the primary focus of the mobile operators, because they pay for the spectrum. Therefore, using unlicensed spectrum with that technology is not supported by all operators. However, the interest may increase once unlicensed LTE technology is ready and deployed.

[38] Interview with an industry expert, January 15, 2018.

[39] Interview with an industry expert, April 18, 2018. For instance, ISO provided a certain period of time for declaring essential patents, which resulted in a situation with three patent pools for a standard; as a response to this licensing situation, the industry created the Alliance for Open Media. Interview with an industry expert, April 4, 2018.

[40] Interview with an industry expert, January 15, 2018.

[41] Industry expert's answers to the questionnaire, received February 15, 2018. Interview with an industry expert, April 18, 2018.

companies,[42] and members joining after the establishment have to accept the operational framework defined by founders, the bylaws and charters always allow for changing the rules when required by the SDOs membership.[43] Examples of such recently erected consortia are Zhaga Consortium and DiiA/DALI Alliance:[44] established only by a few companies, both consortia grew into organizations of about 150 members.[45]

It was also suggested that creation of new SDOs may have negative consequences, especially when a new piece of work can be accommodated in an existent organization.[46] Proliferation of SDOs requires companies to spread their scarce resources and expertise over different entities, and increase their investment uncertainties, which may even create confusion in the market.[47] When the GSM Association initiated work on an audio codec for smartphones, some companies preferred the project to be carried out in 3GPP, where these types of activities traditionally took place: they found that the related specifications should have followed one approval path for staying consistent and being correctly implemented into products, rather than being balkanized over different technical bodies.[48] It is perhaps also for this reason (although it was not mentioned as such by the interviewee) that recent years have witnessed a number of mergers between different SDOs:[49] for instance, some smaller consortia ended up being integrated in the Open Mobile Alliance, which was initially established by only a few entities.[50]

### *Barriers for Participation*

Participation in SDOs generally brings enormous benefits to the industry and public sector due to SDOs' effectiveness, global outreach, and industry reputation;[51] however, some factors may affect stakeholders' decision to join SDOs' membership. In general, IPR policies were named as one of

[42] Interview with an industry expert, January 15, 2018.
[43] Interview with an industry expert, April 18, 2018.
[44] Those were established by members of large consortia, such as Bluetooth SIG. Interview with an industry expert, April 18, 2018.
[45] Ibid.
[46] Interview with an industry expert, January 25, 2018.
[47] Ibid.
[48] Interview with an industry expert, February 19, 2018.
[49] Interview with an industry expert, April 18, 2018.
[50] Interview with an industry expert, February 19, 2018.
[51] Interview with an industry expert, January 23, 2018.

the main factors for preventing effective participation in standards development. Companies that follow open-source or royalty-free business model (typically new players on the market), may be discouraged by ETSI's FRAND policy;[52] to the contrary, companies with a FRAND business model are discouraged from participation in SDOs where IPR policies have adverse effects on their business.[53] Smaller companies were mostly concerned with the amount of royalties they have to pay, and whether IPR policies guarantee fairness and equity.[54]

Other participation barriers commonly mentioned were the availability of a budget, which largely depends on product relevance, company's operational area, and SDOs' participation models; and time.[55] Financing participation in standardization meetings is especially challenging for smaller stakeholders or individuals, which mostly engage in standards development on a voluntary basis.[56] For NSOs, involvement in standardization processes depends on the availability and willingness of their members.[57] But scientific background and human factor also play an important role, especially since, to a certain extent, standardization is akin to politics and requires a trust relationship between participants: to illustrate, lobbying occurs even where a standard's proposal is sufficiently mature.[58] Large Western companies furthermore face challenges to

[52] Although established companies sometimes also operate following the open-source model, they would typically already have experience with the IPR Policy applicable to their standardization activities. Interview with an expert from an SDO, April 4, 2018.

[53] Interview with an industry expert, January 25, 2018; Interview with an industry expert, February 19, 2018; Interview with an industry expert, April 18, 2018. One expert recalled having to convince their company director to participate in an SDO that, at first glance, had an adverse IPR policy. Interview with an industry expert, April 18, 2018.

[54] Interview with an industry expert, February 21, 2018.

[55] Interview with an expert from an NSO, January 19, 2018; Interview with an industry expert, February 19, 2018; Interview with an industry expert, February 21, 2018. Sometimes, the participation model can be mitigated: in forensic cyber standardization, experts may participate without official affiliation, bringing, for instance, unique law enforcement expertise. Interview with experts from cyber police authority, January 11, 2018.

[56] Interview with an environmental management and radiation expert, January 9, 2018. An example is the difference between a large certification company who pays fees and hotels for their representatives, and a private certification consultant who is self-financed.

[57] Interview with an expert from an NSO, January 19, 2018. There may be also difference between NSOs: DIN, for instance, has a business culture to participate in long-term standardization projects, while NEN is more concerned with short-term business profits rather than long-term business profits.

[58] Interview with an industry expert, February 21, 2018.

participate in China's standards development processes due to limited voting rights.[59]

Some barriers for participation are sector-specific: for the telecommunications industry, one of the largest challenges is the rise of ecosystems outside the formal standards (for instance, Android), which appears a well-established practice for software developers.[60] Moreover, different SDOs and industry alliances in wireless telecom sectors maintain their own confidentiality rules, which preclude outsiders from obtaining information on their working programs and contents of standards, crucial for effective cooperation.[61] For internet standardization, effective participation is impossible without command of English, the language of the code, and technical ability to read documents,[62] as well as without remote participation facilities.[63] IETF culture and the way of communication was also noted as one of the challenges newcomers have to overcome:[64] for instance, unlike modern practice, e-mails within IETF are only sent when they contain substantial information.[65]

Also, SDOs' processes may affect stakeholders' decision to participate. To foresee whether their efforts will result in benefits, stakeholders should be able to participate on an understandable basis, which is conditional upon the existence of clear rules.[66] Typically, companies will screen the procedures of a newly formed SDO together with analyzing the probability of market success of its standards,[67] and the value of the

[59] Interview with an industry expert, January 16, 2018; Industry expert's answers to the questionnaire, received April 27, 2018.

[60] Interview with an industry expert, February 19, 2018.

[61] This despite the fact that some SDOs have signed liaisons and partnership agreements, interview with an industry expert, April 18, 2018.

[62] Interview with experts from cyber police authority, January 11, 2018; Interview with an expert from an SDO, January 12, 2018; Interview with an industry expert (former SDO governance bodies member), January 16, 2018.

[63] Interview with an industry expert (former SDO governance bodies member), January 16, 2018.

[64] Interview with an expert from an SDO, January 12, 2018. IETF aimed to address these challenges in South America by teaching how to interact at IETF meetings in their native language, which resulted in increased participation of the South American experts in IETF.

[65] Interview with an expert from an SDO, January 12, 2018.

[66] Interview with an industry expert, January 15, 2018; Interview with an industry expert, February 7, 2018.

[67] Industry expert's answers to the questionnaire, received February 15, 2018.

standard for their business.[68] Each company follows its own internal process for reviewing SDOs' rules,[69] and IPR policies are subject to the most rigid analysis from potential members.[70] In addition, due account is taken of SDOs' antitrust policies, and legal risks that companies may be exposed to by virtue of their involvement in technical discussions.[71] When operational framework of an SDO deviates substantially from the overarching procedural principles, or opens avenues for antitrust abuse, companies would contact the SDO to seek further explanations.[72]

Companies' level of participation and acquiring of leadership positions will depend on how actively an SDO is involved in the sector of their interest.[73] Some large companies, for instance, prefer to participate in SDOs with established infrastructure and a well-functioning secretariat.[74] However, business considerations always prevail: a company will always join an SDO where there is a commercial need to do so.[75] Participating in an SDO's activities is thus a business decision that involves cost-benefit considerations.[76]

Procedural rules other than IPR and antitrust policies were found of less importance when considering participation in an SDO: once a company has established that an SDO develops standards that are relevant and has an acceptable IPR policy, and if there is sufficient funding for that company's involvement in standardization processes, procedural consideration would generally not affect its decision to join the forum.[77]

[68] Although, arguably, the value of a standard is not per se a reason to participate, since the industry will anyways adopt a successful standard. Interview with an industry expert, January 25, 2018.

[69] Interview with an industry expert, January 15, 2018; Interview with an industry expert, January 25, 2018.

[70] Interview with an industry expert, February 19, 2018.

[71] Interview with an industry expert, January 15, 2018; Interview with an industry expert, January 25, 2018.

[72] Interview with an industry expert, January 15, 2018; Interview with an industry expert, June 13, 2018. Some companies follow a "portfolio approach" to decide in which processes they should invest. Interview with an industry expert, January 25, 2018.

[73] Interview with an industry expert, January 25, 2018; Interview with an industry expert, February 19, 2018.

[74] Interview with an industry expert, January 23, 2018.

[75] Interview with an industry expert, February 13, 2018.

[76] Interview with an industry expert, January 25, 2018. Interview with an industry expert, February 19, 2018. However, experts may be willing to get involved in standards development processes of a particular SDO not only with a purpose to influence a standard, but to simply be informed about the standard's content or to network with other experts. Interview with an expert from an NSO, January 19, 2018.

[77] Interview with an industry expert, February 19, 2018.

In that sense, the decision whether to join an SDO is often straightforward and clear.[78] Interviewees shared that most of the times companies find SDOs' rules acceptable[79] and are generally satisfied with procedural guarantees of SDOs where they currently participate, except for specific cases: some stakeholders have raised concerns regarding the updated IEEE policy;[80] others, on the contrary, criticized ETSI's FRAND-based policy for providing little clarity and being too inflexible to adjust to the current needs of the industry.[81]

### *Policy-Making vs Standards Development Processes*

Some experts suggested that governance rules are not subjected to much controversy among SDO membership, since companies will only join an SDO if they are comfortable with the way it is governed.[82] The differences between the two types of processes were accepted since the effect of SDOs' policies is immediate and goes further than the effect of standards, which is mainly indirect and has a reputational risk, but typically would not lead to antitrust accusations or liability claims.[83] And while some experts noted that the "disconnect" between governance and standards development procedures, where it exists, is not justified,[84] others found that differences in voting procedures and quorum are acceptable since they depend on the organization and the gravity of decision that needs to be taken.[85]

SDOs' structure and rules are typically driven by founding companies; other players would join if they consider these rules sufficient, fair, and attractive for their business activities.[86] Nevertheless, the rules can be bent and redeveloped if the SDO's functioning under the existing framework affects its marketability: experts also speak of the operational framework that is being "corrected on its own."[87] Some experts have

[78] Interview an industry expert, April 4, 2018.
[79] Interview with an industry expert, January 15, 2018.
[80] Interview with an industry expert, January 17, 2018.
[81] Interview with an industry expert, February 13, 2018; Interview with an industry expert, February 21, 2018.
[82] Interview with an industry expert, February 13, 2018.
[83] Interview with an industry expert, January 25, 2018.
[84] Interview with an industry expert, January 16, 2018; Interview with an industry expert, January 17, 2018.
[85] Interview with an industry expert, January 23, 2018.
[86] Industry expert's answers to the questionnaire, received April 27, 2018.
[87] Ibid.

even suggested that while firms that have joined only recently have a "pragmatic" approach and may sometimes ignore the established procedural framework, companies that are well settled in an SDO's culture act as watchdogs and ensure that the rules are properly followed.[88] Large members would then negotiate new governance rules, since they possess considerable experience and knowledge in matters related to SDO governance.[89] The other reason why established, large companies are usually involved in drafting SDOs' operational rules is that they have substantial resources and human capacity to engage in SDOs' meetings.[90] For smaller user-stakeholders, governance is typically not an "active discussion."[91] For NSOs, participation in governance processes is not a main task, rather a responsibility to represent interests of their members that are affected by modifications of operational rules, and in particular amendments of IPR policies.[92]

Those not satisfied with the course of discussion on governance processes would also voice their concerns,[93] in particular when a company suspects that the discussion is incompatible with its antitrust policy and may violate competition law.[94] Strategies to intervene include lobbying, e-mail exchange, speaking up at meetings, and making sure that disagreements are noted.[95] Examples of such "protests" shared by the experts included a technical discussion within an SDO that was started by a working group member without having consulted the members of the technical committee above, while the SDO rules prescribed the opposite.[96]

While in reality, changes to operational frameworks are accepted retroactively,[97] they should nevertheless be sufficiently accounted for[98]

88 Interview with an industry expert, February 19, 2018.
89 Ibid.
90 Interview with an industry expert, January 25, 2018.
91 Interview with an industry expert, February 21, 2018.
92 Interview with an expert from an NSO, January 19, 2018.
93 That is, Industry expert's answers to the questionnaire, received April 27, 2018; Interview with an industry expert, June 13, 2018.
94 Interview with an industry expert, January 25, 2018; Interview with an industry expert, January 15, 2018.
95 That is, Industry expert's answers to the questionnaire, received April 27, 2018; Interview with an industry expert, June 13, 2018.
96 Interview with an expert from an NSO, January 19, 2018.
97 Interview with an industry expert, February 7, 2018.
98 Ibid.; Interview with an industry expert, June 13, 2018.

due to the democratic character of SDOs.[99] In this regard, the fundamental standardization principles of openness, transparency, and ability to provide comments are believed to be necessary for both governance and standards development processes.[100] To illustrate, unbalanced IPR policy and unfair treatment during policy drafting are believed to have a discouraging effect on technology contributors, and thus negatively affect standardization results; hence, unlike decision-making on embedded technologies, which sometimes may need to happen rapidly, modifications of IPR policies should be performed with caution, and respect procedural guarantees.[101]

Experts have also shared their experiences with modifications of some SDOs' IPR policies. The controversial IPR Policy of TM Forum, a recently established association for software development, has been eventually modified after a strong protest from the industry.[102] Modifications of the IPR Policy of ZigBee Alliance was a consensus-driven, but also time-consuming, process, which did not escalate to a dispute despite the unhappiness of some companies with the new rules.[103] The amendment of the IETF IPR Policy took about six years' time: a public draft was made available in the RFC and received many comments, but at the last stage of the processes there were only a few comments from the community, and consensus was deemed to be achieved rather easily.[104]

Experts generally noted that there is no difference between the policy-making and standards development processes in ETSI, since the major decisions affecting ETSI's operational framework are taken at the level of the whole membership in the General Assembly, and the Board decided on rather limited and technical issues.[105] Also in IETF, policy-making and standards development processes were confirmed to follow the same model,[106] with some minor differences: for instance, due to concerns of

99 SDOs are suggested to be democratic since they are member-based and governed by contracts; Interview with an industry expert, February 7, 2018.

100 Interview with an industry expert, February 13, 2018.

101 Interview with an industry expert, January 16, 2018.

102 Interview with an industry expert, June 13, 2018.

103 Interview with an industry expert, April 18, 2018.

104 Interview with a legal counsel of an SDO, January 18, 2018.

105 Interview with an industry expert, February 7, 2018; Interview with an expert from an SDO, April 4, 2018.

106 Interview with an expert from an SDO, January 12, 2018; Interview with an industry expert,* January 16, 2018; Interview with a legal counsel of an SDO, January 18, 2018.

dominance, there is a limit to the number of experts affiliated with one company that could be members of IETF's governance bodies.[107] IEEE, while having good technical processes that provide many opportunities for balloting, reviews, and a comment-resolution program, was believed to depart from the WTO criteria in its policy-making.[108] To the contrary, ETSI was praised for its governance processes offering sufficient protection for minority, but criticized for not being flexible enough to accommodate the increasing needs of the industry.[109]

A remarkable differences between policy-making and standards development processes is that the former are mostly attended by lawyers/ business professionals and the latter by engineers,[110] since each of the two processes requires different skills and mindsets.[111] In particular, lawyers are actively involved in drafting operational rules, including IPR policies, of newly established organizations.[112] Imposing governance and accountability questions would unnecessarily burden technical experts and prevent them from being involved in technical decision-making.[113] The number of lawyers and business professionals assigned by a company to participate in SDOs' processes is also smaller than the number of engineers, since technical discussions are more common.[114] That said, sometimes different SDOs may attract different types of participants to their meetings: in (the more political) Internet Corporation for Assigned Names and Numbers (ICANN), for instance, the number of lawyers is larger than in IETF.[115]

[107] Exceptions are made if best qualified candidates appear to be affiliated with the same company. Interview with an expert from an SDO, January 12, 2018.

[108] Interview with an industry expert, January 16, 2018. Apparently, requirements to follow WTO criteria were replaced with the document that states that WTO criteria apply only to standards development. Interview with an expert from an SDO, January 19, 2018.

[109] Interview with an industry expert, February 13, 2018.

[110] Interview with an industry expert,* January 16, 2018; Interview with an industry expert, January 25, 2018; Interview with an industry expert, February 7, 2018; Interview with an industry expert, April 4, 2018. In other words, standards are written "by engineers and for engineers" and SDOs' agreements "by lawyers for lawyers." In a way, this confirms the "technological idealism" of David and Shurmer, 'Formal standard-setting.'

[111] Industry expert's answers to the questionnaire, received April 27, 2018.

[112] Interview with an industry expert, January 25, 2018.

[113] Interview with an expert from an SDO, January 12, 2018.

[114] Industry expert's answers to the questionnaire, received April 27, 2018.

[115] Interview with experts from cyber police authority, January 11, 2018.

### *Procedural Guarantees in SDOs*

Experts generally prefer SDOs that adhere to the procedural principles of the EU Regulation 1025/2012 and "the principles of the WTO."[116] SDOs that comply the six criteria of the TBT Committee Decision were suggested to allow for inclusive participation, timely access to documents, impartiality, and balance the interests, especially the interests of technologies' access and the return on investment, but also to ensure that the selection of technology is objective and based on technical merits (rather than stakeholders' strategic interactions).[117] Concerns regarding the balance in SDOs procedures were suggested to outweigh other procedural principles.[118]

Governance of formal SDOs, such as ISO/IEC and CEN/CENELEC, were found sufficiently transparent, well-established, and hence providing advanced procedural guarantees to the stakeholders; at the same time, it was observed that formal SDOs could not guarantee that the interests of all stakeholders were taken on board via their fast-track processes.[119] Yet, many specifications that have been swiftly drafted in consortia with very limited membership were subject to major revisions once submitted to the formal SDOs.[120] At the same time, 3GPP and IETF were praised for ensuring increased transparency and meaningful participation by sharing drafts of technical documents for participants' review,[121] while IEEE was mentioned by some as lacking transparency and fair appeal systems,[122] and Chinese SDOs as having insufficient procedural guarantees for American and European stakeholders.[123]

By and large, consensus appeared a preferable decision-making model among most of the experts. Some found that consensus encourages stakeholders to make their best effort to resolve objections, while voting opens avenues for strategic behavior[124] and may lead to a situation where controversial questions are decided too soon, without proper

116 Interview with an industry expert, January 15, 2018; Interview with an industry expert, January 16, 2018.

117 Interview with an industry expert, January 16, 2018.

118 Interview with an industry expert, February 7, 2018. Also confirmed in JRC report.

119 Interview with an expert from an NSO, January 19, 2018.

120 Interview with an industry expert, February 19, 2018.

121 Ibid.

122 Interview with an industry expert, January 17, 2018.

123 Interview with an industry expert, January 16, 2018.

124 Interview with an industry expert, April 4, 2018; Interview with an industry expert, February 1, 2018; Interview with an industry expert, April 18, 2018.

deliberations and considerations of all positions.[125] Consensus was suggested to work particularly well in smaller groups, whose composition is transparent and whose decision-making is based on mutual faith, rather than political considerations.[126] For larger standardization groups, and especially SDOs that function based on the national delegation principle, consensus-building is a challenging and lengthy process.[127] For IETF, consensus was mentioned as a necessary prong for openness, and could even be critical in matters such as organization of meetings and events.[128] Even those consortia where leadership has exclusive decision-making rights, are in practice driven by industry consensus: in Bluetooth SIG, the Board of Directors is only concerned with outlining standardization strategies and ensuring that the necessary procedural requirements are fulfilled, while the actual technical definition of standards is left to the SIG's members in the working groups.[129]

More specifically, IETF ensures procedural rights through easy participation in its working groups due to the mailing list and the absence of membership fees, but also due to the fact that its IPR policy does not require specific commitments.[130] Its formal rules are minimized to what is "exactly enough" to achieve a rough consensus and include the judgments of the best technical experts in the field.[131] IETF rules were considered sufficiently flexible to accommodate new developments and believed to guarantee better outcomes:[132] this also related to IPR policies, where some part of the industry may be moving towards royalty-free or open-source licensing approach, requiring the revision of the existent rules.[133]At the same time, informal rules and IETF's extreme openness may sometimes unduly prolong standards development processes.[134]

[125] Interview with an expert from an SDO, January 12, 2018; Interview an industry expert, April 4, 2018.

[126] Interview with an expert from cyber police authority, January 11, 2018.

[127] Interview with an expert from an NSO, January 19, 2018.

[128] For example, when some participants were concerned with a meeting taking place in Singapore for the reason that it did not recognize same-sex marriages, a separate diversity committee was formed. Interview with a legal counsel of an SDO, January 18, 2018.

[129] Interview with an industry expert, April 18, 2018.

[130] Interview with an industry expert,* January 16, 2018.

[131] Interview with an expert from an SDO, January 12, 2018.

[132] In SDOs' involved in internet standardization, this may sometimes include changes to the SDOs' terminology, and not as much to its operational rules: for instance, the term "child pornography" was replaced with "child sexual exploitation." Interview with experts from cyber police authority, January 11, 2018.

[133] Interview with an industry expert, February 13, 2018.

[134] Interview with an expert from an SDO, January 12, 2018.

Moreover, due to its uniqueness, IETF, similar to ICANN, is believed to be an irreplaceable institution for internet governance.[135]

Procedural guarantees in IETF are furthermore secured by the absence of a veto, which precludes standards' capture: this, according to the experts, surpasses IETF's informal processes that sets a low threshold for publishing a technical contribution.[136] Nevertheless, some companies may still attempt to dominate IETF processes, for instance, by sending a large amount of their technical experts to the meetings.[137] Moreover, companies' size, financial background, and degree of involvement in technical processes still appear to matter for their decision-making power within IETF: for instance, to be eligible for NomCom, an expert should have a record of attending IETF working groups' meetings in person, which practically excludes those experts who participate remotely; hence, since NomCom appoints members of some IETF's governing bodies, those who make the selection are typically affiliated with larger companies.[138] To ensure that all interests are taken on board, IETF has recently implemented a requirement for remote participants to formally register for online meetings.[139]

Some experts raised concern regarding ETSI's membership structure based on the units of contribution or companies' turnovers. The "buying vote" practice (weighted voting based on subsidiaries in Europe) may hurt SMEs and non-European companies[140] and allow large companies with high revenues to dominate the voting process.[141] ETSI also allows to "increase" one's voting power by joining through multiple entities: a company with vested interests in the standardization of SIM card formats has joined ETSI Working Group with multiple entities and its proposal gained many votes, although the solution it offered had no industry consensus;[142] likewise, companies employed multiple board members upon their election to the ETSI Board in 2009.[143]

[135] Interview with experts from cyber police authority, January 11, 2018.

[136] Interview with an expert from an SDO, January 12, 2018.

[137] Ibid.

[138] Interview with an industry expert,* January 16, 2018.

[139] Ibid.

[140] Industry expert's answers to the questionnaire, received April 27, 2018.

[141] Interview with an industry expert, February 19, 2018.

[142] Interview with an industry expert, January 17, 2018. Interview with an industry expert, February 19, 2018.

[143] Interview with an expert from an SDO, January 12, 2018.

The design of SDOs processes may indirectly affect the quality of their standards, especially given the asymmetry of information, knowledge, and expertise among the members of larger SDOs: some experts even highlighted those as the reasons why industry leadership may sometimes prefer to develop standards in consortia than in formal organizations.[144] At the same time, the quality of technical work appeared to be monitored by participants of SDOs' working groups: to illustrate, although the informal mechanisms of IETF allows virtually anyone to take part in technical discussions, absurd contributions are generally ignored.[145]

Most of the experts seem to agree that the processes of SDOs where they participate are well drafted with regards to procedural guarantees of stakeholders: as worded by one expert, the challenges are "not in the procedures, but in the way they are applied."[146] Another expert observed that faith and mutual trust among SDOs members is more important than procedural guarantees.[147]

### *IPR Policies*

SDOs' disclosure and licensing rules were addressed by the experts with regard to almost every interview question, including those on procedural guarantees and forum-shifting, and related to both the content of these rules as well as the processes of their drafting. It is evident that different IPR regimes attract different industries: RAND/FRAND are commonly preferred by patent-holders, but may be unappealing for implementors; in turn, royalty-free policies in certain settings may not attract the right technology.[148] Likewise, while some experts found FRAND to be an open commitment and a promise,[149] others found that it should start being adopted to industry changes.[150] Moreover, FRAND and royalty-free-based policies may be differently implemented across the SDOs: in some organizations, royalty-free commitments already arise once a company

[144] Interview with an industry expert, January 25, 2018.
[145] Interview with an expert from an SDO, January 12, 2018.
[146] Interview an industry expert, April 4, 2018.
[147] Interview with experts from cyber police authority, January 11, 2018.
[148] Industry expert's answers to the questionnaire, received April 27, 2018.
[149] Interview with an industry expert, January 23, 2018.
[150] Interview with an industry expert, February 13, 2018; Interview with an industry expert, April 9, 2018; Industry expert's answers to the questionnaire, received April 27, 2018.

joins the forum (i.e., W3C),[151] while in others only when a participant has actually contributed with its technology.[152]

Many experts have also linked IPR policies with procedural guarantees and stated the importance of clear and balanced procedures for their amendments; some have also suggested that FRAND-based organizations are more transparent.[153] According to some experts, IPR policies that are fair should address such issues as the threat of unreasonable injunctions and calculate patent value based on ex ante value of essential technology (thus, before the IPRs were incorporated into a standard).[154] Others expressed the view that due to the industry structure, IPR rules should not be dictated by the majority.[155]

Furthermore, IPR policy may change as the SDO's landscape and membership evolves: from the outset, ETSI's membership did not have much variety and consisted predominantly of operators and manufacturers, later joined by infrastructure providers and handset makers; hence, the policy was agreed upon a much smaller group of participants than ETSI currently accommodates, was driven by different incentives, and did not take into account the increased complexity and surge of patents in the telecoms industry.[156] However, the issue of open-source technologies appears unresolved under the framework of almost all formal SDOs.[157]

Companies may also have different practices with regard to IPRs: some base their business models on patent monetarizing, while others use patent portfolio defensively; moreover, some stakeholders are both patent-holders and implementors.[158] In general, however, all experts appeared to agree that the principles of fairness and transparency are

151 Interview with an industry expert, April 4, 2018.

152 Interview with an industry expert, February 19, 2018. This does not imply that royalty-free groups are in any aspect less successful. Interview with an industry expert, February 13, 2018.

153 Interview with an industry expert, January 17, 2018.

154 Industry expert's answers to the questionnaire, received April 27, 2018.

155 Interview with an industry expert, January 16, 2018; Interview with an industry expert, June 13, 2018.

156 For instance, "license to everyone" was not an issue at that point in time, as it was clear that the license was meant for end-equipment. Interview with an industry expert, April 9, 2018.

157 Interview with an industry expert, January 17, 2018; Interview with an industry expert, January 23, 2018. Yet, it was also noted that incorporation of open source did not get along with WTO principles. Interview with an industry expert, January 16, 2018.

158 Interview with an industry expert, February 13, 2018.

crucial for IPR policies, but also indicated other important elements, such as reciprocity, maintaining the FRAND commitment after sale of the asset/or transfer (in case an SDO is FRAND-based),[159] and a reasonable compensation.[160]

### *Dispute Resolution*

Disputes are mostly resolved in working groups at the committee level, or by internal complaints, and chairs have an important role in ensuring that all disputes are either prevented or settled. Most experts appeared satisfied with these processes. Smaller players that often do not have large investment in R&D, prefer to avert disputes,[161] while larger stakeholders often intervene once they disagree with procedural or technical decisions of a working group.[162] In internet standardization, stakeholders seem to favor "soft enforcement" over strict dispute resolution processes.[163] Dispute resolution mostly include "offline" discussions among stakeholders and seeking compromises: allegedly, it is easier to persuade working group participants to follow a certain solution once it is already supported by the majority.[164]

SDOs generally are not involved in enforcement actions, but their operational frameworks may be used in disputes between their members.[165] Disputes outside SDOs (i.e., disagreements with nonconformity decisions of auditors) are resolved between the parties concerned, without SDOs' involvement.[166] One expert referred to the DVB Forum's policy of forced arbitration, which, however, has never been trigged by its members; this does not mean, in another expert's view, that this policy has been a success, since the absence of disputes may leave some issues unresolved.[167]

Internationally recognized SDOs were commended for having procedures that allow a national body to appeal a decision even in the latest phase of standards development; however, most appeals in CEN/CENELEC and ISO/IEC relate to procedural issues, rather than the

[159] Ibid.; Industry expert's answers to the questionnaire, received April 27, 2018.
[160] Interview with an industry expert, February 13, 2018.
[161] Interview with experts from cyber police authority, January 11, 2018.
[162] Interview with an industry expert, January 25, 2018.
[163] Interview with experts from cyber police authority, January 11, 2018.
[164] Interview with an industry expert, February 7, 2018.
[165] Industry expert's answers to the questionnaire, received February 15, 2018.
[166] Interview with an environmental management and radiation expert, January 9, 2018.
[167] Industry expert's answers to the questionnaire, received April 27, 2018.

content of a standard: the substance of technical documents is left to the discretion of the members and technical experts.[168] Within ETSI, conflicts are preliminarily resolved in working groups, and only when that has proven unsatisfactory, are appealed.[169] In IETF, despite the existence of an appeals procedure, reaching a closure remains a difficult exercise, especially due to the lack of consensus-based dispute resolution methods and attempts to preempt formal dispute resolution procedures by engaging in offline discussions.[170] IEEE was praised for the good functioning of its escalation processes, which facilitated resolution of conflicts in 802.20 committee, where IEEE investigated, heard appeals, and decided to reform the group under new leadership.[171] Disputes that lead to procedural changes were conducted in ECMA, which modified its procedure following complaints regarding the development and adoption of the OXML) standard,[172] and W3C, which agreed to implement a royalty-free-based IPR Policy.[173]

Disputes that relate to infringements of IPRs sometimes result in litigation. In ETSI, court disputes on IPR matters are rather uncommon since the vast majority of conflicts is resolved by (bilateral) agreements.[174] Patent litigation was suggested to be limited in IETF and W3C, in part due to the organizations' culture and – in comparison to telecoms – small number of patents.[175] But generally, court litigation is not a preferred way to settle disputes: its major disadvantage lies in the fact that all relevant documents and communications from ongoing standardization work are put on hold for discovery purposes; hence, regardless of the outcome, litigation negatively affects SDOs' technical activities.[176] In a similar way, fundamental court decisions may impact stakeholders' behavior in SDOs: following the decision in *Rambus*, more attention was paid to when and how were IPR declarations filed;[177] after *Huawei*, ETSI modified its IPR policy to ensure that the FRAND commitments "travels" with the patent once the patent is sold to another

[168] Interview with an expert from an NSO, January 19, 2018.
[169] Interview with an expert from an SDO, April 4, 2018.
[170] Interview with an expert from an SDO, January 12, 2018.
[171] Industry expert's answers to the questionnaire, received April 27, 2018.
[172] Interview with an industry expert, January 23, 2018.
[173] Industry expert's answers to the questionnaire, received April 27, 2018.
[174] Interview with an expert from an SDO, April 4, 2018.
[175] Interview with a legal counsel of an SDO, January 18, 2018.
[176] Industry expert's answers to the questionnaire, received February 15, 2018.
[177] Interview with an industry expert, January 25, 2018.

company;[178] and *James Elliott* affected ETSI with regard to the possible liability claims for ENs that are not operating well.[179]

Curiously, some experts suggested that any failure in a standard or standards development process will be improved by itself simply because a standard will otherwise not be adopted by the majority.[180]

### *Suggested Improvements*

The general agreement seems to be that where and how to modify their processes, voting rules, or membership level should be left to the discretion of the SDOs; however, it was also noted that SDOs should be prepared to adapt to the interests of the industry and offer members an attractive technological forum, while acting within the limits of the WTO criteria.[181] Especially in such fast-developing sectors as telecoms and ICT, SDOs governance should be paced to the needs of the industry for these SDOs to remain relevant: as an example, ECMA's IPR policy was modified to include a royalty-free option to prevent JavaScript standardization from moving to a parallel community.[182] In any event, changes to SDOs operational frameworks may not occur arbitrarily and should always be justified.[183]

When revising their operational frameworks, one of the relevant questions is to what degree of detail, and at what level, should procedures be specified,[184] taking into account the difference of SDOs' landscapes. In formal SDOs, the revision processes should ideally be based on discussions with other SDOs for coordination and cooperation purposes.[185] Modifications may also be required for practical reasons: an example is the change in the Open Mobile Alliance rules on copyrights, which now permit implementing the content of some specifications in the Mission-Critical Push to Talk (MCPTT) initiative of the 3GPP.[186]

Some interviewees suggested that governance models of all SDOs could benefit from opening up and increasing contributions from non-members.[187] Others found that large global SDOs, such as 3GPP, would

[178] Interview with an industry expert, January 15, 2018.
[179] Interview with an expert from an SDO, April 4, 2018.
[180] Industry expert's answers to the questionnaire, received April 27, 2018.
[181] Interview with an industry expert, January 16, 2018.
[182] Interview with an industry expert, January 23, 2018.
[183] Interview with an industry expert, January 16, 2018.
[184] Interview with an industry expert, January 15, 2018.
[185] Ibid.
[186] Interview with an industry expert, February 19, 2018.
[187] Interview with an industry expert, April 4, 2018.

rather benefit from increased decision-making speed and less bureaucracy, and highlighted the need to strike a balance between input (amount of expertise and participants) and output (number of standards) within larger SDOs.[188] Most experts welcomed increased use of open-source models, and advised that SDOs need to manage integrating and provide services to incorporate open-source software development into FRAND-based standards.[189] The issue of open source should especially be addressed by formal SDOs, since in the opposite scenario, they risk losing their grip on standards development, and hence also their relevance for modern standardization activity.[190]

Experts also warned of SDOs' recent tendency to carry out standardization projects in closed groups, or "workshops," which can only be joined at the moment of their establishment, even by the members of SDOs wherein such groups were created.[191] While such a practice may indeed accelerate standards development, it is also opaque; improvements could be made by granting access to information regarding the projects within those groups for every SDO member, and where possible, interested nonmembers, and by allowing them to join the "workshops" even when the group has already been formed.[192] Likewise, SDOs' secretariats were sometimes experienced as being "too institutionalized" and "too active" in top-down initiation of technical work, which risks losing SDOs' membership-driven character: secretariats were invited to pay more attention to stakeholders' requirements and implement a bottom-up approach to technical standardization.[193]

Other general suggestions included improving feedback on parties' communications and complaints regarding technical proposals;[194] implementing processes in formal SDOs to facilitate the adoption of consortia specifications;[195] speeding up technical processes while complying with

[188] At the same time, a high number of participants is a sign of trust in an organization, and the only way to ensure that standards are broadly accepted. Interview with an industry expert, February 7, 2018.

[189] Interview with an industry expert, January 15, 2018.

[190] Interview with an expert from an NSO, January 19, 2018; Interview with an industry expert, April 4, 2018.

[191] Such practices are common in DIN and ETSI, although the latter imposes additional requirements for its members to join; Interview with an industry expert, January 23, 2018.

[192] Interview with an industry expert, January 23, 2018.

[193] Ibid.

[194] Interview with an environmental management and radiation expert, January 9, 2018.

[195] Interview with an expert from an NSO, January 19, 2018.

the overarching procedural principles;[196] leveling requirements for NSOs and other formal SDOs;[197] and facilitating effective remote participation, whereby parties can understand and follow technical processes.[198] It was also acknowledged that in a longer run, the business model for ICT standardization may need to be changed, especially when copyrighted standards that are sold against a fee are referencing open-source elements.[199] Similarly, the current division of membership categories may have lost its functionality, and hence may need simplifications or, even, abolishment.[200]

Furthermore, some experts recognized that ETSI's IPR Policy could no longer be properly applied, in part due to the changed landscape of ICT patents, inconsistencies around FRAND-terminology, and uncertainties with regard to essentiality.[201] It was suggested to introduce a more efficient control over IPR declarations and to improve their quality.[202] Increased transparency in ETSI database would benefit the industry: the poor quality of the database results in a situation where it is unclear whether patents are indeed essential and, if they are, to which standards release.[203] However, increased transparency of the database is challenging to achieve given the differences in patent families or patent systems across the world, and sometimes even the expired essentiality, let alone the obvious question of who is going to bear the costs for the database improvement;[204] moreover, a standard is "never ready," and some solutions may become essential only in future releases.[205]

## Performance of ICT Standards

### *The Loss of Alternatives*

Experts acknowledged competition between SDOs and availability of alternative solutions in ICT standardization. Previous case studies

196 Ibid.
197 Ibid.
198 Interview with an industry expert, January 17, 2018.
199 Interview with an expert from an NSO, January 19, 2018.
200 Interview with an industry expert, January 17, 2018.
201 Interview with an industry expert, February 13, 2018; Interview with an industry expert, April 9, 2018; Industry expert's answers to the questionnaire, received April 27, 2018.
202 Interview with an expert from an SDO, April 4, 2018.
203 Interview with an industry expert, January 16, 2018.
204 Some companies, for instance, prefer not to make use of the database, but rather provide explanations to their licensees, explaining the value of portfolios. Interview with an industry expert, January 16, 2018.
205 Interview with an industry expert, February 19, 2018.

demonstrated that at some point in time, standards developed in the prominent SDOs were mostly unsuccessfully challenged by competing alternatives.[206] For instance, promulgation of TCP/IP was jeopardized by ISO's Open Systems Interconnection (OSI) – a seven-layer model of network architecture developed in the late 1970s. Although OSI initially gained global endorsement from governments, solutions developed by ISO were less effective than those offered by IETF's informal protocols, in part due to the slow pace of ISO's standardization processes.[207] Likewise, W3C's shift to XHTML was unsuccessful; the SDO eventually decided to proceed with the HTML5 specifications, which in the meanwhile were developed by a WHATWG consortium.[208] To the contrary, the first low-cost, low-power, short-range technology was introduced by the infrared data interconnection standards (IrDA), but was swiftly found impractical since the type of connection it offered depended upon the line of sight between devices;[209] IrDA was soon replaced by the Bluetooth standard for unlicensed 2.45 GHz band, developed through cooperation between a number of companies in the Bluetooth SIG.

Experts provided different reasons for the failure of alternatives to established standards. The Worldwide Interoperability for Microwave Access (WiMAX), an initiative within the IEEE, did not differ very much from 4G LTE standard crafted in 3GPP, at least on basic technological grounds: both standards were using the same orthogonal frequency-division multiplexing (OFDM) radio technology and had a comparable performance.[210] LTE was eventually found superior as it offered capabilities to rollout the technology, for instance, by introducing specified voice codec and improving handover between sessions.[211] Moreover, the LTE standard followed the paths of the already established set of specifications within the 3GPP,[212] building on existing infrastructure and continuing the GSM evolution: it incorporated previous technicalities and knowledge borne within the ETSI/3GPP ecosystem,[213] including

[206] See, among others, JRC Report, Halpin, 'The crisis of standardizing DRM'; Russel, '"Rough consensus and running code"'; B. DeLacey, K. Herman, D. Kiron and J. Lerner, 'Strategic behavior in standard-setting organizations' (2006) Harvard NOM Working Paper No. 903214; Keil, 'De facto standardization'.

[207] For an elaborative case study, see Russel, "Rough consensus and running code."

[208] See Halpin, 'The crisis of standardizing DRM', p. 14.

[209] Keil, 'De facto standardization', 208.

[210] Interview with an industry expert, February 1, 2018; Interview with an industry expert, February 19, 2018.

[211] Interview with an industry expert, February 19, 2018.

[212] Interview with an industry expert, April 18, 2018.

[213] Interview with an expert from an SDO, April 4, 2018.

relevant proprietary technology, and ensured backwards compatibility with earlier generations of cellular standards.[214] Furthermore, the commercial model for cellular technologies was largely set by mobile network operators, who had already invested in 3GPP technologies and even publicly announced their intention to follow LTE standard:[215] as a result, WiMAX gained support only from a part of the industry,[216] and could never reach the same coverage and global acceptance as 3GPP's LTE.[217]

ETSI's HiperLAN, despite its initial technological supremacy,[218] was never able to achieve the commercial success of its US counterpart, IEEE's Wi-Fi (802.11). The major players on the market were already supporting the 802.11 standard – which also explains, in part, why some elements of the HiperLAN were implemented into the 802.11 series.[219] Since Wi-Fi technology standardized in IEEE was already dominating the markets,[220] HiperLAN was purely too late to attract the industry.[221] At the same time, some experts believed that HiperLAN was more complex and not well suited for unlicensed spectrum, while the access protocol defined by 802.11 was simply "good enough."[222] Also HomeRF, created as a response to a slow and balkanized standardization processes within the 802.11 Working Group,[223] while running on devices that were priced lower than the devices for Wi-Fi specifications, could not win the competition with Wi-Fi: by mid 2000, when HomeRF-supporting devices became commercially available, the WLAN market had already switched to the 802.11b.[224]

### *Standards' Uptake by Industry and Markets*

Since ICT standards are voluntary, their uptake by the market will largely depend on whether they achieve the objectives they pursue, that is, the

214 Industry expert's answers to the questionnaire, received April 27, 2018.

215 Interview with an industry expert, February 1, 2018. Interview with an industry expert, February 19, 2018.

216 Interview with an industry expert, April 18, 2018.

217 Interview with an industry expert, February 7, 2018.

218 K. J. Negus and A. Petrick, 'History of wireless local area networks (WLANs) in the unlicensed band' (2009) 11 *info* 36–56 at 43.

219 Ibid.

220 Interview with an industry expert, February 7, 2018.

221 Interview with an industry expert, January 17, 2018.

222 Interview with an industry expert, February 13, 2018.

223 See Negus and Petrick, 'History of wireless local area networks'.

224 Ibid., 48.

intended level of technological connectivity or interoperability. This is not surprising, since the market is unlikely to follow a standard that is not sufficiently effective to address its demands; by the same token, regulators will not refer to an ineffective private standard, and would even consider governmental alternatives if they are more adequate to fulfil the intended objectives. The resilience of ICT standards thus depends on their effectiveness and fulfilment of technical requirements.

While referring to "successful" rather than "effective" standards or SDOs, experts explained that standards are almost never predestined for global implementation: the success of SDOs is usually not taken for granted at the moment of their establishment,[225] and only about 25 percent of standards achieve the means they pursue *and* are accepted by the markets.[226] It is also quite common for standards to become successful at a later stage,[227] especially when they are created sooner than the industry has expected or has been prepared for, which was the case with the IP Multimedia Sub System (IMS) and the Enhanced Data Rates for GSM Evolution (EDGE) standards.[228] Some experts took the view that standards that are published are already by definition "successful."[229]

In general, standards' success relies on compliance with users' requirements,[230] the common interest of SDO's members to bring new technology on the market, and the choice of the right momentum to introduce that technology.[231] Past experiences in cellular mobile industry demonstrated that time and technical domain are two crucial elements of standards' success.[232] And yet, superior and complex technologies do not always win the battle for the market: factors such as consumer preferences, first-mover advantage of a standard, "locking-in" the industry, or even the price of a standard[233] should also be taken into account.

From the perspective of companies on the downstream market, standards are successful only when the sale of products running on those

[225] Interview with an industry expert, February 1, 2018.
[226] Interview with an industry expert, January 17, 2018.
[227] Interview with an industry expert, February 19, 2018.
[228] Interview with an industry expert, February 1, 2018.
[229] Industry expert's answers to the questionnaire, received April 27, 2018.
[230] In this regard, users may not always be sure about their requirements and preferences, which adds additional challenges for technology developers. Interview with an industry expert, February 1, 2018.
[231] Interview with an industry expert, January 15, 2018.
[232] Interview with an industry expert, January 17, 2018.
[233] Ibid.

standards is high.[234] Elements of standards' success may likewise vary per sector: for instance, forensic internet standards are typically employed by governments, whereas the requirements on standards' substance are set by industry: in this regard, standards developed in IETF and ICANN are believed to achieve – although slowly – the means they pursue, simply because there is no alternative to influence internet governance.[235] In turn, the success of web standards lies in their open nature as well as royalty-free licensing of patents incorporated in those standards, although proprietary standards with royalties may achieve industry recognition when their scope is clear.[236]

Some experts suggested that standardization initiatives driven by companies whose business model is focused on the maximum deployment of their patents may fail since some technologies, despite their quality and maturity, may simply not be welcomed on the market.[237] MPEG codec, arguably, did not have a proper view on how to resolve and avoid IPR issues; High Efficiency Video Coding (HEVC) codec was developed in a RAND working group, where uncertain licensing costs and patent pools fueled dissatisfaction of the industry.[238] In this regard, AV1, an open, royalty-free video codec recently developed by Open Media Alliance, is believed to offer increased technological advancement compared to the HEVC, while being available to more companies.[239]

While quality is a prerequisite for standards' success,[240] a standard's adoption on the market also depends on its suitability to resolve technical issues,[241] timely availability of the qualitative solutions it proposes,[242] and the achievement of critical mass at the early stages of its deployment.[243] Other "success factors" mentioned by the experts were: existence of competing standards (and their possible elimination due to the slow development process), publicity about standardized technologies,[244]

[234] Interview with an industry expert, April 18, 2018.
[235] Interview with experts from cyber police authority, January 11, 2018.
[236] Interview with an industry expert, April 4, 2018.
[237] Interview with an industry expert, April 18, 2018.
[238] Interview with an industry expert, April 4, 2018.
[239] Ibid.
[240] Interview with an industry expert, April 18, 2018; Interview with an industry expert, February 13, 2018.
[241] Interview with an industry expert, January 25, 2018.
[242] Industry expert's answers to the questionnaire, received April 27, 2018.
[243] Interview with an industry expert, January 23, 2018.
[244] Interview with an industry expert, January 25, 2018.

markets' preferences, recognizable trademark;[245] reputation of standardizing parties[246] and – perhaps the most important – industry belief that the standard enshrines the best possible technology and is promising in a long-term future.[247]

Experts also highlighted that global promulgation of ICT standards is dependent on the interoperable nature of electronic products: devices manufactured by different suppliers constitute a part of a larger ecosystem provided by interconnectivity, in which they need to "communicate" and exchange information.[248] To illustrate, while products supporting ZigBee standard owe their success to the standard's maturity and availability of silicon solutions, ZigBee has also gained in popularity due to the high sale volumes of electronic devices implementing the standard.[249] In this regard, it is also not uncommon for a standardized technology to grow into a service and to create the need for a specific sort of interoperability, as it was the case with the Short Message Service (SMS).[250] Some standards have developed a "life of their own" and are used for other purposes than pursued by their creation, such as GSM's successors, addressing their own part of the market and, at the same time, leaving sufficient room for new technologies.[251] A standard's success thus depends on the demand for products running on it, and vice versa.

### *Procedural Guarantees and Standards Uptake*

Procedural guarantees in SDOs were not mentioned as the main prongs of standards' effectiveness, but neither were they completely overlooked. One expert stated that institutional design of standard-setting committees plays a role in SDOs' ability to create a "win-win situation" for both standards creators and users: however, standardization should merely be viewed as a business tool, and not a goal in itself,[252] which makes SDOs facilitators of business transactions among interested parties. In that sense, standards' success also depends on the (additional) services, that

245 Interview with an industry expert, January 23, 2018.
246 Ibid.
247 Interview with an industry expert, February 13, 2018.
248 Interview with an industry expert, February 19, 2018.
249 Interview with an industry expert, April 18, 2018.
250 Interview with an industry expert, January 17, 2018.
251 Interview with an industry expert, April 18, 2018.
252 Interview with an industry expert, January 15, 2018.

is, testing, certification, and educational programs, offered by SDOs to their members.[253]

Standards crafted in formal European or global SDOs, such as CEN, CENELEC, ISO, and IEC, increase their chance of success since they are by definition endorsed by governmental organizations during well-established and transparent processes, which enhances these standards' quality and consistency; legitimacy gained by this recognition may be thwarted by the so-called fast-track procedures offered by these institutions.[254] This is especially the case in the field of ICT, characterized by a sheer abundance of informal consortia that are rarely focused on national representation and legitimacy aspects, but on having shorter development time and allowing for achieving consensus with a limited group of actors.[255] Companies may strategically join multiple standardization fora to observe which technology is winning.[256] This represents an attempt to accelerate deployment of new technologies as a response to the slow processes of formal SDOs: endorsement of standards developed in informal bodies through a fast-track process of a formal SDO legitimizes the process of their development by opening up the standard for comments from a broader community.[257]

3GPP's institutional set up was praised for allowing different opinions and accepting technical proposals from various companies, which facilitates the achievement of a truly global solution.[258] Also IETF was mentioned as having well-functioning governance and procedures: some experts attributed the popularity of the transmission control protocols to IETF's institutional setting and culture that did not preclude any actor from putting forward technical proposals or publishing a draft

[253] Interview with an industry expert, April 18, 2018, on file with the author; Industry expert's answers to the questionnaire, received February 15, 2018.

[254] Interview with an expert from an NSO, January 19, 2018.

[255] Ibid.; Interview with an industry expert, February 19, 2018. The author notes that it is not clear from the interviews whether experts found that consortia exist because ISO standards are ineffective, or ISO standards are ineffective because of the consortia. To the author's opinion, both statements hold.

[256] Interview with an expert from an NSO, January 19, 2018, on file with the author.

[257] An example provided is the standard for compact disk, which initially was controlled by two companies, but was eventually opened up as an IEC standard, Interview with an industry expert, February 19, 2018.

[258] Interview with an industry expert, January 17, 2018; Interview with an industry expert, February 7, 2018.

specification ensuring that the input was broad enough to satisfy the community's need for functioning protocols and networks.[259]

The probability of standards' success may also be identified based on the composition of a standards development group: the more common interests the participants have, the more likely it is that the standard they develop will be widely adopted.[260] In this regard, increased openness and transparency were believed to contribute to standards' success but also cause drawbacks in standards development processes.[261] Indeed, one of the main challenges accompanying Bluetooth specifications was the enormous success of the SIG among the industry: the more players joined the promoters group, the more difficult it became to align their interests, which in turn affected the pace of standards development.[262] At the same time, the fact that the initial promoters had a prominent position on the target markets sent a signal to those markets that the developed technology has a high probability of success, encouraging its adoption.[263] Moreover, the SIG's semi-open structure, where the promoters' group is strictly limited and adopter group extremely open, represented a combination of control and market reputation of closed platforms and market diffusion and standard promulgation advantages of open platforms.[264]

Procedural guarantees are thus not necessarily sufficient to define standards' effectiveness,[265] and standards' success is almost never a matter of an institutional framework alone, but mostly of industry adoption.[266] That said, some experts believed that SDO governance fall under a broader picture to define successful SDOs that companies are comfortable to join,[267] and that procedural elements may not be crucial at the initial stages of standards development; they seem to become relevant when the standard is adopted.[268] And while it is impossible to see at the beginning of standardization processes whether a standard will

[259] Interview with an expert from an SDO, January 12, 2018; Interview with an industry expert,* January 16, 2018; Interview with a legal counsel of an SDO, January 18, 2018.
[260] Interview with an industry expert, January 15, 2018.
[261] Interview with an expert from an SDO, April 4, 2018.
[262] Keil, 'De facto standardization', 208–9.
[263] Ibid., 211.
[264] Ibid.
[265] Interview with an industry expert, January 15, 2018; Interview with an industry expert, January 23, 2018.
[266] Industry expert's answers to the questionnaire, received February 15, 2018.
[267] Interview with an industry expert, February 13, 2018.
[268] Interview with an industry expert, February 19, 2018.

indeed become successful, participants would typically discover the flaws before the standard is finalized and try to correct them or, ultimately, resume the processes in a different setting.[269]

Does this imply that procedural safeguards put forward by the regulatory frameworks are of trivial importance? Each expert was asked whether, in their opinion, it is possible to have an effective standard developed by ill-defined procedures that do not respect the principles of due process. As a first reaction, experts agreed that such a standard will be successful if the market pressure is high enough, emphasizing the markets' power to decide which standard is effective, and which is not. On a second thought, however, it was suggested that lack of procedural guarantees will diminish the input from all relevant actors, which will result in less technological maturity of a standard and, as a consequence, diminish its effectiveness. A standard that is not mature, correct, or complete, is less likely to be interoperable and will attract neither industry nor consumers. Standards development processes that exclude parties by definition create incentives to establish a competing standard; in turn, a process that is open for inclusion of a broad range of interests and provides opportunities to contribute and to make changes makes other parties more inclined to accept the outcome, even when the amendments they suggested have not been realized.[270]

## Observations and Takeaways from the Interviews

Although the aforementioned considerations represent the views of a limited subset of the actors involved in ICT standardization, and are sometimes of anecdotal evidence, they indicate these actors' preferences and tendencies and allow for some observations. As self-regulatory bodies, SDOs may differ in the implementation of due process principles into their operational frameworks; these differences become more apparent in practice, and as such depend on both exogenous and endogenous factors, including legal constraints, market preferences, and membership. In this regard, SDOs operating in the ICT sector are distinctive due to, among other factors, increased consortia activity, interdependence of their technical work (especially in the IoT standardization), an IPR-intensive environment, and the far-reaching network effects of their standards.

[269] Industry expert's answers to the questionnaire, received April 27, 2018.
[270] Interview with an industry expert, February 19, 2018.

In seems that in such a highly technical environment, procedural guarantees are rarely perceived as barriers for SDO participation, unless they are discouraging IPR contributions for specific sectors. Joining an SDO remains a commercial decision, and processes become relevant only when they affect companies' commercial purposes. In all likelihood, this is different for noncommercial stakeholders who pursue noncommercial objectives by participating in global standardization. Transparency and coherence are sometimes challenging in the ICT environment due to SDOs' confidentiality rules. Openness and participation may also face difficulties due to the lack of technological and linguistic knowledge, especially by non-Western experts. Some SDOs, however, address this issue by launching local educational initiatives, which illustrates how openness and transparency can be targeted through other procedural principles, in this case, (assistance to) developing countries.

Among all procedural principles, experts appear to attach the most value to balance and avoidance of dominance. Even when SDOs' practices appear to run afoul of due process, modifications of their rules and procedures should be carried out with consent from, and upon an agreement with, its membership, in order to preclude SDOs from being hijacked by one interest group.[271] Avoidance of dominance becomes particularly important when SDOs' processes give rise to antitrust concerns – due to potential liability of SDOs, but also individual liability of their members. Antitrust liability is thus a strong factor contributing to compliance with due process.

The threat of liability and increased costs may also explain why disputes within SDOs rarely make it to litigation. By and large, procedural questions are resolved within the governance bodies and technical committees of SDOs according to their internal procedures, without any "checks" by external actors. This seems to sit well with the experts, who generally view procedural disagreements as internal matters of SDOs.

When an SDO does not fulfill the expectations of (some) stakeholders, the tendency appears to establish a new, specialized group or consortium, rather than switching to an already existent SDO; often, standards developed in such a group will be eventually returned to the SDO in question. It is thus questionable whether the threat of forum-switching is

[271] Almost everyone except for one interviewee suggested it; that person, however, asserted that changes would be made as necessary, that the organization will make them happen as a natural process, which still indicates certain consent, or approval, at the higher level. Industry expert's answers to the questionnaire, received April 27, 2018.

credible and may incentivize SDOs to modify their procedures: past examples demonstrate that "voting with the feet" does not occur that often. Especially since the global adoption of a standard is facilitated by broad industry participation in its development and, given the commercial importance for companies to be engaged in standard-setting processes, moving an entire standardization project to another organization seems unlikely.

With regard to procedural guarantees, experts appeared to praise the WTO principles of TBT Committee Decision, however without explaining whether and why should these principles apply for every type of SDO and for both policy-making and technical processes. This observation is remarkable, since it indicates that the WTO principles have evolved into the "threshold" for legitimacy in private standardization communities and are stretched to their governance and even IPR policies (which, in turn, is not revealed from the analysis of the regulatory frameworks). Hence, interpretation of the principles is more important for the industry than the intention of the regulatory frameworks from which these principles are derived.

Experts' views provide no unilateral answer to which governance model should be considered as the best one but seem to suggest that the processes should be clear and predictable, while at the same time flexible and responsive to industry advancement. Procedural rules should be "sufficiently good," and the markets are left to decide whether standards developed according to these processes are "good enough" for their global adoption. In the complex environment of ICT standardization, SDOs' processes are believed to be "self-correcting," and their quality relies on industry acceptance, experts' prudence, and technical logic.

SDOs' processes thus enable technical work in a manner that suits SDOs' particular setting and their members, and facilitate fast solutions and better implementation, which eventually reflects on the quality of standards. Standards' adoption appears conditional on broad input from the industry, but this input can take many forms and is not limited to "active and effective" participation. Commercial success of many standards was mainly a consequence of resolving collective action problems by getting the relevant players – mostly private companies, but sometimes also governments or even individuals – to agree on both technical and policy issues surrounding standardization processes.

# 12

# Revisiting the Legitimacy of ICT Standardization

While there are many analytical lenses to study legitimacy, in a multi-layered regulatory environment, legitimacy of the rule-making power depends upon its origins and effects.[1] Studies on management and organizational studies suggests that standards are legitimized by their voluntary nature, cooperative and inclusive standard-setting process, and the ability to serve potential users,[2] but also the quality of SDOs' decision-making processes.[3] In the context of transnational private regulation, it is the combination of private autonomy to adopt SDOs' standards and the procedural requirements according to which they are developed that legitimizes compliance with these standards.[4] Scholars also suggested that legitimacy of SDOs is multifaceted and is achieved through compliance with legal norms as well as through market forces.[5]

Each of these approaches does justice to the complexity of legitimacy of private regulation in the sense that it accentuates the linkages and interdependencies between different legitimization techniques. They also allow for further observation that legitimacy has both theoretical and empirical accounts and that, depending on the normative lens through which one assesses SDOs' rule-making, these accounts can be in contradiction or in harmony.

While legitimacy may assume a different meaning among engineers, managers, and lawyers, three types of legitimacy have been defined recurrently by the interviewed experts: legitimacy derived from

[1] J. Black, 'Constructing and contesting legitimacy'; Cafaggi, 'New foundations', p. 15.
[2] Botzem and Dobusch, 'Standardization cycles'; Boström and Tamm Hallström, 'NGO power'; Brunsson, 'Organizations, markets and standardization', p. 23.
[3] C. Joerges, H. Schepel and E. Vos, 'The law's problems with involvement of non-governmental actors in Europe's legislative processes: the case of standardization under the New Approach', EUI Working Paper No. 99/9, p. 12.
[4] Cafaggi, 'The many features'.
[5] JRC Report, p. 128.

compliance with the applicable law; legitimacy derived from the institutional characteristics of SDOs; and legitimacy derived from the technical expertise of standards developers. This largely follows the pattern of legitimacy in private rule-making, bearing on the authority of SDOs and their technical and political performance.

## Public Law Legitimacy

It is not uncommon for privately driven regulation to seek and obtain legitimacy through public law mechanisms. Standards for business conduct are legitimized through their implementation in States' regulatory policies, which provide enforcement mechanisms to ensure that these standards are complied with.[6] Legitimacy of EU private regulatory arrangements is achieved ex post through EU free movement and competition rules.[7] Transnational professional associations derive their legitimacy from participation of domestic private bodies in their decision-making:[8] in a transnational setting, States' role is one of the catalysts that coordinate and support various regulatory activities.[9]

As discussed in Chapter 1, voluntary standards that are endorsed in public law, or by organizations recognized in (inter)national law, acquire a binding force and increased legitimacy. Such recognition occurs, for instance, through the publication of a reference to a HES in the OJ of the EU, or through incorporation by reference of a private voluntary standard by US regulatory agencies, or the endorsement by (inter)national courts and tribunals. Approval by democratic bodies, such as parliaments or governmental institutions, may compensate for nondemocratic rule-making of SDOs,[10] and thus also pay due regard to public interest.

[6] D. Vogel, 'The private regulation of global corporate conduct', in W. Mattli and N. Woods (eds.), *The Politics of Global Regulation* (Princeton: Princeton University Press, 2009), p. 153.

[7] Mataija, *Private Regulation*, p. 17.

[8] Whereas legitimacy of national, self-regulated professional associations is achieved through an explicit transferal of powers from public bodies to such associations. See R. B. Stewart, 'Enforcement of transnational public regulation' (2011) in EUI Working Papers, Robert Schuman Centre for Advanced Studies, Private Regulation Series-06, RSCAS 2011/49.

[9] Abbott and Snidal, 'The governance triangle'.

[10] See JRC Report, p. 127.

Governmental endorsement appears as an important legitimation element even in very narrowly specialized scientific domains. For instance, it has been once suggested that ICANN is an inappropriate forum to discuss internet governance since it is driven by private parties and, allegedly, does not take into account the concerns of States.[11] The CASE standards for forensic language, while developed by expert community, have presumably gained their legitimacy and wide support among the stakeholders due to the involvement of governmental agencies in its administration.[12] This does not take away, however, that governmental endorsement of an industry activity may be prone to lobbying by private firms.[13]

Endorsement through public law is often presented in the regulatory frameworks and in practice as the main mechanism for legitimization of private standards. SDOs whose authority is indisputable from the perspective of those conferring the regulatory power, and those on whom this power is exercised, are trusted more easily, but this does not suffice for input legitimacy of their rule-making. The broad formulation of regulatory frameworks, and the continued reluctance of States to stretch their procedural principles to private standards bodies, entrusts SDOs with the political quality of their input, which in turn depends on the dynamics and interactions between stakeholders that are predominantly commercial actors with vested interests in SDOs' technical and governance processes. Input legitimacy in SDOs thus relies on the "democracy of experts" catalyzed by the interplay between public law and SDOs' institutional and procedural settings.

## Procedural Legitimacy

Legitimacy can also be derived from the procedural properties of non-State regulation. In transnational governance, legitimacy arises from participatory mechanisms that represent fair, transparent, accessible, and open processes, and that also offer tools to handle objections and

[11] Schneiderman, *Modern Standardization*, p. 6.

[12] This is an assumption of the author, based on the rationale that governments may not feel completely comfortable to fully delegate forensic standardization to private actors.

[13] An example provided by one of the experts was a long-time rejection of the Dutch government to accept the danger of asbestos, allegedly due to the strong lobby of private companies. Interview with an environmental management and radiation expert, January 9, 2018, on file with the author.

include third parties in decision-making.[14] Fairness and justice in procedure provides space for hybridity and opens avenues for alternatives, arguably enhancing the quality of regulatory outcomes.[15] For global governance organizations, procedural legitimacy claims can be observed from information available on websites, such as reports, working programs, and decisions of their governance bodies,[16] which echoes the requirement of transparency.

Due process principles for standardization discussed in this book aim to ensure that the outcomes of SDOs processes are legitimate under a certain set of legal rules; in this context, procedural legitimacy is linked to public law legitimacy. These principles also safeguard a balance of interests in SDOs and, ideally, protect standards development from being dominated by a single (group of) interest; in this sense, procedural legitimacy also contributes to standards' quality and facilitates their uptake by the market, for standards that favor only certain (type of) stakeholders would ultimately not be adopted at the global level.

To illustrate, standards developed in an open process of a formal organization may sometimes be accepted on the market more easily, as opposed to proprietary alternatives. In the late 1990s, the battle for the 56K modem standard raged between X2 and Flex, two symmetric network technologies supported by two different groups of firms.[17] Industry's reluctance to agree on a unified standard resulted in market fragmentation and increased transaction costs.[18] The solution came from ITU, whose V.90 specification became widely used in computer equipment and facilitated the rapid growth of the market.[19] Despite its slow, government-driven process and lack of enforcement power on a national level, ITU managed to offer infrastructure for the resolution of IPR issues[20] and attracted the support of all major industry players, even

[14] Mattli and Woods, 'In whose benefit?' p. 4; S. Botzem and S. Quack, 'Contested rules and shifting boundaries: international standard-setting in accounting', in M. Djelic and K. Sahlin-Andersson (eds.), *Transnational Governance: Institutional Dynamics of Regulation* (Cambridge: Cambridge University Press, 2006), p. 284.

[15] Berman, *Global Legal Pluralism*, pp. 16, 163.

[16] See J. Steffek, 'Discursive legitimation in environmental governance' (2009) 11 *Forest Policy and Economics* 313–18.

[17] X2 was supported by US Robotics and Flex, which was developed later, by Rockwell, Lucent and Motorola.

[18] See Greenstein and Rysman, 'Coordination costs and standard setting'.

[19] Ibid., p. 5.

[20] Note that resolution of IPR issues was also one of the main factors of ETSI's success in developing GSM, as opposed to national arrangements. In this regard, one of the main

though the SDO could not actually guarantee the fulfillment of its scheduling claims and the new standard was incompatible with both X2 and Flex.[21]

Interestingly, the success of ITU's V.90 is underpinned by reasons directly opposite to those that experts considered crucial for the promulgation of Bluetooth specifications. Parties involved in the definition of V.90 technical specifications were willing to accelerate the process since they believed that the 56K modems would be rapidly obscured by broadband technologies and that the market opportunities for deploying 56K modems would be short-lived.[22] In the case of Bluetooth specifications, however, it was the belief in long-term relevance of the Bluetooth technology that incentivized the members to work on its development and, subsequently, to adopt it for their hardware devices.[23]

Next to the "external" procedural principles, SDOs processes should follow the SDOs' "internal" rules, which are tailor-made for every organization and accepted by members when joining an SDO. Adherence to these rules can be scrutinized by SDOs' governance bodies, for instance, by means of appeal processes against an alleged breach of SDO's rules (i.e., IEEE-SA IPR Policy Update case study) and rectified through the corrective measures available under the SDOs' operational frameworks. Noncompliance with SDOs' internal rules may be challenged in courts as a breach of contract (i.e., *TruePosition, Inc.* v. *LM Ericsson Tel* case study). By the same token, compliance with external procedural rules can be safeguarded by SDOs themselves (i.e., IEEE-SA IPR Policy Update; DRM EME approval in W3C case studies) as well as scrutinized by courts (i.e., *EMC Development, NSS Labs vs. Symantec).* These possibilities for "internal" and "external" review arguably strengthen the importance of procedural legitimacy in standardization.

challenges in GSM development was the refusal of Motorola, the largest SEP holder, to make general declarations on licensing of its SEPs and instead offering cross-licensing agreements, which risked monopolization by firms who could afford Motorola's technology. Since GSM was one of the first standards whose development was impeded by licensing practices, there was, at that point in time, no official policy or guidelines that would govern the inclusion of SEP into technical specifications. See R. Bekkers, G. Duysters and B. Verspagen, 'Intellectual property rights, strategic technology agreements and market structure: the case of GSM' (2002) 31 *Research Policy* 1141–61.

[21] Greenstein and Rysman, 'Coordination costs and standard setting', p. 10.

[22] Ibid., p. 17, n. 10.

[23] Interview with an industry expert, April 18, 2018.

Procedural legitimacy amounts to throughput legitimacy in its attention to the quality of the processes on which SDOs base their rule-making authority. But considering only the procedural principles and their implementation by SDOs presents a rather limited view on throughput legitimacy, a view that overlooks the very processes of SDOs acquiring their regulatory power. These, in turn, are rarely taken into account by practitioners because of the general presumption of SDOs' public law legitimacy; they are equally overlooked by scholars because private and informal bodies such as ICT SDOs are typically outsourced from the realm of law and regulation.

Another fallacy would be assuming that as voluntary associations, SDOs are triggered to hold themselves to high procedural norms due to the existence of regulatory alternatives. SDOs may indeed compete in the early stages of standards development, but due to financial, organizational, and personal investments of their members, the threat of a standardization activity moving to another SDO becomes less credible the more a standard is progressing into the development and release phases.[24] This does not necessarily contradict the self-improving character of SDOs' processes, since SDOs' members would challenge the processes that they deem to be of low quality, and oppose the decisions they deem unfair; but this is only possible to the extent that SDOs enable an independent review of their procedures or appeal of their decisions. The fact that SDOs generally prefer the disputes to be handled internally and by their own governance bodies, while ensuring technical expertise and lowering SDOs' costs, also jeopardizes independence when the appeals are handled by nonlawyers, or even by members who may have vested interests in the outcomes of the procedure. Submitting SDOs' processes to an "external" review instead of SDOs' governance bodies increases their throughput, but also input legitimacy, since it allows including public interest and societal concerns in otherwise purely technical considerations.

Even when a regulatory institution supplies extensive participatory mechanisms and provides for inclusive procedures, the legitimacy of its rule-making should not be taken for granted, especially when it does not satisfy the "demand side" of regulation.[25] Compliance with a set of procedural requirements does not immediately assure flawless

[24] See Delimatsis et al., 'Strategic behaviour in standards development organizations'.

[25] See Mattli and Woods, 'In whose benefit?'.

implementation of standards,[26] nor does it guarantee standards' acceptance on global markets. And even if public and procedural legitimacy contribute to input and throughput legitimacy, they are nearly meaningless in the ICT ecosystem without the specific knowledge and experience that is required to develop a standard.

## Epistemic Legitimacy

Legitimation of private regulation can also occur through decision-making that is driven by specific expertise. To manage complex, rapidly evolving regulatory fields, rule-makers should have specialized technological knowledge and skills, typically possessed by narrowly trained actors.[27] In some particular domains, such expertise-driven regulatory schemes, despite being voluntary, may nevertheless be preferred over formal arrangements.[28]

In global politics, the absence of expertise may risk the regulatory outcomes not to achieve the ends pursued by the institution, which is likely to shatter the belief of norm-receivers and affect their compliance with the rules established by this institution, eventually rendering regulation ineffective.[29] Legitimacy of industry-driven normative schemes is premised on the relevant knowledge and expertise claims behind the regulatory results, and on shared norms and values of the epistemic community defining the rules.[30] To achieve epistemic legitimacy, expertise in organizations should be genuinely present, and decision-making in organizations should be based on expert considerations and fall within the scope of the expertise.[31] At the same time, organizations that are

[26] See also Wiegmann et al., 'Multi-mode standardization', p. 1375.

[27] M. Djelic and K. Sahlin-Andersson, 'Introduction: a world of governance: the rise of transnational regulation', in M. Djelic and K. Sahlin-Andersson (eds.), *Transnational Governance: Institutional Dynamics of Regulation* (Cambridge: Cambridge University Press, 2006), p. 7; Shapiro, '"Deliberative," "independent" technocracy', p. 343.

[28] For instance, the European Network of Forensic Science Institutes prefers that all forensic labs use ISO standards; however, due to the differences [in their regulatory systems and operations of their labs], Member States often prefer the use of best practices. Interview with experts from cyber police authority, January 11, 2018.

[29] In this regard, see F. Scharpf, 'Problem-solving effectiveness and democratic accountability in the EU' (2003) MPIfG Working Paper 03/1; I. Clark, 'Legitimacy in a global order' (2003) 29 *Review of International Studies* 75–95; I. Hurd, 'Legitimacy and authority in international politics' (1999) 53 *International Organization* 379–408.

[30] Bexell, 'Global governance', pp. 291–3; Djelic and Sahlin-Andersson, 'Introduction: a world of governance', p. 7.

[31] JRC Report, p. 125.

epistemically legitimate should be capable of generating effective rules by means of providing opportunities for discussions and evaluation of various views and interests, promoting diversity and reducing the risk of opportunistic interventions.[32]

It is incontestable that standardization is driven by technical experts. Scientific-based decision-making is endorsed in many, if not all, SDOs and was emphasized by the interviewed experts. Even SDOs' management and administration staff usually have a technical background.[33] This combined expertise drives stakeholders to SDOs and that ensures that SDOs' processes result in high-quality, technological-experts-based solutions. From this vantage point, it is the relevant expertise that guarantees SDOs' performance, and thus their output legitimacy.

While this type of legitimacy appears the most valuable in ICT standardization, it also has its flaws. A common limitation to expertise-based decision-making in SDOs is that standards development, despite being considered as a purely engineering exercise, in practice still includes political and commercial considerations, and may even be influenced by individuals whose real motivates are impossible to verify. This puts into question in whose interest do SDOs truly act and challenges their rule-making authority and, by this means, also the quality of their standards. Hence, output legitimacy cannot thrive solely on expertise and requires procedural legitimacy and, to the extent that it enables interest representation, public law legitimacy.

Another drawback of relying on epistemic legitimacy is the lack of external scrutiny. While technical issues in standards development can be addressed by the working groups' chairs of SDOs, they cannot, and should not, be subjected to review by courts:[34] the opposite will undermine the scientific character of SDOs' processes and cause frustration among technical experts.

Ultimately, in non-State governance, epistemic regulation is likely to represent the perspectives of a narrow interest group,[35] which creates tensions with inclusive regulation and democratic control. A suggested solution to have a democratically driven community "coordinating"

[32] Keohane, 'The contingent legitimacy of multilateralism', p. 15.

[33] JRC Report, p. 128.

[34] Recall the case *EMC Development*, where the CJEU looked at CEN's processes, rather than the technical contents of the standard.

[35] Shapiro, '"Deliberative," "independent" technocracy', p. 343.

experts' work ("experts on tap and not on top") would not be feasible in a complex technological setting where the ultimate decision-maker is required to possess the knowledge of complex technical issues.[36] Epistemic regulation should thus be designed in processes that protect wider interest groups and prevent concertation of power, in a way compensating for the democratic deficit.

## Practical Approach to Legitimacy of ICT Standardization

Standards are legitimized through endorsement by authorities, SDOs' compliance with the applicable procedural rules, expertise-driven decision-making, and acceptance by the markets. And whereas all these elements are equally relevant, no single form of legitimacy would suffice. Different types of legitimacy complement and avert each other simultaneously, and further case-specific analyses would be required to establish whether and how are particular standardization schemes legitimized from the perspective of various stakeholders.

It is reasonable to assume that because of their voluntary nature, legitimacy of ICT standards would predominantly be derived from their effectiveness and market uptake. At first glance, this crucial element of legitimacy appears to rely entirely on market forces and industry preferences; however, standards acceptance also seems to have procedural dimension. As suggested by the interviewed experts, it is the combination of inclusive and open procedures, possibility to review decisions, transparency, and balance of interests that improves standards' quality and ultimately ensures their success. And while compliance with procedural principles does not seem crucial for the global acceptance of ICT standards, it feeds both their legitimacy and effectiveness.

That said, it is possible that ICT standards differ from standards in other sectors, such as labor or environment, where increased public law scrutiny would be more desirable due to the overarching public interest concerns. It is also possible that with the evolvement of ICT standards into stronger regulatory norms, additional "external" scrutiny by public sector would be required to strengthen their input legitimacy. This, however, is an issue that should be further elaborated on by regulatory authorities, that should work in tandem with SDOs to prevent the regulatory capture of their processes

[36] Ibid.

while ensuring that standards development also takes into account a wide range of the relevant interests.

Considerations regarding best practices in the industry with regard to standards' legitimacy and effectiveness question whether increased compliance with due process in ICT standardization is desirable. An argument in favor of stricter adherence to procedural rules is the need to safeguard public interest and to ensure that the decisions taken by SDOs would benefit the wider community, and not only its fraction. Expertise-driven rule-making intrinsically lacks representation of all relevant interests, not to mention that, in reality, SDOs appear to be driven by large companies. Yet, ICT standardization is evolving from a purely technical activity to a form of private governance that affects the wider society. Given this public interest function, ICT SDOs should offer increased procedural and substantive safeguards that ensure legitimacy and effectiveness of their standards, as well as their compliance with the applicable regulatory requirements. To exist as effective regulatory institutions, SDOs require independence and representativeness to guarantee openness and due process, and expertise and operational capacity for effective regulation.[37] Hence, from the viewpoint of law, SDOs' accountability should be provided by increased participation, access to dispute resolution, and balance of interests.

It is also true, however, that a "one size fits all" approach to procedural guarantees does not appear feasible when analyzing SDOs' operational frameworks, which differ significantly due to their historical background, institutional features, and preferences of their membership. The prevailing opinion among the experts seems that, apart from separate cases and suggested minor improvements, the ICT standardization system generally complies with due process principles *as interpreted by the wider industry*, and that any changes to the current landscape may disturb the work of a well-established, expertise-driven ecosystem.

What then should the role of governments be in the private, self-regulatory processes of ICT standardization? Governmental actors can be involved in ICT standardization by means of a public–private partnership, where governmental authorities and SDOs interact to clarify and

[37] See Abbott and Snidal, 'The governance triangle', p. 46.

develop applicable legal rules and institutional norms. Governments can also provide ex post control by scrutinizing SDOs' procedures against due process requirements, for instance, when selecting a private standard to be referenced in legislation. Stronger governmental involvement, even though it is likely to contribute to public law legitimacy of ICT standards by safeguarding public interest and addressing human rights concerns, may also diminish their epistemic, and possibly also procedural legitimacy: due process requirements are formulated as "best practice" efforts and provide SDOs' with sufficient margin for their implementation. Stakeholders may perceive such governmental interference and efforts to clarify SDOs' processes as an attempt to intervene in SDOs' self-regulation, which may result in their withdrawal from collective standards development and by this means, ultimately affect the quality of standards.

## SYNOPSIS

What ensures the resilience of SDOs and grants legitimacy to their standards: SDOs' compliance with the applicable regulatory requirements, inclusiveness of their operational processes, or their technological supremacy? Each of these elements have a role to play when it comes to SDOs' legitimacy and effectiveness, and no single element is sufficient. The interviewed experts seem to agree that the self-regulatory nature of SDOs, their flexibility to adapt to market needs, and the technical excellence of their membership trump procedural principles. When viewed from the lens of private governance, however, ICT standardization should be subjected to increased due process. Indeed, when considering the emerging regulatory role of ICT standardization, epistemic legitimacy may not suffice: SDOs need to take due consideration of the variety of interests affected by their standards and provide sufficient mechanisms to challenge the decision-making of their bodies and officials while, at the same time, ensuring that their technical processes do not get stalled.

While in standards development committees, technological considerations generally outweigh procedural concerns, it does not necessarily mean that the two are contradictory, since balanced and inclusive processes have a positive effect on standards' quality. From the legal viewpoint, compliance with procedural principles endows SDOs with public law legitimacy as well as procedural legitimacy. Due process holds SDOs to a higher standard of good governance, shields them from legal liability and, in part, compensates for the democratic deficit of their rule-making. From the viewpoint of practitioners, compliance with procedural requirements does not appear as essential as the technical features of standards, yet it contributes to standards' quality and effectiveness, and hence also to their epistemic legitimacy. This, however, does not imply that procedural legitimacy is sufficient to guarantee the effectiveness of standards as a form of private governance.[38] Due process and technical decision-making are thus not mutually exclusive, provided that procedural requirements are adjusted to the needs of the particular sector and industry.

The observations of this empirical study furthermore challenge some concepts and perceptions that traditionally pertain to standardization. Firstly, while standards development processes are believed to be guided by consensus, SDOs appear to attach more significance to balance and lack of dominance. Indeed, the requirement of "balance" may be subject to different interpretations: some scholars suggested that the principle of balance in the context of antitrust law requires SDOs to promote a balanced representation of appropriately defined categories of interests and is therefore different from the requirement to provide safeguards against dominance.[39] This book submits that the requirement of balance is first and foremost meant to ensure that standardization processes are not hijacked by one group of stakeholders, regardless of whether they are in a horizontal or vertical relationship with other groups, since a standard tilted towards one group of

[38] A similar conclusion with regard to procedural legitimacy and success of global governance regimes was reached by Besheim and Dingwerth, who suggest considering the complexity of global governance, the fact that the importance of procedural legitimacy varies across different stages of governance processes, and that different stakeholders may attach different values to procedural legitimacy. M. Besheim and S. Dingwerth, 'Procedural legitimacy and private transnational governance: are the good ones doing better?' (June 2008) SFB-Governance Working Paper Series No. 14, at p. 26. It should be noted, however, that while deliberation indeed promotes the sense of legitimacy, it may also legitimize bad decisions – hence, involving a larger group of stakeholders in decision-making may sometimes even decrease the quality of these decisions. C. R. Sunstein, *Infotopia: How Many Minds Produce Knowledge* (New York: Oxford University Press, 2006), p. 56.

[39] See J. Baron and P. Larouche, 'Antitrust and balance of interests in standards development: lessons from *NSS Labs. v. Symantec*' (September 2019) 2 *Competition Policy International* 2–10, who view balance as a vertical relationship between interest categories of groups, and dominance as a horizontal relationship between competing technology.

interests while excluding others is less likely to achieve the means it pursues.[40]

Secondly, while due account should be given to competitive forces in standardization, conflicts among SDO members seem to arise not merely from the very fact of rivalry, but when a (group of) stakeholder(s) is excluded, or alleges being excluded, from SDOs' decision-making processes. This is because, apart from procedural issues, exclusion also has technical and business consequences for those affected by a particular standard or having vested interests in standards development. The negative consequences of exclusion are furthermore aggravated when it triggers liability of an SDO and its members, since those who are not party to the conflict become embroiled in it.

Finally, the question remains whether SDOs are appropriate platforms for discussing societal concerns. While SDOs' status of organizations concerned merely with engineering issues is challenged by the increased regulatory and societal importance of ICT standards, many industry experts still view them as purely technical organizations. Subjecting SDOs' processes to an external review may thus be perceived by SDOs as a disturbing interference into their processes, and their standardization activities may then risk moving to even less regulated platforms with fewer procedural guarantees. The potential endorsement of such standards by formal SDOs may not compensate for procedural shortcomings during their development, especially in case these standards are implemented by a large subset of the industry. The redefined regulatory role of ICT SDOs can only be embraced if there is a shift in the mentality of SDOs' participants.

[40] For instance, an international standard ISO 1581-2, which was supposed to set the appropriate level of biocide tributyltin used in antifouling paints so that the paints used for ships do not disturb the hormone level of water organisms, appeared to be based on inaccurate calculations and to ignore environmental concerns; unsurprisingly, the development of this standard was dominated by large paint producers. A. Gottlieb, H. Verheul and H. De Vries, 'Project Verbetering formele normalisatieproces – CASE ISO 15181: paints and varnishes – determination of release rate of biocides in antifouling paints' (2003) Delft: Ministry of Economic Affairs.

# Conclusion

> Dierdre Kostick: We are becoming a board of lawyers focusing on process, rather than on engineering. Let's focus on engineering. Does the severity of the problems with the documents warrant reducing the status of the documents?
>
> Scott Bradner: Yes, we are needing to focus on process, so that the standards setting process appears fair. We cannot dismiss the rules that we have made for ourselves.[1]

In April 2020, the Council of State, the highest Administrative Court of the Netherlands, issued a decision in an appeal filed against a decree of a Dutch municipality that allowed placement of a transmission tower in a relatively isolated area.[2] The plaintiffs, a group of civilians sensitive to electromagnetic radiation, argued that the municipality, and later also the lower court, did not take into account the adverse effects that the tower placement would have on their health. The Council sided with the municipality, noting that the level of radiation produced by the transmission tower fell within the internationally established scientific norms and that there were no scientific conclusions that would justify the plaintiffs' claims. Hence, according to the Council, the municipality reasoned correctly when balancing between the objectives of the improvement of mobile coverage and the potential adverse effects resulting from the proximity of transmission tower.

While this judgment does not directly relate to ICT standards, and regardless of one's views on radiation concerns and on scientific evidence supporting or refuting them, it illustrates the important societal, commercial, and regulatory dynamics of the increasing need for connectivity.

[1] D. Perkins, IAB considerations in appeal SNMPv2 SMI (March 1996), available at www.iab.org/appeals/1996-2/appeal-snmpv2-smi-appeal-by-mr-david-t-perkins-iab-consideration-march-1996/.

[2] Raad van State, Uitspraak 201903780/1/A1, ECLI:NL:RVS:2020:924.

ICT standards are the enablers of this connectivity; escaping their reach and scope is practically impossible due to the need for continuous, seamless connection between networks and devices – a new normative order created by the networks of technical infrastructure[3] and in which, unlike in Lessig's universe, decisions are carried out not by computers but by companies and individuals. This normative order comes with its limitations, with the "democracy of experts" replacing parliamentary democracy, with a blurred distinction between technical and commercial motives, and with engineers steering the regulatory decision-making.

This normative order also comes with trust. Trust that legislators place onto the fairness and inclusiveness of private regulators; trust that private regulatory bodies place on their members' expertise; trust of experts that the wider community will adopt the rules they have created and, finally, trust of the community that the legislator or judiciary will intervene if things go wrong. The ecosystem of ICT standardization is built on the network of trust and relies on the interplay between the different layers of regulation, many of which remain invisible. Decisions taken at any of these levels inevitably affect the other levels, as decisions taken by one type of stakeholders in the past affect the others in the future. Due process principles are just but one example of convoluted trust mechanisms on which ICT standardization relies.

This book is a first holistic attempt to provide a systemic and in-depth account of the legal and regulatory landscape in which the most prominent rule-making bodies in the ICT sector operate. Its conclusion that the national, regional, and international frameworks lag the evolution of ICT standardization would not surprise legal scholars. But an even bigger problem is the continuous reluctance of States to use the ambiguous formulation of the law in favor of enforcing due process and enhancing accountability of SDOs.

Given the tremendous regulatory freedom that SDOs enjoy, further conclusion that their processes are not, or not always, shielded from abuse and partiality is also not astonishing. In this network of trust, SDOs' confidence in their processes can easily clash with the confidence of legislators into their self-regulatory capacity. But this does not seem to bother SDOs, since the input, throughput, and output legitimacy of their standards is linked to the desires and conditions of their membership,

[3] See B. Kingsbury, 'Infrastructure and InfraReg: on rousing the international law "Wizards of Is"' (2019) 8 *Cambridge International Law Journal* 171–86.

and not those of the legislator. Indeed, to survive as private rule-makers, SDOs need their demos.

It would be reductive to believe that changing this entrenched regulatory arrangement would solve the problems of legitimacy and fill in all existing accountability gaps. Similar to the emergence of consortia as a response to the institutionalization and formalization of SDOs, tightening the regulatory muscle around SDOs' processes will most probably be met with hesitancy and averseness by the industry. SDOs know it, and so do the legislators, and both structure their rules accordingly.

This does not mean that SDOs' institutional and operational framework cannot change; conversely, demands for changes in governance modalities, and the counter-demands to undo them, are attributes of a healthy and resilient institutional ecosystem. Initially, procedural requirements for national standardization committees merely ensured that standards are not adopted over objections; nowadays, the applicable legal frameworks also refer to the principles that are more of administrative nature, such as appeal and review. These changes are also noticeable in SDOs' institutional architecture and their membership, which reflects the commercialization of the internet and redefinition of global technology leadership.[4]

In the current ecosystem, SDOs' processes should be improved "from within," starting with opening up their governance processes, clarifying the repercussions of noncompliance with procedural requirements and strengthening the feedback mechanisms that their procedures provide. This means, at the very least, implementing functioning and independent appeal mechanisms where their decisions, technical and procedural, can be challenged; where stakeholders can make their voice heard; and where an independent panel can perform weighing of procedural principles in a specific context. Such an appeal body will not be able to accommodate all views and address all interests, especially when those interests are far in the normative chain of ICT standardization; in this regard, SDOs should not stand in the way of subjecting their procedures to the judicial review, leaving the ultimate balancing between public and private to courts rather than to engineers.

That said, regardless of the mechanisms used by SDOs to enhance due process, procedural guarantees are only useful when stakeholders are aware of them and are familiar with their functioning. Naturally, there

[4] See Nickerson and zur Muelen, 'The ecology of standards processes'.

is a considerable risk that promoting due process mechanisms among SDOs' participants may overload the governance bodies of SDOs, resulting in expanding SDOs' administrative and management staff and thus, increasing the costs for their members; in the long run, however, it will reduce incentives to abuse SDOs' processes.

## Outlook on ICT Standardization and Global Trade

Technical harmonization has always been essential for international trade. Standards were high on the States' trade agenda when concluding multilateral trade agreements[5] as well as during the Brexit negotiations.[6] With growing digitalization, the role of ICT standards in international trade will increase even more, most likely questioning the WTO's status quo regarding SDOs developing such standards and triggering such widespread concerns as openness of ISBs, fairness towards developing countries, and informed participation in standards bodies. Another question that may arise relates to the protection of intellectual property offered by the TRIPS Agreement: recently, the EU filed a request for consultations at the WTO against Chinese policy prohibiting SEP holders from enforcing their patents in non-Chinese courts (the so-called "anti-suit injunctions").[7]

As any type of standardization, ICT standardization is susceptible to geopolitical developments. In this regard, States' political agenda can influence international competition in ICT standardization. The example of 5G demonstrates that rivalry for technological leadership does not only occur between companies, but also between States, and may even influence national innovation policies.[8] Unlike previous efforts in wireless standardization, IoT and 5G standardization is characterized by increasingly active participation of Chinese companies which, despite

[5] European Parliament, 'Trans-Pacific Partnership: geopolitical implications for EU-US Relations' (2016), available at www.europarl.europa.eu/meetdocs/2014_2019/documents/d-us/dv/03_1_tppstudy_/03_1_tppstudy_en.pdf.

[6] European Commission, Notice to Stakeholders, 'Withdrawal of the United Kingdom and EU food law and EU rules on quality schemes' (March 20, 2019) REV2, available at https://ec.europa.eu/info/sites/info/files/eu_food_law_en.pdf.

[7] Request for Consultations by the European Union (February 18, 2022), available at https://trade.ec.europa.eu/doclib/docs/2022/february/tradoc_160051.pdf.

[8] European Commission, '2021 rolling plan for ICT standardization', available at https://joinup.ec.europa.eu/collection/rolling plan ict standardisation/rolling plan 2021; 117th Congress, United States Innovation and Competition Act of 2021, S.1260 (adopted June 8, 2021).

being recent market entrants, have already established themselves as the leaders of future ICT standardization. At the same time, China's past endeavors to promote their home grown standards nationally and globally as a part of China's indigenous innovation policy have given rise to concerns of protectionism and unfair trading practices.[9] Global introduction of such standards as TD-SCDMA, EVD, and WAPI, although not crowned with success, demonstrated China's long-term strategy to lead global ICT standardization.[10]

The increasing importance of ICT standards for global trade and investment is also apparent from the Belt and Road Initiative (BRI) – China's long-term policy and investment program aiming to connect and integrate African and Asian countries into world trade.[11] Among other things, BRI aims to achieve "integration by infrastructure"; one of BRI's cornerstones, connectivity, directly relies on ICT standards, which are the main enablers of digital infrastructure. China's leading role in supplying these standards will arguably create larger controversies[12] and will spark off a wider academic debate.[13]

Geopolitical tensions in ICT standardization increase once countries adopt legal measures that influence relationships with foreign companies and, as a consequence, restrict their innovation capabilities. For instance, a number of Western governments have pledged to exclude China-based Huawei from participating in building their national 5G infrastructure due to security concerns related to Huawei's hardware,[14] while in 2018, the US prohibited its federal agencies from purchasing telecommunica-

[9] Such tension between "techno-nationalism" and "techno-globalism" still shapes industrial policies of many States and, in particular, in emerging economies, where governments employ a great variety of means to promote indigenous innovation. M. Murphree and D. Breznitz, 'Indigenous digital technology standards for development: the case of China' (2018) 1 *Journal of International Business Policy* 234–52.

[10] Murphree and Breznitz, 'Indigenous digital technology'; Wu, 'Interplay between patents and standards'; Gibson, 'Globalization and technology standards game'.

[11] For the official policy documents, see https://eng.yidaiyilu.gov.cn/info/iList.jsp?cat_id=10059&cur_page=1.

[12] E.g., Hoffmann et al., 'Standardising the splinternet'.

[13] See M. E. Erie and T. Streinz, 'The Beijing effect: China's "Digital Silk Road" as transnational data governance' (2021) 54 *NYU Journal of International Law and Politics* 1–92.

[14] See, for instance, Joint Media Release, 'Government provides 5G security guidance to Australian carriers' (August 23, 2018), available at www.minister.communications.gov.au/minister/mitch-fifield/news/government-provides-5g-security-guidance-australian-carriers.

tions equipment and services supplied by Chinese manufacturers.[15] In this light, the designation of Huawei and its affiliates on the US Export Administration Regulation (EAR) entity list (August 2019) was not met with an enthusiasm by US companies, for which Huawei is the largest trading partner. And, while restrictions on Huawei's participation in 5G standards developments have been lifted following the June 2020 clarifications of the US Commerce Department,[16] the questions regarding the actions that SDOs should take in case one of their participants is subjected to restrictions under national law, as well as their liability for the failure to take actions, still remained.

## Future Research Agenda

The need for standardization research in the context of various disciplines is ever-growing and is becoming increasingly relevant for lawyers. Legal research on ICT standards may advance traditional fields as antitrust, administrative law or trade law, but also span to private (and) transnational regulation. As a few possible paths, future studies may broaden and deepen the findings of this book by examining how modifications of SDOs' operational frameworks affected different groups of actors; study the appropriateness of SDOs in dealing with nontechnical issues; or focus on the birth and death of SDOs in a historical and institutional context, illustrating how procedural safeguards have evolved with time. Standardization as a research topic can also be approached from different angles, including geopolitical, institutional, and individual perspectives.

In particular, standardization scholarship and practice would benefit from uncovering the experience of *all* stakeholders participating in SDOs, providing an even more holistic picture of SDOs' compliance with due process principles and offering more constructive suggestions with regard to improvement of procedural guarantees in SDOs. Such an analysis goes beyond the scoping review of SDOs' procedures and embraces systematic observations of technical meetings as well as well-founded empirical predictions for the consequences of institutional changes within SDOs. It would require a high level of interdisciplinarity and should be ideally performed not only by lawyers, but also statisticians, political scientists, economists, and engineers with a profound

[15] See n. 6 in Part II and accompanied text.
[16] 85 FR 36719, 15 C.F.R 744 (June 18, 2020).

knowledge and understandings of complex technical issues, while also taking into account the specifics of particular organizations and their different roles in SDOs, for instance, leadership in their committees and governance bodies and individual reasons for participation.

Recognizing ICT standards as elements of global governance and as the metamorphosis of the current regulatory order presents methodological and normative avenues to examine the limits of private ordering. This book is just the beginning of the long journey into the mechanics and fundamentals of standardization.

# Annex I

## List of Interviews

Note: All interview transcripts and notes are on file with the author.

1. Interview with an environmental management and radiation expert, January 9, 2018.
2. Interview with experts from cyber police authority, January 11, 2018.
3. Interview with an expert from an SDO, January 12, 2018.
4. Interview with an industry expert, January 15, 2018.
5. Interview with an industry expert, January 16, 2018.
6. Interview with an industry expert* (former SDO governance bodies member), January 16, 2018.
7. Interview with an industry expert, January 17, 2018.
8. Interview with a legal counsel of an SDO, January 18, 2018.
9. Interview with an expert from an NSO, January 19, 2018.
10. Interview with an expert from an SDO, January 19, 2018.
11. Interview with an industry expert, January 23, 2018.
12. Interview with an industry expert, January 25, 2018.
13. Interview with an industry expert, February 1, 2018.
14. Interview with an industry expert, February 7, 2018.
15. Interview with an industry expert, February 13, 2018.
16. Industry expert's answers to the questionnaire, received February 15, 2018.
17. Interview with an industry expert, February 19, 2018.
18. Interview with an industry expert, February 21, 2018.
19. Interview with an expert from an SDO, April 4, 2018.
20. Interview with an industry expert, April 4, 2018.
21. Interview with an industry expert, April 9, 2018.
22. Interview with an industry expert, April 18, 2018.
23. Industry expert's answers to the questionnaire, received April 27, 2018.
24. Interview with an industry expert, June 13, 2018.

* Two different interviews with two different industry experts on the same date (16 January).

# BIBLIOGRAPHY

## Books and Edited Volumes


Auby, J. B. (ed.), *The Future of Administrative Law* (Paris: LexisNexis SA, 2019)

Bartosch, A., Braun, J., Koenig, C. and Romes, M. (eds.), *EC Competition and Telecommunications Law* (The Hague and London: Kluwer Law International, 2009)

Berman, H. J., *Law and Revolution: The Formation of the Western Legal Tradition* (Cambridge, MA: Harvard University Press, 1983)

Berman, P. S., *Global Legal Pluralism: A Jurisprudence of Law beyond Borders* (Cambridge: Cambridge University Press, 2012)

Bolin, S. (ed.), *The Standards Edge: Future Generations* (Ann Arbor: Sheridan Press, 2005)

Brunsson, N. and Jacobsson, B. (eds.), *A World of Standards* (New York: Oxford University Press, 2000)

Büthe, T. and Mattli, W., *The New Global Rulers: The Privatization of Regulation in the World Economy* (Princeton: Princeton University Press, 2011)

Cassese, S., Carotti, B., Casini, L., Macchi, M., MacDonald, E. and Savino, M. (eds.), *Global Administrative Law: Cases, Materials, Issues*, 2nd ed. (Rome: IRPA/IILJ, 2008)

Contreras, J. L. (ed.), *The Cambridge Handbook of Technical Standardization Law: Competition, Antitrust and Patents* (Cambridge: Cambridge University Press, 2018)

*The Cambridge Handbook of Technical Standardization Law: Further Intersection of Public and Private Law* (Cambridge: Cambridge University Press, 2019)

Contreras, J. L. and Jacob, M. (eds.), *Patent Pledges: Global Perspectives on Patent Law's Private Ordering Frontier* (Cheltenham: Edward Elgar, 2017)

Cornes, R. and Sandler, T., *The Theory of Externalities, Public Goods, and Club Goods* (Cambridge: Cambridge University Press, 1996)

Cutler, C., *Private Power and Global Authority: Transnational Merchant Law in the Global Political Economy* (Cambridge: Cambridge University Press, 2003)

Dasgupta, P. and Stoneman, P. (eds.), *Economic Policy and Technological Performance* (Cambridge: Cambridge University Press, 1987)

Delimatsis, P. (ed.), *The Law, Economics and Politics of International Standardization* (Cambridge: Cambridge University Press, 2015)

Delimatsis, P., Bijlmakers, S. and Borowicz, M. K. (eds.), *The Evolution of Transnational Rule-makers through Crises* (Cambridge: Cambridge University Press, forthcoming)

DeNardis, L., *The Global War for Internet Governance* (New Haven: Yale University Press, 2014)

*The Internet in Everything: Freedom and Security in a World with No Off Switch* (New Haven and London: Yale University Press, 2020)

(ed.), *Opening Standards: The Global Politics of Interoperability* (Cambridge, MA: MIT Press, 2011)

Dixit, A., *Lawlessness and Economics: Alternative Modes of Governance* (Princeton: Princeton University Press, 2004)

Djelic, M. and Sahlin-Andersson, K. (eds.), *Transnational Governance: Institutional Dynamics of Regulation* (Cambridge: Cambridge University Press, 2006)

Du, M., *The Regulation of Product Standards in World Trade Law* (Oxford: Hart Publishing, 2020)

Eliantonio, M. and Cauffman, C. (eds.), *The Legitimacy of Standardization as a Regulatory Technique in the EU: A Cross-disciplinary and Multi-level Analysis* (Cheltenham and Northampton: Edward Elgar Publishing, 2020)

Franck, T. M., *The Power of Legitimacy among Nations* (Oxford: Oxford University Press, 1990)

Goldsmith, J. and Wu, T., *Who Controls the Internet? Illusions of a Borderless World* (Oxford: Oxford University Press, 2006)

Hall, P. A. and Soskic, D. (eds.), *Varieties of Capitalism* (Oxford: Oxford University Press, 2001)

Harcourt, A., Christou, G. and Simpson, S., *Global Standard Setting in Internet Governance* (Oxford: Oxford University Press, 2020)

Held, D. and Koenig-Archibugi, M. (eds.), *Taming Globalization: Frontiers of Governance* (Oxford: Polity Press, 2003)

Hurrelmann, A., Schneider, S. and Steffek, J. (eds.), *Legitimacy in an Age of Global Politics* (London: Palgrave Macmillan, 2007)

Joerges, C. and Petersmann, E.-U. (eds.), *Constitutionalism, Multilevel Trade Governance and Social Regulation* (Oxford: Hart Publishing, 2006)

Keohane, R. O., *After Hegemony* (Princeton: Princeton University Press, 1984)

van Leeuwen, B., *European Standardization of Services and Its Impact on Private Law: Paradoxes of Convergence* (Oxford: Bloomsbury Publishing, 2017)

Lessig, L., *Codes and Other Laws of Cyberspace* (New York: Basic Books, 1999)

Lundqvist, B., *Standardization under EU Competition Rules and US Antitrust Laws: The Rise and Limits of Self-Regulation* (Cheltenham: Edward Elgar, 2014)

Mataija, M., *Private Regulation and the Internal Market: Sports, Legal Services and Standard Setting in EU Economic Law* (Oxford: Oxford University Press, 2016)

Matsushita, M., Schoenenbaum, T. J. and Mavroidis, P. C., *The World Trade Organization: Law, Practice, and Policy* (Oxford: Oxford International Law Library, 2015)

Mattli, W. and Woods, N. (eds.), *The Politics of Global Regulation* (Princeton: Princeton University Press, 2009)

Mavroidis, P., *Trade in Goods* (Oxford: Oxford University Press, 2012)

Mueller, D., *Public Choice III* (Cambridge: Cambridge University Press, 2003)

Murphy, C. and Yates, J., *The International Organization for Standardization (ISO): Global Governance through Voluntary Consensus* (London: Routledge, 2009)

Olson, M., *The Logic of Collective Action: Public Goods and the Theory of Groups* (Cambridge: Harvard University Press, 1965)

Ostrom, E., *Governing the Commons: The Evolution of Institutions for Collective Action* (Cambridge: Cambridge University Press, 1990)

Parker, C., Scott, C., Lacey, N. and Braithwaite, J. (eds.), *Regulating Law* (Oxford: Oxford University Press, 2004)

Peters, A., Koechlin, L., Foester, T. and Fenner Zinkernagel, G. (eds.), *Non-State Actors as Standard Setters* (Cambridge: Cambridge University Press, 2009)

Robert, H. M. and Robert, S. C., *Robert's Rules of Order Newly Revised*, 11th ed. (Boston: Da Capo Press, 2011)

Rogers, E. M., *Diffusion of Innovations: Modifications of a Model for Telecommunications* (New York: The Free Press New York, 1995)

Russel, A. L., *Open Standards and the Digital Age: History, Ideology, and Networks* (New York: Cambridge University Press, 2014)

Scharpf, F., *Governing in Europe: Effective and Democratic?* (Oxford: Oxford University Press, 1999)

Schepel, H., *The Constitution of Private Governance: Product Standards in the Regulation of Integrating Markets* (Oxford and Portland: Hart Publishing, 2005)

Schneiderman, R., *Modern Standardization: Case Studies at the Crossroads of Technology, Economics and Politics*, Standards Information Network (Hoboken: John Wiley & Sons, 2015)

Scholte, J. A. (ed.), *Building Global Democracy: Civil Society and Accountable Global Governance* (Cambridge: Cambridge University Press, 2011)

Shapiro, C. and Varian, H. W., *Information Rules: A Strategic Guide to the Network Economy* (Cambridge, MA: Harvard Business Review Press, 1998)

Sunstein, C. R., *Infotopia: How Many Minds Produce Knowledge* (New York: Oxford University Press, 2006)

Ullrich, H., Hilty, R. M., Lamping, M. and Drexl, J. (eds.), *TRIPS plus 20. From Trade Rules to Market Principles MPI Studies on Intellectual Property and Competition Law* (New York: Springer, 2016)

Weiss, T. G. and Thakur, R., *The UN and Global Governance: An Unfinished Journey* (Bloomington: Indiana University Press, 2010)

Whish, R. and Bailey, D., *Competition Law* (New York: Oxford University Press, 2015)

Wijckmans, F. and Tuytschaever, F., *Vertical Agreements in EU Competition Law* (Oxford: Oxford University Press, 2011)

Yates, J. and Murphy, C. N., *Engineering Rules: Global Standard Setting since 1880* (Baltimore: John Hopkins University Press, 2019)

Yin, R. K., *Case Study Research: Design and Methods*, 3rd ed. (Thousand Oaks: Sage Publications, 2003)

## Journal Articles

van Aaken, A. and Chambers, R., 'The accountability and independence of international election observers' (2009) 6 *International Organizations Law Review* 541–80

Abbott, K. W. and Snidal, D., 'Hard and soft law in international governance' (2000) 54 *International organizations* 421–56

'International "standards" and international governance' (2011) 8 *Journal of European Public Policy* 345–70

Alchian, A. A. and Demsetz, H., 'Production, information costs and economic organizations' (1972) 62 *American Economic Review* 777–95

An, B., 'Intellectual property rights in information and communications technology standardization: highly profiled disputes and collaboration potentials between the United States and China' (2009) 45 *Texas International Law Journal* 175–99

Austin, M. T. and Milner, H. V., 'Strategies of European standardization' (2001) 8 *Journal of European Public Policy* 411–31

Baron, J. and Gupta, K., 'Unpacking 3GPP standards' (2018) 27 *Journal of Economics and Management Strategy* 433–61

Baron, J. and Larouche, P., 'Antitrust and balance of interests in standards development: lessons from *NSS Labs. v. Symantec*' (September 2019) 2 *Competition Policy International* 2–10

Baron, J., Ménière, Y. and Pohlmann, T., 'Standards, consortia and innovation' (2014) 36 *International Journal of Industrial Organization* 22–35

Baron, J. A. and Pohlmann, T., 'Who cooperates in standards consortia: rivals or complementors?' (2013) 9 *Journal of Competition Law and Economics* 905–29

Bartley, T., 'Institutional emergence in an era of globalization: the rise of transnational private regulation of labor and environmental conditions' (2009) 113 *American Journal of Sociology* 297–351

Bekkers, R., Duysters, G. and Verspagen, B., 'Intellectual property rights, strategic technology agreements and market structure: the case of GSM' (2002) 31 *Research Policy* 1141–61

Benvenisti, E., 'The interplay between actors as determinant of the evolution of administrative law in international institutions' (2005) 68 *Law and Contemporary Problems* 319–40

Berger, T., 'Balancing barriers to trade and technical standards: potential impact on ICT industries' (2015) 17 *International Trade and Business Law Review* 315

Bernstein, L., 'Opting out of the legal system: extralegal contractual relations in the diamond industry' (1992) 21 *Journal of Legal Studies* 115–57

'Private commercial law in the cotton industry: creating cooperation through rules, norms and institutions' (2001) 99 *Michigan Law Review* 1724–90

Bernstein, S. and Hannah, E., 'Non-state global standard-setting and the WTO: legitimacy and the need for regulatory space' (2008) 11 *Journal of International Economic Law* 575–608

Bexell, M., 'Global governance, legitimacy and (de-)legitimation' (2014) 11 *Globalization* 289–99

Biddle, B., Curci, F. X., Haslach, T. F., Marchant, G. E., Askland, A. and Gaudet, L., 'The expanding role and importance of standards in the information and communications technology industry' (2012) 52 *Jurimetrics* 177–208

Blind, K. and Gauch, S., 'Trends in ICT standards in European standardization bodies and standards consortia' (2008) 32 *Telecommunications Policy* 503–13

Bodansky, D., 'The legitimacy of international governance: a coming challenge for international environmental law?' (1999) 93 *American Journal of International Law* 596–624

Borghetti, J. S. Nikolic, I. and Petit, N., 'FRAND licensing levels under EU law' (2021) 17 *European Competition Journal* 205–68

Boström, M. and Tamm Hallström, K., 'Global multi-stakeholder standard setters: how fragile are they?' (2013) 9 *Journal of Global Ethics* 93–110

'NGO power in global social and environmental standard-setting' (2010) 10 *Global Environmental Politics* 36–59

Botzem, S. and Dobusch, L., 'Standardization cycles: a process perspective on the formation and diffusion of transnational standards' (2012) 33 *Organizational Studies* 735–60

Bovens, M., 'Analysing and accessing accountability: a conceptual framework' (2007) 13 *European Law Review* 447–68

Bovens, M., Schillemans, T. and 't Hart, P., 'Does public accountability work? an assessment tool' (2008) 86 *Public Administration* 225–42

Bremer, E. S., 'American and European perspectives on private standards in public law' (2016) 91 *Tulane Law Review* 325–70

'On the costs of private standards in public law' (2015) 61 *Kansas Law Review* 279–333

Brunsson, N., Rasche, A. and Seidl, D., 'The dynamics of standardization: three perspectives on standards in organization studies' (2012) 33 *Organizational Studies* 613–32

Buchannan, A. and Keohane, R. O., 'The legitimacy of global governance institutions' (2006) 20 *Ethics and International Affairs* 405–37

Buratti, C., Conti, A., Dardari, D. and Verdone, R., 'An overview on wireless sensor networks technology and evolution' (2009) 9 *Sensors* 6869–96

Burk, D. L. and Gillespie, T. L., 'Autonomy and morality in DRM and anti-circumvention law' (2006) 4 *TripleC* 239–4

Büthe, T., 'Engineering uncontestedness? The origins and institutional development of the International Electrotechnical Commission (IEC)' (2010) 12 *Business and Politics* 1–62

'The globalization of health and safety standards: delegation of regulatory authority in the SPS Agreement of 1994 Agreement Establishing the World Trade Organization' (2008) 71 *Law and Contemporary Problems* 219–55

Cabral, L. and Salant, D., 'Evolving technologies and standards regulation' (2014) 36 *International Journal of Industrial Organization* 48–56

Cafaggi, F., 'The many features of transnational private rule-making: unexplored relationships between custom, jura mercatorum and global private regulation' (2015) 36 *University of Pennsylvania Journal of International Law* 875–938

'New foundations of transnational private regulation' (2011) 38 *Journal of Law and Society* 20–49

Cafaggi, F. and Janczuk, A., 'Private regulation and legal integration: the European example' (2010) 12 *Business and Politics* (3), 1–40

Callies, G. P. and Renner, M., 'Between law and social norms: the evolution of global governance' (2009) 22 *Ratio Juris* 260–80

Cannataci, J. A. and Bonnici, J. P. M., 'Can self-regulation satisfy the transnational requisite of successful internet regulation?' (2010) 17 *International Review of Law Computers & Technology* 51–61

Cantero Gamito, M., 'Europeanization through standardization: ICT and telecommunications' (2018) 37 *Yearbook of European Law* 395–423

Cassese, S., 'Administrative law without the state? The challenge of global regulation' (2005) 37 *N.Y.U. International Law and Politics* 663–94

Cath, C. and Floridi, L., 'The design of internet architecture by the Internet Engineering Task Force (IETF) and human rights' (2017) 23 *Science and Engineering Ethics* 449–68

Chappatte, P., 'FRAND Commitments: the case for antitrust intervention' (2009) 5 *European Competition Journal* 319–46

Chiao, B., Lerner, J. and Tirole, J., 'The rules of standard-setting organizations: an empirical analysis' (2007) 38 *The RAND Journal of Economics* 905–30

Clark, I., 'Legitimacy in a global order' (2003) 29 *Review of International Studies* 75–95

Conde Gallego, B. and Drexl, J., 'IoT connectivity standards: how adaptive is the current SEP regulatory framework?' (2019) 50 *IIC – International Review of Intellectual Propertly and Competition Law* 135–56

Contreras, J. L., 'Divergent patterns of engagement in internet standardization: Japan, Korea and China' (2014) 38 *Telecommunications Policy* 916–34

'From private ordering to public law: the legal frameworks governing Standards-Essential Patents' (2017) 30 *Harvard Journal of Law and Technology* 211–31

'A tale of two layers: patents, standardization and the internet' (2016) 93 *Denver Law Review* 853–95

'Understanding "balance" requirement for standards-development organizations' (2019) 2 *CPI Antitrust Chronicle* 1–16

Cunningham, L. A., 'Private standards in public law: copyright, lawmaking and the case of accounting' (2005) 104 *Michigan Law Review* 291–344

Curran, P., 'Standard-setting organizations: patents, price fixing, and per se legality' (2003) 70 *The University of Chicago Law Review* 983–1009

Cusumano, M. A., Mylonadis, Y. and Rosenbloom, R. S., 'Strategic maneuvering and mass-market dynamics: the triumph of VHS over beta' (1992) 66 *Business History Review* 51–94

Cutler, A. C., 'The legitimacy of private transnational governance: experts and the transnational market for force' (2010) 8 *Socio-Economic Review* 157–85

Daubs, M. S., 'HTML5, Digital Rights Management (DRM) and the rhetoric of openness' (2017) 3 *Journal of Media Critiques* 77–94

David, P. A. and Greenstein, S., 'The economics of compatibility standards: an introduction to recent research' (1990) 1 *Economics of Innovation and New Technology* 3–41

David, P. A. and Shurmer, M., 'Formal standard-setting for global telecommunications and information services: towards an institutional regime transformation?' (1996) 20 *Telecommunications Policy* 789–815

De Vries, H., 'Standardization – what's in a name?' (1997) 4 *Terminology – International Journal of Theoretical and Applied Issues in Specialized Communication* 55–83

Delcamp, H. R. and Leiponen, A., 'Innovating standards through informal consortia: the case of wireless telecommunications' (2014) 36 *International Journal of Industrial Organization* 36–47

Delimatsis, P., 'The future of transnational self-regulation enforcement and compliance in professional services' (2017) 40 *Hasting International and Comparative Law Review* 1–67

'Global standard-setting 2.0: how the WTO spotlights ISO and impacts the transnational standard-setting process' (2018) 28 *Duke Journal of Comparative and International Law* 273–326

Delimatsis, P., Kanevskaia, O. and Verghese, Z. G., 'Strategic behaviour in standards development organizations in times of crisis' (2021) 2 *Texas Intellectual Property Law Journal* 127–85

Dimitriou, N., Sarakis, L., Loukatos, D., Kormentzas, G. and Skianis, C., 'Vertical Handover (VHO) framework for future collaborative wireless networks' (2011) 21 *International Journal of Network Management* 548–64

Dixit, A., 'Governance institutions and economic activity' (2009) 99 *American Economic Review* 5–24

'Trade expansion and contract enforcement' (2003) 111 *Journal of Political Economy* 1293–317

Dolmans, M., 'Standards for standards' (2002) 26 *Fordham International Law Journal* 163–208

Du, D. and Deng, F., 'International standards as global public goods in the world trading system' (2016) 43 *Legal Issues of Economic Integration* 113–44

Eliantonio, M. and Medzmariashvili, M., 'Hybridity under scrutiny: how European standardization shakes the foundations of EU constitutional and internal market law' (2017) 44 *Legal Issues of Economic Integration* 323–35

van den Ende, J., Van den Kaa, G., Den Uijl, S. and De Vries, H. J., 'The paradox of standard flexibility: the effects of co-evolution between standard and inter-organizational network' (2012) 33 *Organization Studies* 705–36

Erie, M. E. and Streinz, T. 'The Beijing effect: China's "Digital Silk Road" as transnational data governance' (2021) 54 *NYU Journal of International Law and Politics* 1–92

Erman, E., 'Global political legitimacy beyond justice and democracy?' (2016) 8 *International Theory* 29–62

Farina, E. M. M. Q., Gutman, G. E., Lavarello, P. J., Nunes, R. and Reardon, T., 'Private and public milk standards in Argentina and Brazil' (2005) 30 *Food Policy* 302–15

Farrell, J. and Saloner, G., 'Coordination through committees and markets' (1998) 19 *The RAND Journal of Economics* 235–52

Farrell, J., Hayes, J., Shapiro, C. and Sullivan, T., 'Standard setting, patents, and hold-up' (2007) 74 *Antitrust Law Review* 603–70

Fisher, E., 'Transparency and administrative law: a critical evolution' (2010) 63 *Current Legal Problems* 272–314

Fontanelli, F., 'ISO and Codex standards and international trade law: what gets said is not what's heard' (2011) 60 *International and Comparative Law Quarterly* 895–932

Fuentelsaz, L., Maicas, J. P. and Polo, Y., 'Switching costs, network effects, and competition in the European mobile telecommunications industry' (2012) 23 *Information Systems Research* 93–108

Funk, J. L. and Methe, D. T., 'Market- and committee-based mechanisms in the creation and diffusion of global industry standards: the case of mobile communication' (2001) 30 *Research Policy* 589–610

Gandal, N. Salant, D. and Waverman, L., 'Standards in wireless telephone networks' (2003) 27 *Telecommunications Policy* 325–32

Garud, R. and Kumaraswamy, A., 'Changing competitive dynamics in network industries: an exploration of Sun Microsystems' open systems strategy' (1993) 14 *Strategic Management* 351–69

Geradin, D., 'The European Commission policy towards the licensing of standard-essential patents: where do we stand?' (2013) 9 *Journal of Competition Law and Economics* 1125–45

van Gestel, R. and Micklitz, H., 'European integration through standardization: how judicial review is breaking down the club house of private standardization bodies' (2013) 50 *Common Market Law Review* 145–81

Gibson, C. S., 'Globalization and technology standards game: balancing concerns of protectionism and intellectual property in international standards' (2007) 22 *Berkley Technology Law Review* 1403–84

Ginsburg, D. H., Owings, T. M. and Wright, J. D., 'Enjoining injunctions: the case against antitrust liability for standard essential patent holders who seek injunctions' (2014) 14 *The Antitrust Source* 1–7

Goerke, L. and Holler, M., 'Strategic standardization in Europe: a public choice perspective' (1998) 6 *European Journal of Law and Economics* 95–112

Goodin, R. E., 'Enfranchising all affected interests and its alternatives' (2007) 35 *Philosophy and Public Affairs* 40–68

Grant, R. W. and Keohane, R. O., 'Accountability and abuses of power in world politics' (2005) 99 *American Political Science Review* 29–43

Greif, A., Milgrom, P. and Weingast, B., 'Coordination, commitment and enforcement: the case of the merchant guild' (1994) 102 *The Journal of Political Economy* 745–76

Gulbrandsen, L. H., 'Accountability arrangements in non-state standards organizations: instrumental design and imitation' (2008) 15 *Organization* 563–83

Gunningham, N. and Rees, J., 'Industry self-regulation: an institutional perspective' (1997) 19 *Law and Policy* 363–414

Gupta, K., 'The patent policy debate in a high-tech world' (2013) 9 *Journal of Competition Law and Economics* 827–58

Gupta, K. and Effraimidis, G., 'IEEE patent policy revisions: an empirical examination of impact' (2019) 64 *The Antitrust Bulletin* 151–71

Hadfield, G. K. and Weingast, B. R., 'What is law? A coordination model of the characteristics of legal order' (2012) 4 *Journal of Legal Analysis* 471–514

Harlow, C., 'Global administrative law: the quest for principles and values' (2006) 17 *The European Journal of International Law* 187–214

Hart, O., Shleifer, A. and Vishny, R. W., 'The proper scope of government: theory and an application to prisons' (1997) 112 *Quarterly Journal of Economics* 1127–61

Héritier, A. and Eckert, S., 'New modes of governance in the shadow of hierarchy: self-regulation by industry in Europe' (2007) 28 *Journal of Public Policy* 113–38

Hettne, J., 'Standards, barriers to trade and EU internal market rules: need for a renewed approach?' (2017) 44 *Legal Issues of Economic Integration* 409–20

Hinricher, J., 'The law-making of the International Telecommunication Union (ITU): providing a new source of international law?' (2004) 64 *ZaöR* 489–501

Hoffinger, R., 'The 2015 DOJ IEEE business review letter: the triumph of industrial policy preferences over law and evidence' (2015) 3 *CPI Antitrust Chronicle* 1–24

Hoffmann, S., Lazanski, D. and Taylor, E., 'Standardising the splinternet: how China's technical standards could fragment the Internet' (2020) 5 *Journal of Cyber Policy* 239–64

Homiller, D., 'Patent misuse in patent pool licensing: from national harrow to "the nine no-nos" to not likely' (2006) 5 *Duke Law and Technology Review* 1–21

Howse, R. and Teitel, R., 'Beyond compliance: rethinking why international law really matters' (2010) 1 *Global Policy* 127–36

Hurd, I., 'Legitimacy and authority in international politics' (1999) 53 *International Organization* 379–408

Hurrell, A., 'Legitimacy and the use of force: can the circle be squared?' (2005) 31 *Review of International Studies* 15–32

Jakobsen, K. A., 'Revisiting standard-setting organizations' patent policies' (2004) 3 *Northwestern Journal of Technology and Intellectual Property* 43–60

Kallestrup, M., 'Stakeholder participation in European standardization: a mapping and an assessment of three categories of regulation' (2017) 44 *Legal Issues of Economic Integration* 381–94

Kanevskaia, O., 'ICT standards bodies and international trade: what role for the WTO' (2022) 56(3) *Journal of World Trade* 429–52

Kappos, D. and (The Honorable) Michel, P. R., 'The smallest salable patent-practicing unit: observations on its origins, development, and future' (2018) 32 *Berkley Technology Law Journal* 1433–56

Karachalios, K., 'Fundamental uncertainty at the intersection between patents and standards' (November/December 2015) *The Patent Lawyer* 33–5

Keil, T., 'De facto standardization through alliances: lessons from Bluetooth' (2002) 26 *Telecommunications Policy* 205–13

Kindleberger, C. P., 'Standards as public, collective and private goods' (1983) 36 *Kyklos* 377–96

Kingsbury, B., 'Infrastructure and InfraReg: on rousing the international law "Wizards of Is"' (2019) 8 *Cambridge International Law Journal* 171–86

Kingsbury, B., Krisch, N. and Stewart, R. B., 'The emergence of global administrative law' (2005) 68 *Law and Contemporary Problems* 15–61

Koenig-Archibugi, M., 'How to diagnose democratic deficits in global politics: the use of the "all-affected" principle' (2017) 9 *International Theory* 171–202

Lane, C., 'The social regulation of inter-firm relations in Britain and Germany: market rules, legal norms and technical standards' (1997) 21 *Cambridge Journal of Economics* 197–215

Larouche, P. and Schuett, F., 'Repeated interactions in standard setting' (2018) 28 *Journal of Economics and Management Strategy* 488–509

Larrain Aylwin, M. and Prüfer, J., 'Trade associations, lobbying and endogenous institutions' (2015) 7 *Journal of Legal Analysis* 467–516

Layne-Farrar, A. and Stark, R., 'License to all or access to all? A law and economics assessment of standard development organizations' licensing rules' (2020) 88 *George Washington Law Review* 1307–49

Layne-Farrar, A., Llobet, G. and Padilla, J., 'Payment and participation: the incentive to join cooperating standard setting efforts' (2014) 23 *Journal of Economics and Management Strategy* 24–49

Lazanski, D., 'Governance in international technical standards making: a tripartite model' (2019) 4 *Journal of Cyber Policy* 362–79

Lee, J., 'Implementing the FRAND standard in China' (2016) 19 *Venderbilt Journal of Entertainment & Technology Law* 37–85

Leiponen, A., 'Competing through cooperation: the organization of standard setting in wireless telecommunications' (2008) 54 *Management Science* 1904–19

Lemley, M. A., 'Intellectual property rights and standard-setting organizations' (2002) 90 *California Law Review* 1889–980

Lemley, M.A. and Shapiro, C. 'Patent holdup and royalty stacking' (2007) 85 *Texas Law Review* 1991–2049

Lerner, J. and Tirole, J., 'A model of forum shopping' (2006) 96 *American Economic Review* 1091–113

'Standard-essential patents' (2015) 123 *Journal of Political Economy* 547–86

Lindsay, M. A. and Karachalios, K., 'Updating a patent policy: the IEE experience' (2015) 3 *CPI Antitrust Chronicle* 1–6

Liu, H. W., 'International standards in flux: a Balkanized ICT standard-setting paradigm and its implications for the WTO' (2014) 13 *Journal of International Economic Law* 551–600

Lundqvist, B., 'European harmonized standards as "part of EU law": the implications of the *James Elliott* case for copyright protection and, possibly, for EU competition law' (2017) 44 *Legal Issues of Economic Integration* 421–36

Markus, M. L., Steinfield, C. W. and Wigard, R. T. 'Industry-wide information systems standardization as collective action: the case of the U.S. residential mortgage industry' (2006) 30 *MIS Quarterly* 439–65

Masten, S. E. and Prüfer, J., 'On the evolution of collective enforcement institutions: communities and courts' (2014) 43 *Journal of Legal Studies* 359–400

Mataija, M., 'Leveraging trade law for governance reform: the impact of the WTO agreement on technical barriers to trade on private standard-setting' (2019) 2 *European Review of Private Law* 293–318

Matsushita, M., 'The structural impediments initiative: an example of bilateral trade negotiation' (1991) 12 *Michigan Journal of International Law* 436–49

Mattli, W. and Büthe, T., 'Setting international standards: technological rationality or primacy of power' (2003) 56 *World Politics* 1–42

Mavroidis, P. C., 'Last mile for tuna (to a safe harbour): what is the TBT Agreement all about?' (2019) 30 *The European Journal of International Law* 279–301

Mavroidis, P. C. and Wolfe, R., 'Private standards and the WTO: reclusive no more' (2017) 16 *World Trade Review* 1–24

Mazzoleni, R. and Nelson, R. R., 'The benefits and costs of strong patent protection: a contribution to the current debate' (1998) 27 *Research Policy* 273–84

McRae, D., 'Measuring the effectiveness of WTO dispute settlement system' (2008) 3 *Asian Journal of WTO & International Health Law and Policy* 1–20

Medzmariashvili, M., 'Delegation of rulemaking power to European standards organizations: reconsidered' (2017) 44 *Legal Issues of Economic Integration* 353–66

Meidinger, E., 'Administrative law of global private–public regulation: the case of forestry' (2006) 17 *European Journal of International Law* 47–87

Meyer, J. W. and Rowan, B., 'Institutional organizations: formal structure as myth and ceremony' (1977) 83 *American Journal of Sociology* 340–63

Milgrom, P., North, D. C. and Weingast, B. R., 'The role of institutions in the revival of trade: the law merchant, private judges, and the champagne fairs' (199) 2 *Economics and Politics* 1–23

Moravczik, A., 'Is there a "democratic deficit" in world politics? a framework for analysis' (2004) 39 *Government and Opposition* 336–63

Muir, A., 'The race to safety: how private lawmaking and voluntary-standard adoption can inspire a global regime that strengthens and harmonizes product safety standards' (2016) 23 *Indiana Journal of Global Legal Studies* 323–47

Mulgan, R., 'Accountability: an ever-expanding concept?' (2000) 78 *Public Administration* 555–73

Murphree, M. and Breznitz, D., 'Indigenous digital technology standards for development: the case of China' (2018) 1 *Journal of International Business Policy* 234–52

Nanni, R., 'The "China" question in mobile Internet standard-making: insights from expert interviews' (2021) 45 *Telecommunications Policy* 1–12

Nanz, P. and Steffek, J. 'Global governance, participation and the public sphere' (2004) 39 *Government and Opposition* 314–35

Nadvi, K., 'Global standards, global governance and the organization of global value chains' (2008) 8 *Journal of Economic Geography* 323–43

Negus, K. J. and Petrick, A., 'History of wireless local area networks (WLANs) in the unlicensed band' (2009) 11 *info* 36–56

Nickerson, J. F. and zur Muelen, M., 'The ecology of standards processes: insights from internet standards making' (2006) 20 *MIS Quarterly, Special Issue on Standards Making* 467–88

Noel, M. and Schankerman, M., 'Strategic patenting and software innovation' (2013) 61 *The Journal of Industrial Economics* 481–520

Nollkaemper, P. A. and Curtin, D., 'Conceptualizing accountability in international and European law' (2007) 36 *Netherlands Yearbook of International Law* 3–20

Okediji, R., 'Legal innovation in international intellectual property relations: revisiting twenty-one years of the TRIPS agreement' (2014) 36 *University of Pennsylvania Journal of International Law* 191

O'Neill, K., Balsiger, J. and VanDeveer, S. D., 'Actors, norms, and impact: recent international cooperation theory and the influence of the agent-structure debate' (2004) 7 *Annual Review of Political Science* 149–75

Oshri, I. and Weeber, C., 'Cooperation and competition standard-setting activities in the digitalized era: the case of wireless information devices' (2006) 18 *Technology Analysis and Strategic Management* 265–83

Park, S., 'Quantitative analysis of network externalities in competing technologies: the VCR case' (2004) 86 *The Review of Economics and Statistics* 937–45

Partiti, E., 'What use of an unloaded gun? The substantive discipline of the WTO TBT code of good practice and its application to private standards pursuing public objectives' (2017) 20 *Journal of International Economic Law* 829–54

Pauwelyn, J., Wessel, R. A. and Wouters, J., 'When structures become shackles: stagnation and dynamics in international law-making' (2014) 25 *The European Journal of International Law* 733–63

Pelkmans, J., 'The new approach to technical harmonization and standardization' (1987) XXV *Journal of Common Market Studies* (3), 249–69

Petit, N., 'The IEEE-SA revised patent policy and its definition of "reasonable" rates: a transatlantic antitrust divide?' (2017) 27 *Fordham Intellectual Property, Media and Entertainment Law Journal* 211–51

'Injunctions for FRAND-pledged SEPs: the quest for an appropriate test of abuse under Art. 102 TFEU' (2017) 9 *European Competition Journal* 677–719

Pohlmann, T., 'The evolution of ICT standards consortia' (2014) 93 *Digiworld Economic Journal* 17–40

Pusceddu, P., 'Hic sunt dracones? Mapping the legal framework of China's innovation policy: standardization and IPRs' (2020) 51 *International Review of Intellectual Property and Competition Law* 559–93

Ragavan, S., Murphy, B. and Dave, R., 'FRAND v. compulsory licensing: the lesser of the two evils' (2016) 14 *Duke Law & Technology Review* 83–120

Rubin, J. L., 'Patents, antitrust and rivalry in standard-setting' (2007) 38 *Rutgers Law Journal* 509–38

Russel, A., '"Rough consensus and running code" and the internet-OSI standard wars' (2006) 28 *IEEE Annals of the History of Computing* 48–61

Rysman, M. and Simcoe, T., 'Patents and the performance of voluntary standard-setting organizations' (2008) 54 *Management Science* 1920–34

Samuelson, P. A., 'The pure theory of public expenditures' (1954) 36 *The Review of Economics and Statistics* 387–9

Schepel, H., 'New approach to new approach: the juridification of harmonized standards in EU law' (2013) 12 *Maastricht Journal of European and Comparative Law* 521–33

Schmidt, V., 'Democracy and legitimacy in the European Union revisited: input, output and "throughput"' (2013) 61 *Political Studies* 2–22

Schmidt, V. and Wood, M., 'Conceptualizing throughput legitimacy: procedural mechanisms of accountability, transparency, inclusiveness and openness in EU governance' (2019) 97 *Public Administration* 727–40

Scott, C., Cafaggi, F. and Senden, L., 'The conceptual and constitutional challenge of transnational private regulation' (2011) 38 *Journal of Law and Society* 1–19

Senden, L., 'The constitutional fit of european standardization put to the test' (2017) 44 *Legal Issues of Economic Integration* 337–52

Shanin, J., 'The European Union's performance in the International Telecommunications Union' (2011) 33 *Journal of European Integration* 683–98

Shapiro, C., 'Navigating the patent thicket: cross licenses, patent pools, and standard setting' (2001) 1 *Innovation Policy and the Economy* 119–50

Shapiro, C. and Lemley, M., 'The role of antitrust in preventing patent holdup' (2020) 168 *University of Pennsylvania Law Review* 2019–63

Shapiro, M., '"Deliberative," "independent" technocracy v. democratic politics: will the globe echo the EU?' (2005) 68 *Law and Contemporary Problems* 341–56

Sheremata, W. A., 'Competing through innovation in network markets: strategies for challengers' (2004) 29 *The Academy of Management Review* 359–77

Sidak, J. G., 'The antitrust division's devaluation of standard-essential patents' (2015) 48 *The Georgetown Law Journal Online* 48–73

Simcoe, T., 'Standard setting committees: consensus governance for shared technology platforms' (2012) 102 *American Economic Review* 305–36

Smith, H. E., 'Property as platform: coordinating standards as technological innovation' (2013) 9 *Journal of Competition Law and Economics* 1057–89

Spulber, D. F., 'Innovation economics: the interplay among technology standards, competitive conduct, and economic performance' (2013) 9 *Journal of Competition Law and Economics* 777–825

Staiger, R. W. and Sykes, A., 'International trade, national treatment and domestic regulation' (2011) 40 *Journal of Legal Studies* 149–203

Stasavage, D., 'Open-door or closed-door? transparency in domestic and international bargaining' (2004) 58 *International Organization* 667–703

Steffek, J., 'Discursive legitimation in environmental governance' (2009) 11 *Forest Policy and Economics* 313–18

'The output legitimacy of international organizations and the global public interest' (2015) 7 *International Theory* 263–93

Stewart, R. B., 'Remedying disregard in global regulatory governance: accountability, participation and responsiveness' (2014) 108 *The American Journal of International Law* 211–70

Stringham, E., 'The extralegal development of securities trading in seventeenth-century Amsterdam' (2003) 43 *The Quarterly Review of Economics and Finance* 321–44

Sun, N., 'Piercing the veil of national security: does China's banking IT security regulation violate the TBT agreement' (2016) 11 *Asian Journal of WTO and International Health Law and Policy* 395–436

Swinnen, J. and Vandermoortele, T., 'Trade and the political economy of standards' (2012) 11 *World Trade Review* 390–400

Sykes, A. O., 'Regulatory consistency requirements in international trade' (2017) 49 *Arizona State Law Journal* 821–66

Teubner, L. K., Henkel, J. and Bekkers, R., 'Industry consortia in mobile telecommunications standards setting: purpose, organization and diversity' (2021) 45 *Telecommunications Policy* 1–20

Trachtman, J. P., 'Toward open recognition? Standardization and regional integration under Article XXIV of GATT' (2003) 6 *Journal of International Economic Law* 459–92

Trubek, D. M., 'The political economy of the rule of law: the challenge of the new developmental state' (2009) 1 *Hague Journal on the Rule of Law* 28–32

Tsang, K. F. and Lee, J. A., 'Unfriendly choice of law in FRAND' (2019) 59 *Virginia Journal of International Law* 220–305

Tushman, M. and Rosenkopf, L., 'Organizational determinants of technological change: towards a sociology of technological evolution' (1992) 14 *Research in Organizational Behaviour* 311–47

Ullrich, H., 'Expansionist intellectual property protection and reductionist competition rules: a TRIPS perspective' (2004) 7 *Journal of International Economic Law* 401–30

Verbruggen, P., 'Good governance of private standardization and the role of tort law' (2019) 2 *European Review of Private Law* 319–52

'Introduction: regulating private regulators: understanding the role of private law' (2019) 2 *European Review of Private Law* 175–96

Verbruggen, P. and van Leeuwen, B., 'The liability of notified bodies under the EU's new approach' (2018) 43 *European Law Review* (3), 394–498

Vincent, C. and Camp, J., 'Looking to the internet for models of governance' (2004) 6 *Ethics and Information Technology* 161–73

Volpato, A., 'Harmonised standards before the ECJ: *James Elliott Construction*' (2017) 54 *Common Market Law Review* 591–603

Weiser, P. J., 'Internet governance, standard setting and self-regulation' (2001) 28 *Northern Kentucky Law Review* 822–46

Weiss, M. and Sirbu, M., 'Technological choice in voluntary standards committees: an empirical analysis' (1990) 1 *Economics of Innovation and New Technologies* 111–33

Weitzel, T., Beimborn, D. and König, W., 'A unified economic model of standard diffusion: the impact of standardization cost, network effects, and network topology' (2006) 30 *MIS Quarterly* 489–514

Werle, R., 'Institutional aspects of standardization – jurisdictional conflicts and the choice of standardization organizations' (2001) 8 *Journal of European Public Policy* 392–410

Werle, R. and Iversen, E.J., 'Promoting legitimacy in technical standardization' (2006) 2 *Science, Technology and Innovation Studies* 19–39

Wiegmann, P., Blind, K. and De Vries, H., 'Multi-mode standardization: a critical review and a research agenda' (2017) 46 *Research Policy* 1370–86

Williamson, O. E., 'Transaction-cost economics: the governance of contractual relations' (1979) 22 *The Journal of Law and Economics* 233–61

'The economics of governance' (2005) 95 *American Economic Review* 1–18

Wouters, J. and Geraets, D., 'Private food standards and the World Trade Organization: some legal considerations' (2012) 11 *World Trade Review* 479–89

Zingales, N. and Kanevskaia, O., 'The IEEE-SA patent policy update under the lens of EU competition law' (2016) 12 *European Competition Journal* 195–235

van der Zee, E., 'Disciplining private standards under the SPS and TBT agreement: a plea for market-state procedural guidelines' (2018) 52 *Journal of World Trade* 393–414

## Working Papers and Unpublished Material

Baron, J. and Kanevskaia, O., 'Global competition for leadership positions in standards development organizations" (March 2021)

Baron, J. and Pohlmann, T., 'Mapping standards to patents using databases of declared standard-essential patents and systems of technological classification' (2015)

Bekkers, R. and West, J., 'IPR standardization policies and strategic patenting in UMTS' (2008) in *Proceedings of 25th DRUID Celebration Conference*, Copenhagen, June 17–20, 2008

Besheim, M. and Dingwerth, S., 'Procedural legitimacy and private transnational governance: are the good ones doing better?' (June 2008) SFB-Governance Working Paper Series No. 14

Biddle, B., White, A. and Woods, S., 'How many standards in a laptop? (and other empirical questions)' (2010) in *Proceedings from K-2010: ITU Kaleidoscope Academic Conference – Beyond the Internet? Innovations and for Future Networks and Services*, Pune, India, December 13–15, 2010

Black, J., 'Calling regulators to account: challenges, capacities and prospects' (2012) LSE Law, Society and Economy Working Papers 15/2012

'Constructing and contesting legitimacy and accountability in polycentric regulatory regimes' (2008) LSE Law, Society and Economy Working Papers, n. 02-2008

'Learning from regulatory disasters' (2014) LSE Law, Society and Economy Working Papers 24/2014

Cafaggi, F., 'A comparative analysis of transnational private regulation: legitimacy, quality, effectiveness and enforcement' (2014) EUI Department of Law Research Paper No. 2014/145

Coglianese, A. and Mendelson, E., 'Meta-regulation and self-regulation' (2012) U of Penn Law School, Public Law Research Paper No. 12-11

Contreras, J., 'Intellectual property pools and aggregation' (2021) University of Utah College of Law Research Paper No. 408

Curtin, D. and. Senden, L., 'Public accountability of transnational private regulation: chimera or reality?' (2011) Amsterdam Centre for European Law and Governance Working Paper Series 2011-06

DeLacey, B., Herman, K., Kiron, D. and Lerner, J., 'Strategic behavior in standard-setting organizations' (2006) Harvard NOM Working Paper No. 903214

Delimatsis, P., 'Into the abyss of standard-setting: an analysis of procedural and substantive guarantees within ISO' (November 2014) TILEC Discussion Paper 0042-2014

Ernst, D., 'America's voluntary standards system: a "best practice" model for innovation policy?' (February 2012) East-West Center Working Paper No. 128

'Indigenous innovation and globalization. The challenge for China's standardization strategy' (2011), available at www.eastwestcenter.org/sites/default/files/private/ernstindigenousinnovation.pdf

Ernst, D. and Martin, S, 'Adjusting to the global knowledge economy? Recent developments in China's WAPI Standard' (2010) Unpublished manuscript, East-West Center, Honolulu.

Franck, T. M., 'Democracy, legitimacy and the rule of law: linkages' (1999) Working Paper 2, New York University School of Law Public Law and Legal Theory Working Papers Series

Geradin, D., Layne-Farrar, A. and Padilla, J., 'Royalty stacking in high tech industries: separating myth from reality' (2007) CEPR Discussion Paper No. DP6091

Greenstein, S. M. and Rysman, M., 'Coordination costs and standard setting: lessons from 56K modems' (2004) Center for the Study of Industrial Organization Working Paper #0056

Gupta, K., 'The role of SMEs and startups in standards development' (2017)

Gupta, K. and Snyder, M., 'Smart phone litigation and standard essential patents' (2014) Working Paper Series No. 14006, Hoover Institution Working Group on Intellectual Property, Innovation, and Prosperity Stanford University

Hachez, N. and Wouters, J., 'Promoting the rule of law: a benchmarks approach' (2013) KU Leuven Centre for Global Governance Studies Working Paper No. 105

Halpin, H., 'The crisis of standardizing DRM: the case of W3C encrypted media extensions' (2017) in *Proceedings of the 7th International Conference, SPACE 2017*, Goa, India, December 13–17, 2017

Joerges, C., Schepel, H. and Vos, E., 'The law's problems with involvement of non-governmental actors in Europe's legislative processes: the case of standardization under the new approach' (1999) EUI Working Paper No. 99/9

Katznelson, R., 'Perilous deviations from FRAND harmony: operational pitfalls of the 2015 IEEE patent policy' (2015) in *Proceedings of IEEE 9th International Conference on Standardization and Innovation in Information Technology (SIIT)*

Keohane, R. O., 'The contingent legitimacy of multilateralism' (2006) GARNET Working Paper No. 09/06

Kleinhans, J. P., '5G vs. national security: a European perspective' (February 2019)

Lindsay, M. A., Business review letter request to Assistant Attorney General, W. J. Baer (September 30, 2014)

Madnick, S. E., 'The misguided silver bullet: what XML will and will NOT do to help information integration' (2001) Sloan Working Paper 4185-01

Mallinson, K., 'Development of innovative new standards jeopardised by IEEE patent policy' (September 2017)

Murphy, C. and Yates, J., 'Coordinating international standards: the formation of the ISO' (2006)

Ohana, G., 'Diversity in standards development: a response to Katznelson' (2015) in *Proceedings of IEEE 9th International Conference on Standardization and Innovation in Information Technology (SIIT)*

Pauwelyn, J., Wessel, R. A. and Wouters, J., 'Global governance as public authority: structures, contestation and normative change' (2011) Jean Monnet Working Paper No. 06/11

Ping, W., 'A brief history of standards and standardization organizations: a Chinese perspective' (2011) East-West Center Working Papers: Economic Series No. 117

Pohlmann, T., 'Empirical study on patenting and standardization activity in IEEE' (March 2017) IPlytics GmbH

Price, M. E. and Verhulst, S. G., 'In search of the self: charting the course of self-regulation on the internet in a global environment' (2000) Cardozo Law School, Public Law Working Paper No. 015

Purnhagen, K., 'Voluntary "new approach" technical standards are subject to judicial scrutiny by the CJEU!: the remarkable CJEU judgment "Elliott" on private standards' (2017) 2017/05 Wageningen Working Papers in Law and Governance

Scharpf, F., 'Problem-solving effectiveness and democratic accountability in the EU' (2003) MPIfG Working Paper 03/1

Stewart, R. D., 'Enforcement of transnational public regulation' (2011) in EUI Working Papers, Robert Schuman Centre for Advanced Studies, Private Regulation Series-06, RSCAS 2011/49

Stoll, T., 'Are you still in? The impact of licensing requirements on the composition of standards setting organizations' (2014) Max Planck Institute for Innovation and Competition Research Paper No. 14

Tabarés-Gutiérrez, R., 'Taking a glance at the history of HTML5', in K. Jacobs and K. Blind (eds.), *EURAS Proceedings 2017. Digitalization: Challenge and Opportunity for Standardisation* (Aachen: Verlaghaus Mainz GmbH, 2017), pp. T351–66

Thorstensen, V., Weissinger, R. and Sun, X., 'Private standards: implications for trade, development and governance' (2015) Think Piece of E15 Initiative on Regulatory Systems Coherence, International Centre for Trade and Sustainable Development

Verbruggen, P. W. J. and Paiement, P. M., 'Transnational private regulation', in *Oxford Bibliographies in Political Science* (July 2017), available at www.oxfordbibliographies.com/view/document/obo-9780199756223/obo-9780199756223-0226.xml

Weiler, J., 'The rule of lawyers and the ethos of diplomats: reflections on the internal and external legitimacy of WTO dispute settlement' (2000) Harvard Jean Monnet Working Paper 9/00

Werle, R., 'Standards in the international telecommunications regime' (2001) Hamburg Institute of International Economics (HWWA) Discussion Paper 157

Wijkstrom, E. and McDaniels, D., 'International standards and the WTO TBT Agreement: improving governance for regulatory alignment' (2013) World Trade Organization Staff Working Paper ERSD-2013-06

Wu, X., 'Interplay between patents and standards in the information and communication technology (ICT) sector and its relevance to the implementation of the WTO agreements' (2017) WTO Working Paper ERSD – 2017-08

Yu, P. K. , "The sweet and sour story of Chinese intellectual property rights" (2004) Paper commissioned for the ESRC Research Seminar Series on "Intellectual property rights, economic development and social welfare: what does history tell us", Queen Mary Intellectual Property Research Institute, University of London

## Reports and Studies

Baron, J., Contreras, J. L., Husovec, M., Larouche, P. and Thumm, N., 'Making the rules: the governance of standard development organizations and their policies on intellectual property rights' (2019) JRC Science for Policy Report, EUR 29655 EN, available at https://publications.jrc.ec.europa.eu/repository/bitstream/JRC115004/sdo_governance_final_electronic_version.pdf

Bekkers, R. and Updegrove, A., *A Study of IPR Policies and Practices of a Representative Group of Standards Setting Organizations Worldwide*, updated version (Washington, DC: National Academies of Science, 2013)

Breznitz, D. and Murphree, M., 'The rise of China in technology standards: new norms in old institutions (2013) Report, available at www.uscc.gov/sites/default/files/Research/RiseofChinainTechnologyStandards.pdf

Contreras, J., 'An empirical study of the effects of ex ante licensing disclosure policies on the development of voluntary technical standards' (2011) Conducted for the National Institute of Standards and Technology (NIST), US Department of Commerce

Gottlieb, A., Verheul, H. and De Vries, H., 'Project Verbetering formele normalisatieproces – CASE ISO 15181: paints and varnishes – determination of release rate of biocides in antifouling paints' (2003) Delft: Ministry of Economic Affairs

IPlytics, 'Who is leading in the 5G patent race? Analysis on declared standard essential patents, 3GPP contributions and attendance data' (February 2019)

Schepel, H. and Falke, J., 'Legal aspects of standardization in Member States of the EC and EFTA, volume 1' (February 25, 2000) European Commission Publications

Schwab, K., 'The fourth industrial revolution: what it means, how to respond' (World Economic Forum, 2016), available at www.weforum.org/agenda/2016/01/the-fourth-industrial-revolution-what-it-means-and-how-to-respond/)

## European Union Publications

### *European Commission*

'2019 rolling plan for ICT standardization' (March 2019)

'2021 rolling plan for ICT standardization' (March 2021)

'The convergence of the telecommunications, media and information technology sectors, and the implications for regulation' (1999) COM (1999) 108 final, available at http://aei.pitt.edu/983/1/telecom_convergence_gp_follow_COM_99_108.pdf

'An EU strategy on standardization. Setting global standards in support of a resilient, green and digital EU Single Market' (February 2022) COM (2022) 31
'Independent review of the European standardization system', Final Report of the European Commission, Directorate-General for Internal Market, Industry, Entrepreneurship and SMEs (March 2015)
Notice to Stakeholders, 'Withdrawal of the United Kingdom and EU food law and EU rules on quality schemes' (March 20, 2019) REV2
'Setting out the EU approach to Standard Essential Patents' (November 29, 2017) COM (2017) 712 final.

### *European Parliament*

Europol, 'Position paper of 5G' (April 10, 2019) EDOC #1038503
NIS Cooperation Group, 'EU coordinated risk assessment of the cybersecurity of 5G networks' (October 9, 2019)
'Trans-Pacific Partnership: geopolitical implications for EU-US Relations' (2016)

## US Publications

### *NIST*

'Interagency report on strategic U.S. government engagement in international standardization to achieve U.S. objectives for cybersecurity' (2015) NIST Interagency Report 8074, vol. 1
'NIST framework and roadmap for smart grid interoperability standards, release 1.0' (January 2010) NIST Special Publication 1108

### *US Department of Justice*

117th Congress, United States Innovation and Competition Act of 2021, S.1260 (adopted June 8, 2021)
'Can there be a "one-world approach" to competition law?' Remarks of principal Deputy Assistant Attorney General Renata B. Hesse at the Chatham House Conference on Globalization of Competition Policy (2016)
R. Hesse, Remarks as prepared for the Global Competition Review (GCR) Live IP & Antitrust USA Conference, 'A year in the life of the joint DOJ-PTO policy statement on remedies for F/RAND encumbered standards-essential patents' (March 25, 2014)
IEEE-SA Request for Business Review Letter to the US Department of Justice, Antitrust Division (November 29, 2006)
Response to the Institute of Electrical and Electronics Engineers, Inc.'s request for business review letter (April 30, 2007)

Response to Vmebus International Trade Association (VITA)'s request for business review letter (October 30, 2006)

US Trade Representative, '2005 report to Congress on China's WTO compliance' (2005)

## Selected Periodicals

Doctorow, C., 'Boring, complex and important: a recipe for the web's dire future' (September 21, 2017) *Wired*, available at www.wired.co.uk/article/w3c-eff-open-standards-web-cory-doctorow

Lawson, S., 'Clouds hang low over Chinese WLAN standard' (December 19, 2003) *Computerworld*, available at www.computerworld.com/article/2804354/clouds-hang-low-over-chinese-wlan-standard

Layne-Farrar, A., Why patent holdout is not just a fancy name for plain old patent infringement' (February 2016) *Competition Policy International*, available at www.competitionpolicyinternational.com/why-patent-holdout-is-not-just-a-fancy-name-for-plain-old-patent-infringement

Nylen, L., 'Electrical Engineer Institute's new Wi-Fi measures won't get American national standards designation' (March 2019) *Mlex*, available at https://mlexmarketinsight.com/insights-center/editors-picks/antitrust/cross-jurisdiction/electrical-engineer-institutes-new-wifi-measures-wont-get-american-national-standard-designation

O'Brien, D., 'Lowering your standards: DRM and the future of the W3C' (October 2, 2013) available at www.eff.org/deeplinks/2013/10/lowering-your-standards

Way, J., 'A brief history of HTML5' (December 6, 2011), available at https://code.tutsplus.com/articles/a-brief-history-of-html5--net-23064

## Main Online Sources

ANSI: www.ansi.org/
Bluetooth SIG: www.bluetooth.com/
CEN/CENELEC: www.cencenelec.eu/Pages/default.aspx
EC: https://ec.europa.eu/growth/single-market/european-standards_en
ETSI: www.etsi.org/
IEEE(-SA): www.ieee.org/ and https://standards.ieee.org/
IETF: www.ietf.org/
ISO: www.iso.org/
ISOC: www.internetsociety.org/
ITU: www.itu.int/
NIST: www.nist.gov/
W3C: www.w3.org/
WTO: www.wto.org/

## Main SDOs Governing Documents

### *3GPP*

3GPP Partnership Agreement (December 4, 1998)

3GPP Working Procedures (April 29, 2021)

### *Bluetooth SIG*

Bluetooth SIG Membership Agreement (Version 3.0, May 2017)

Bluetooth Specification Management Process Document (December 29, 2020)

Bylaws of Bluetooth SIG, Inc. (2012)

Bylaws of Bluetooth SIG, Inc. (May 17, 2019)

Fourth Amended and Restated Certificate of Incorporation of Bluetooth SIG, Inc.

### *ETSI*

ETSI Directives (Version 44, December 21, 2021)

ETSI Intellectual Property Rights Policy, Annex 6 ETSI Rules of Procedures (December 1, 2021)

ETSI Guide on Intellectual Property Rights (IPRs), Version adopted by Board #133 (June 10, 2021)

ETSI Rules of Procedure, Version approved by a Specially Convened Meeting of the ETSI General Assembly (December 1, 2021)

ETSI Statutes, Version approved by a Specially Convened Meeting of the ETSI General Assembly (December 1, 2021)

ETSI Technical Working Procedures, Version adopted by Board #134 (October 18, 2021)

Guidelines for the Implementation of Annex 2 of the Rules of Procedure, Version adopted by General Assembly #58 (November 30, 2011)

### *IEC*

IEC Statutes and Rules of Procedure (2021 edition, 2021)

### *IEEE*

IEEE Certificate of Incorporation (1993)

IEEE Constitution and Bylaws (2022)

## *IEEE-SA*

IEEE-SA Operations Manual (February 2022)
IEEE-SA Standards Board Bylaws (February 2022)
IEEE-SA Standards Board Operations Manual (January 2022)

## *IETF*

'Charter of the Internet Architecture Board (IAB)', Carpenter, B. (ed.) (May 2000) RCF28050
'IAB, IESG, and IAOC selection, confirmation, and recall process: operation of the nominating and recall committees', Kucherawy, M. (ed.), (January 2015) RFC 7437
'An IESG Charter', Alvestrand, H. (ed.) (February 2004) RFC 3710
'Intellectual property rights in IETF technology', Bradner, S. (ed.) (March 2005) RFC 3979
'Intellectual property rights in IETF Technology', Bradner, S. and Contreras, L. (eds.) (May 2017) BCP 79
'Structure of the IETF Administrative Support Activity (IASA)', Austein, R. (ed.) (April 2005) BCP 101
'The Tao of IETF: a novice's guide to the internet engineering task force', Hoffman, P. (ed.) (2019)
'Update to RFC 3777 to clarify nominating committee eligibility of IETF leadership', Leiba, B. (ed.) (January 2013) RCP 6859
'What makes for a successful protocol' Thaler, D. (July 2008)
'Clarification of the third-party disclosure procedure in RFC 3979', Narten, T. (ed.) (April 2007) RFC 4879
IETF Working Group Guidelines and Procedures (September 1998), Bradner, S. (ed.) RCP 2418
'The internet standards process – revision 2', C. Huitema and P. Gross (eds.) (March 1994) RFC 1602
'The internet standards process – revision 3', Bradner, S. (ed.) (October 1996) RFC 2026

## *ISO*

ISO Statutes (20th ed., 2022)
ISO/IEC Directives Part 1 (12th ed., 2021)
ISO/IEC Guide 2, Standardization and Related Activities – General Vocabulary (2004)
ISO/IEC Guide 21-1, Regional or National Adoption of International Standards and Other International Deliverables – Part 1: Adoption of International Standards (1st ed., 2005)

ISO/IEC Guide 59 – Code of Good Practice for Standardization (1st ed., 1994)

ISO/IEC Guide 59 – ISO and IEC Recommended Practices for Standardization by National Bodies (2nd ed., 2019)

### *ITU*

Common Patent Policy for ITU-T/ITU-R/ISO/IEC (2006)

Constitution and Convention of the International Telecommunication Union adopted by the 2018 Plenipotentiary Conference (2018 edition, 2019), available at www.itu.int/en/history/Pages/ConstitutionAndConvention.aspx

IEC/ISO/ITU, Guidelines for Implementation of the Common Patent Policy for ITU-T/ITU-R/ISO/IEC (November 2018)

### *W3C*

Draft International World Wide Web Consortium Member Agreement (2021)

W3C Patent Policy, D. J. Weitzner (ed.) (February 2004)

World Wide Web Consortium Process Document, C. M. Nevile (ed.) (March 2017)

## Other

### *ANSI*

ANSI, 'Accredited Standards Developers' (January 10, 2022)

ANSI Essential Requirements, Due Process Requirements for American National Standards' (edition: January 2022)

ANSI procedures for U.S. participation in the international standards activities of ISO' (January 2019)

Overview of the US Standardization System: voluntary consensus standards and conformity assessment activities' (2007)

### *CEN/CENELEC*

CEN-CENELEC's position paper 'Standard essential patents and fair, reasonable and non-discriminatory commitments' (September 2016)

CEN/CENELEC position on the consequences of the judgment of the European Court of Justice on *James Elliott Construction Limited* v. *Asphalt Limited* (2017)

## *OECD*

'The internet of things: seizing the benefits and addressing the challenges' (May 24, 2016) (DSTI/ICCP/CISP(2015)3/FINAL)

'Measuring regulatory performance: evaluating the impact of regulation and regulatory policy' (August 2012) Expert Paper No. 1 by C. Coglianese, available at www.oecd.org/gov/regulatory-policy/1_coglianese%20web.pdf

'Standard setting' (March 8, 2011) (DAF/COMP (2010)

## *Miscellaneous*

Arkko, J. 'Diversity' (April 2013) available at www.ietf.org/blog/diversity

Boyera, S. 'The mobile web in developing countries: the next step' (2006) available at www.w3.org/2006/12/digital_divide/public.html

Daniel, I. D. (ed.) 'WTO TBT Standards Code criteria applied to W3C' (July 12, 2009)

The IAB reply to the European ICT questionnaire, 'Impact assessment study on the "standardization package." Request for information from forums and consortiums' (2011) available at: https://www.iab.org/wp-content/IAB-uploads/2011/03/2010-02-05-IAB-Response-Euro-ICT-Questionnaire.pdf

Infographic: The 5 Core Principles of OpenStand', available at https://open-stand.org/

'Open letter from Just Net Coalition to Sir Tim Berners-Lee seeking his urgent intervention to stop acceptance of Encrypted Media Extensions as a W3C standard' (April 12, 2017)

Perkins, D., IAB considerations in appeal SNMPv2 SMI (March 1996), available at www.iab.org/appeals/1996-2/appeal-snmpv2-smi-appeal-by-mr-david-t-perkins-iab-consideration-march-1996/

United Nations Forum on Sustainability Standards (UNFSS), 'Voluntary Sustainability Standards' (2013)

WTO, 'Trade and public policies: a closer look at non-tariff measures in the 21st century', World Trade Report (2012)

# INDEX

www.ingramcontent.com/pod-product-compliance
Lightning Source LLC
Chambersburg PA
CBHW061558260225
22529CB00004BA/30
*9781009300575*